Man to Man

The Missorium of Theodosius I (388 C.E.)
Real Academia de la Historia, Madrid / Shutterstock.com

Man to Man
Desire, Homosociality, and Authority in Late-Roman Manhood

Mark Masterson

 The Ohio State University Press · Columbus

Copyright © 2014 by The Ohio State University.
All rights reserved.

Library of Congress Cataloging-in-Publication Data
Masterson, Mark.
  Man to man : desire, homosociality, and authority in late-Roman manhood / Mark Masterson.
     pages cm
  Includes bibliographical references and index.
  ISBN 978-0-8142-1268-4 (hardback) — ISBN 0-8142-1268-9 (cloth) — ISBN 978-0-8142-9372-0 (cd-rom) — ISBN 0-8142-9372-7 (cd-rom) — ISBN 978-0-8142-7352-4 (ebook) — ISBN 0-8142-7352-1 (ebook)
  1. Homosexuality—Rome—History. 2. Patron and client—Rome—History. 3. Authority—Rome—History. 4. Elite (Social sciences)—Rome—History. I. Title.
  HQ76.2.R6M372014
  306.76'6093763dc23
                    2014008795

Cover image: Emperor Theodosius II / Gold Solidus (CE 408–450). Obverse: Theodosius II, head and bust. Reverse: Roma, helmeted and seated. Courtesy of The Classics Museum of Victoria University of Wellington, New Zealand

Cover design by Laurence J. Nozik
Text design by Juliet Williams
Type set in Adobe Garamond

∞ The paper used in this publication meets the minimum requirements of the American National Standard for Information Sciences—Permanence of Paper for Printed Library Materials. ANSI Z39.48–1992.

9   8   7   6   5   4   3   2   1

CONTENTS

Acknowledgments · vii
List of Abbreviations · ix
List of Emperors · xi

Introduction · 1
Summary of This Book's Contents · 1
Prospect for This Book · 3
Two Men: Setting the Scene · 6
Law and the Knowingness of Authority · 19
A Metaphor for Admirability · 30
Summation and Prior Scholarship on Late-Roman Manhood · 34

Chapter One · Emperor Julian's Marcus Aurelius · 41
Introduction · 41
Platonic Glamour in the *Caesares* · 45
Saloustios and Julian on the Proper Use of Myths · 62
The Making of Julian's Authority in *Against Heracleius* · 72
Ioulianos Mythoumenos · 79
Conclusion · 84

Chapter Two · Athanasius' Antony · 90
Introduction · 90
Sources and Athanasius' Métier · 93
Antony the Legible · 98
Figuring Antony · 112
Two Treatises · 127
Conclusion · 135

Chapter Three · **Ammianus' Emperors** — 138
  Introduction — 138
  Adventus — 142
  Imperial Signature — 147
  Aeternitas in the *Res Gestae* and Beyond — 149
  Not a Civil Emperor — 154
  Declinatio and Emperor — 156
  Conclusion — 164

Conclusion — 170

Bibliography — 179
Index Locorum — 207
General Index — 213

ACKNOWLEDGMENTS

I received much help on this project that has stretched over many years.

Thanks, therefore, to Steven Smith, Simon Perris, and the anonymous readers provided by The Ohio State University Press for reading and commenting on the entire typescript; to Clifford Ando, Joseph Boone, Virginia Burrus, Stephanie Cobb, Dorota Dutsch, Mathew Kuefler, Kristina Meinking, Judith Perkins, Sara Phang, Nancy Rabinowitz, Jeff Tatum, and Greg Thalmann for reading portions of this work in its various manifestations; to Shadi Bartsch, Diana Burton, Mark Edwards, Tony Cuttriss, John Davidson, Alex Drummond, Helen Fitzgerald, Bruce Frier, Philip Gisondi, Jill Harries, Tania Hayes, Deborah Hollingsworth, Alison Keith, Jerzy Linderski, Chris Marshall, Christabel Marshall, Jen Oliver, Lynn Peace, Arthur Pomeroy, Carl Rubino, Fran Scoble, Emily Simons, Judy Stacey, Mark Stephenson, Kristen Strohmeyer, Hannah Tokona, Deborah Willis, and David Wray for advice and support; to members of the Classics Programme and the Faculty of Humanities and Social Sciences at Victoria University of Wellington; to Judy Deuling for help with obtaining the images for the cover and for teaching relief a couple years ago; to the memories of Marcia Masterson and William Masterson; to Eugene O'Connor for being a genial, knowledgeable, and dependable editor; to Sharon James for providing crucial advice at a critical time; to Barbara Gold for advice on the manuscript and for support and friendship, for which I am most grateful, over the years; to Amy Richlin, who has been a wonderful intellectual and personal presence in my life.

And, lastly, to Timothy Heartt for believing and following with love.

ABBREVIATIONS

4H	Claudian, *Panegyricus de Quarto Consulatu Honorii Augusti*
6H	Claudian, *Panegyricus de Sexto Consulatu Honorii Augusti*
Amm.	Ammianus Marcellinus
Anon. Lat.	Anonymous, *De Physiognomonia Liber*
Apophth. Patr.	*Apophthegmata Patrum*
Arch.	Cicero, *Pro Archia Poeta*
Chrm.	*Charmides*
CIL	*Corpus Inscriptionum Latinarum*
Claud.	Claudian
CTh.	*Codex Theodosianus*
Fat.	Cicero, *De Fato*
Gent.	Athanasius, *Contra Gentes*
Hist. Monach.	Anonymous, *Historia Monachorum*
IE	Claudian, *In Eutropium*
ILS	*Inscriptiones Latinae Selectae* (ed. Dessau)
Inc.	Athanasius, *De Incarnatione*
Jul.	emperor Julian
Lampe	Lampe and Liddel, *A Patristic Greek Lexicon*
LSJ	Liddell, Scott, Jones, and McKenzie, *A Greek–English Lexicon*
Lucr.	Lucretius, *De Rerum Natura*
Myst.	Iamblichus, *De Mysteriis*
OLD	*Oxford Latin Dictionary*

Or.	*Oration*
Pacat.	(Latinus) Pacatus (Drepanius)
Pan. Lat.	*Panegyrici Latini*
PG	*Patrologia Graeca*
Phdr.	*Phaedrus*
Phlb.	*Philebus*
PL	*Patrologia Latina*
Pl.	Plato
Plot.	Plotinus, *Enneades*
R.	*The Republic* (Plato)
RE	*Realencyclopädie der classischen Altertumswissenschaft* (Pauly-Wissowa)
Reg. Pachom.	Jerome, *Interpretatio Regulae Sancti Pachomii*
Smp.	*Symposium*
TLG	*Thesaurus Linguae Graecae*
TLL	*Thesaurus Linguae Latinae*
Tusc.	Cicero, *Tusculan Disputations*
Victric.	Victricius, *De Laude Sanctorum*

LIST OF EMPERORS

Constantine I (the Great) dies in 337
Constantine II (337–340)
Constans (337–350)
Constantius II (337–361)
Julian (360–363)
Jovian (363–364)
Valentinian I (364–375 [West])
Valens (364–378 [East])
Gratian (367–383 [West])
Valentinian II (375–392 [West])
Theodosius I (379–395 [East + West])
Arcadius (383–408 [East])
Honorius (393–423 [West])
Constantius III (421 [West])
Theodosius II (408–450 [East])
Valentinian III (423–455 [West])

INTRODUCTION

SUMMARY OF THIS BOOK'S CONTENTS

This book's subject is same-sex desire between men and the connection it has to elite men's homosociality and the making of masculine authority in late antiquity (the later fourth century and into the fifth, to be precise). Late-ancient law, a saint's life, historiography, philosophy, theology, oratory, and poetry provide the source material. Overt expressions of same-sex desire appear in these sources and there is ample evidence of its covert presence too. Whether overt or covert, same-sex desire played constituent and complex roles in the contexts of elite men's homosociality and the construction of manly authority. Given that late-ancient sources often report that same-sex desire between men was not manly and the secondary literature of recent decades has in large part been content to relay these statements as definitive, the pairing of same-sex desire with late-ancient manhood may seem surprising. But as will be shown, the evidence is there. Late-ancient manhood does not mirror a caricature of modern manhood that says masculinity and same-sex desire have nothing in common. But how did this situation which calls for this study come about? Why has this evidence fallen from consideration in recent decades? It was, albeit briefly, considered not too long ago.

In a ground-breaking work from 1980, *Christianity, Social Tolerance, and Homosexuality,* John Boswell considered same-sex desire between men. His strategy, however, of identifying instances of homosexuality and gay people in late antiquity and the Middle Ages came increasingly to be seen as anachronistic and problematic. His search now seems naïve, though current critics should remember that today's naïveté will be revealed in time.[1] And it seems too that no sooner was same-sex desire in late antiquity discovered, than it was straightaway lost.

Michel Foucault's problematization and historicization of sexuality in 1978 and the rise of social constructionism in the 1980s were powerful contributing factors leading to the disappearance of discussion of same-sex desire between men from studies of late antiquity (and this loss ironically occurred during a time of growing interest in and discussion of sexuality across the humanities). With Boswell's discovery of gay people in late antiquity rejected as essentialist (if it was mentioned at all), there was a concomitant feeling that same-sex desire could not be reified or emphasized such that it might be seen or, perhaps, be *misunderstood* as a defining element of identity among late-ancient men. Furthermore, scholars following Foucault's problematic lead in the second and third volumes of *The History of Sexuality* (1985, 1986), in which he is often an uncritical reader of protreptic literature, have tended to present norms contained in exhortations to "good" behavior as credibly thorough discussions of desire and sexual behavior in late antiquity. Taking protreptic literature as a foundation for description of realities of ancient gender and sex intensified the tendency fostered by the rise of social constructionism toward making same-sex desire among men invisible in accounts of late antiquity: the definition of a man from the sources says that this is no man if he enjoys such a thing as being penetrated—and so discussion is over before it starts, and this result is a flow-on effect from the definition of manhood offered by the late ancients and accepted as unproblematic by many modern scholars.

Rejecting the often explicit late-ancient assertion (and the all too often complicit scholarly consensus) that same-sex desire among men must be considered apart from manhood allows its importance in the homosocial world of elite manhood to be seen. Instead of being separate from manhood, same-sex desire was a conspicuous vehicle for expressing friendship, patronage, solidarity, and other important relationships among elite men in late antiquity. The evocation of this desire and its possible attendant corporeal satisfactions made it a compelling metaphor for friendship. A man's grandeur, his *auctoritas* or *axiōma*/ἀξίωμα, could also be portrayed

---

1. See Mathew Kuefler's discussion (2006) for a narrative of the scholarly reception of Boswell's work.

metaphorically, and with some paradox, as sexual attractiveness, and the substantial status differences often seen in late antiquity could be rendered less formidable by a superior using amatory language to address an inferior. At the same time, however, there was ambivalence, to say the least, about same-sex desire and sexual behavior between men (as there had been in previous centuries and as there would be in centuries to come), and same-sex sexual behavior was criminalized as it had never been before. Still, while rejection and condemnation may seem to indicate a decisive distancing between authority and this desire and behavior, authority gained power from maintaining a relation to them. Demonstrating knowledge of the actual mechanics of same-sex sexual behavior suggested to a witness that there was nothing unknown to authority making the demonstration: authority that knew of forbidden same-sex desire and scandalous masculine sexual pleasure could project its power pretty much anywhere. This startling dissonance between positive uses of same-sex desire between men and its criminalization in one and the same moment—a dissonance which discussions privileging normative definitions of manhood are unable to address—requires further investigation, and this book supplies it.

PROSPECT FOR THIS BOOK

This introduction continues with discussion of two elite men of senatorial status, Nummius Aemilianus Dexter and Paulinus of Nola. This discussion considers the ways same-sex desire can be seen, or posited as operative, among the educated elite men of the later empire. Of key importance are the pronounced homosociality of this milieu (substantially that of the emperor's bureaucracy) and the expressions of same-sex desire, emerging in the fine-weave of communication and enabled by the education or *paideia* required of elite men, that metaphorize friendships between men. Leaving behind these two men, the introduction then passes to the innovative fourth-century legislation against same-sex sexual behavior. This legislation reveals authority to be in possession of knowledge about masculine desire and pleasure that might seem scandalous. But quite far from being a scandal, this knowledge builds the power of the authorities who know the ways of desire and the mechanics of sex between men. Same-sex desire also emerges in the contexts of the status differences often seen in late antiquity. The glory of an emperor or holy man is metaphorized as same-sex sexual attractiveness, or a subordinate is hailed with amatory language. Expressions of love and desire wish away asymmetries of status and rank.

The introduction concludes with how paradox engendered by the counterintuitive presence of same-sex desire in late-ancient manhood intensifies the very much alive masculine ambition to transcend the body, memorialized in Platonic philosophy and passed down in the perduring association of man with mind and woman with body. Depicting masculine friendship and admirability through same-sex sexual tropes and building authority through signaling knowledge of the obscene mechanics of male same-sex sexual behavior harness corporeal vitality to depict masculinized transcendence via paradox. This paradox recalls the penchant of late-Platonic philosophy to discover, in a way that moves beyond logic, transcendently pure value in the impure and non-transcendent physical world. And this is not all. The use of this desire and pleasure to glamorize late-ancient men and indicate far-reaching powers of authority reveals an interesting perspective on this desire. Able to be employed in positive ways, even as they are regarded as something bad, and their vitality valued, desire and sexual pleasure between men are things that exist prior to and are transcendent of a moral system that would capture and judge them. They are available to be repurposed by those who believe that the transcendent is mysterious and beyond human morals. This particular position was one that some late-ancient thinkers (e.g., Athanasius) found unacceptable, while others were conflicted (Ammianus) or accepting (the late Platonists to varying degrees).

Changing the focus to the late Platonists, the first chapter makes two works of the emperor Julian, *Caesares* and the seventh oration (*Against Heracleius*), centerpieces of investigations both of masculine same-sex sexual attractiveness as a metaphor for masculine admirability and of the late-ancient theoretical basis for the use of the carnal to represent worthiness and admirability. In a passage from *Caesares* well regarded as intertextual with Plato, Julian tropes the admirability of his predecessor, emperor Marcus Aurelius, as same-sex sexual attractiveness. This paradoxical troping would have been visible to anyone with even just a moderate amount of *paideia* under his or her belt: knowledge of Plato brings a sexual subtext to the surface. Discussion anchored in Julian's seventh oration suggests that this apparently counterproductive troping of masculine admirability is an example of the paradoxical use of material things to signify grandeur, a procedure often seen in late antiquity. Julian's discussion in this oration of the value paradoxically attributed to carnal and sexy myths—value not decreased but amplified by their somatic content—shows that invocation of the material could have an elevating and indeed electrifying effect on masculine glamour. The generally positive role for same-sex desire and same-sex sexual attractiveness seen in the first chapter is not, however, the whole story for same-sex desire, homosociality, and the making of masculine authority in late antiquity.

In chapter two the rejection of same-sex desire in the works of Athanasius (the *Vita Antonii* in particular) exists alongside a subtly indicated knowledge of the bodily experience of male same-sex desire and pleasure. Athanasius has no use for metaphorizations of masculine authority as same-sex sexual attractiveness, and friendly relations between men don't appear as a subject in and of themselves in the *vita*. All the same, knowledge of male same-sex sexual activity increases Athanasius' authority, for it appears that there is nowhere that his projecting authority, invasive and knowledgeable, cannot go. Athanasius resembles the lawmakers discussed in the introduction to the book.

The third chapter is a discussion of the emperor as seen by the historiographer Ammianus Marcellinus. Close analysis of Ammianus' language in his *Res Gestae* reveals the implication of same-sex desire with homosociality and authority. Ammianus wants the emperor to be glamorously transcendent of this world—set free from the need to relate with subordinates via a workable homosociality—and yet he is ambivalent about the autocratic abandon transcendence seemingly encourages. A symptom of Ammianus' ambivalence is the appearance of the ancient and well-known discourse of tyrannical effeminacy in the fine weave of his language; Ammianus attributes sexual passivity to the emperor Constantius II, whose glorious transcendence curdles into tyranny, while he praises emperor Julian for his understanding treatment of his subjects, consistent with an upright and hard dedication to civility. It may seem that Ammianus has an attitude toward same-sex desire among men close to the one held by Athanasius, who sees same-sex desire and attractiveness as things worthless in themselves and only useful to him to the extent that demonstration of knowledge about them makes him appear a more authoritative judge of human life. Such an impression would be incorrect. When the twenty-four-year-old Julian is made *caesar*, Ammianus observes that Julian's eyes are "terrible with loveliness" or, perhaps, "awe-inspiring on account of the power of Venus" (*Res Gestae* 15.8.16: *venustate terribiles*), and the audience gazing upon and affected by this terrible beauty, this epiphany of the goddess of love and desire, is the soldiery.

In both chapters two and three, the disquiet that Athanasius and Ammianus exhibit in the face of the inexplicability of the transcendent is also a point of discussion. Understood in theorizations surveyed in the first chapter as approachable through an embrace of opposites that surpasses terrestrial efforts to understand it, the transcendent on this basis is unsatisfactory to both Athanasius and Ammianus. Disquiet leads both authors to reject the mystery of the transcendent to varying degrees. Their rejection of mystery, which amounts to a thorough-going rationalization of the transcendent, causes perceived physical effects in the here and now. In the case of Athanasius, same-sex desire and the potential for pleasure in being penetrated become endemic to all male human bodies. For Ammianus, the emperor who embodies imperial grandeur the best (Constantius II) is at the same time depicted as irredeemably effeminate via physicalizing metaphors, while Julian, his proposed model emperor and impenetrable, loses touch with the transcendent in its mysterious aspect.

The evidence of three chapters teaches that same-sex desire and unease over possible masculine interest in being penetrated lead to various responses, all of which maintain connections to late-ancient masculine aspirations to glamour and transcendence. The perception of the transcendent's paradoxical presence in this world enables positive symbolic uses of same-sex sexual attractiveness in late-ancient men's homosociality in some thinkers. Other thinkers, less relaxed, reject the positive use of same-sex desire and same-sex sexual attractiveness (Athanasius) or display ambivalence about it (Ammianus).

TWO MEN: SETTING THE SCENE

The late-ancient senate provides an excellent starting place for an investigation of elite manhood's relationship to same-sex desire, homosociality, and the making of authority. The number of senators burgeoned in the fourth century, and senatorial status was the *telos* toward which hereditary elites, new men, and men from the military all strove.[2] Generalizations drawn from observation of the late-ancient senate are therefore applicable to a wide variety of elite men (and this focus on the senate produces a base-line and context for the detailed work to come in chapters one, two, and three).[3] In order to substantiate these claims about men of senatorial status, there now follow two sketches of men of the late fourth-century C.E. senate who

---

2. Salzman 2002: 39 (cf. 31–33, 41–42).
3. The literature on the late-ancient senate is vast. The following are useful: Chastagnol 1982a: 265–78, and 1982b; Heather 1998; Jones 1964; Marcone 1998; Matthews 1975; Näf 1995. In 2000, a special issue (33.3) of *Arethusa* appeared on elites in late antiquity. Each piece in this issue, to varying degrees, considers the senate. In an important monograph, Salzman provides a detailed account (2002: 19–61) of the evolution of the senatorial aristocracy in the western parts of the empire in the third and (especially) fourth centuries.

embody the qualities of elite Roman men and whose relations with other elite men are typical of this special time in the history of the Roman state. One of these men is a new man, from a relatively humble background, and the other, of senatorial stock, is lofty indeed. They may have met in Milan in the 380s.[4] Whether they did or not, they would have understood each other, not only because they were born relatively near one another but also, and especially, because of their similar educations and acculturation to the canons of elite Roman manhood. First, then, the new man.

Nummius Aemilianus Dexter[5] was born in the middle of the fourth century in Spain. His father, Pacianus, was bishop of Barcino (Barcelona). Dexter was of no considerable rank to begin with, but he vaulted from relatively humble origins to go on to a brilliant career in the imperial government. His advancement was likely helped by association with the Theodosian family from Spain which came to imperial power as the Valentinians progressively faded in the latter decades of the fourth century. It was a good time for important men from Spain. The Theodosians would provide emperors to the empire until the middle of the next century, and those who had attached themselves to Theodosius' star did well. Dexter's advancement is also attributable to his level of education or *paideia*.

This expensive education, years-long training in literature, rhetoric, and even philosophy, was substantially the preserve of the wealthy. *Paideia* made boys into men whose superiority and social dominance appeared the most natural thing in the world.[6] *Paideia* was key for a man to prosper at elite levels in the Roman empire, and this was never more true than in the later centuries of the empire. Peter Brown remarks on how this shared education helped men understand one another in the context of governing the empire:

> Through a shared *paideia,* [elite educated men in the later empire] could set up a system of instant communication with men who were, often, total strangers to them. They signaled, above all, that they were approach-

---

4. Matthews 1975: 153 (cf. Trout 1999: 91).

5. Jones 1971: 251 *Dexter* 3; Humphries 2009: 99; Matthews 1975: 133–34; Rebenich 1992: 125–26, 214–15 and 2002: 24; Salzman 2002: 91, 104, 117, 298.

6. Watts 2006: 2; Gleason 1995: 164. For the structure of ancient education (grammar, rhetoric, and, finally, philosophy), see Marrou 1956: passim, but 265ff. and Cribiore 2001: *passim*, but 37–44. Edward Watts has recently and often written helpfully on late-ancient education (2005a, 2005b, 2006, 2010). Christians in the fourth century were conflicted about the role that pagan literature was to play in their lives as educated persons. See Anthony Kaldellis' discussion (2007: 120–72) for a presentation of the issues. For the "philosophical education," i.e., the specific curriculum that created many of the deep thinkers of late antiquity, see Athanassiadi 2002; Lamberton 2001; Cameron 1998: 680–82.

able and that they knew the rules of the game. As a "fellow servant of the Muses," no administrator could mistake a compliment or ignore a challenge posed to him as a classical reminiscence. (1992: 40[7])

Indeed, the importance of *paideia* to elite men in the later Roman Empire cannot be overstated, and it only grew as the fourth century passed into the fifth.[8]

As important as *paideia* was for forming and articulating the profile of a successful elite man, and as much as the graces of education told everyone that this was a man to whom all ought to listen, the abilities conferred by *paideia* were also connected to material advantages. Mastery of *paideia* was, to take a significant example, the *sine qua non* for service to the emperor in the bureaucracies. In 360, at *Codex Theodosianus* 14.1.1,[9] emperor Constantius II and Julian (while he was still *caesar*) specified that clear evidence of literary studies and flawless linguistic style were required of all who aspired to imperial service.[10] Delivering a panegyric before the emperor and/or a reputation gained through published works could be significant milestones on the way to a lofty career in imperial administration.[11]

In the case of Dexter there is good evidence of his level of education. In the first place, there is his brilliant career; without the polishing of *paideia*,

---

7. Cf. Salzman 2002: 42, 48; Bouffartigue 1992: 585–90.

8. For discussions of the importance and pervasiveness of *paideia* in late antiquity, see, e.g., Brown 1992 (*passim*); Cameron 1998 (*passim*); Cribiore 2001 and 2009; Heather 1998 and 1994a: 181–86; Jones 1964: 577–78; Kaldellis 2007: 120–72; Kaster 1988 (*passim*); Lenski 2002: 269–70; Marcone 1998: 364; Matthews 1975 (*passim*); Rapp 2000: 387, 399; Salzman 2000: 353–54; Van Dam 2002: 80–94, 160–62, and 2003 (*passim*); Wormald 1976: 218. Noel Lenski (2002: 92–97, 371) tellingly notes that emperor Valens' lack of conspicuous educational attainment made relations with the highly educated elites of Asia Minor difficult and put him at a disadvantage *vis-à-vis* the usurper Procopius. André Chastagnol provides a useful list of the intellectual and literary pursuits of various Praetorian Prefects of Rome (1960: 453).

9. Discussion of the *Codex Theodosianus* as a source appears below.

10. Kaldellis 2007: 154–55; for more on the necessity of expert training in literature and rhetoric for a career in the late-ancient bureaucracies: Corcoran 1996: *passim,* but 92–94 296–97; Brown 1992; Cameron 1998: 673–79; Halsall 2004: 21–25; Harries 1999: 56–59 and 1988; Heather 1994a: 181–86; Honoré 1998; Kelly 1994; Matthews 2000a: *passim*, but 177 (*quaestors*); Millar 1977: 83–101, 203–28; Vessey 2003.

11. Sivan 1993: 79. Symmachus arguably launched his career with two panegyrics to Valentinian I and one to Gratian at Trier in 369/370. He was soon made *comes tertii ordinis* and then proconsul in Africa (Matthews 1975: 32, 86). Soon after delivering a panegyric to emperor Julian in which he offered thanks for his consulship (*Pan. Lat.* 11 [3]), Claudius Mamertinus went on to become praetorian prefect in Italy in 362, and Latinus Pacatus Drepanius "won the proconsulship, and afterwards court office in the East, having delivered a panegyric [*Pan. Lat.* 12 (2)] for the emperor at Rome, in 389" (Matthews 1975: 86). Indeed, the entire corpus of the *Panegyrici Latini* is testament to this economy of praise. Such performances were not done for charity; material benefits followed them. See, too, MacCormack 1981 and 1975.

Dexter never would have had it. Second, at *De Viris Illustribus* 132 (a collection, written in the 390s, of 135 brief biographies of Christian men who wrote something worthy of memory from the time of the martyrs up to the current day), Jerome reports that Dexter wrote a universal or world history (*omnimoda historia*). Jerome also dedicated this popular work of his to Dexter. Significantly, Jerome wrote *De Viris Illustribus* to document the presence of learning among the fathers and men of the church, thus underscoring the importance of *paideia*. Indeed, both Dexter and his father Pacianus are listed in the work: Dexter, as noted above, at 132 and Pacianus at 106.

And what a career this education and connections to the ruling house enabled. Swept east in Theodosius' triumphant wake, Dexter was far from home, the governor of the province of Asia in the 380s. After his retirement, the province erected a statue to him, their former governor, in Barcino, the base for which survives as *CIL* 2.4512. In 387, Dexter achieved bureaucratic splendor in the office of *comes rerum privatarum*. Not content with making his mark in the East, this Spaniard was later the highly prestigious Praetorian Prefect of Italy in 395. Administration of this prefecture was the glorious cap to a career that left him a senator of the highest grade. The number of senators grew in the fourth century and Dexter's career should be seen in the context of this increase; his career path was not exceptional but, instead, exemplary of a changing situation.

As noted above, the late fourth and early fifth centuries were a special time in the history of the empire. The latter part of the fourth century saw substantial change in the composition of elites. Focusing on the senate makes perception of this large (and rather unwieldy) transformation somewhat manageable. At the beginning of the century the senators totaled about six hundred, and senatorial status was, in any case, hereditary.[12] By the end of the century this status was no longer just hereditary.[13] It could also be acquired by service to the emperor and, in the year 400, there were about six thousand administrative jobs in the empire that would secure senatorial status for their holders.[14] In addition to this general increase, there had been creation of a whole new senate in Constantinople.[15] Arnaldo Marcone notes that there was an "opening-up of new channels of social mobility, which permitted unexpected opportunities for advancement" (1998:

---

12. Heather 1998: 184; Jones 1964: 525.
13. Jones 1964: 525–29.
14. Heather 1998: 190; see Noel Lenski's discussion (with much bibliography) of the raising up of educated bureaucrats and military men to senatorial parity with those who had this status by birth during the reigns of Valentinian I (364–375) and Valens (364–378) (2002: 56–67 [esp. 63–67]).
15. Chastagnol 1982a: 227–34; Dagron 1974: 119–210 (chapters 4–6); Heather 1994b; Skinner 2000.

338). One of course could not count on being plucked from obscurity—far from it—but for the lucky and educated there were good opportunities to exploit and, compared to the past, there was a plethora of them. At the fourth century's end, birth, although still valuable, was not the determinant it had been for elite success.

A further demotion for elites who inherited senatorial status occurred with the coming of a system of precedence within the senatorial order. By 400, every man of senatorial rank would have held one of the three following ranks (lowest to highest): *clarissimus*/λαμπρότατος[16] ("most bright"), *spectabilis*/σπεκταβίλιος[17] (or περίβλεπτος[18]) ("well-worth looking at"), and *illustris*/ἰλλούστριος[19] ("utterly illuminated").[20] Only the lowest, *clarissimus*, was hereditary and the other two more lofty titles were bestowed only through service.[21] Those men who were made *spectabiles* and *illustres* came to possess privileges, such as exemption from *munera sordida* (i.e., contribution of goods, services and money to meet various needs identified by the central government) that mere *clarissimi* could not avoid.[22] Furthermore, these terms designating precedence, with their appeals to light and spectacle that are veritable visual lures, are a culmination of developments in the portrayal of honor. J. E. Lendon draws attention to the fact that, for both Latin and Greek speakers in the earlier empire, glory (*gloria*) was a shining thing (1997: 274 [Latin], 278–79 [Greek]). While these terms are the result of the processes of centuries, the fact that they refer to something beyond this earth, i.e., the transcendent, must be kept in mind: inasmuch as they connect bureaucratic elites to the transcendent, these appellations are of a piece with panegyrical figurations of holy men and emperors.

So then, the relatively humbly-born Dexter, after working his way across the empire in successively higher positions, ended his life (probably back in Spain) as an important personage indeed. Holding the office of praetorian prefect would have made Dexter *illustris* and from then on his family would be *clarissimus,* with the possibility that his descendants could become *spectabiles* or *illustres* through service, as Dexter had done. He exploited the opportunity afforded him by the coming of the Theodosian imperial family.

---

16. Mason 1974: 65, 179; Millar 1983: 91; Jones 1964: 1228.
17. *LSJ* Supplement 1996.
18. *LSJ* Supplement 1996.
19. Jones 1964: 1229; *Lampe* 1961.
20. Of the three terms, *clarissimus* and *illustris* are well attested in the fourth century, and *spectabilis,* less visible in the sources, is establishing itself by 400. For more, see Chastagnol 1992: 293–324; Gizewski 2012; Groß-Albenhausen 2012a and b; Hirschfeld 1901; Jones 1964: 528–30; Löhken 1982: 112–34; Salzman 2002: 37–38.
21. Jones 1964: 529, 1221; *CTh.* 6.4.10 (originally from 356 c.e.).
22. *CTh.* 11.16.15 (originally from 382); Jones 1964: 452.

Without mastery of *paideia* (of which there is strong evidence), the opportunity would have come to nothing, however. Because of this mastery he was able to function far from home, finding common ground with the men with whom he worked. Educated and lofty with the abstract and celestializing title of *illustris,* Dexter functioned successfully in the male *homosocial* spaces of the administrative structures in which he served.

A word about homosociality will be welcome at this moment. The adjective "homosocial" and the related noun, "homosociality," made a decisive arrival in studies of sex and gender with the appearance in 1985 of *Between Men: English Literature and Male Homosocial Desire* by Eve Kosofsky Sedgwick. Sedgwick wrote that "'homosocial' is a word [that] describes social bonds between persons of the same sex; it is a neologism, obviously formed by analogy with 'homosexual,' and just as obviously meant to be distinguished from 'homosexual'" (1). Mongrels of Greek and Latin (as is "homosexual"), "homosocial" and "homosociality" refer to same-sex relations broadly construed.[23] Hence, male homosociality designates connections between men forged through rivalry or in friendship, and it also most assuredly includes in its ambit sexual acts between men. Displacing the anachronistic and not to be crossed frontier separating homosexuality from heterosexuality, homosociality proposes a terrain that includes a range of intertwining/overlapping social relationships: hostility, cooperation, friendship, and erotic relations. This terrain is most hospitable to the late-ancient evidence surveyed in this book, especially as this is a time before homosexuality, as would be recognizable now, existed.[24] Thinking in terms of homosociality enables discussion of the demonstrable continuity in late antiquity between friendship and same-sex desire without employing the more problematic terms "homosexual" or "gay"; homosociality keeps the focus on the evidence at hand and is a less invasive and less anachronistic hermeneutic instrument.[25]

---

23. The mongrel nature of these terms is perhaps less objectionable than usual. Their nature in the case of this study employing Greek and Latin sources is, at the very least, poetically appropriate.

24. For the beginnings of "homosexuality" in the nineteenth century, see Foucault (1978) and Halperin (1990: 15–40; 2002a). In a persuasive study of changes in the representation of masculinity in painting around the time of the French Revolution, Abigail Solomon-Godeau remarks on the usefulness of homosociality as a concept: "Homosociality may include homosexual acts or meanings within its purchase, but is in no way limited to them. The more nuanced, flexible and inclusive meanings of homosociality are, moreover, of greater descriptive utility in discussing works of arts made, historically speaking, before homosexuality" (1997: 29).

25. Erik Gunderson (2000) and Richard King (2004, 2006) both feature extensive use of homosociality as a guiding concept in their discussions of ancient manhood. Also see my book chapter on Antony and Paul the Simple (2006) and my general discussion of issues attending the study of ancient masculinity (2013).

Homosocial and homosociality are useful terms for considering, for example, the ever-growing structure of advancement for men of *paideia* in the fourth century and into the fifth: the bureaucracy. Dedicated to the emperor's service and always creating more senators, the bureaucracy moved men around the empire. Well described as homosocial, the bureaucracy was permeated by competition, friendship, and words of same-sex desire. It is a mistake to view the realization of manhood in this homosocial context as primarily agonistic; the bureaucracy was often marked by cooperation and relation. The man with whom another man wanted a connection might be portrayed, via metaphor, as sexually desirable and the connection depicted, again by metaphor, as an erotic one (and with no diminution of status on either side). This is not to say that there was no competition or *agōn* to be had in this system. There was. But the man making his way could not act as though he were involved in a zero-sum game in which there was nothing but honor for winners and shame for losers. Relations of patronage and travel far from home demanded something more in the tool-kit for career success than winning at all costs with submission for thee and not for me. The reality for late-Roman men, at least in these burgeoning senatorial circles, is not captured by models of the Roman manhood of earlier centuries. Those models propose a strong honor-shame dynamic that gives pride of place to sexual penetration as a metaphor for political power, with honor doled out to the penetrators/political winners and shame to the passive men/political losers.[26]

Now the second sketch—this one of a man whose origins were not as humble. *Paideia* again is important, and the role of same-sex desire in male homosocial relations is abundantly in evidence.

Born in Burdigala (Bordeaux) probably a few years before 355, Meropius Pontius Paulinus,[27] best known as Paulinus of Nola, was of senatorial stock, wealthy, and well educated. His teacher was the famous poet and political figure, Ausonius. Paulinus' extensive surviving writings show a supple mind in command of its intellectual inheritance. His political career, while not as brilliant as Dexter's, was all the same estimable.[28] In 378 or just before, he was suffect consul, and in 381 he was *consularis* (or proconsul) of Campania. After 381, he made his way back to Burdigala where he had a spell

---

26. For strong statements both of the importance of penetration as an indicator of masculine authority and of the loss of honor incurred by being penetrated in earlier Rome, see Parker 1997, Richlin 1997 and 1992a, Walters 1997, or Williams 1999.

27. Jones 1971: 681–83 *Paulinus* 21.

28. Trout 1999 and Conybeare 2000 were useful in the crafting of the coming remarks on Paulinus' career and life.

of leisure (*otium*) that was considered appropriate after the task (*negotium*) of office holding. Office holding was important for senators to burnish their credentials and to gain the desired appellations of *spectabilis* or *illustris* through service.[29] But time away to manage estates and cultivate civilized pursuits (including writing works that would demonstrate literary mastery) was a *desideratum* for reasons of duty and pleasure. Paulinus' return to the quiet of Burdigala should be seen in this light.[30]

In the later 380s, Paulinus married a wealthy Spanish heiress by the name of Therasia, and shortly thereafter moved to northern Spain with her. Also around this time, misfortune struck twice. Paulinus' brother was killed, and this seemed for a time to presage difficulties for his property and even his person. Whatever the danger was, however, it apparently dissipated. Then he and Therasia lost their baby son, Celsus, when he was only eight days old. Sometime later, Therasia and Paulinus redefined their marriage as one in which sexual relations would not play a part, and they also began to give away their possessions and embrace asceticism. In 394, Paulinus became a priest in Barcino and, in the next year, he and Therasia moved to Nola in Campania, where Paulinus, first as priest and then as bishop, tended the shrine of St. Felix and superintended a building program there. Paulinus died at Nola in 431.

Throughout his adult life, Paulinus wrote poetry and exchanged letters with other important men in the empire, e.g., Augustine, Sulpicius Severus, Victricius, and, of course, Ausonius. The highly intertextual verse letters to and from Ausonius are famous, even notorious, for their sublimated and not so sublimated expressions of same-sex desire. While these letters are perhaps hyperbolic in this respect, they are not unparalleled; similar warmth can be found elsewhere in the late-ancient record. It is also important to remember that these letters were not private in the way modern letters are; they were "sophisticated textual performances" meant to advertise both the connection between writer and recipient and the writer's mastery of *paideia*.[31] Hence, these letters are representative of an important aspect of late-Roman men's homosociality on the basis of this public role. Brief remarks on a verse letter written by Ausonius (*Epistulae* 23/24[32]) and Paulinus' response (his *Epistulae* 11) suggest what is going on in these letters.

---

29. It seems probable that Paulinus gained the title of *spectabilis* through being *consularis* in Campania (Chastagnol 1960: 433).

30. Cameron 2011: 396–98; Matthews 1975: 1–12, 17–18; Salzman 2002: 44–49. In a discussion of emperor Julian, Susanna Elm (2012: 72–75) underscores the politicized complexion that *otium* often possessed.

31. Ebbeler 2009: 272.

32. *Epistulae* 24 is an expanded version of 23.

Writing most probably around the year 390, Ausonius concludes *Epistulae* 23 (at line 52 [=24.124]) with direct quotation of line 108 of Virgil's eighth eclogue: "Are we to believe this or do the very ones who love contrive dreams for themselves?" (*Credimus? An qui amant ipsi sibi somnia fingunt?*).[33] The context for this line in Virgil's poem is the conclusion of the second of two songs offered by two shepherds, Damon and Alphesiboeus. Line 108 is the second to last line of the poem and it concludes Alphesiboeus' offering: a song of desire[34] that functions as a binding spell which seemingly accompanies ritual action performed by Amaryllis to make her man, Daphnis, come back. Line 108 is Amaryllis' words as she wonders whether her song and rite have been successful: she hears the dog barking! It seems that someone may be at the door (107)! Ausonius quotes *Ecl.* 8.108 after visualizing, at length, Paulinus coming from far away and making his way through town to Ausonius' very door. Ausonius is talking to himself: "and passing by his own properties, now! now! let him knock on your door! Are we to believe this or do the very ones who love contrive dreams for themselves?" (*Ep.* 23.51–52 [=24.123–24]: *et sua praeteriens iam iam tua limina pulsat! / Credimus? An qui amant ipsi sibi somnia fingunt?*). Making use of glamorous Virgil, Ausonius offers the carnal—undeniably in the past and perhaps in a moment if the spell has worked—relation between Amaryllis and Daphnis as a metaphor for his friendship with Paulinus: their relation has a similar intensity. It is impossible to overstate the significance of the intertextuality of the end of this poem of Ausonius with Virgil's. Given the direct quotation and similarity of content *and* the centrality of Virgil to late-ancient *paideia*, these observations just made, in all their detail, are emphatically plausible ones for Paulinus to have made, and other late-ancient readers (or hearers) of this verse letter too.

It is appropriate to speak now of intertextuality and its use in an investigation such as this one. The existence of an educated and engaged late-ancient readership in possession of *paideia* is assumed throughout this book. Such an assumption is logical given that possession of *paideia* was necessary for success among late-ancient elites. It also is relevant that the period of the fourth century into the early fifth century was a time of considerable renewal of and innovation in literature and rhetoric. This efflorescence did not occur in the absence of an appreciative and engaged audience. Assuming the prevalence of a high level of education in elite circles and relying on a reasonable hypothesis of widespread engaged reading, the scholar should regard late-ancient texts' intertextuality with earlier texts as eminently inter-

---

33. This translation, as are all in this book, is my own.
34. 8.83; 8.89.

pretable. The claim is that recognition now of likely awareness then of an author's manipulation of his textual inheritance and posited late-ancient readers' perceptions—some of which an author would have anticipated and still others that might have surprised him—are reasonably regarded as valuable, if always to some degree contestable, data. Perceptible links with prior literature—perceptible because of the high level of education among late-ancient elites—enable perceptions of meaning on the basis of a text's similarity to and difference from older texts.

A frequent point of difficulty as regards intertextuality is its indeterminacy. It is a fact that, while the author writes his texts and indeed arguably sets out (and even has the intention) to quote, say, Plato or Homer, any intertextuality-dependent meaning that emerges requires competence in the reader. In the absence of readerly competence, the author's intention counts for nothing. It is also conceivable that readers may make meanings on the basis of perceived relations with other texts that might puzzle an author and even run counter to his intentions (could they be known, and they cannot). In other words, all manner of conclusions are possible. All the same, while certainty is not possible, persuasive cases are there to be made and the intertextuality of late-ancient productions with earlier works is a resource for the scholar.[35]

If return is now made to the poetic correspondence of Ausonius and Paulinus, it will be seen that Paulinus also associates friendship with desire and carnality in his ardent response to Ausonius, *Epistulae* 11. There is, for example, an audacious *double-entendre* toward the end of the following passage in which Paulinus figures a reproach from Ausonius as a sexual assault:

> Continuata meae durare silentia linguae
> te numquam tacito memoras placitamque latebris
> desidiam exprobras neglectaeque insuper addis
> crimen amicitiae formidatamque iugalem
> obicis et durum iacis in mea viscera versum.

You remind me that extended silences of my tongue grow hard/long (*durare*), while you have not been silent at all. You find fault with my

---

35. I have found the following helpful in coming to an understanding of intertextuality: Conte 1986, Edmunds 2001, Fowler 2000: 115–37, and Hinds 1998. Interpretation of the intertextuality of late-ancient texts, which Cameron (1998: 705–7) has recommended to scholars of late antiquity, is not that common in the secondary literature, though this is changing. For examples, see Børtnes 2000, Kelly 2008, Knight 2005, MacCormack 1998, Masterson 2010, Mastrangelo 2008, or Roberts 1985.

pleasing laziness in hiding places. You add, in addition a charge laid on account of a friendship untended. You throw it in my teeth that a yoke-mate is feared. You pitch into my very vitals a hard . . . verse (*durum iacis in mea viscera versum*). (*Ep.* 11.1–5)

Paulinus restates Ausonius' complaints about the fact that he has been writing letters that have been unanswered, while Paulinus has been at his ease on his estates. Furthermore, Ausonius has accused Paulinus of not behaving as a friend should and Paulinus' wife, Therasia (the "yoke-mate"), is one to be feared: is she interfering with their friendship? Then comes the *double-entendre* (which is prefigured by *durare* in line one). The second clause in line five starts with the adjective meaning hard (*durum*) and then moves to the pitching into the vitals (an action which can certainly hold sexual meaning[36]). The imagination may run wild until the word "verse" (*versum*) arrives at the end of the line to attempt to make it all innocent, but this is an insufficient remedy. The "damage" has been done, for the reader has been on a journey and memory will abide. The not to be spoken pain (or is it pleasure?) of being penetrated is called to mind briefly; the verse may be hard but who doesn't like poetry?[37] Besides, Ausonius' Virgil's Amaryllis has her own abiding memories and ones to come too, if Daphnis is at her door.

In addition, words appear later in Paulinus' letter that would certainly indicate a love relation (more than likely with sexual union), if they passed between a man and a woman:

[As long as I live,] I will see you with my heart, I will embrace you, everywhere present to me, with my pious mind. And when released from this bodily prison, I fly away from earth, in whatever heaven the father of all

---

36. *Viscus* in the plural, as here, can refer to internal organs of men and women and to spaces within the body (*OLD* 3a and b). "Until the swords of the fatherland make their way into the bowels (*in viscera*) of Caesar, Pompey will be unavenged" is Lucan's thought at *Bellum Civile* 10.528–29 (*dum patrii veniant in viscera Caesaris enses / Magnus inultus erit*). Also of interest and from the sixth century, Maximinus at *Elegies* 3.31 uses *viscera* to designate the genitals of a young woman who yearns for her boyfriend (who is also the narrative voice in the poem) to have sex with her: "Then *as her innermost parts* were panting, she looks for me everywhere" (*Tunc me* visceribus *per totum quaerit anhelis*). But most to the point, there was a developed discourse in Latin poetry of *viscera* being able to refer to the male rectum in a sexual sense (Adams 1982: 116). At *Priapea* 25.6 (first-century c.e.), the anonymous author uses the phrase *intra viscera* to designate the promised anal penetration of a fruit-thief by Priapus (the minor god of gardens) and there is a similar (and notorious) moment in Juvenal at *Satires* 9.43.

37. Cf. Catullus 116.8, where he figures his poetry as a weapon capable of penetrating an opponent.

places me, there too I will hold you in my mind. The end which will ease me from my body will not ease me from your love. (*Ep.* 11.55–62)[38]

Paulinus' words, which can be called, *mutatis mutandis,* romantic, provoke reflection now. While it will no longer do to describe these poems in terms of "gay love," as Boswell did in 1980 (133–34), it will do to assert that Paulinus metaphorizes his friendship with Ausonius as a love relation, complete with physical union, because it makes for an intense metaphor. In remarks tailored to Paulinus' prose letters but also relevant to the verse letters to Ausonius, Catherine Conybeare notes that the "letters express the love of friends, which reflects and is enriched by Christ's love; in loving a friend more fully, one will also love Christ more fully, and hence become more fully Christian" (2000: 16). Friendship for Paulinus was part of the universe of Christ's love and devotion to friends was a way to participate truly in this love. The more intense he could make this devotion, and calling to mind erotic relations was a way to secure maximal intensity, then all the more would the friendship so portrayed express the intense and limitless goodness of Christ and the Christian life. Thoughts and feelings that elsewhere would excite censure can be evoked because their carnal intensity makes them assertive metaphors (even for something, i.e., Christian friendship that is often thought, then and now, to be distant from erotic relations between men).

Comparison of the sketch of Paulinus' life with that of Dexter brings out aspects they have in common, and the greater knowledge about the life of Paulinus suggests what to infer often about Dexter's. In the first place, and like Dexter, Paulinus served the emperor and service probably raised him from *clarissimus* to *spectabilis.* Dexter, on the other hand, made it all the way to *illustris.* Dexter and Paulinus both possessed high levels of education. The contours of his career and Jerome's report suggest the extent of Dexter's *paideia,* and Paulinus' writings and career reveal his. Furthermore, and once again like Dexter, Paulinus traveled. He left his home and functioned elsewhere. *Paideia* of course enabled such travel, but there needed to be a certain canniness around homosocial relations. The paucity of sources

---

38. videbo corde, mente complectar pia
  ubique praesentem mihi.
  et cum solutus corporali carcere
  terraque provolavero,
  quo me locarit axe communis pater
  illic quoque animo te geram.
  neque finis idem, qui meo me corpore,
  et amore laxabit tuo.

about Dexter (and especially of sources from his own hand) does not allow much consideration of the ways in which this travelling and formation of important relations with other men may have worked. The case with Paulinus is quite different, as has been seen in the foregoing sketch.

Paulinus speaks about his relations with his male friends through amorous and carnal metaphors. The metaphoric use of same-sex desire to talk about the depth and power of male friendship is not hard to understand. Paulinus uses the immediacy of erotic connection as a compelling metaphor to underscore the importance of his relations with other men: it is deployment of hyperbole to secure maximum emphasis. This metaphoric use is also easy to understand because of the pronounced isometry between love and alliance/mentorship: erotic relations and friendship share similarities, and this was recognized as far back as Aristotle,[39] to say nothing of Plato. At the same time, the use of erotic relations as a metaphor flows naturally from the education that late-ancient elite men received. Both the Latin and Greek canons featured high-status works that gave late-ancient men erotic language to employ when they spoke of their relations with one another. As just seen in the case of Paulinus and Ausonius, a poem by Virgil provides inspiration and a medium. In the Greek sources, pederasty prevalent in sources from golden-age Athens functions similarly as a bank of images and language, as a look at a letter by "emperor Julian" to the philosopher Iamblichus (77 [Wright 1980b/1923] / 183 [Bidez/Cumont 1922])[40] or an oration (his fourth) by the real emperor Julian will show.[41]

But same-sex desire and same-sex sexual pleasure provide more than a compelling metaphor for friendship. There is an integral relation between same-sex desire and the projection and portrayal of masculine authority in

---

39. See my discussion (2010: 83–84; 86–90) of friendship in relation to erotic relations (with frequent reference to Aristotle's positions) in emperor Julian's fourth oration.

40. Passed down in the corpus of emperor Julian's works and dating most likely from the first decades of the fourth century, *Ep.* 77 (Wright 1980b/1923) / 183 (Bidez and Cumont 1922) is a letter from "emperor Julian" (not the emperor, who more than likely had not even been born when Iamblichus died) to Iamblichus that features extraordinarily warm language. This letter is the source for one of the fragments of Sappho (Frag. 48 [Lobel and Page 1955]) at 446C, and, at 448C, "Julian" makes reference to the double-bodied beings from Plato's *Symposium* (echoing language from *Smp.* 191C) who were separated by Zeus and who were subsequently in danger of dying of grief until intercourse was made possible through the remolding of human bodies. For more on the dating and authorship of letter 77/183, see Barnes 1978.

41. For the employment of same-sex desire to metaphorize friendship through the use of Plato and Theocritus in emperor Julian's fourth oration (which dates from the 350s), see my discussion from 2010. Chapter one of this book features extended consideration of the presence of same-sex desire in Julian's *Caesares* via intertextuality with Plato. Also see Børtnes (2000) for Gregory of Nazianzus' use of Plato's language of same-sex desire to metaphorize masculine friendship in his funeral oration for Basil of Caesarea.

late antiquity. Analysis to come will show same-sex desire playing two further roles:

- Demonstration of knowledge of the physical realities of male same-sex desire and pleasure makes authority more credible. The supreme knowingness of authority, projecting itself anywhere it pleases, has cognizance of these forbidden things.
- Expression of same-sex desire provides a metaphor to portray late-Roman men's admirability and the power of their *auctoritas* or *axiōma*/ ἀξίωμα.[42] As amatory language goes "up" in contexts of social asymmetry to metaphorize a superior's grandeur, it also goes "down" in these contexts to show a lofty one's esteem for a social inferior.

As a way into considering these further facets to the role of same-sex desire in late-Roman men's homosociality, attention now turns to the hostility directed at this desire and pleasure. The continuity between homosocial togetherness and same-sex sexual connection exemplified in Paulinus' and Ausonius' letters in some respects seems from another world when action in law is considered.

LAW AND THE KNOWINGNESS OF AUTHORITY

In the early 390s, three Roman emperors signed their names to a letter or *epistula* (with the force of law) condemning the male prostitutes in the city of Rome to be burned in public. Although the heated and florid language is metaphorical, anal penetration is clearly exercising their imperial majesties. The consistory or privy council of the lead emperor, Theodosius I (his colleagues Valentinian II and Arcadius, aged 19 and 12 respectively, were more figureheads than active presences at this time[43]), likely composed the

---

42. For ἀξίωμα as a Greek synonym for *auctoritas* in late antiquity, here is the following:
    - *TLL* 2.1213.69–70,
    - consideration of the entire entries for ἀξίωμα in *LSJ* and *Lampe* and close attention (in *Lampe*) to 1a (honor for persons; cf. Eunapius, *Lives of the Philosophers* 6.5.4.6/465 [Wright 2005/1921: 394], 8.1.5.1/481 [Wright 2005/1921: 462]), 4b.i (civil office; cf. Eunapius, *The Chronicle after Dexippus* 65.1), and 4.b.iii (episcopal office; cf. Julian *Ep.* 58/17 [Bidez and Cumont 1922/Wright 1980b/1923]) suggest that this word's combination of valuation and office makes it an apt synonym,
    - and there is, finally, emperor Augustus translating *auctoritas* directly as ἀξίωμα at *Res Gestae* 34.3.
43. Resident in Gaul and indeed not allowed to leave, Valentinian II was dominated (with

epistula. Virius Nicomachus Flavianus, the quaestor and leading member of Theodosius' consistory, may have been the author of the actual words,[44] which are rhetorically elaborate and sophisticated.[45] Providing a dramatic contrast to the warm words between Paulinus and Ausonius and written at nearly the same time, the *epistula* came from the masculine homosocial space of the consistory:

> Emperors Valentinian [II], Theodosius [I], and Arcadius [send these words] to Orientius, the *vicarius* of the city of Rome: "Orientius, most dear and delightful to us (*k[arissime] ac iuc[undissime] nobis*), we do not endure (*non patimur*) that the city of Rome, the mother of all virtues/ manly excellences (*virtutum omnium matrem*), be fouled any longer by the contamination of effeminized shame in a man (*in viro*) and that the ancient founders' rustic strength—made exiguous through the people broken with softness—incur abuse either in the time of the founders or in the time of the emperors. Therefore all those who practice sexual debauchery by condemning their manly body (*virile corpus*) that they refashioned in a womanly way through the yielding (*patientia*) proper to the other sex, and having no difference from women—all these, having been arrested, as the monstrousness of this sexual debauchery demands, and having been led forth from all the brothels of men (*virorum lupanaribus*) (It shames even to say it!), Your Experience (which will be praised) will punish with the avenging powers of flame as the people watch, so that all may understand that the abode of the manly soul (*virilis animae*) must be sacrosanct (*sacrosanctum*) to all and that not without the highest penalty will he who disgustingly has lost his own [sex] attain to a sex not his own." Posted in the Hall of Minerva on the fourteenth of May [in 390]. (*Mosaicarum et Romanarum Legum Collatio* 5.3.1–2)[46]

Theodosius' agreement) by the general Arbogast; otherwise, it would be possible to imagine him as more active, and Arcadius was obviously too young to exercise political authority.

44. Honoré 1998: 58, 14.

45. E.g., the law's 97 words contain but two sentences, both of which are syntactically complex; there is word play (discussed below) around the words *patior* and *patientia;* alliteration toward the end of the second sentence: *sine summo supplicio,* etc.

46. IMPP. VALENTINIANUS THEODOSIUS ET ARCADIUS Auggg. ad Orientium vicarium urbis Romae. 1. Non patimur urbem Romam virtutum omnium matrem diutius effeminati in viro pudoris contaminatione foedari et agreste illud a priscis conditoribus robur fracta molliter plebe tenuatum convicium saeculis vel conditorum inrogare vel principum, Orienti k[arissime] ac iuc[undissime] nobis. 2. Laudanda igitur Experientia Tua omnes, quibus flagiti usus est virile corpus muliebriter constitutum alieni sexus damnare patientia nihilque discretum habere cum feminis, occupatos, ut flagitii poscit inmanitas, atque omnibus eductos, pudet dicere, virorum lupanaribus spectante populo flammae vindicibus expiabit, ut universi intellegant sacrosanctum cunctis esse de-

Written in two lavish sentences, this letter survives through the fact that it caught the attention of the unknown compiler of a collection of Mosaic regulations from the Old Testament combined with opinions of Roman jurists, the *Mosaicarum et Romanarum Legum Collatio* (henceforth *Collatio* or *Coll.*).[47] A radically shortened version of the law appeared a little less than fifty years later in the legal compilation known as the *Codex Theodosianus* (henceforth the *Codex* or *CTh.*) and this version had great currency in centuries to come because of its appearance in the *Codex:*

> The same three emperors [i.e., Valentinian II, Theodosius I, and Arcadius send these words] to Orientius, the *vicarius* of the city of Rome: "All those who practice sexual debauchery by condemning their manly body (*virile corpus*) that they refashioned in a womanly way through the yielding (*patientia*) proper to the other sex—for they seem to maintain no distinction from women—they, through the avenging powers of flame, will pay for so high a crime while the people watch." Posted on August 6 in the forum of Trajan in the consulships of emperor Valentinian (his fourth) and Neoterius. (*CTh.* 9.7.6)[48]

---

bere hospitium virilis animae nec sine summo supplicio alienum expetisse sexum qui suum turpiter perdidisset. Prop. pr. id. Maias Romae in atrio Minervae [a. 390].

(Note: Frakes [2011: 170] proposes a different text at four spots, none of which much affect the argument to be pursued:

IMPPP. for *IMPP.*,
in viris for *in viro*,
flagitiosus luxus for *flagiti usus,*
and
flammis for *flammae.*)

47. A collection of documents from Roman law and excerpts from the Old Testament, the *Mosaicarum et Romanarum Legum Collatio* was unparalleled, and questions remain about the purpose of the work. It is also of uncertain date. Most of the internal evidence suggests that it was compiled in the early fourth century. The inclusion of this *epistula* (which then appears in shortened form in the *Codex Theodosianus* as 9.7.6) necessitates either that this section is a later addition or that the *Collatio* itself was compiled after 390. Agreeing with the general scholarly consensus, I regard the *Collatio* as datable to the very late fourth century. For further discussion of this work, see Frakes 2011 and 2002; Matthews 2000a: 277–79; Corcoran 1996: 11, nn. 27–28; Harries 1998: 67–70 (detailed and helpful remarks on content, dating, and manuscript history [and now Frakes 2011]); Honoré 1998: 8 n. 65; Robinson 1997: 65; Liebs 1987: 162–74.

A further thing to note about the *Collatio* is the debate since the 1930s over whether it is a work coming from a Christian or Jewish perspective. The apparent scholarly consensus has gone back and forth on this question, and Frakes (2011: 129–40 and 2006: 129–37; cf. Rutgers 1995: 210–11), whose position is that the anonymous author was Christian, provides helpful surveys of the swings of the pendulum. Rutgers has recently argued at length for Jewish authorship (1995, 210–53) and Jacobs (2006) presents a case for Christian authorship.

48. Idem AAA. Orientio vicario urbis Romae: Omnes, quibus flagitii usus est virile corpus muliebriter constitutum alieni sexus damnare patientia, nihil enim discretum videntur habere cum

Noting differences between the *epistula* and its edited version from the *Codex* is revealing, but before proceeding it is necessary to discuss the compilation of the *Codex*.

The *Codex Theodosianus* is a massive compilation of laws (more than 2500 of them) meant to sum up legal thought since the advent of the Christian emperors. The original dates of the various documents contained in the *Codex* extend from 313 to 437. A project of emperor Theodosius II (hence the name *Codex Theodosianus*), the idea was to collect from all over the empire various rescripts, *epistulae, decreta, edicta,* and *orationes* and edit them so that a "sacred generality" (*sacra generalitas*) could be distilled from them, as is specified in the code itself at 1.1.5. *CTh.* 1.1.5 also named a board of men, one a resplendent *illustris* and the rest bright *spectabiles*, who did the editing that brought into light the *sacra generalitas* latent in the unedited documents. The resulting compilation, the *Codex* (most of which is still extant) along with two prior law codes, those of Gregorius and Hermogenianus (both of which are substantially lost), were meant to "contribute to a further volume, a comprehensive manual of law which would be a true guide to life, a *magisterium vitae* [*CTh.* 1.1.5] for future generations" (Matthews 2000a: 10). This last volume, the *magisterium vitae*, was not written, arguably, until emperor Justinian's efforts in the next century, while the *Codex Theodosianus*, of course, was. John Matthews describes the process of its composition:

> It will be recalled that in the law of 429 [*CTh.* 1.1.5] they [the editors] were instructed to excerpt points of substance in the texts of laws, to classify the excerpts under relevant titles, dividing texts between titles where appropriate, and to abbreviate texts by omitting superfluous wording not relevant to the point of law in question. In the law of 435 [*CTh.* 1.1.6], they were given authority to make additions where necessary, to clarify ambiguous passages, and to emend texts to remove incongruities. (2000a, 129)

The completed code was then presented by the East to the West and came into effect on New Year's Day in 439.[49]

---

feminis, huiusmodi scelus spectante populo flammae vindicibus expiabunt. Pp. in foro Traiani VIII id. Aug. Valentiniano A. IIII et Neoterio conss. (I thank Bruce Frier and Amy Richlin for their advice on this translation.).

49. See Harries (1999: 21–23) for a clear and concise description of the genesis of the Code and indeed see all of both Harries (1999) and Matthews (2000a) for the code in general. See Honoré (1998) and Garnsey and Humfress (2001: 52–64) also.

As noted above, direct comparison of *Collatio* 5.3 and *CTh.* 9.7.6 is revealing. In the first place, the later document does not specify that it is a matter of executing prostituted male slaves (for it would have been slaves who were working in the brothels). Now all men who would be sexually passive are liable to be executed (and perhaps their partners in crime, as it were, though the language of *CTh.* 9.7.6 is vague on this point). Furthermore, the later version lacks the expansive rhetoric of the earlier one. Gone now are references to Rome being mother of all virtues/manly excellences, the rustic strength of the ancient founders, and other comments from the deluxe first sentence. Missing too are the warm homosocial address to Orientius ("most dear and delightful to us") and the mention of sacrosanctity ("the abode of the manly soul must be sacrosanct [*sacrosanctum*]"). Further reflection suggests, however, that the homosociality and sanctity may not be lost, but are present in different form: the board of male colleagues *worked together* to bring the *sacra generalitas* into evidence, and the entire operation was, in any case, overseen by the *consecrate* emperor, Theodosius II, whose name graces the compilation.

The harsh penalty of burning in *Collatio* 5.3 and *CTh.* 9.7.6 is a dreadful innovation on what had been the case in previous centuries. Roman men's sexual dissidence, if it was punished at all, was subject either to informal disapproval or on occasion to the following substantial, although not as dire, penalties: the inability to speak in court, loss of half of one's goods and the inability to make testamentary distribution of the rest.[50] There would have been no concern in those earlier days, of course, for a prostituted slave, and late antiquity is a long way from Seneca the Younger, who merely advised against *amicitia* or a relation of patronage with a male prostitute.[51]

This severe penalty for male sexual dissidence is not without precedent in the fourth century, however; the *Codex* contains a law, originally from 342, that could be a regulation enacted against weddings between men:

> Emperors Constantius [II] and Constans [send these words] to the people: "When a man weds as a woman, what should this 'woman,' who would abandon manhood [*lit.* men], want when sex has lost its place? When there is this crime which it does no good to know, when Venus is changed into another form, when love is sought and is not seen—we order that the laws rise up, that Law be armed with an avenging sword, so that these infamous ones be brought low by well-wrought punishments, [all of them] who are

---

50. Richlin 1993: 560.
51. *De Beneficiis* 2.21.1–2; McGinn 1998: 44.

guilty or who will be." Given on December 4 in Milan, posted in Rome on December 16 in the third consulship of emperor Constantius (II) and in the second of emperor Constans. (*CTh.* 9.7.3)[52]

While imprecise in specification of the penalty for these perhaps illegally-wed[53] pairs, violent punishment awaits guilty ones. The increased savagery of penalties for passive male same-sex sexual behavior, which attracted legal sanction inconsistently in the past, was a manifestation of an increasing preference in the later empire for harsher legal penalties. Ramsay MacMullen (1990) points out that the number of crimes punishable by death more than quadrupled between 200 and 400 C.E. (with three-quarters of the increase occurring in the fourth century). While numbers are deceptive because of the vagaries of evidence's survival, they are nonetheless evocative. And it was not just male same-sex sexual behavior; adultery and *stuprum* (sexual relations with unmarried free persons) attracted the penalty of execution. Writing in the 390s in his *Res Gestae,* the historiographer Ammianus Marcellinus speaks of the execution of persons of both sexes for adultery

---

52. IMPP. CONSTANTIUS et CONSTANS AA. ad populum. Cum vir nubit in feminam, femina viros proiectura quid cupiat, ubi sexus perdidit locum, ubi scelus est id, quod non proficit scire, ubi Venus mutatur in alteram formam, ubi amor quaeritur, nec videtur, iubemus insurgere leges, armari iura gladio ultore, ut exquisitis poenis subdantur infames, qui sunt vel qui futuri sunt rei. Dat. prid. non. Dec. Mediolano, proposita Romae xvii kal. Ianuar. Constantio iii et Constante ii aa. conss.

53. As can be well imagined, there is debate about what kind of relation is at issue. John Boswell twice (1980: 123; 1994: 85–86) argues that this law outlawed marriages between men; he also favors a reading different from the one printed above (i.e., *Cum vir nubit in feminam viros porrecturam, quid cupiat . . .* ["when a man weds as a woman who would offer herself to men, what should he want . . . "]; see Craig Williams' discussion [1999: 362–63]). The use of the word *nubo*, which precisely designates taking the woman's part in a wedding, supports Boswell's perception. On the other hand, Danilo Dalla (1987: 63 n.2; [cf. 170; indeed see discussion of both *CTh.* 9.7.3 and 9.7.6 on 165–84]) and Eva Cantarella (1992: 175–76) maintain that the use of *nubo* is not literal, but metaphorical (Harper [2013: 152–53] is in substantial agreement with this position). Mathew Kuefler makes the interesting suggestion that marriages between intact and eunuch men were at issue (2001: 101–102). Frakes (2011: 266) draws attention to the reputation, reported by Zonaras, that Constans, one of the signatory emperors, had for being interested sexually in lads and young men (*Epitome Historiarum* Lib. 13–18, pg. 32.16–17: μειρακίσκων καὶ νεανίσκων). This law was possibly a highly ironic enactment, especially as one of the verbs Zonaras uses may be saying that "they [the lads and young men] would be made kinsmen" (pg. 32.17: ᾠκείωντο [was this some sort of brotherhood?]); cf. Harper (2013: 284, n. 28) for more ancient *loci* reporting the sexual irregularities of emperor Constans. In any case, given the current (and, until recently, inconceivable) debate about and actual changes to the definition of marriage in the West, on the one hand, and the possible metaphorical nature of the language in this law, on the other, I am content to say that I cannot decide what is at issue beyond same-sex sexual activity, and I am (even strongly) impatient with the certainty of those who think that male/male weddings of some kind could *not* be at issue. In any case, if the reception of this law is considered, the fact that its very language would have called to mind in late antiquity marriages between men is beyond debate and a point of interest.

and *stuprum* in Rome in 370–71.⁵⁴ A law originally from 339 C.E., *CTh.* 11.36.4, condemns adulterers either to be sewn up in a sack and thrown in a river (the fate of parricides) or to be burned.⁵⁵ Prior to the fourth century, the worst punishments for adultery had been loss of property and *relegatio* (banishment to an island).⁵⁶

Merely to attribute the violence of the penalty specified in *CTh.* 9.7.6 to the late-ancient tendency to punish illegal actions more violently, as another instance of pervasive "judicial savagery," as MacMullen said in 1990, is to identify part of the cause for this increasing legal severity as the whole reason. The targets in the *epistula* from the *Collatio* were male prostitutes. The excision of their mention, which criminalized this sexual behavior for all men, came later with the *Codex* in the late 430s. The significance of the *epistula* is that it is concerned with male and not female prostitutes; proper masculine gender performance is at issue. The frequent use of the word *vir* (man) and derivatives from it in the *epistula* underscore this. The abbreviation in *CTh.* 9.7.6 suggests in addition that the basic concern of the law, which the editors of the *Codex* would have called its *sacra generalitas* (*CTh.* 1.1.5), was manhood and prohibition of sexual activity between adult men. The contrast between the respective fates of male and female prostitutes is instructive too. At the end of his book on Roman prostitution, when Thomas McGinn looks forward toward developments in late antiquity, he notes that female prostitutes are regarded in a number of late-ancient Christian representations as capable of being redeemed and, indeed, of attaining impressive heights of sanctity.⁵⁷ No such discourse emerged about male prostitutes; the reality was the opposite.

Regarding an idea of proper manly behavior as the *sacra generalitas* identified by Theodosius' illustrious board underscores the significance of the use of *vir* (and derivatives) in both laws. The *epistula* fixates on this normative and evocative noun and its related adjective, *virilis,* through mention of the "brothels of men" (*lupanaria virorum*) and of sexual dissidence appearing in manly bodies (*corpora virilia*) and manly souls (*animae viriles*) and, indeed, through the possibly pornographic phrase, "in a man" (*in viro*). The designation of Rome as the "mother of all virtues/manly excellences"

---

54. *Res Gestae* 28.1.16 (adultery); 28.1.28 (adultery and *stuprum*).
55. See Evans-Grubbs (1995: 216–25) for further discussion of the penalties exacted in late antiquity for adultery.
56. Gardner 1991: 128.
57. McGinn 1998: 348; see Virginia Burrus' (2004: 128–46) discussion of two prostitutes (Mary, Niece of Abraham, and Pelagia) whose seductiveness and degradation make them especially attractive objects for divine love. Burrus remarks of Mary: "Even God cannot resist the alluring saint. In—not despite—her 'sin,' she is perfected" (137).

(*virtutum omnium matrem*) further intensifies the emphasis on manhood, as *virtus* had a long association with men and manhood.⁵⁸ *CTh.* 9.7.6 speaks too of the manly body.

An ancient man (Latin *vir*; Greek *anēr*/ἀνήρ), according to many of the sources and in the secondary literature generally deferential to these sources, follows the rules. He is an impenetrable penetrator in sex and honors the local customs in dress and deportment. The opposite of the *vir/anēr*, as the sources have often hastened to add, is the *cinaedus*. The *cinaedus*, or *kinaidos* (κίναιδος) in Greek, is a free adult male who enjoys the passive role in sex, and it is generally assumed that he will lack gender conformity in his dress and behavior.⁵⁹ The anonymous author of the fourth-century Latin physiognomy, who is therefore contemporary with both *Collatio* 5.3 and Ausonius and Paulinus, makes reference to a story about the philosopher Cleanthes (*floruit* third century B.C.E.) who identifies a *cinaedus* through hearing the man's sneeze. The phraseology is significant. The author says that the man "confessed through his sudden sneeze that he was no man" (*Anon. Lat.* 11: *sternutamento subito virum se non esse confessus est*). Of course the word *cinaedus* does not occur here but ample discussion of *cinaedi* elsewhere in this work (e.g., *Anon. Lat.* 55) shows that a *cinaedus* is at issue. This conclusion is bolstered by the fact that Anonymous presents, as noted above, an abbreviated version of a story about the philosopher Cleanthes, fuller renditions of which can be found in Diogenes Laertius (third century C.E.) and Dio Chrysostom (40–c.112 C.E.; *Or.* 33.53–54). In both of these versions, the Greek word, *kinaidos*/κίναιδος, appears. Here is Diogenes Laertius' version of the story:

> While [Cleanthes] was speaking about Zeno—that he was such as to quickly grasp character from its outward appearance—it is said that some mischievous young men led before him a *kinaidos* who had been made rugged in the great outdoors, and they asked [Cleanthes] to reveal [what he could] about [the *kinaidos*'] character, but, being thoroughly at a loss, he told the man to leave. But as he was leaving, he sneezed. Cleanthes said, "I have him [now]—he is *soft*" [i.e., a *kinaidos*]. (7.173)⁶⁰

---

58. Kuefler 2001; McDonnell 2006.
59. See Halperin 2002b for an energetic presentation (that includes consideration of late-ancient evidence) of this view of the *cinaedus*/κίναιδος.
60. Λέγεται δὲ φάσκοντος αὐτοῦ κατὰ Ζήνωνα καταληπτὸν εἶναι τὸ ἦθος ἐξ εἴδους νεανίσκους τινὰς εὐτραπέλους ἀγαγεῖν πρὸς αὐτὸν κίναιδον ἐσκληραγωγημένον ἐν ἀγρῷ καὶ ἀξιοῦν ἀποφαίνεσθαι περὶ τοῦ ἤθους, τὸν δὲ διαπορούμενον κελεῦσαι ἀπιέναι τὸν ἄνθρωπον· ὡς δὲ ἀπιὼν ἐκεῖνος ἔπταρεν, ἔχω, εἶπεν, αὐτόν, ὁ Κλεάνθης· μαλακός ἐστι.
(See Gleason's discussion of all the above [1995, 76–81].).

Often showing great deference to points of view discovered in the sources, scholarship on ancient masculinity frequently seems to follow in the footsteps of the anonymous physiognomist and Cleanthes. The sneeze explodes with the truth and significance that set a scholar's agenda. Men who don't follow the rules for dress and sexual activity often wind up as footnotes or foils to "real" men in discussions of ancient manhood,[61] and a frequent feature of scholars' discussions of gender in late antiquity is a lack of accounting for same-sex desire and same-sex sexual behavior at moments when it might be expected.[62] The sources say these men are not men, and the judgment is accepted. And the sources are beguiling. They offer evidence and interpretative schemata for understanding it at the same time. It is, of course, crucial to understand what the norms say, but they are not the whole story.

What is being investigated here requires both distance from asserted norms and attention to what is not said, or not quite said. The shapes are dim and the structures are complex and contradictory; that which is denied and reviled is embraced, and even known from the unpromising and surely indirect evidence of, say, a sneeze. And, in this context, recourse to the

---

61. Brown 1988; Corbeill 1996; Edwards 1993; Gleason 1995; Halperin 1990; Parker 1997; Richlin 1992a, 1997; Williams 1999/2010; Winkler 1990.

62. For example, Kate Cooper (1992, 1996, 2007, 2009; see, too, Cooper and Leyser 2000), writing on gender in the later empire, focuses energetically on late-ancient men's interests in women. She also, with success, reveals the contours of honor and esteem that a sexually active elite *mater familias* could command in the later empire (2007). Men's same-sex desire does not interest her and remains outside of any detailed consideration, and this in spite of her concentrated attention on late-ancient men's homosociality. Peter Brown's important *Body and Society* (1988) mentions same-sex desire a total of five times in the course of its 500 plus pages. In an important article from 1996, Gillian Clark quotes Augustine's *Confessions* 2.2.2 (a moment of undeniable same-sex desire *and* same-sex sexual activity) and effaces the same-sex dimension of the passage to use it in discussions of the body and mind/soul and of the relations between men and women. In two studies not on gender, but relevant in the present instance, Dennis Trout's (1999) and Catherine Conybeare's (2000) excellent books on Paulinus don't say anything substantive about same-sex desire.

Kyle Harper's *From Shame to Sin* (2013) came too late into my hands for detailed engagement. Suffice it to make a few observations. He pays considerable attention to same-sex desire throughout his book on the transformation of sexual ethics in the Roman empire over the period of the 100s to the 500s. His focus in the case of same-sex desire in late antiquity is on legislation and regulation in the contexts of changing attitudes to slaves and the development of a Christianized ethos of sexual behavior (see 141–58, and, especially, 141–43 [*Collatio* 5.3], 153–55 [*Collatio* 5.3 and *CTh.* 9.7.6], and 152–53 [*CTh.* 9.7.3]). Composing a narrative that, once it reaches the fourth century, looks to the *telos* of Justinian's repressions and grows ever darker, Harper does not have time for nuances and counter narratives to be found in the sources and, indeed, in the interested passions and claims to authority of the legislators: his story is about the construction of an oppressive discourse. That said, his suggestion that proper sexual activity (i.e., "'natural' sex") in late antiquity "is reorganized around the gender of the partner rather than the role of the sexual actor" (139) impresses me as worth measuring against the evidence and arguments presented in this book.

name of the *cinaedus* must be resisted. Conjuring the *cinaedus* will have a totalizing effect and have him, a perfect embodiment of deviance, facing the supposedly utterly different *vir*, a perfect embodiment of compliance, across, perhaps, a no-man's land that no logic or words can cross, finesse, or eliminate. The coexistence of Paulinus' *Ep.* 11 with the *sacra generalitas* of *CTh.* 9.7.6 strongly suggests that thinking in terms of *cinaedus* and *vir* will be a hermeneutic strategy too blunt for discussing same-sex desire among men in late antiquity: the *vir* cuts a more complex figure. Furthermore, setting the adversarial and totalizing figures of *cinaedus* and *vir* against each other does not keep faith with a complex reality recognized within the (highly hostile to same-sex desire) confines of *Collatio* 5.3 and *CTh.* 9.7.6.

While it is perhaps arguing a bit from a noisy silence (for there are words), it is significant that, instead of the more neutral term *homo*, *Collatio* 5.3 features *vir* and related words, and *CTh.* 9.7.6 speaks of the *virile corpus*. The evidence from the anonymous physiognomist and elsewhere suggests that *vir* would be precisely the wrong word. Societal expectations for elite men had inflected the word *vir* for centuries, and it is a word omnipresent in the *Codex* (appearing over two hundred times).[63] Also a frequent word in the *Codex* and appearing over 130 times, *homo* indicates a human of either sex[64] and generally lacks the presupposition of status that *vir* possesses.[65] Of course, many hands wrote the original versions of the laws, and there was the editing to secure *sacra generalitas* for the *Codex*. But, inasmuch as there were expectations among the writers about the meanings of words in the legal corpus and, just as importantly, expectations present among those reading, it is interesting that *vir* and related words, and not *homo*, are the words used in both the *epistula* and the later law. *Homo* would more naturally designate a man, probably enslaved, who is discovered working in a brothel.

The result is that the appearance of the word *vir* attributes a desire for men to men. The late-ancient conception of "man" can contain such things, and, although the imperial majesties, consistory, and, eventually, editorial board of Theodosius II are not happy about it, this state of affairs is nonetheless recognized by all involved (and by Theodosius' board most of all). Of course, this is not to say, either, that this is an innovative liberatory proclamation. It is hardly that: execution is on the agenda. Rather, if the deployment of *vir* in *Collatio* 5.3 is read against expectations for its

---

63. See Gradenwitz (1970/1925: 277–78) for a list of occurrences of *vir* in the *Codex*.
64. E.g., 5.7.2.pr.
65. E.g., 16.6.4.pr., but 16.8.22; see Gradenwitz (1970/1925: 99) for a list of occurrences of *homo* in the *Codex*.

meaning recoverable from other sources (and exemplified by Anonymous' presentation of the sneeze of revelation), late-ancient disagreement about the meaning of *vir* becomes visible. Instead of thinking this an example of late-ancient careless prolixity, for the sheer frequency of the word (and derivatives of it) in the *Codex* suggests intent, it is preferable to squint through the glare of the pyre of prohibition and, taking the emperors and their staffs, *viri* all, at their words, consider this desire a possibility for late-ancient *viri* that the emperors recognize, and that the emperors wish to be seen recognizing. While they rely on the notion that such behavior is a thing not to be done by *viri*, the rhetorically elaborate excess of the writing in the *epistula* indicates interest, and the *enargeia* of the depiction of same-sex sexual behavior in it demonstrate that masculine imperial authority has the expertise and experience to rule on such a thing.

Attentive reading of *Collatio* 5.3 reveals images of same-sex copulation: *virorum lupanaribus* ("the brothels of men") and, with but minimal pressure, *in viro* ("in a man"). In addition, the perceptible word play around the verb *patior* and the related noun *patientia* brings to mind a male-to-male sexual encounter. The verb coming first (*non patimur*, "we do not endure") is rendered a *double-entendre* when "the yielding proper to the other sex" (*alieni sexus . . . patientia*) arrives in the second sentence, for the verb *patior*, in an ancient idiom still alive in late antiquity, is part of the phrase used to designate what a man experiences when he allows another man to penetrate him anally: *pati muliebria* (*lit.* "to endure womanly things").[66] The emperors have comprehensive knowledge of this thing, while, at the same time, they push it away, entrusting it to their *vir*, the "most dear and delightful" Orientius whom they punningly address as "Your Experience,"[67] to handle.[68]

While at first perhaps a cause for pause, this state of affairs is ultimately not so surprising. Authority (*auctoritas*/ἀξίωμα), if it is to be convincing, needs to show itself knowledgeable about forbidden things. It must pull them close even as it pretends to an insurmountable distance from them. Authority will brandish what it disavows. Some formulations of Slavoj Žižek are useful for thinking about the empowering display of forbidden matters. He is alive to the way ostensibly decorous authorities can have

---

66. E.g., Augustine, *De Mendacio* 9.15; for more, see *TLL* 10.1 731.63–732.25.

67. The address, *Experientia Tua*, appears elsewhere in the *Codex*: 3.32.2 [320s], 8.5.57 [397], 10.10.16 [382], 12.1.126 [392], 16.5.28 [395], 16.10.8 [382].

68. Incitement to visualization similar to *Collatio* 5.3 occurs at *CTh.* 9.7.3 when a man marries as a woman does. What is going on "when Venus is changed into another form, when love is sought and is not seen" (*Ubi Venus mutatur in alteram formam, ubi amor quaeritur, nec videtur*)? The reader or listener has been given an invitation to imagine or even remember.

an obscured investment in what they say they cannot abide. Authorities interested in the control of their own and, especially, others' bodily urges maintain a connection to these urges nonetheless. Žižek speaks of a denying law that remains intimate with that which it would deny: the "judicial domain" is penetrated by "vital" forces (Žižek 1991: 147). It could be said that the display of authority on the part of these three co-emperors is "smeared by an obscene vitality" that causes their profiles and their *epistula* to "[assume] the features of a heterogeneous, inconsistent *bricolage* penetrated with enjoyment" (Žižek 1991: 149). Unforgiving authority's profile is faceted by the sexy carnality of life that calls law into existence, makes law necessary, and this authority grows more powerful through the faceting: there is nowhere that this authority cannot go and there is nothing it cannot or will refuse to see. It entertains even that which is not proper for it to entertain, parasitically supping on and drawing power from life's realities.[69]

A METAPHOR FOR ADMIRABILITY

In addition to functioning as a metaphor for friendship and as disavowed and yet brandished knowledge that increased the credibility of authority, same-sex desire, expressed by one man for another, also served as a metaphor for the admirability of the man who was (at least metaphorically) so

---

69. It is also possible to think of the *epistula* as something of a dodge. Pleasure in forbidden same-sex unions is displaced into a trumpeting of regulation that indulges in visualization of that which is taboo (cf. Gunderson [2003: 235] for a similar dynamic in first-century C.E. declamation). Still another way to think about these words from the sacred emperors is that disavowed desire shapes the *epistula* by its explicit absence. The desire and the known (but disavowed) masculine potentiality for passive desire "register[s] itself *negatively* in [this legal] speech," appearing not as confession but as prohibition (Copjec 1994: 14 [emphasis in original]). Also possibly visible are continuities between this embrace of forbidden carnality, which bolsters this authority that speaks of its sacred nature, and the ritual religious obscenity of previous centuries. Earlier in the Roman empire and republic and in Greece, contexts religious to various degrees were marked by obscenity (by which is meant the utterance of words and/or the revelation of body parts that were not supposed to appear outside of private situations, if there at all). Ritual contexts such as the Eleusinian Mysteries had obscenity associated with them and, in literature that featured obscenity, an association with religion is easily found. The frequently obscene plays of Aristophanes were presented at the *Lenaia* (a religious festival), and the lyric or satirical poetry of a Roman *vates*, who had religious aspirations himself (a *vates* can be a poet or seer), often featured obscenity (see Henderson [1991: 13–17] for Athenian festivals, and see Richlin 1992a for the *vates* [8–9; 31, 210], Roman festivals [9–10], and discussion of earlier Roman notions of obscenity [1–31]). Obscenity made the one who displayed it in religious contexts more powerful in earlier centuries, and consecrate imperial authority knowledgeably calling to mind explicit carnality seems an echo of this. For obscenity in late antiquity, see Shanzer 2006 and my forthcoming article, "Authoritative Obscenity in Iamblichus and Arnobius."

desired. If a man's *auctoritas* or *axiōma*/ἀξίωμα was worthy, then this worthiness could be troped as one man's attractiveness to another man. Expressions of same-sex desire performed the function of increasing the grandeur of a superior or raising the status of an inferior; these expressions confirmed or finessed hierarchy.

In Jerome's *Vita Pauli*, for example, Antony of the Desert casts himself as the locked-out lover, and time spent with Paul of the Desert is depicted as time spent with a beloved.[70] For more than six hours before Paul's locked door, Antony pleads:

> You know quite well who I am, from where and why I have come. I know that I don't deserve to see you. All the same I will not leave until I see you. You who welcome beasts, why do you repel a man? I have sought and I have found; I pound so that it may be opened. And if I don't get what I seek, here—here—(*hic, hic*) I shall die at your doorstep. Surely you will bury [me] even when I am a corpse? (9.5)[71]

Citing prior scholarship that sees Antony "playing Romeo to Paul's Juliet," Virginia Burrus sees the opening moves of the eventual communion of these two saints as an "almost parodically groping rite of courtship" (2004: 30). Indeed, as it is the case that Antony complains outside the locked door of his desired one, thoughts may turn to the many *paraklausithyra* in the erotic poetry of centuries previous. The repetition of "here" (*hic, hic*) certainly recalls the staginess of earlier Roman erotic poetry.[72] Furthermore,

---

70. Jerome wrote the *Vita Pauli* in the 370s, and in it he tells the story of Paul of the desert. A fanciful and thought-provoking work, the *vita* was clearly meant to be an answer to Athanasius' influential *Vita Antonii* from the previous decade.

71. Qui sim, unde, cur venerim, nosti. Scio me non mereri conspectum tuum, tamen nisi videro, non recedam. Qui bestias suscipis, hominem cur repellis? Quaesivi, et inveni, pulso ut aperiatur; quod si non impetro, hic, hic moriar ante postes tuos: certe sepelies vel cadaver? (I thank Amy Richlin for advice on this translation.)

72. See, e.g., Horace *Odes* 3.26 (line six in particular):

> Vixi puellis nuper idoneus
> et militavi non sine gloria:
>   nunc arma defunctumque bello
>   barbiton hic paries habebit,
> laevom marinae qui Veneris latus   5
>   custodit: **hic, hic** ponite lucida
>   funalia et vectis et arcus
>   oppositis foribus minacis.
> o quae beatam diva tenes Cyprum et
> Memphin carentem Sithonia nive,   10
>   regina, sublimi flagello
>   tange Chloen semel arrogantem.

when Antony threatens suicide if he is not admitted, Jerome's text may bring to mind the scene of boyish cruelty to the importuning lover exemplified by Theocritus' *Idyll* 23. In this poem, the lover, driven to despair by rejection, commits suicide by hanging himself in front of the locked door of the boy's house (49–53). A late-ancient reader sensitive to these intertextual dynamics through *paideia* will perceive Jerome figuring the respect and reverence that Antony had for Paul as same-sex desire.

In his *Lives of the Philosophers* (a set of linked biographies of learned men and one woman probably written in the late fourth or early fifth century), Eunapius metaphorizes the regard that disciples/comrades (*homilētai* [ὁμιληταί] / *hetairoi* [ἑταῖροι]) have for the various charismatic philosophers he depicts as a sexual and even fetishizing regard. A short way into this work, Eunapius admits that he has not captured all the details he wanted to about the men whose lives he will narrate. As he does so, he thematizes his devotion as erotic and suggests that the fragments of the illustrious lives he presents should be regarded as fetishized women's clothing or jewelry:

> This much, then, I emphatically place on record, and knowing full well that some things have perhaps escaped me, but other things have not. And if, although expending much thought and effort on this, namely that there might be a continuous and definite account of the lives of the most celebrated of philosophers and rhetoricians—if I then fell short of my ambition, I have had the same experience as those who love madly with consuming flames. For they, seeing their beloved herself and the chilling beauty of her appearance, look down, lacking the strength to look at what they desire and being utterly dazzled. But if they see her sandal or necklace or earring, heartened by these, they send forth their souls into the sight and melt at the vision, being able to see and love the symbols of beauty more easily than the beauty itself. (2.2.1.1–2.2.5.1; 454–55 [Wright 2005/1921: 348–50])[73]

> Until recently I have lived, suitable for the girls, and I have served under arms not without glory. Now this wall will possess the arms and lyre used up in battling—the wall which guards the left side of marine Venus. **Here, here** set down the gleaming torches, the bars, and the bows (*sc.* of Cupid)—things that threaten opposing doors. O goddess, who possesses Cyprus and Memphis free of Sithonian (Thracian) snows, O queen, please flick Chloe, for once uncooperative, with your sublime lash.

73. Καὶ ταῦτά γε εἰς μνήμην ἐγὼ τίθεμαι, τοῦτο συνορῶν, ὅτι τὰ μὲν ἔλαθεν ἴσως ἡμᾶς, τὰ δὲ οὐκ ἔλαθεν. ἐκείνου δὲ καίπερ πολλὴν ποιούμενος φροντίδα καὶ σπουδήν, τοῦ συνεχῆ καὶ περιγεγραμμένην εἰς ἀκρίβειαν ἱστορίαν τινὰ λαβεῖν τοῦ φιλοσόφου καὶ ῥητορικοῦ βίου τῶν ἀρίστων ἀνδρῶν, εἶτα οὐ τυγχάνων τῆς ἐπιθυμίας, ταὐτόν τι τοῖς ἐρῶσιν ἐμμανῶς καὶ περιφλέκτως ἔπαθον. καὶ γὰρ ἐκεῖνοι, τὴν μὲν ἐρωμένην αὐτὴν ὁρῶντες καὶ τὸ περίψυκτον ἐν τῷ φαινομένῳ κάλλος, κάτω νεύουσιν, ὃ ζητοῦσιν ἰδεῖν ἐξασθενοῦντες, καὶ περιλαμπόμενοι· ἐὰν δὲ πέδιλον αὐτῆς ἢ πλόκιον

Eunapius invokes the urgency of a physical response to express his regard for the generational succession of philosophers.⁷⁴ Also, there is more than a passing similarity between Eunapius' invocation of erotics and the various sublimations of eroticism in the *Symposium*⁷⁵ and other works of Plato. Indeed, since Plato's works arguably had achieved scriptural status by late antiquity,⁷⁶ this invocation of erotics calls to mind scenarios replete with same-sex desire that were as close as the nearest (and readily available) copy of the *Phaedrus, Philebus*, or, of course, *Symposium*.

In addition to providing a metaphor to depict the admirability of a magnificent man, the language of same-sex desire was useful for raising the status of inferiors. This language arguably finessed hierarchy, making status differences seem less steep through an appeal to something outside of these differences. The language of erotic regard often performs this function in the law codes. The hailing of Orientius by the emperors as "most dear and delightful" in *Collatio* 5.3 lessens the effects of hierarchy and, of course, shows affection. *Karissime* and *carissime* (merely alternate spellings) appear a number of times in the *Codex* as part of direct addresses by one or more emperors to inferiors.⁷⁷ There is further warm language in the Sirmondian Constitutions⁷⁸ and in the *Novellae* of Theodosius II and Valentinian III.⁷⁹ In these legal collections, two set phrases occur repeatedly. At times, the emperors will address an inferior as "brother most beloved"

ἢ ἐλλόβιον ἴδωσιν, ἐκείνων καταθαρσοῦντες, τὴν ψυχήν τε τῇ ὄψει προσαφιᾶσι καὶ κατατήκονται πρὸς τῷ θεάματι, τὰ σύμβολα τοῦ κάλλους μᾶλλον ἢ τὸ κάλλος ὁρᾶν ἀνεχόμενοι καὶ στέργοντες.

74. Cf. Patricia Cox Miller's remarks:

> Using the simile of the lover, Eunapius describes his narrative enterprise in terms that are not only erotically emotional but also aesthetic; his biographical sketches are to be read as "symbols of beauty" that evoke beauty itself, the philosophical tradition to which his subjects belonged. (2000a: 213 [cf. 236])

Miller sees the text's aesthetic dimensions rendered more urgent by the evocation of erotics. Clothing and jewelry, which inspire an erotically fetishistic investment, designate the entire succession of philosophers starting from Plato, the "golden chain" (*chrysē seira*/χρυσῆ σειρά [2000a: 213; citing Fowden 1982: 34]). Miller's views contrast with and complement the interests of the present analysis which sees same-sex desire being used both to metaphorize masculine admirability and to draw a portrait of homosociality that has a somatic urgency to it.

75. See for example, the so-called "ladder of love" in the *Symposium* at 210A–211C.

76. Miller 2000a: 212; G. Shaw 1995: 8.

77. *Karissime* in the *Codex*: 1.15.13, 1.16.9, 3.18.1, 6.30.1, 6.35.6, 7.4.1, 7.22.11, 8.11.5, 9.21.9, 9.27.5, 11.30.52, 12.1.27, 12.6.17, 12.9.2, 13.1.13, 15.1.5, 15.1.22, 15.1.33, and 16.5.44; *carissime* occurs at 15.1.4.

78. The Sirmondian Constitutions are full versions of legislation that in a number of cases appeared in edited form in the *Codex*.

79. The *Novellae* are laws that these emperors issued too late for them to make it into the *Codex* or after it came into effect in 439.

(*frater amantissime*),⁸⁰ and at other times they will address him as "parent most dear and most beloved" (*parens karissime atque amantissime*).⁸¹

SUMMATION AND PRIOR SCHOLARSHIP ON LATE-ROMAN MANHOOD

So then: in late antiquity same-sex desire and pleasure among men

- provided a metaphor for important friendships, relying on isometry between friendly and erotic relations and often assuming recognition of references to texts well known through *paideia*,
- comprised a disavowed and yet brandished knowledge of forbidden pleasure and desire that increased authority's credibility, and
- provided once again a metaphor (also often drawn from texts learned in the course of education) to speak of another man's grandeur or to finesse hierarchy.

Same-sex desire, accordingly, was an important element in late-ancient men's understanding of their homosociality, providing a logical metaphor to portray symmetrical friendship. It also proved valuable to the projection of masculine authority through its demonstration of authority's vital and knowledgeable reach to regulate forbidden pleasures and desire; the demonstrated understanding of the mechanics of male to male sexual behav-

---

80. "*frater amantissime*" (the date of issue is in brackets):

- Sirmondian Constitutions: *none*
- *Novellae* of Theodosius II: 5.1 [438], 19 [440], 21 [441], 24 [443], 25 [444]
- *Novellae* of Valentinian III: 6.3 [444], 7.3 [447], 24 [447], 28 [449], 30 [450]

See Corcoran (1996: 335–36) for more examples of affectionate language in law and related documents.

81. "*parens karissime atque amantissime*" (the date of issue is in brackets):

- Sirmondian Constitutions: 1 [333], 2 [405], 7 [380/1], 9 [408], 12 [407], 14 [409], 16 [408]
- *Novellae* of Theodosius II: 1 [438], 3 [438], 4 [438], 5.2 [439], 5.3 [441], 7.1 [439], 7.2 [440], 7.3 [440], 7.4 [441], 8 [439], 9 [439], 10.1 [439], 10.2 [439], 11 [439], 12 [439], 13 [439], 14 [439], 15.2 [444], 16 [439], 17.1 [439], 17.2 [444], 18 [439], 20 [440], 22.1 [442], 22.2 [443], 23 [443], 26 [444]
- *Novellae* of Valentinian III: 1.1 [438], 1.2 [440/1], 2.2 [442], 2.3 [443], 2.4 [454], 3 [439], 4 [440], 6.1 [440], 6.2 [443], 7.1 [440], 7.2 [442], 8.1 [440], 8.2 [441], 10 [441], 11 [443], 12 [443], 13 [445], 14 [444], 17 [445], 19 [445], 20 [445], 21.1 [446], 21.2 [446], 22 [446], 23 [447], 25 [447], 26 [448], 27 [449], 29 [450], 31 [451], 32 [451], 33 [451], 34 [451], 35 [452], 36 [452]

ior increased authority's power and grandeur, as it was therefore clear that there was no place where this authority could not or would not go. The language of same-sex desire also provided a lively metaphor for the respect owed a superior, or, making the steep status divisions in late antiquity more livable, for the esteem in which an inferior was held. At the same time, however, law and less formal statements, e.g., the anonymous Latin physiognomy, condemn such desire and pleasures and regard them as inimical to manhood. Hence, there is the possibly contradictory, but better seen as paradoxical, situation of same-sex desire and pleasure being useful for representation of authority and power, even as they are decried in identical milieux as (indicative of) deplorable weaknesses.

This conflicted situation, which can be characterized as a clash between reality and morality, i.e., masculine realities prove irresistible to authorities who simultaneously find fault with them, generates effects in turn. This play of aspects in conflict increases the otherworldliness of the resulting masculine profile. According to earthbound systems of moral evaluation, late-ancient elite Roman manhood should be questionable because its grandeur is secured through degradation; height, so to speak, is attained via depth. This dynamic recalls the paradoxical valuation of materiality in late-Platonic philosophy. The transcendently pure can be paradoxically present in this bounded and contingent world, and the failure of reason to account for this state of affairs is a strong proof of this fact. It is best, therefore, to understand this conflicted situation around same-sex desire as a dynamo that increases grandeur in a similar fashion. This situation also suggests that masculine grandeur is best measured according to a scale of valuation whose coordinates are otherworldly. The conflict between the positive evocations of same-sex sexual attraction/activity and the condemning *sacra generalitas* of *CTh.* 9.7.6 can only be resolved in some place beyond human morals and the laws of this world.

This vision of late-Roman manhood characterized by paradox and having a connection to things beyond this world, or the transcendent, has antecedents in the secondary literature on late-Roman men and manhood. Taking a cue from Maud Gleason's (1995) survey of the paradoxically successful career of Favorinus, the second-century eunuch *rhetor*, Virginia Burrus (2000) drew a picture of late-Roman manhood in which she paid close attention to paradoxical moments in it. She provided, for example, an interesting discussion of Ambrose's adoption of feminine modes of self-presentation in order to project an uncanny *persona* capable of thwarting imperial will.[82] In 2001, Mathew Kuefler saw paradox at the heart

---

82. 2000: 138–140.

of Christianized masculinity in late antiquity; the title of his book, *The Manly Eunuch*, was indicative. In his analysis, the eunuch figured as both a symbol for a progressively weakened classical manhood[83] and for the manhood he saw taking its place (and which achieved its ideal in the continent monk[84]). Kuefler also discussed Christian bishops figuring themselves as brides of Christ.[85] This figuration was old by late antiquity and ultimately derived from centuries of exegesis, Christian and Jewish, of the *Song of Songs*, where the Israelites and Yahweh were envisioned as beloved and lover respectively. Kuefler remarked that "we can only begin to imagine, for example, what a writer like Ambrose thought or felt about his masculine identity as he more than once hinted at the erotic pleasure of being a bride of Christ and then used the image to describe himself" (2001: 239). Helpful for the present argument are Burrus' and Kuefler's highlighting, e.g., of a virtually cross-dressing bishop putting an emperor in his place and a man imagining himself as Christ's bride; both Burrus and Kuefler demonstrated some of the manifest complexities that mark late-Roman elite manhood. Also helpful is Kuefler's notion of male productivity withering into eunuchism that was then reinterpreted as manhood paradoxically drawing strength from its impotence.

The secondary literature on men in late antiquity has also laid great emphasis on the idea of manhood as transcendent, as having a connection to things beyond this world. In 1971, Peter Brown presented the influential thesis that Christian holy men, as mediators between this world and the next, were virtual patrons of the communities with which they interacted.[86] Claudia Rapp outlined in 2005 three interconnected modes of epis-

---

83. "The threat to masculinity in late antiquity posed by the growing distance between expectation and reality—between the military ideal of manliness and the actual collapse of the empire, between the centrality of political office to aristocratic identity and the political impotence of the aristocracy, between the ideal of patriarchal marital and familial authority and declining *patria potestas*—all could be reconciled through the creation of a kind of counterculture that interpreted disjunction as paradox and was invigorated by its dissociation from traditional standards rather than frustrated by it. The use of paradox allowed Christian men to claim real manliness in apparent unmanliness" (2001: 209) Also see pp. 70–76 for discussion of ways in which emperor Constantine's legislation weakened the legal rights of fathers and husbands over female relatives and wives.

84. "[Monks'] easy appropriation of the identities [newly] crafted for Christian men in late antiquity—soldiers of Christ, brides of Christ, eunuchs for the sake of the kingdom of Heaven—affirmed their assumption of the new ideal. In larger terms, the physical eunuch had symbolically demonstrated the disintegration of the traditional model of masculinity. The monk, in contrast, proved the success of the Christian ideology of masculinity, embracing its paradox of manliness in unmanliness, even if it was a eunuch's embrace" (2001: 282).

85. 2001: 137–42; for Christ's frequent role as Bridegroom for women in late antiquity, see Jerome's *Epistle* 22, Shaw (1998: 248–52), Miller (1993/2001).

86. A frequent touchstone in Brown's work, the holy man and other elite religious men as me-

copal authority: pragmatic, ascetic, and spiritual. Pragmatic authority was institutional and an attribute of the office of bishop. Perceptible practices of bodily control caused ascetic authority to accumulate. Spiritual authority, an invisible and unearned gift from God, was the *sine qua non* of truly effective bishops. According to Rapp's analytical schema, the bishop with spiritual authority was touched by divinity and therefore possessed, by definition, the ability to transcend that was an attribute of Brown's holy man.

Gleason looked forward to late antiquity and remarked about elite male self-fashioning:

> Late antiquity begins when these status seekers [i.e., elite men looking to be preeminent in politics and rhetoric] start to draw on extra-social sources of validation, bypassing the approval of their peers to a hitherto unparalleled extent, a scenario that fostered the eccentric behavior of larger-than-life personalities in the fourth century, the age of Antony, Athanasius, Constantine, and Julian. (1995: 166)

Gleason's point was that one of the marks of late-ancient manhood was a decreased emphasis on building status in relation to one's peers. Men secured *auctoritas* or *axiōma*/ἀξίωμα through drawing accreditation from something larger than the group of locals, though the locals did in the end remain a key audience to impress with this display that had something uncanny and otherworldly about it.[87] Building on this insight of Gleason, Burrus presented an account of late-ancient manhood that arose from her analysis of the assertively orthodox Christologies and other writings of Athanasius, Gregory of Nyssa and Ambrose. The late-ancient explications of Christ's nature (and those of the Father and Spirit) made the nature of the son of God a *telos* for a manhood now possessing a transcendent dimension not present to the same extent in prior models of manhood, e.g., *miles, pater, senator, orator*, et al. (2000: 5).

Of course, the idea that manhood was related to something beyond this world—that it was transcendent—was an intensification of the association of men with the mind and women with the body. This dichotomization by gender was old by late antiquity, as were the following similar dichotomizations: mind/rationality/activity describing the male and body/

---

diators between earth and heaven featured quite emphatically in *The Making of Late Antiquity* (1978). Brown has modified his thoughts since then. See Brown (1987: 9 and 1992: 62–63) and Cameron's (1999) discussion of the evolution of his thinking.

87. As Burrus (2000: 21) observed in her consideration of Gleason's remarks.

irrationality/passivity describing the female.⁸⁸ Transcendence had an aura of masculinity about it given these long-lived conceptualizations. Not surprisingly, the primary literature is replete with descriptions of miraculous behavior or attributes attesting to the otherworldly nature of masculine *auctoritas*/ἀξίωμα. Eunapius reports that the philosopher Iamblichus would levitate and at times turn golden as he prayed.⁸⁹ Emperor Julian often applies the term "divine" or "godlike" (θεῖος) to him.⁹⁰ Athanasius depicts the famous Antony of the desert in the *Vita Antonii* in possession of a connection to God through his solitary practices of self-denial. And it was not just holy men who had these connections; similar characteristics were attributed to late-ancient elite men in general. Senatorial elites, described as *clarissimi, spectabiles,* and *illustres,* possessed distinction that was given the quality of light. Their *auctoritas* or ἀξίωμα shone. It was no more, and no less, hallucinatory than the "spiritual authority" belonging to bishops or the golden light pouring off Iamblichus' body. Calling the male body "sacrosanct" in *Collatio* 5.3 is thus another example of the ambitions of late-Roman manhood to connect with things not of this world. Mention of *Collatio* 5.3 returns the argument to the connection between late-Roman manhood's ambitions to transcendence and same-sex desire.

Any individual Roman man would have found same-sex desire and pleasure compelling or repugnant or somewhere in between and, likewise, would have found their prohibition limiting or irrelevant or, again, somewhere in between. But whatever the case, this desire and pleasure were things experienced directly, feared, and/or intellectually understood (it does not matter which of these and it can be more than one), and the concern to limit them by legal and less formal means shows the following: they occasioned interest and they had a constituency. Same-sex desire was *a fact,* and as a fact, it could hold whatever moral valence was desired, as existence is prior to morals in this case at least. The reality of it *usually* being regarded a

---

88. For the relation between male and female in the writings of Greek philosophers, see Lloyd (1993: 2–7, 18–28) and duBois 1988. For the continuation of this dynamic in late antiquity, see, e.g., Ruether 1974; Burrus 2000: 47–58. The persistence of these discourses made the late-ancient holy woman a remarkable exception that proves the rule. For examples, see the stories of Amma Sara (*Apophthegmata Patrum,* Sara 4 [*PG* 65 420C-D 41–48]; Castelli 1991b) and Sosipatra (*Lives of the Philosophers* 6.6.5–10.5 [Wright 2005/1921: 399–419]; Civiletti 2007: 384–417; Penella 1990: 58–62; Lanzi 2004). See also general remarks by Clark (1998: 176–77) and Kuefler (2001: 236–38).

89. *Lives of the Philosophers* 5.1.8 (Wright 2005/1921: 458/364); see extended discussion of this passage with comparanda and bibliography in Civiletti 2007: 326–34 (nn. 105 and 106). For more on the frequent appearance of light at the point of connection between a theurgist/philosopher and the divine, see Lewy 1978/1956: 467–71; Cremer 1969: 104–6; Sodano 1984: 255–57.

90. Bouffartigue 1992: 76–78; Wright 1980c/1896: 41–42. For more on the non-Christian holy man, see Athanassiadi 2002; Cox 1983: 17–30; Fowden 1982; Miller 2000a.

bad thing meant that it was, through the logic of the embrace of opposites, an attractive vehicle for expressing the transcendent and for suggesting that a man had a connection to things not of this earth. A dangerous and real thing, same-sex desire also excited imaginations and regulation and was subject to appropriation. This desire and pleasure made everything they touched more lively on account of the corporeal excitement they occasioned (hence their use in the depiction of friendship and admirability).

A further point to keep in mind is that even as this fascinating material was used, and the fact that it was forbidden was often a key attraction, the authoritative and manly sources were careful about the nature of its visibility as it was being deployed. When the use of this desire was positive (e.g., in the case of friendship and admirability), it was a metaphor: homosocial connection was expressed in ways that indicated knowledge of forbidden pleasure and desire, the direct force of which was deflected via metaphor. When this desire was reviled, it was prohibited, even as the lawmakers likewise indicated knowledge, limning the presence of even extravagant experience of forbidden corporeal realities.

Focusing on pleasure and knowledge themselves will further clarify this varying visibility. In the case of approving uses of same-sex desire and pleasure, the physical results of this desire's achieving its aim were downplayed but *pleasure* remained front and center through the happy affect in the metaphor. In the case of *knowledgeable* prohibition, the messy mechanics of manly coupling were *known,* and shown to be known, and it was pleasure that was erased: there is no fun or love to be had here. Paulinus soft-pedals the mechanics of same-sex sexual activity in preference for love, and the imperial consistories, when they forbid, deny that affection attends sex between men (*CTh.* 9.7.3: "when love is sought and is not seen" [*ubi amor quaeritur, nec videtur*]). One thing that both these discourses share is that the reality of same-sex desire and pleasure is called to mind and then repurposed amid ambivalence and variously expressed moral judgment, i.e., metaphorization or prohibition. This dynamic of the evocation of the real for positive or negative purposes and the subsequent application of morality reveals a number of things.

In the first place, this dynamic reveals that that which is real and existent is prioritized. The real thing attracts attention, and the moral strictures are reactive and secondary. Furthermore, the results of this frequent use of same-sex desire and pleasure to define friendship and homosociality and to build authority by men who would, in word at least, condemn same-sex intimacies are that they see same-sex desire and pleasure partially free of morality. The necessary corollary to this temporal prioritization of same-sex desire and its relative freedom from morality is the existence of a transcendent realm that is indifferent to earthly morals and strictures, and this realm, when embodied by carnal same-sex desire and pleasure, is, in all its indifference, close at hand and ready to lend a metaphor to friendship and life to *auctoritas*.

ONE

Emperor Julian's Marcus Aurelius

INTRODUCTION

In a passage from Iamblichus' *De Mysteriis*,[1] a treatise in ten books in which he re-theorizes pagan religious practice as theurgy ("God-Work"; *theourgia*/ θεουργία), the late third-/early-fourth-century philosopher describes how the divine makes its way from still singularity into increasing motion and differentiation; he shows how the transcendent manifests in this world. In the context of considering the connections between same-sex desire, homosociality, and the making of authority among late-ancient men, the Platonizing and, indeed, Platonic vocabulary is worth taking time over because of the importance of Plato in *paideia* in late antiquity. Terribly interesting too is the manifestation of beauty as manliness at the passage's end:

---

1. A new edition of this work appeared in the Budé series in 2013. The new title appearing on the cover is *Réponse à Porphyre* with the old title, *De Mysteriis*, in parentheses. As this treatise is Iamblichus' detailed response to Porphyry about the theoretical basis of his philosophy, the new title is sensible. Inside the book, however, the editors favor a different title for the work, "An Answer from Abamon" (Ἀβάμωνος Ἀπόκρισις), Abamon being the persona of an Egyptian priest that Iamblichus adopted when addressing Porphyry, who had started a dialogue with him taking the name of Anebo (also an Egyptian name). The words ΑΒΑΜΩΝΟΣ ΑΠΟΚΡΙΣΙΣ appear at the top of each of the 217 pages of the Greek text. I find this puzzling, and, while I have consulted this edition (its page and line numbers appear in brackets) and favor its readings, I have decided to retain *De Mysteriis* (*Myst.*) as the title.

Besides these characteristics [of ever increasing motion and differentiation (2.3.72–73 [54.4–55.2])], things divine flash forth a sort of irresistible/uncanny beauty, seizing those beholding it with wonder, providing a divinely sweet cheerfulness, manifesting itself with unspeakable symmetry, and transcending the fitting attractiveness of all other forms. The blessed visions of archangels also themselves have an extremity of beauty, but it is not at all as unspeakable and wonderful as that of the divine. The beauty of angels already divides up into parts the beauty that it receives from the archangels. The spirits of the daemons and heroes appearing in direct visions, each of them, possess beauty in distinct forms: the beauty which is arrayed in words determining essence is daemonic, and the beauty showing itself as manliness/courage is heroic. . . . (*Myst.* 2.3.73 [55.3–17])[2]

"A sort of irresistible or uncanny beauty" (*kallos hoion amēchanon*/κάλλος οἷον ἀμήχανον) flashes forth from divinity (*ta . . . theia*/τὰ . . . θεῖα). This beauty moves through the archangels, angels, and thence to the daemons and heroes as a signal manifestation of each. The material world participates with rising increments of contingency and perishability. Although this beauty expresses itself in increasingly less direct ways, the divine source of this beauty remains in view through Iamblichus' metaphors of light and vision. Beauty (*kallos*/κάλλος, *to kalon*/τὸ καλόν) "flashes forth" (*apastraptei*/ἀπαστράπτει), "transcend[s] the fitting attractiveness of all other forms," and ultimately is evident in epiphanies of the spirits (*autoptika pneumata*/αὐτοπτικὰ πνεύματα) of daemons and heroes. In the case of daemons, this irresistible or uncanny beauty is a thing arrayed/arranged (*diakosmēthen*/διακοσμηθέν)—significantly *diakosmeō*/διακοσμέω is a word not only used in philosophical contexts,[3] but also in military ones (e.g., *Iliad* 2.126 or 2.476) and ones related to beauty—in speech that depicts essence, thereby asssociating logic and philosophy with beauty both military and fetching. Finally, this beauty appears in heroes, manifesting as manliness or courage (*tēn andrian*/τὴν ἀνδρίαν).

---

2. Πρὸς δὴ τούτοις τοῖς ἰδιώμασι τὰ μὲν θεῖα κάλλος οἷον ἀμήχανον ἀπαστράπτει, θαύματι μὲν κατέχον τοὺς ὁρῶντας, θεσπεσίαν δ' εὐφροσύνην παρεχόμενον, ἀρρήτῳ δὲ τῇ συμμετρίᾳ ἀναφαινόμενον, ἐξῃρημένον δ' ἀπὸ τῶν ἄλλων εἰδῶν τῆς εὐπρεπείᾳ· τὰ δὲ τῶν ἀρχαγγέλων μακάρια θεάματα μέγιστον μὲν ἔχει καὶ αὐτὰ τὸ κάλλος, οὐ μὴν ἔτι γ' ὁμοίως ἄρρητον καὶ θαυμαστὸν ὥσπερ τὸ θεῖον· τὰ δὲ τῶν ἀγγέλων μεριστῶς ἤδη διαιρεῖ τὸ καλὸν ὅπερ ἀπὸ τῶν ἀρχαγγέλων παραδέχεται· τὰ δαιμόνια δὲ καὶ τὰ ἡρωϊκὰ αὐτοπτικὰ πνεύματα ἐν εἴδεσι μὲν ὡρισμένοις ἔχει τὸ κάλλος ἀμφότερα, οὐ μὴν ἀλλὰ τὸ μὲν ἐν λόγοις τοῖς τὴν οὐσίαν ἀφορίζουσι διακοσμηθέν ἐστι δαιμόνιον, τὸ δ' ἐπιδεικνύμενον τὴν ἀνδρίαν ἡρωϊκόν. . . .

3. E.g., one meaning of *diakosmeō* (*LSJ* I.3) according to the Stoics is the reordering of the world order after its destruction in an *ekpurōsis* (ἐκπύρωσις).

Iamblichus here asserts the presence of the transcendent in the material world, and a notable manifestation of this presence is divinity's beautiful appearance in the social field as *andria* (manliness or courage). The resultant gleaming *andria* possesses divine attributes and, further, Iamblichus' use of *kallos amēchanon* suggests the presence of same-sex desire. A primary meaning of *kallos* is physical beauty that attracts desire, and men comprise the presumed audience for the *De Mysteriis*. But perhaps even more important, the phrase *kallos amēchanon* makes a notorious appearance at the end of Plato's *Symposium* when Alcibiades tells the story of his attempt to seduce Socrates.[4] A reader in possession of *paideia* will likely think of Plato's text when this phrase appears and remember this scene with its intriguingly unexpected contours of same-sex desire. Recollection of Plato thematizes same-sex desire as an essential companion to *kallos amēchanon*, and, admiration of *andria* is metaphorized powerfully by a story that includes, and even incites, corporeal arousal. Admiration metaphorized in this way provides an additional support to Iamblichus' assertion of the transcendent's presence in this world. The inappropriateness of same-sex desire as a medium—its corporeality in the case of the divine and the possibility of an "unmanly" submission in the case of manhood—proposes that the universe and an admirable man are governed by forces that cannot be explained in terms that will avoid contradiction. And this surely is Iamblichus' claim about how to think about the social, for this passage is ontological and, indeed, "daemonic" in its presentation of the essence of paradoxically related levels of reality, a reality that, as it acquires contingency and mortality, might be said to "[assume] the features of a heterogeneous, inconsistent *bricolage*," whose burgeoning liveliness becomes an incitement to "enjoyment" (Žižek 1991: 149).

If the foregoing reading of same-sex desire and attractivenes into this passage from Iamblichus is to be persuasive, it needs parallels and an investigation into why the evocation of same-sex desire as a metaphor for the admirability of manhood would have been an effective strategy in late antiquity. To these ends, and building on what has already been said in the introduction to this book, there will shortly be discussion of emperor Julian's use in his *Caesares* of the same phrase Iamblichus uses, *kallos amēchanon*, in order to gauge its remarkable effects. As does Iamblichus, Julian invokes the *Symposium* at the carnal and transgressive moment of Alcibiades with Socrates. This intertextuality infuses Julian's portrait of Marcus Aurelius with a narration of same-sex desire. It will be also

---

4. This episode from the *Symposium* is discussed in detail below.

suggested that Julian's text at this point should be read with the *Charmides* (as could Iamblichus' for that matter), for the eponymous hero of this dialogue and object of Socrates' (supposed?) desire is arguably in possession of *kallos amēchanon* too. Since *kallos amēchanon* in the *Symposium* is an attribute of the desired Socrates and, in the *Charmides,* belongs to Charmides who is the object of Socrates' (supposed) desire, a narrative of an adult masculine sexual persona, who can be either subject or object of same-sex desire, is called to mind. To the extent readers of Julian's text will want to associate proper manhood with being the impenetrable penetrator in sexual relations, this vision of masculine versatility is a scandalous and even impossible one. The undecidability of sexual roles, i.e., inability to determine who is penetrator and who is penetrated, means that the asymmetry claimed for male/male sexuality in antiquity is not present in the case of Julian's Marcus Aurelius. A picture emerges of an idealized Marcus (and an ideal Socrates too) insouciantly separated from the protocols of penetrator and penetrated, subject and object of desire, honor and shame. Indeed, the "impossible" carnal desire of one man for another is offered for contemplation, and its transfixing, forbidden liveliness glamourizes Marcus' *auctoritas* or *axiōma*/ἀξίωμα. The chapter concludes with both Plotinus' use of *kallos amēchanon* to designate the emperor and discussion of the Missorium plate of Theodosius I. This massive and famous silver plate has both emperors and, significantly, cupids on it.

In between these discussions featuring *kallos amēchanon* associated with authoritative men, however, is an argument to show why an evocation of same-sex desire to glamourize manhood would have been effective, for it is the case that such a procedure is counterintuitive, given the presumption of shame accompanying penetration. Plato, as all, then and now, would agree, is wonderful, but, at the very least to a scholarly orthodoxy wedded to the idea that penetrating is an essential mark of manhood, it seems that something unmanly is happening to some man, if the intertexts are allowed their interpretability. Since the argument is that the intertextuality with Plato increases masculine glamour through importing the liveliness of actual life, and because the evocation of what is forbidden increases this glamour through the late-ancient love of paradox, an explanation of the mechanism involved will be welcome, if not necessary.

Given the widespread late-ancient penchant for enlivening paradox, there is more than one way to make this explanation. The retheorization of late-ancient pagan religious practice, i.e., *material* devotional practices like sacrifice are the way to a *dematerialized* transcendent, might have provided one corollary example of the mechanism posited for this valuation of same-sex desire. The theorization of the effects of relics, i.e., treasured bits and pieces of a saint's body and clothing are able to be, miraculously, the saint him- or herself on earth even as they are in heaven at the same time, could have provided another. However, since Julian's *Caesares*—a work which Julian characterizes as a *mythos*—is the centerpiece of the first part of the chapter, his defense of myths in his seventh oration (with the addition of Saloustios' *De Deis et Mundo*) has been chosen.

In the seventh oration, Julian provides a powerful example of a discourse that features an embrace of what is forbidden to underscore value and engineer transcendent glamour. Conveying nothing less than divine truth, the myths, whose surfaces of violence and sex are hardly in line with community norms, are valuable, and, the more objectionable they are, the more value they possess. This oration, in which Julian takes to task late-ancient Cynics in general and one late-ancient Cynic in particular, Heracleius (hence the title of the oration, *Against Heracleius*), is doubly useful in the present investigation of late-ancient manhood's relation to forbidden same-sex desire: paradox is visible not only in the valuation of myths, it also marks the speaking voice and persona of Julian himself in both the speech itself and in the *mythos* he tells of his own life. One moment he is critical of allegory and indirection in speech, and then, in the next, he praises them to the skies. Now he is mightily concerned that Cynics have been disregarding the opinions of society, and then he quotes with approval the Cynic maxim, "Give a new stamp to the currency" (*paracharaxon to nomisma*/παραχάραξον τὸ νόμισμα). This maxim recommends a challenge to society's ideas, because the impression that the *mores* of society make on human life are an imposture that must be erased in preference to what is real and true to the substance that has been defaced. In his discussion of this maxim (and another one not specific to the Cynics, "Know yourself" [*gnōthi sauton*/γνῶθι σαυτόν]), Julian recommends that the man who has ambitions to be wise consider what he is in reality, and not what society tells him he is, as he lives a life that aims at brilliant virtue. There is a scale of value extending beyond society; it is the liveliness of things that exist and are connected to the transcendent that matters, and not the judgements of society on both them and the man.

PLATONIC GLAMOUR IN THE *CAESARES*

In a passage from the moderately satiric and most Lucianic of all his works, the *Caesares* (also known as the *Kronia* and, significantly, *Symposium*), emperor Julian offers a portrait of emperor Marcus Aurelius in which he depicts his predecessor's glorious connection to the transcendent. In this portrait Julian also depicts Marcus' same-sex sexual attractiveness by means of Platonic intertexts. This intertextuality has a number of effects. In the first place, Julian infuses the portrait with a narrative of same-sex desire transgressive of the norms, well known to scholars of antiquity, of activity and passivity; it is not possible to tell whether Marcus' attractiveness should inspire in the reader a desire to penetrate or to be penetrated. Second, the collocation of authoritative glamour and same-sex sexual attractiveness is a further instance of masculine admirability metaphorized by sexual attractiveness to add to those already discussed in the introduction to this book. Lastly, the paradoxical embrace of the forbidden makes Marcus uncanny and therefore all the more transcendent.

Julian begins this work from late 362 with a conversation (10.1/306A–307A) between himself and (probably) his friend Saloustios at the time of the festival of the *Saturnalia* or *Kronia*.[5] Coming at the end of the year, the *Saturnalia* was a festival in which there were parties, gifts, role reversals, and the allowance of license for lower-status members of society. In his first words, Julian presents himself not wanting to speak nonsense and not being able to get into the spirit of the holiday, for, he says, he has no talent for being amusing. His friend notes that boors construct amusements laboriously. Agreeing, Julian proposes instead to tell a "myth" (10.1.11/306B: *mythos*/μῦθος) that he says Hermes told him (10.1.21/307A). He promises that this myth will be an amusement appropriate to the season and that it will contain "perhaps many things worth hearing."[6] Julian's friend rejoins: "I agree, reckoning with you and your

---

5. There is debate about precisely who this friend is. Saloustios/Saturninius Secundus Salutius (the probable author of *De Deis et Mundo*) is considered a possibility because Julian dedicated his prose hymn to Helios to him on the grounds that he, Julian says, thought the earlier-written *Kronia* to be worth something (11.44.4–5/157C: ἐπεί σοι καὶ τὸ πρότερον εἰς τὰ Κρόνια γεγραμμένον ἡμῖν οὐ παντάπασιν ἀπόβλητον ἐφάνη). Much hangs on whether or not the *Kronia* mentioned is the same as the *Caesares* and there is the additional problem of the fact that showing appreciation for a work does not of necessity make one a character in the work in question. Still, given Saloustios' showing up as addressee in the hymn to Helios and as an overwhelming presence in Oration 4, he is a likely addressee at this moment. Sardiello (2000: 85) provides a way into this debate. See, too, Baldwin 1978: 452–53; Gilliam 1967: 205; and Pack 1946: 152, 154.

6. But since it is necessary to obey the law of the god [of the festival], do you wish that I tell you by way of entertainment a myth in which there are perhaps many things worth hearing? (10.1.10–12/306B)

Ἐπεὶ δὲ χρὴ τῷ νόμῳ πείθεσθαι τοῦ θεοῦ, βούλει σοι ἐν παιδιᾶς μέρει μῦθον διεξέλθω πολλὰ ἴσως ἔχοντα ἀκοῆς ἄξια;

esteemed, or, rather, the universally esteemed Plato: many things were pursued zealously by him through myths."⁷

This exchange raises questions about how to interpret the *Caesares*. Julian presents this work as an entertainment and it does not lack for entertaining aspects, but the invocation of Plato and his myths suggests that deeper reflections on its contents are warranted. After all, although he disparages myths in the *Republic*,⁸ Plato nonetheless presents the effective "Myth of Er" in the same work.⁹ Also important is the fact that one of the subtitles of the *Caesares* is *Symposium*. There are structural similarities between this work and Plato's dialogue.¹⁰ Like Plato's dialogue, the *Caesares* features six major speeches. In the *Symposium*, the line-up is Phaedrus, Pausanias, Eryximachus, Agathon, Aristophanes, and Socrates, while the *Caesares* presents Julius Caesar, Alexander the Great, Augustus, Trajan, Marcus Aurelius, and Constantine. Furthermore, Silenus, whose satiric commentary figures prominently in Julian's work, is also present in the *Symposium*; Alcibiades compares Socrates to him a number of times.¹¹ These connections to Plato's iconic work suggest that taking this amusement seriously is worthwhile.

The focus on Marcus Aurelius in the work also counsels an earnest approach to the *Caesares*. In the first place, Julian clearly regards Marcus Aurelius as an ideal for himself in both this work and others.¹² Furthermore, it is an emperor who speaks and depicts himself looking forward to having the martial god Mithras as his patron deity upon his death (10.38.16–21/336C), which is paralleled by the various emperors taking gods as their patrons at the end of the work, including Zeus and Kronos by Marcus Aurelius.¹³ This anticipated patronage also recalls Julian's imperial predecessors' associations with gods—a practice old by the fourth century. In sum, the connection of the *Caesares* to Julian's own identification with Marcus

---

7. 10.1.15–17/306C: ἀκόλουθα σοί τε καὶ φίλῳ τῷ σῷ, μᾶλλον δὲ τῷ κοινῷ, Πλάτωνι διανοούμενος, αὐτῷ πολλὰ ἐν μύθοις ἐσπούδασται.

8. 2.377E–3.392A.

9. 10.614B–621D.

10. The similarities between the *Caesares* and Plato's *Symposium* are an accepted part of an approach to this work of Julian. See, e.g., Sardiello 2000: xi; Müller 1998: 39–40.

11. 215A ff., 216D, and 221E.

12. In addition to the passage to be discussed below (10.17/317C–D), there is evidence of Julian's intense admiration for Marcus Aurelius in the *Caesares* at 10.34/333B and 10.34–35/334A–B. Ammianus Marcellinus notes that Julian took Marcus Aurelius as his model at 16.1.4. See Sardiello 2000: 128; Müller 1998: 38; Hunt 1995; Smith 1995: 42, 170; Bouffartigue 1992: 73; Bowersock 1982: 172; Athanassiadi 1981: 200, 224; Baldwin 1978: 466; Lacombrade 2003/1965: 15 and 1967 for more on Julian's idealizing of Marcus Aurelius in the *Caesares* and other works.

13. 10.37.11–12/335D.

Aurelius, along with the stated Platonic agenda, lend force to Julian's assertion that there are "things worth hearing" here[14]: the glamour secured for Marcus Aurelius through attribution of same-sex sexual attractiveness to him (via *kallos amēchanon*) occurs in a philosophizing text about emperors by an emperor who identified himself with Marcus Aurelius. Julian suggests in this work who and what he, a glamorous emperor, is and how he should be regarded.

The *Caesares* tells the story of a banquet Romulus, the first king of Rome, put on in heaven for the gods and rulers of Rome from Julius Caesar onward. As all the rulers enter the banquet hall, most are allowed a place at the table but a few, judged unworthy, are sent away (e.g., Caligula [10.6/310A–B], Nero [10.6/310C], Commodus [10.9/312B–C], Caracalla [10.10/312D], Elegabalus [10.10/313A]). When the feast is ready, Hermes, with Zeus' agreement, proposes a speech contest between the various emperors, who are called "heroes."[15] At this point, Herakles interjects that it is hardly fair or explicable that his own Alexander the Great has not been summoned to this gathering of great leaders from the past. Zeus approves the addition of Alexander, who takes the place denied Caracalla.

In due course, the number of eligible contestants is narrowed to six: Julius Caesar, Alexander the Great, Augustus, Trajan, Marcus Aurelius, and Constantine. Each of the rulers then presents his case and faces examination on the question as to why he should be considered the greatest leader. All the rulers face considerable jibing from Silenus. At the conclusion of the contest, the overweening and imperial temperaments of the first four stand revealed, and Constantine, speaking sixth, has been tarred with the brush of being a lover of pleasure.[16] Marcus Aurelius (having spoken fifth) is declared the winner. When asked what he thought the "most beautiful ambition in life" (*kalliston . . . tou biou telos*/κάλλιστον . . . τοῦ βίου

---

14. R. A. Pack suggested that there

> is no reason for refusing to take the writer at his word when he asserts that his taste does not normally run to jesting; rather, one can well believe that the austere emperor had no real enthusiasm for Saturnalian fooleries, but that, while certain ideas or motives appropriate to the Saturnalia were thrust upon him, so to speak, by the occasion, he still retained in this piece something of the spirit as well as the external framework of a μῦθος [of the sort Plato would employ] (1946: 154).

Pack also identified serious philosophical aspects in the *Caesares*. Julian may be at his ease in this work, but it reflects in broad outline late-Platonic conceptions of the cosmos, especially in the spatial registration of the gods above the emperors and the setting of the banquet just below the moon.

15. 10.16.2–4/316A: αὐτῶν δὲ τῶν ἡρώων ἐδόκει τῷ Ἑρμῇ διαπειρᾶσθαι καὶ τῷ Διὶ τοῦτο οὐκ ἀπὸ γνώμης ἦν . . . .

16. See Amerise 2002 for more on Julian's depiction of Constantine.

τέλος) was, he answered that he had always striven to be like the gods.[17] This answer is not surprising nor is it a surprise that he was judged the best, given the intensely admiring portrait Julian draws of him prior to the contest's commencement:

> When summoned, Marcus entered looking excessively dignified and having eyes and face somewhat drawn from his labors. Displaying in his very self an irresistible/uncanny beauty (*kallos* . . . *amēchanon*/κάλλος . . . ἀμήχανον[18]) through the very fact that he offered himself up unadorned and unbeautified. His beard, in any case, was long and his dress was simple

---

17. 10.34.12.–15/333B–C:

> Then Hermes looked at Marcus and said, "And you, Verus, what did you think the most beautiful ambition in life was?" He answered gently and modestly, "To imitate the gods."
>
> Καὶ ὁ Ἑρμῆς βλέψας εἰς τὸν Μάρκον· "Σοὶ δέ," εἶπεν, "ὦ Βῆρε, τί κάλλιστον ἐδόκει τοῦ βίου τέλος εἶναι;" καὶ ὃς ἠρέμα καὶ σωφρόνως· "Τὸ μιμεῖσθαι," ἔφη, "τοὺς θεούς."

18. In the Budé edition and Sardiello 2000, the word *amachon* (ἀμάχον) appears instead of *amēchanon* (ἀμήχανον). In agreement with Wright (1969/1913) and F. Müller (1998)—both of whom follow Hertlein in his preference for this reading from manuscript M—, I prefer *amēchanon*. Both words occur roughly the same number of times in Julian's œuvre. *Amachon* is seen eight times and *amēchanon* nine, if my choice is followed here. If the reading in the Budé and Sardiello is favored, these numbers are reversed, of course. *Amēchanon* is preferable because of its association with beauty in the prose hymn to Helios and indeed with the general feeling of the impossible or hard to comprehend (3.11.10/62B; 3.11.42/63B; 4.5.28/247A; 5.2.5/269D; 9.10.4/189B) and the divine (2.12.4/118A; 11.5.14/132D) that attends Julian's use of the word. There are also, conclusively in my view, the Platonic intertexts and, indeed, arguable intertextuality with Plotinus (*Enneads* 5.5.3.1–15; discussed at the end of this chapter), and with Iamblichus (discussed at the chapter's start).

Amachon, on the other hand, appears (with one exception) only in military contexts in Julian's works (1.30.12/37C; 1.12.11/16D; 1.21.13/26C; 1.30.4/37B; 3.10.4/60D; 3.27.9/84B; 10.21.15/321B) and refers to the notion that the warrior/army in question cannot be defeated. The single use of *amachon* that departs from its usual martial meaning characterizes the hunger and loneliness that the young Hercules had to endure as "most invincible" enemies (7.14.23/219D: *amachōtatois*/ἀμαχωτάτοις). Sardiello (2000: 129) makes a case for *amachos* on the basis of the phrase, *kallos amachon*, being less common and through noting parallels in Libanius, Menander (the playwright), Aelian, and John Chrysostom—the last of whom perhaps splits the difference as he speaks of the beauty (*kallos*) of God that is both *amachos* and *amēchanos*:

> And first of all, there is the beauty (*kallos*) of that blessed and unblemished nature that is, thus, somehow irresistible/uncanny (*amēchanon*) and invincible (*amachon*), overbounding all language/logic and escaping all thought. Whenever you hear of beauty [in this context], don't assume anything bodily, beloved, but rather some incorporeal notion and an unutterable magnificence. (*Expositiones in Psalmos* 160.32–38)
>
> Καὶ πρῶτον, τὸ κάλλος τῆς μακαρίας ἐκείνης καὶ ἀκηράτου φύσεως, ὅτι ἀμήχανον οὕτω πώς ἐστι καὶ ἄμαχον, καὶ πάντα ὑπερβαῖνον λόγον, καὶ πᾶσαν ἐκφεῦγον διάνοιαν. Κάλλος δὲ ὅταν ἀκούσῃς, μηδὲν σωματικὸν ὑποπτεύσῃς, ἀγαπητέ, ἀλλὰ ἀσωμάτων τινὰ δόξαν καὶ μεγαλοπρέπειαν ἄφραστον.

and sober, and from fasting his body was exceedingly shiny and transparent, just like, I suppose, light itself, most pure and stainless. (10.17.15–22/317C–D)[19]

Although Marcus is of the second century historically, Julian makes him appear late-ancient. Jean Bouffartigue (1992: 74) notes that Marcus' diaphanous body transforms him into a stand-in for a late-Platonic sage. As he enters, there is also evidence of hard work and fasting: now an ascetic, Marcus accumulates *auctoritas*/ἀξίωμα this way too.[20] This accumulation is rendered hyperbolic by the perception of light. The light-filled terms for late-ancient senatorial elites, *clarissimi*, *spectabiles*, and *illustres*, are relevant here, as is Eunapius' story of Iamblichus' body and clothing acquiring a gold hue when he was at his devotions.[21] The theurgist, the late-ancient practitioner of pagan religious practice (prayer and sacrifice), was also often figured as bathed in light.[22] This rendering of Marcus also recalls descriptions of saints' relics being filled with light.[23] Indeed, Victricius, in his *De*

---

19. Ἐπεὶ δὲ καὶ ὁ Μάρκος κληθεὶς παρῆλθε, σεμνὸς ἄγαν, ὑπὸ τῶν πόνων ἔχων τά τε ὄμματα καὶ τὸ πρόσωπον ὑπό τι συνεσταλμένον, κάλλος δὲ ἀμήχανον ἐν αὐτῷ τούτῳ δεικνύων, ἐν ᾧ παρεῖχεν ἑαυτὸν ἄκομψον καὶ ἀκαλλώπιστον· ἥ τε γὰρ ὑπήνη βαθεῖα παντάπασιν ἦν αὐτῷ καὶ τὰ ἱμάτια λιτὰ καὶ σώφρονα, καὶ ὑπὸ τῆς ἐνδείας τῶν τροφῶν ἦν αὐτῷ τὸ σῶμα διαυγέστατον καὶ διαφανέστατον ὥσπερ αὐτὸ οἶμαι τὸ καθαρώτατον καὶ εἰλικρινέστατον φῶς.

20. John Dillon (1998) discusses asceticism in Platonism (cf. Claudia Rapp [2005] on the ascetic authority of bishops).

21. Eunapius, *Lives of the Philosophers* 5.1.8 (Wright 2005/1921: 458/364); see Civiletti (2007: 326–34 [esp. 333–34]) for discussion of many instances of a light-filled and/or golden appearance attributed to notable men in late antiquity. See, too, Struck (2004: 227–29) and Goulet (2001: 47) on the glorious light-filled impression the fifth-century philosopher Proclus makes in the biography Marinus wrote of him (*Vita Procli* 3). On a related note, Brown (1981: 73) draws attention to Paulinus' characterization of the martyred saint Felix as a star; Paulinus says of Felix that "the martyr is at once a star at his shrine and a remedy for those who worship [him]" (*Carm.* 19.15: *martyr stella loci simul et medicina colentum est*).

22. Iamblichus, *Myst.* 1.12.41 [31.9–15]:

> Therefore, by means of this [divine] will, the gods, being benevolent and gracious, shine their light generously upon the theurgists, calling their souls up into themselves and orchestrating oneness/unity with themselves for them, accustoming them—while they are yet in bodies—to be detached from bodies and to be turned around to their [i.e., the gods'] eternal and noetic principle.

Διὰ τῆς τοιαύτης οὖν βουλήσεως ἀφθόνως οἱ θεοὶ τὸ φῶς ἐπιλάμπουσιν εὐμενεῖς ὄντες καὶ ἵλεῳ τοῖς θεουργοῖς, τάς τε ψυχὰς αὐτῶν εἰς ἑαυτοὺς ἀνακαλούμενοι καὶ τὴν ἕνωσιν αὐταῖς τὴν πρὸς ἑαυτοὺς χορηγοῦντες, ἐθίζοντές τε αὐτὰς καὶ ἔτι ἐν σώματι οὔσας ἀφίστασθαι τῶν σωμάτων, ἐπὶ δὲ τὴν ἀίδιον καὶ νοητὴν ἑαυτῶν ἀρχὴν περιάγεσθαι.

23. Miller discusses Victricius' using light as a metaphor to describe saints' relics:

> In order to make spiritual sense of the sight of body-fragments—that is to say, in order to evoke the whole [of the divine] in the part—[Victricius] needed a metaphor that was

Laude Sanctorum, depicts the arrival of relics to Rotomagus (Rouen) in the mid 390s as an imperial *adventus.*[24] In both cases, there is a ceremonial arrival of *res mortales,* relics or an emperor, that have been sacralized.[25] The representational ambitions of Eunapius in his *Lives of the Philosophers* and the anonymous author of the *Historia Monachorum* (both writing about 400 C.E.) and the expectations they had of their readers certainly apply here. Quoting John Onians, Patricia Cox Miller writes that

> petitioning the visual imagination of the spectator . . . marked the biographical literature of this period [sc. the *Lives of the Philosophers* and the *Historia Monachorum*], as authors invited readers to "see" holiness in the bodies of their heroes. Indeed, an increase in the ability to "see more than was there" . . . seems characteristic of [this] cultural scene. . . . (2005c: 24)

And so, even though this representation of Marcus Aurelius is contained within a somewhat jocular context, the contours of Julian's flattering portrait are of a piece with the glorifications of emperors, sages and ascetics, and relics seen elsewhere in late-ancient sources. Indeed, the resemblance between this passage and the excerpt from the *De Mysteriis* that began this chapter is striking: heroes, light, and irresistible/uncanny beauty (*kallos amēchanon*) are present in both.

The *kallos amēchanon* with which Julian endows Marcus rewards concentrated attention. In Julian's many works the noun, *kallos,* possesses a variety of meanings. It often refers to the physical beauty of either men or women.[26] Moral excellence, as had been the case for centuries, is also an attribute of *kallos.* As noted above, Hermes asked Marcus Aurelius what he thought the most beautiful ambition in life was. Julian also has occasion to mention the "beauty of deeds" and "true beauty of the soul"[27] and in the following passage from the opening to the first panegyric to Constantius II

---

powerful enough to rival an actual body. He found it in the metaphor of light, which appears in a variety of guises in his sermon: as the radiance of fire, the brightness of the sun, and the sparkle of jewels. (2005b: 47 [cf. 2000b: 226-27, 234-35])

Cf. Lamberton's remarks on Plotinus' resort to light to describe the One (1986: 90).

24. Victric. 3 (pp. 379–80 in G. Clark 1999). In her discussion of this work, Gillian Clark remarks that "it is now the martyrs who make a triumphal entry with the insignia of imperial power, who impose judicial torture to force a confession from evil spirits, who will give official guidance on righteous and unlawful living, and who will both pardon and judge those who do wrong" (1999: 372). See, too, Brown (1981: 98–101), Miller (2005b: 49 and 2005c: 29–30), and Hunter (1999: 424).

25. See chapter three for discussion of Ammianus Marcellinus' famous depiction of the *adventus* of Constantius II to Rome in 357.

26. E.g., 1.7.16/9B; 1.35.37–38/43D; 2.5.13/109C; 2.5.20/109D; 2.17.32/127D; 12.14.11–12/346A.

27. 1.38.16/47B: κάλλος πράξεων; 12.20.38/351A: ψυχῆς ἀληθινὸν κάλλος.

(employing the for all practical purposes identical substantive form of the adjective *kalos*), Julian shows the close association that beauty can have with moral excellence, here denoted by the word *aretē*:

> There is an ancient directive taught by him who first revealed philosophy to men [it is unclear whom Julian has in mind] and it goes thus: all who are looking to virtue (*aretēn*/ἀρετήν) and beauty/the beautiful (*to kalon*/ τὸ καλόν) must make it a habit in their words, deeds, and dealings with others, in short, in all affairs of life, great and small, to aim in every way at beauty (*tou kalou*/τοῦ καλοῦ). Now who of those who have a mind would deny that virtue (*aretē*/ἀρετή) is the most beautiful (*kalliston*/κάλλιστον) thing of all? (1.2.1–7/3C–D)[28]

In addition to earthly beauty and moral excellence, *kallos* also designates cosmic transcendent beauty. In the context of quantifying an understanding of this *kallos* of Marcus Aurelius, whose body Julian compares to light, it is of interest that Julian associates transcendent beauty with the sun/ Helios in his prose hymn to this god.[29] He repeatedly notes that the sun god is the source of the noetic/intelligible[30] beauty that illumines the visible world.[31] And in the eighth oration (the prose hymn to the Mother of the Gods[32]), the bestowal of form on a formless world that Julian represents

---

28. Νόμος ἐστὶ παλαιὸς παρὰ τοῦ πρώτου φιλοσοφίαν ἀνθρώποις φήναντος οὑτωσὶ κείμενος· ἅπαντας πρὸς τὴν ἀρετὴν καὶ πρὸς τὸ καλὸν βλέποντας ἐπιτηδεύειν ἐν λόγοις, ἐν ἔργοις, ἐν ξυνουσίαις, ἐπὶ πᾶσιν ἁπλῶς τοῖς κατὰ τὸν βίον μικροῖς καὶ μείζοσι τοῦ καλοῦ πάντως ἐφίεσθαι. Πάντων δὲ ὅτι κάλλιστον ἀρετή, τίς ἂν ἡμῖν τῶν νοῦν ἐχόντων ἀμφισβητήσειε;

29. Written in 362, the eleventh oration, the prose hymn *To King Helios*, shows Helios associated with the absolute and inaccessible, while also placed in the sensible world as both the visible sun and mediator between this world and the absolute. Among Julian's salient preoccupations in this oration are the connections between the invisible and visible, the transcendent and embodied, and the soul and body (e.g., 11.37/152B). For more on this oration, see Elm 2012: 286–99; Smith 2012; Smith 1995: 139–59; Athanassiadi 1981: 147–52.

30. Within late-Platonic thought generally (and *quot scriptores, tot historiae*), there is the sensible world in which humans live and then "above" are what the late Platonists call the intellectual (*noeros*/ νοερός) and intelligible (*noētos*/νοητός) hypostases (and "above" these is the One). Gods who have dealings with the sensible world populate the intellectual hypostasis. When saying that the sun is the source of the beauty that sheds its radiance on the world, Julian places the sun or Helios in the intellectual hypostasis. Gods in the intelligible hypostasis are beyond human ken, as is, of course, the One. For more on Late Platonism (or Neoplatonism), see, e.g., Rappe 2000, Sells 1994, Lilla 1992, or Wallis 1995/1972.

31. 11.43.9/156D: μεταδιδοὺς τῷ φαινομένῳ παντὶ τοῦ νοητοῦ κάλλους, cf., e.g., 11.24.7– 8/145A; 11.24.10/145A; 11.24.16/145B; 11.30.5/149A; 11.43.5/156D.

32. Julian probably composed Oration 8 in the spring of 362. It consists, for the most part, of a searching reading of the myth of Attis and the Mother of the Gods (aka Cybele—a name which Julian does not use in the oration). There is a lengthy section at the end of the oration in which Julian discusses which foods can be eaten to secure ritual purity. The combination of the relentlessly corpo-

allegorically through the demigod Attis' fevered self-castration is a bringing of beauty (*kallos*) to the mire that is this earthly domain:

> But is not Attis the one who not long ago was out of his mind, but who is now through his castration the one called wise? Yes, out of his mind because he preferred matter and presides over generation, but wise because he adorned and transformed this dung [our earth], with such beauty [*kallos*/κάλλος] as no human art or intelligence could imitate. (8.19.23–28/179C–D)[33]

Accordingly, then, Julian's use of the word *kallos* calls to mind a number of things at once: physical beauty of persons, moral excellence, and powers emanating from the cosmos. But Marcus' beauty is also irresistible or uncanny, *amēchanon*. This adjective proves to be interesting.

In Julian's œuvre, *amēchanos* often conveys a notion of divine, or nearly divine, invincibility. It accordingly is most useful in panegyrical situations, and not surprisingly appears in Julian's speech of praise to empress Eusebia, the wife of Constantius II. Julian asserts that Constantius took care that was *amēchanos* to ensure that he and his brother Gallus were not killed when the rest of his side of the family was slaughtered in 337 after Constantine I died:

> He seized me from dangers so great that not even "a man in the strength of his youth" [*Iliad* 12.382] could have, indeed, successfully fled away from them, unless he obtained some means of safety divine and irresistible/uncanny (*amēchanou*/ἀμηχάνου). (2.12.2–4/117D–118A)[34]

Julian also uses this word to designate things that defeat human efforts to understand how they work: *amēchanos* twice denotes, in hyperbolic fashion,

---

real story of the demi-god Attis (which Julian ambitiously presents as an allegory of the constitution of a proper subjectivity, of the suitable arrangement of ritual practices, *and* of the structure of the universe) with the concerns with purity through diet makes for a juxtaposition whose combination of the material and transcendent is utterly late-ancient. Broadly considered, the oration displays a mixture of solicitude for individual persons, seen within the expansive context of the universe, and a program for traditional religious renewal in the empire. For more on this work, see Elm 2012: 118–36; Liebeschuetz 2012; Smith 1995: 159–62, 171–78; Cosi 1986; Athanassiadi-Fowden 1981: 141–48; Bowersock 1978.

33. Ἄττις δὲ οὐχ οὗτός ἐστιν ὁ μικρῷ πρόσθεν ἄφρων, νῦν δὲ ἀκούων διὰ τὴν ἐκτομὴν σοφός; Ἄφρων μὲν ὅτι τὴν ὕλην εἵλατο καὶ τὴν γένεσιν ἐπιτροπεύει, σοφὸς δὲ ὅτι τὸ σκύβαλον τοῦτο εἰς κάλλος ἐκόσμησε καὶ τοσοῦτον μετέστησεν ὅσον οὐδεμία μιμήσαιτο ἀνθρώπων τέχνη καὶ σύνεσις.

34. κινδύνων τε ἐξήρπασε τηλικούτων, οὓς "οὐδὲ ἡβῶν ἀνὴρ" εὖ μάλα διαφύγοι μὴ θείας τινὸς καὶ ἀμηχάνου σωτηρίας τυχών.

military divisions that are not able to be reckoned up in Julian's second panegyric to Constantius.[35] *Amēchanos* is the speed of thought in the consolation Julian wrote to himself on the departure of his friend Saloustios,[36] and, in a moment of self-panegyric in the "Letter to the Athenians," Julian characterizes the velocity of his crossing the empire's North after he was declared emperor as *amēchanos*.[37]

Amēchanos also appears, showing an extension from the meanings hitherto offered for it, when Julian speaks of the human body in his oration, *To the Uneducated Cynics*[38]:

> Now then, there are parts of a body such as eyes, feet, and hands but also hair, nails, and excrement—a sort of class of superfluities—that accompany them, and without these things the human body is an impossible (*amēchanon*/ἀμήχανον) thing. (9.10.1–4/189B)[39]

If the body were not to include that which is destined to flake, fall off, or be expelled (and this is tantamount to envisioning a body that will neither decay nor exhibit natural processes), then this body, irresistible/uncanny to intellection, will no longer be human: it will be divine.

Applying the adjective *amēchanos* to Marcus Aurelius' *kallos*, Julian attributes to it, then, uncanniness, impossibility, irresistibility, and divinity—which is to underscore what is present already in the word *kallos*. But there remains another facet to *amēchanos* and it appears in the Helios hymn. The beauty (*kallos*) that emanates into the world from the One comes into existence in company with an irresistible or uncanny (*amēchanos*) power:

> [A]t any rate, this uncompounded cause of the whole universe (in accordance with the primal creative essence that abides in it) revealing to all

---

35. 3.11.10/62B; 3.11.42/63B.
36. 4.5.28/247A.
37. 5.2.5/269D: ἀμηχάνῳ τάχει.
38. Julian wrote his ninth oration, *To the Uneducated Cynics*, mid-year in 362. It was a sequel to the seventh oration, which is discussed later in this chapter. This work was an "instructional treatise on how to lead a life pleasing to the gods, this time [as opposed to the more polemical orientation of the seventh oration] by pointing out how one ought to prepare for the true philosophical life, in contrast to that led by uneducated Cynics" (Elm 2012: 136). Julian recommends much *paideia* and is critical of what he sees as the Cynics' overemphasis on the body and neglect of the mind. Also see Elm 2012: 136–39; Marcone 2012; Billerbeck 1996: 216–20; Krueger 1996: 232–34; Smith 1995: 49–90; Athanassiadi-Fowden 1981: 137–41.
39. Οὐκοῦν ἐπειδὴ σώματος μέρη μέν ἐστιν, οἷον ὀφθαλμοί, πόδες, χεῖρες, ἄλλα γε ἐπισυμβαίνει, τρίχες, ὄνυχες, ῥύπος, τοιούτων περιττωμάτων γένος, ὧν ἄνευ σῶμα ἀνθρώπινον ἀμήχανον εἶναι.

things in existence beauty (*kallous*/κάλλους), perfection, oneness/unity, and irresistible/uncanny (*amēchanou*/ἀμηχάνου) power—[this uncompounded cause] brought forth into the light Helios, the greatest god, proceeding from himself and in all things like unto himself, as middle cause out of the middle, intellectual, and demiurgic causes. (11.5.12–17/ 132D–133A)[40]

The primal uncompounded cause produces the god Helios/the sun as the middle term linking all things in the universe to one another.[41] For Julian the sun is both a physical object (in the sky sending material warmth) but also a transcendent entity remote from this material world, associated not only with the gods of the Pantheon but also with the principle of reality transcendent even of them. Both sensible (disclosing things to sight and giving warmth), and yet utterly evanescent and instantaneous in its action, light is the perfect attribute for this god who is both physical body in the sky *and* transcendent entity. The combination of light, beauty, and irresistibility attending Helios strongly recalls the *kallos amēchanon* of Marcus Aurelius and what Iamblichus says about divinity.

Not only intertextual with Iamblichus' *De Mysteriis*, *kallos amēchanon* in the *Caesares* is also intertextual with Plato's *Symposium* and *Charmides*. A further instance of Julian's frequent engagement with Plato throughout his writings,[42] intertextuality with these highly glamorous Platonic texts puts a further sheen on an already otherworldly Marcus. The contents of this dazzlement are worth close inspection. Plato does not function merely as a gorgeous accessory; this intertextuality with Plato was interpretable then, because of *paideia,* and, of course, now. Reading this section of the *Caesares* with Plato creates Marcus Aurelius as both the Socrates of Alcibiades' longing in the *Symposium* and the Charmides of Socrates' (possible) longing in the *Charmides*. Marcus' masculine transcendent glamour is inflected with same-sex sexual attractiveness, and, to the extent that Marcus is associated with Socrates, who is both subject and object of desire, and of

---

40. αὕτη δὴ οὖν ἡ μονοειδὴς τῶν ὅλων αἰτία, πᾶσι τοῖς οὖσιν ἐξηγουμένη κάλλους τε καὶ τελειότητος ἑνώσεώς τε καὶ δυνάμεως ἀμηχάνου, κατὰ τὴν ἐν αὐτῇ μένουσαν πρωτουργὸν οὐσίαν, μέσον ἐκ μέσων τῶν νοερῶν καὶ δημιουργικῶν αἰτιῶν Ἥλιον θεὸν μέγιστον ἀνέφηνεν ἐξ ἑαυτοῦ πάντα ὅμοιον [ἐν] ἑαυτῷ.

41. For more on the middleness (μεσότης) of Helios and his consequent mediating function, see 11.13.11–14.5/138D–139A. Also see Elm (2012: 293–97) and Smith (1995: 148–51).

42. While dubious about the depth of Julian's knowledge of Plato, Bouffartigue (1992: 170–97) lists 81 references to Plato throughout Julian's works. The passages discussed here don't appear in Bouffartigue's helpful survey. The addition of these increases Bouffartigue's total of 81 to at least 82, if not 83 (if *amēchanon* is regarded as attached to both the *Symposium* and *Charmides*).

course with the exorbitantly good-looking object, Charmides, then to this extent Marcus is likewise both subject and object of desire.[43]

Before proceeding with the argument, however, it is necessary to explain why same-sex desire, instead of pederastic desire, is the term used in this discussion based in Plato's texts. In the first place, the perceptible intertextuality of Julian's text with those of Plato is an employment of golden-age Athenian pederasty to speak of relations between men: both Marcus Aurelius and the presumed audience for the *Caesares* are adult men. The desire rendered visible in Julian's text, stripped of asymmetries of age, is no longer pederastic and better described as same-sex. Second, it is true that if Plato's texts were the sole object in view, pederastic desire, as it is commonly understood, would be the correct term for the most part. Male/male desire in the Platonic corpus is generally desire of an older male for a younger one; prevalent are the asymmetries of age, societal position, and, it seems, sexual role. That said, this picture of Platonic same-sex desire from the secondary literature, while acceptable much of the time, is overconfident. Alcibiades' attempt at seduction (to be seen shortly) problematizes the asymmetries asserted for Platonic pederasty. Agathon and Pausanias, both adult, appear in the *Symposium,* and their doing so puts the question to the insistence that it was an adolescent on the verge of manhood and a man with a full beard who exhaust the visibility of male/male sexual desire in representations from the Platonic corpus and, indeed, Athens.[44] The *kallos amēchanon* that Julian takes from Plato and attributes to Marcus Aurelius also raises this question: associated with both Socrates *and* Charmides, Marcus comes to seem both subject (*erastēs*) and object (*erōmenos*) of desire. Awareness, in late antiquity and now, of Plato at the point of reception of Julian's text makes perceptible same-sex desire that lacks the supposedly necessary asymmetries of age and activity, the presence of which is already under some question in Plato's text anyway. Hence, speaking of male same-

---

43. The *Charmides* also appears in Julian's fourth oration, his self-consolation on the departure of his friend Salutius (=Saloustios). See my "Erotics and Friendship in Emperor Julian's Fourth Oration" (2010) for an extended discussion of this oration.

44. For the presence of asymmetry in sexual role and in age in Athenian pederasty, see, e.g., Halperin 1990, Winkler 1990, or Dover 1978. With some controversy, James Davidson has twice (2001, 2007) asserted (*contra* this orthodoxy) that scholars have found too much sexual activity, and anal penetration especially, in the works of Plato (while Davidson does for the most part leave in place asymmetry of age). The asymmetries dear to the orthodoxy are often perceptible in Plato's works, and the presence of sexual activity is undeniable both if relevant *comparanda* such as Aristophanes are brought to bear, and if the possibility of (nearly) complete ironization of expressions of desire is sensibly rejected. In any case, evidence of the indeterminacy of real life is visible in Plato's works. Depictions of desire and sexual agency on the part of young men who are supposed to be passive according to the norms are there to be seen.

sex desire is a more accurate way to proceed, as a normative understanding of Athenian pederasty is not sufficient to explain the phenomena under discussion in Julian's text or, some of the time, in the texts of Plato.

Toward the end of the *Symposium,* a boisterously drunk Alcibiades bursts into the party. He tells tales and hearkens back to the time he wanted to seduce Socrates. In his narration, Alcibiades tells Socrates he will give his body to him because Socrates is the only man worthy to be his lover. Alcibiades is willing to take teasing from persons who just don't understand, for he knows that such an association will make him a better person. Socrates refuses the offer on the basis of a characteristic (for him) hierarchicization of embodied and disembodied beauties, speaking of his own disembodied *amēchanon kallos* as greater than Alcibiades' own embodied *kallos.* Socrates, however, also characteristically undercuts this hierarchicization through the "ironical simplicity"[45] that inflects his reply. Alcibiades speaks first:

> "'I would be ashamed much more before thoughtful persons at not gratifying such a man [as you] than I would be ashamed before the many unthoughtful ones when I had gratified him.' Having heard me out, he [Socrates] responded with that pronounced and customary ironical simplicity of his: 'My dear Alcibiades, it seems likely that you are not incorrect, if what you are saying about me is true and there is some power in me through which you can be made better. You would surely be seeing in me some irresistible/uncanny beauty (*amēchanon . . . kallos*/ἀμήχανον . . . κάλλος) and one decisively surpassing the handsomeness you possess. And if you're trying to barter your own beauty for the beauty you have found in me, you are aiming to get much from me for but a little: you're trying to exchange the semblance of beauty for the thing itself, in truth *bronze for gold* [sc. *Iliad* 6.232–36]." (*Smp.* 218D–219A)[46]

Socrates' remarks about hierarchized beauties might at first seem all too familiar, in essence a mini-replay of the "ladder of love" (210A–211C) that

---

45. "Ironical simplicity" is Michael Joyce's apt phrase from his translation of the *Symposium* (Hamilton and Cairns 1971: 570).
46. "'ἐγὼ δὴ τοιούτῳ ἀνδρὶ πολὺ μᾶλλον ἂν μὴ χαριζόμενος αἰσχυνοίμην τοὺς φρονίμους, ἢ χαριζόμενος τούς τε πολλοὺς καὶ ἄφρονας.' Καὶ οὗτος ἀκούσας μάλα εἰρωνικῶς καὶ σφόδρα ἑαυτοῦ τε καὶ εἰωθότως ἔλεξεν, ''Ω φίλε Ἀλκιβιάδη, κινδυνεύεις τῷ ὄντι οὐ φαῦλος εἶναι, εἴπερ ἀληθῆ τυγχάνει ὄντα ἃ λέγεις περὶ ἐμοῦ, καί τις ἔστ' ἐν ἐμοὶ δύναμις δι' ἧς ἂν σὺ γένοιο ἀμείνων· ἀμήχανόν τοι κάλλος ὁρῴης ἂν ἐν ἐμοὶ καὶ τῆς παρὰ σοὶ εὐμορφίας πάμπολυ διαφέρον. εἰ δὴ καθορῶν αὐτὸ κοινώσασθαί τέ μοι ἐπιχειρεῖς καὶ ἀλλάξασθαι κάλλος ἀντὶ κάλλους, οὐκ ὀλίγῳ μου πλεονεκτεῖν διανοῇ, ἀλλ' ἀντὶ δόξης ἀλήθειαν καλῶν κτᾶσθαι ἐπιχειρεῖς καὶ τῷ ὄντι *χρύσεα χαλκείων διαμείβεσθαι νοεῖς*.'"

featured earlier in Diotima's remarks. But the "ironical simplicity" and what happens next indicate complexities; hearing Socrates' protestations as coy, Alcibiades moves in to take what he thinks he has made his own:

> "Having heard and spoken these things, and having shot my arrows, as it were, I thought that he had been wounded. And having gotten up and not allowing him to say another word, I wrapped my cloak around him. . . . "
> (*Smp.* 219B)[47]

The "ironical simplicity" of Socrates' reply naturally signals, for it is ironic, something at odds with the surface meaning of the words. Alcibiades accordingly makes his move which accomplishes nothing, as is known. But Alcibiades' sexual strike-out does not matter for the present analysis. Socrates' ironic mode raises questions about how serious he is about his disembodied *amēchanon kallos* and suggests how much stock others are putting in his ostensible valuation of it; why otherwise would Alcibiades suspect that this might be a moment for saying one thing while meaning another? The hierarchy of disembodied beauty and its physical counterpart is ironized: it seems that where the former is the latter is never far away. Indeed, it appears possible to climb up *and* down the ladder of love. It is of course possible that Alcibiades is lying.[48] But even if this interesting interpretative position is taken up, abstract and physical beauties remain entangled in unstable counterpoint in a canonic work of great influence in late antiquity. And the fact of this unstable counterpoint is the point to take away: this disembodied *amēchanon kallos* found itself in company with a sexual approach and encouraged it.

Kallos amēchanon is also found in the *Charmides*, when the extravagantly handsome Charmides discountenances Socrates with a glance that is *amēchanon*. Indeed, seemingly with only the greatest of efforts does this dialogue settle in and down to being an inconclusive, and ironic, investigation of temperance (*sōphrosynē*).

When Charmides arrives at the palaestra of Taureas (the setting for the dialogue[49] and, therefore both a homosocial and [potentially] sexually charged place where males exercised in various stages of undress[50]),

---

47. Ἐγὼ μὲν δὴ ταῦτα ἀκούσας τε καὶ εἰπών, καὶ ἀφεὶς ὥσπερ βέλη, τετρῶσθαι αὐτὸν ᾤμην· καὶ ἀναστάς γε, οὐδ' ἐπιτρέψας τούτῳ εἰπεῖν οὐδὲν ἔτι, ἀμφιέσας τὸ ἱμάτιον τὸ ἐμαυτοῦ τοῦτον. . . .

48. Mark Jordan (2006: 29–32) considers the interesting ramifications of understanding Alcibiades' speech as a misrepresentation.

49. *Chrm.* 153A.

50. The following exchange between Chaerephon and Socrates underscores that the palaestra was a place where the removal of clothing was unremarkable:

Socrates admits that "[Charmides] appeared marvelous to him on account of his stature and his beauty (*kallos*/κάλλος)."[51] Chaerephon soon makes a similar point, saying that Charmides' form is "all-beautiful" (154D: *pankalos*/πάγκαλος). Hearing that Charmides has a headache and wanting to get closer, Socrates decides to pass himself off as a doctor in possession of a remedy. Interested in relief, Charmides comes over and sits down, expectant. Socrates seems at a loss for words.[52] Charmides then gives Socrates a glance that is irresistible/uncanny (*amēchanon*/ἀμήχανον),[53] and Socrates, in the midst of these difficulties, happens to get a provocative glance inside Charmides' cloak:

> [A]nd then, my noble friend, I saw what was inside his cloak and I was set ablaze. I was no longer in possession of myself . . . but all the same, since he had asked if I knew the remedy for his head, I somehow and with difficulty answered that I knew it. (*Chrm.* 155D-E)[54]

Now off his game, Socrates finds it hard to proceed with dialectic, and then, in time, the dialogue with pronounced irony turns into a lengthy and inconclusive discussion of *sōphrosynē*. The macro-motion of the dialogue suggests that it is difficult to move from the physical to the transcendent. Both remain in play and finality is not reached.[55] Indeed, the remedy that

---

"What does the young man [Charmides] look like to you, Socrates?" [Chaerephon] said. "Handsome face, no?" "Super!" I said. "Yet," he continued, "if he should be willing to disrobe [today], you will utterly forget his face, so all-beautiful is he as regards his form." (*Chrm.* 154D)

Τί σοι φαίνεται ὁ νεανίσκος, ἔφη, ὦ Σώκρατες; οὐκ εὐπρόσωπος; Ὑπερφυῶς, ἦν δ' ἐγώ. Οὗτος μέντοι, ἔφη, εἰ ἐθέλοι ἀποδῦναι, δόξει σοι ἀπρόσωπος εἶναι· οὕτως τὸ εἶδος πάγκαλός ἐστιν.

51. *Chrm.* 154C: ἐκεῖνος ἐμοὶ θαυμαστὸς ἐφάνη τό τε μέγεθος καὶ τὸ κάλλος.
52. *Chrm.* 155C:

> Coming over, he [Charmides] sat between me and Critias and then I was indeed at a loss, my friend, and my former boldness had been knocked out of me—the boldness that I had that it would be possible for me to speak with him with consummate ease.

ὁ δ' ἐλθὼν μεταξὺ ἐμοῦ τε καὶ τοῦ Κριτίου ἐκαθέζετο. ἐνταῦθα μέντοι, ὦ φίλε, ἐγὼ ἤδη ἠπόρουν, καί μου ἡ πρόσθεν θρασύτης ἐξεκέκοπτο, ἣν εἶχον ἐγὼ ὡς πάνυ ῥᾳδίως αὐτῷ διαλεξόμενος.

53. *Chrm.* 155D: he gazed upon me with those eyes of his with a sort of irresistible/uncanny (*amēchanon*) look . . . (ἐνέβλεψέ τέ μοι τοῖς ὀφθαλμοῖς ἀμήχανόν τι οἷον . . .)
54. τότε δή, ὦ γεννάδα, εἶδόν τε τὰ ἐντὸς τοῦ ἱματίου καὶ ἐφλεγόμην καὶ οὐκέτ' ἐν ἐμαυτῷ ἦν . . . ὅμως δὲ αὐτοῦ ἐρωτήσαντος, εἰ ἐπισταίμην τὸ τῆς κεφαλῆς φάρμακον, μόγις πως ἀπεκρινάμην ὅτι ἐπισταίμην.
55. Of course, Socrates is not *really* completely laid low by lust. But the conceit of this dialogue is that sexual desire (and desire between males at that) is able to disable the pursuit of virtue, even

Socrates offers Charmides for his headache can likewise be seen as a metaphor for this macro-motion. The remedy consists of a leaf (*phyllon*/φύλλον) and a spell (*epōidē*/ἐπῳδή), which shows that this therapy has material and immaterial aspects to it, both of which are necessary for it to be efficacious.⁵⁶ Alcibiades' embodied and Socrates' disembodied beauties may come to mind at this point; similar to what happens in the *Symposium*, the *Charmides* features an enmeshment of the physical and the transcendent.⁵⁷

---

as it is connected over and over to just such a thing: at the beginning of the dialogue, Socrates asks "about the young men, whether any of them might be excelling in wisdom, beauty, or both" (153D: περί ... τῶν νέων, εἴ τινες ἐν αὐτοῖς διαφέροντες ἢ σοφίᾳ ἢ κάλλει ἢ ἀμφοτέροις ἐγγεγονότες εἶεν). This dialogue is, in a sense, typical of Plato, a tribute to the connection of desire for wisdom with that for bodies.

56. *Chrm.* 155E.

57. *Kallos amēchanon* is in Plato's *Republic* at 6.509A. In the lead-in to this passage, Socrates explains to Glaukon how the soul betters itself by focusing on things beyond the material world (6.508D). He also speaks of "the Good" as the source of knowledge and truth and how it is greater than both of them. He employs a metaphor of the sun and its relation to light and vision to explain how the Good is related to knowledge and truth:

> But with regard to knowledge and truth, just as in the present instance it is right to consider light and vision sun-like but it is an error to believe that they are the sun, it is right to consider these two good-like, but it is not right to believe that either of them is the Good, and even more must the enduring existence of the Good be honored. (*R.* 6.508E–509A)

> ἐπιστήμην δὲ καὶ ἀλήθειαν, ὥσπερ ἐκεῖ φῶς τε καὶ ὄψιν ἡλιοειδῆ μὲν νομίζειν ὀρθόν, ἥλιον δ' ἡγεῖσθαι οὐκ ὀρθῶς ἔχει, οὕτω καὶ ἐνταῦθα ἀγαθοειδῆ μὲν νομίζειν ταῦτ' ἀμφότερα ὀρθόν, ἀγαθὸν δὲ ἡγεῖσθαι ὁπότερον αὐτῶν οὐκ ὀρθόν, ἀλλ' ἔτι μειζόνως τιμητέον τὴν τοῦ ἀγαθοῦ ἕξιν.

Given that *kallos amēchanon* appears presently, the mention of light suggests that this passage also could have been in Julian's mind (and that this passage could have come into the mind of an educated late-ancient reader of the *Caesares*). In any case, that which follows is revelatory of the enmeshment of this phrase, *kallos amēchanon*, in an erotic dynamic, even as it designates the transcendent. Having heard the words above, Glaukon remarks:

> "You speak of an irresistible/uncanny beauty (*amēchanon kallos*)," he said, "if it gives us knowledge and truth, and yet it is above/beyond them in beauty (*kallei*). You surely don't say that it is pleasure." (*R.* 6.509A)

> Ἀμήχανον κάλλος, ἔφη, λέγεις, εἰ ἐπιστήμην μὲν καὶ ἀλήθειαν παρέχει, αὐτὸ δ' ὑπὲρ ταῦτα κάλλει ἐστίν· οὐ γὰρ δήπου σύ γε ἡδονὴν αὐτὸ λέγεις.

Glaukon's jump to pleasure (*hēdonē*/ἡδονή), more than likely physical, is difficult to square with the thrust of the text up to this point. Has Glaukon not been listening as carefully as he might have? Socrates has been insisting that value is something beyond physical things. Socrates' immediate reaction (509A: "Hush!" [*euphēmei*/εὐφήμει]) shows that Glaukon has said something that he should not have. But said it he did and his saying so underlines the way in which this particular phrase, *kallos amēchanon*, even as it seems to designate things disembodied, puts the corporeal in play. And so, the connection between disembodied virtue and the physical, and surely tending in the direction of sexual matters on account of the use of the word *hēdonē*, is present here as it is in both the *Symposium* and *Charmides*. Once again, awareness of a Platonic intertext suggests a physical and erotic dimension to the admiration of Julian's Marcus Aurelius.

When both intertexts inflect an understanding of Julian's Marcus Aurelius (one moment Marcus is Socrates and the next he is Charmides), Julian will be seen to trope admiration for his hero as same-sex desire and to borrow the intensity of sexual excitement—for the corporeal remains in play—to render his predecessor even more glamorous. It is a borrowing, via intertextual means, of the real and existent to make his hero and admiration for him more lively and compelling. Since Marcus, an adult male, appears to be both subject and object of desire, however, does this glamorization of his masculine profile perhaps promise part-time shameful passivity? In a word, no. As there seems to be no shame here and instead a profusion of honor, looking for losers to blame and winners to crown is a mistake. The protocols of honor and shame asserted for ancient male/male sexual desire and relations don't inform these intertextual dynamics. But the question of honor/shame aside, men having it off with men was not an approved activity either. The question may be asked as to why evocation of these real pleasures and desires should add to the sheen—otherworldly like "light itself, most pure and stainless"—of Marcus Aurelius' *auctoritas* or *axiōma*/ἀξίωμα.

A quick answer to this question is that use of paradox to depict the transcendent and holy was just in the air. Matter was an expression of the transcendent in Iamblichus' reformulation of the pagan religious practices of prayer and blood sacrifice as theurgy.[58] The transcendent worthiness of a saint was said to be present in the fragmentary materiality of his or her relics.[59] It would be possible, accordingly, to compare the paradoxical use

---

58. Reacting to the devaluation of matter by the late-Platonists Plotinus and Porphyry, Iamblichus put Platonism on a new footing that, going forward, saw matter as paradoxically implicated in the transcendent (and *vice-versa*). Sacrifice and the material practices of pagan worship were now theurgy, or "God-Work," which could put religious persons in touch with sacred and transcendent divinity in a way not able to be described logically. Shaw puts it well: "Iamblichan Platonism, with its emphasis on theurgy, succeeded in incorporating pagan religious rites into the intellectual edifice of Platonism while, at the same time, infusing the Platonic school with the vitality of popular cultic practices" (1995: 17). For general discussion of theurgy, see Shaw 1985 and 1993 (in addition to 1995); Struck 2004: 210–213; Van Liefferinge 1999; Johnston 1997; Smith 1995: 91–113; Luck 1989; Fowden 1986: 116–41 and 1982; Wallis 1995/1972: 100–123; Lewy 1978/1956; *RE: Theurgie*. Dodds (1951: 283–93), superseded in the matter of the distinction between magic and theurgy, is helpful on the mechanics of sacrifice and ritual conceived as theurgy.

59. Similar to the theorization of theurgy (and, as will be seen, that of myths), the discourse around the veneration of saints and their relics, developing in the course of the fourth century, identified a series of coincidences between the physical (profane) with transcendent (sacred). There was an existent economy that guaranteed that what one saw, whether, say, dried blood or bone, was something greater. There was a connection between this world and the next; a way to the transcendent holiness of the saints was through their poor remains, their relics. Victricius' late fourth-century sermon, *De Laude Sanctorum*, is a key text in this regard. For discussion of this work and of relics more generally, see Brown 1981; Miller 1998a, 2000b, 2004, 2005b: passim, but 44–50, 2005c: passim,

of disavowed pleasure and desire to theorizations of theurgy and relics. But since Julian calls the *Caesares* a *mythos*, the discourse around the valuing of myths fits better (and makes poetic sense). The process of rescuing myths from disapprobation entailed finding indubitable value in physical matters (including sexual ones) that were usually the object of moralizing solicitude. The treatise, *De Deis et Mundo*, of Julian's friend, Saloustios, and Julian's own seventh oration (*Against Heracleius*) provide accounts of the paradoxical value myths have. Julian's seventh oration also features masculine self-presentation—embodied by a representation of the cynic Diogenes and by Julian himself in his speaking voice and in the *mythos* he tells of his life—that ignores the opinions of society to hitch its star to a reality lively and paradoxically beyond earthly morals. Indeed, the impression that Julian makes in the seventh oration recalls the idealized portrait he offers of Marcus Aurelius in *Caesares:* the liveliness of the corporeal in counterpoint with the celestial creates a paradoxical glamour that is most assuredly irresistible and transcendent because earthbound logic cannot account for it.

SALOUSTIOS AND JULIAN ON THE PROPER USE OF MYTHS

There had been questions raised about the appropriateness of myths from an early date in antiquity, and indeed well before Rome was much of anything.[60] Myths feature care-free carnality, criminality, and lack of control: things hardly to be encouraged among mere mortals. Plato famously questions the value of myths in the *Republic* but, within this work and others, he uses mythic material and modes to illustrate and present his arguments.[61] But even as questions were raised over the centuries, the stories of the Olympic pantheon, and the crude ones especially, never lacked for apologists. If something seemed immoral or too carnal, this was a call for further interpretation and not wholesale rejection.[62] What to do with and about myths were critical questions because of the centrality of mythic

---

but 27–30; G. Clark 1999; Hunter 1999.

60. E.g., Xenophanes faults myths for their anthropomorphism in the sixth century B.C.E.

61. E.g., *R.* 2.377E–3.392A (con) with 10.614B–621D (pro [the "Myth" of Er]); also see Collobert et al. 2012.

62. Feeney (1991) provides an overview of the mixed reactions that the adulteries and other connivances of the Olympians evoked in ancient readers and critics. Also see Brisson (2004) for the debates in and between the various philosophical schools over the value of myths. Lamberton's (1986) discussion of the reception of Homer among the late-Platonists is illuminating on the status of myths in late antiquity.

material to the ancient world in all its facets: in addition to their role in religion, myths provided a storehouse of images and metaphors in constant use in all media, and major texts learned in *paideia* were drenched in myth.

With the coming of Christian ascendancy, the status of myths and the stories of the Olympic Pantheon became more problematic. There were wholesale attacks on myths in works such as Arnobius' *Adversus Gentes* (c. 300) and Firmicus Maternus' *De Errore Profanarum Religionum* (mid-fourth century). In response, late-Platonists intensified interpretive pressure on myths, in essence doubling down on prior approaches: contradiction was no longer something to be explained away but, rather, to be embraced. The late-ancient defense of myths not only tolerates the disjunction between surface aspect (obscenity) and asserted value (sanctity) of the myths, but finds this disjunction a choice indicator of the transcendent. As is the case with other discourses that could have been discussed in this context (i.e., justifications of theurgy, theorizations of the effects of relics), there is embrace of things that could be regarded as bad. This embrace reveals a realm indifferent to and greater than earthly moral strictures and understandings. Hence, the defense of these stories recalls the late-ancient embrace of same-sex desire and pleasure as a way to metaphorize manly admirability. This defense also increases authority's credibility in a way similar to how brandishing knowledge of same-sex sexual behavior makes prohibiting authority grander: not limited by strictures of society, it is able to go anywhere.

In *De Deis et Mundo,* a short treatise written in the mid-fourth century on the gods, their relation to the world, and pagan religious practice, Saloustios defends myths.[63] Saloustios is probably the major political figure, Saturninius Secundus Salutius,[64] and, as noted above, perhaps Julian's conversation partner in the *Caesares*. After stating that myths are divine (3.2: *theioi*/θεῖοι) in their nature, he asserts that words spoken about the

---

63. Nock's (1926) lavish introduction to *De Deis et Mundo* and Clarke (1998: 341–47) were helpful for formulating this discussion of Saloustios (and the one of Julian's seventh oration to follow). See Lamberton (1986: 139–43) also.

64. I believe it likely that Saloustios is Saturninius Secundus Salutius, Julian's friend and an important man in the empire, to whom the army offered the imperial throne right after Julian's death. There is debate, however. While there is authoritative opinion that Saloustios is Saturninius Secundus Salutius (e.g., Clarke 1998: 347–50; Rochefort 2003/1960: x–xxi; Nock 1926: ci), a mid-fourth-century political figure from Gaul, Flavius Sallustius has proponents (e.g., Jones 1971: 796), and still others regard the question as open (e.g., Brisson 2009). As the text is in Greek and the authorship question is not a burning one for the present argument, Saloustios, a transliteration of the Greek that appears in the text and which is a Greek rendering of either Salutius or Sallustius, is used.

gods will resemble them (3.2⁶⁵) and explains how this resemblance manifests itself:

> The myths imitate the gods themselves according to what is speakable and unspeakable, according to what is invisible and visible, according to what is obvious and hidden; they also imitate the goodness of the gods—because, just as the gods have made the good from perceptible things for all persons and have made good things from things intellectual for the wise alone, so then the myths say to all that the gods exist but what they are and what their nature is, they say these things to those able to know alone. (3.3)⁶⁶

The likeness of myths to divinity registers in ways that can and cannot be articulated; myths have a pervasive and incomprehensible relationship to divinity, although the wisest can come to a rough estimation of its shape. Saloustios' ambiguous language gestures to something existing outside the scope of human intellect and experience.

Continuing, Saloustios explains how myths force the mind into interpretation. Not just inert stories, they compel the mind to realization of sublime truth through their paradoxical embodiment of transcendent divinity:

> But why have they spoken of adulteries, thefts, the binding of fathers, and other strangeness in the myths? Or is this also worthy to wonder over, namely, that on account of apparent strangeness the soul straightaway supposes the words a veil and believes the truth to be something unspeakable? (3.4)⁶⁷

Having posed a question as to why these stories are told at all, Saloustios answers it: these obscene and disreputable stories, out of place and strange, cause the soul to read them in ways opposite to their manifest content.⁶⁸ Saloustios' formulation also turns the dynamic of veiling on its

---

65. ἐχρῆν καὶ τοὺς περὶ θεῶν λόγους ὁμοίους εἶναι ἐκείνοις.

66. αὐτοὺς μὲν οὖν τοὺς θεοὺς κατὰ τὸ ῥητόν τε καὶ ἄρρητον, ἀφανές τε καὶ φανερόν, σαφές τε καὶ κρυπτόμενον οἱ μῦθοι μιμοῦνται, <καὶ> τὴν τῶν θεῶν ἀγαθότητα, ὅτι ὥσπερ ἐκεῖνοι τὰ μὲν ἐκ τῶν αἰσθητῶν ἀγαθὰ κοινὰ πᾶσιν ἐποίησαν, τὰ δὲ ἐκ τῶν νοητῶν μόνοις τοῖς ἔμφροσιν, οὕτως οἱ μῦθοι τὸ μὲν εἶναι Θεοὺς πρὸς ἅπαντας λέγουσι, τίνες δὲ οὗτοι καὶ ὁποῖοι τοῖς δυναμένοις <μόνοις> εἰδέναι.

67. ἀλλὰ διὰ τί μοιχείας καὶ κλοπὰς καὶ πατέρων δεσμοὺς καὶ τὴν ἄλλην ἀτοπίαν ἐν τοῖς μύθοις εἰρήκασιν; ἢ καὶ τοῦτο ἄξιον θαύματος, ἵνα διὰ τῆς φαινομένης ἀτοπίας εὐθὺς ἡ ψυχὴ τοὺς μὲν λόγους ἡγήσηται προκαλύμματα, τὸ δὲ ἀληθὲς ἀπόρρητον εἶναι νομίσῃ;

68. Cf. Clarke 1998: 341; Lamberton 1986: 141.

head. Saloustios offers a surfeit of violence and bodily excess to function as a "chaste" covering for the unspeakable. The thing which is not able to be spoken is veiled by that which must not be spoken: the unspeakable unknowable is, as a result, metaphorized by the obscene.[69]

It is worth emphasizing what has been occurring here. An embrace of the morally suspect enables an approach to what would normally be considered moral: divinity. A scale of value extending beyond earthbound morality, intellects, and experience is present. Saloustios translates the corporeal and material out of the earthly moral economy (where prevailing assumptions often associate them with immorality) into a transcendent existent one: an assertion about ontology forecloses ethical questions about myths. The moral concerns that carnal mythical scenes can evoke are beside the point as the myths lead the mind to perception of the more capacious reality, whose contours are greater than earthbound intellects and morals can comprehend.[70] The use of disavowed carnality recalls the way late-ancient manhood gains glamour and draws strength from its involvement with same-sex desire. The enlivening effects of corporeality direct the mind to value understood, through the power of paradox, as transcendent of corporeality. In his seventh oration, Julian also discusses this paradoxical dynamic and offers more details on its workings.

Written in early 362, Julian's seventh oration, *Against Heracleius,* is a riposte to Heracleius, a Cynic who declaimed a myth at an imperial function. Hearers of Heracleius' myth of Zeus and Pan understood these gods to be figures allegorical of Heracleius and Julian respectively (7.23/234C–D).[71] Julian's taking exception to this allegorical myth leads him into reflections on how to understand and use myths. His notions accord with those of Saloustios. For Julian too, myths are paradoxically valuable through the fact that the more objectionable or puzzling their surface content, the more treasurable they are: paradox and puzzling incongruities indicate value and summon interpretation. Also, sprinkled throughout the speech are reflections on the Cynic way of life and a presentation of the Cynics, Diogenes and Crates, as free of the strictures of society and, yet, curiously deco-

---

69. Cf. Clarke 1998: 344–45.

70. Writing in the next century in Latin, Macrobius approaches myths in a similar way. He worries more, though, about the possible obscene content, preferring to reject stories out of hand (*Comm. In Somn. Scip.* 1.2.11). But even as he does so, he inflects his philosophizing with the carnal to such an extent that his comments meant to explain Nature call to mind a striptease and references to the father gods, castrated and not, call to mind male genitalia (*Comm. In Somn. Scip.* 1.2.17–18).

71. Heracleius' speech does not survive. Rochefort offers an ambitious reconstruction of it (2003/1963: 35–36).

rous and pious (e.g., 7.8–9/212C–214A). Julian offers them as examples of a proper philosopher (and it is no coincidence that they resemble Julian). Julian contrasts these "good" Cynics to "bad" Cynics, Philiscus and Oenomaus (e.g., 7.6/210C–211A; 7.8/212A), and, of course, Heracleius. Even as he endorses the Cynic notion of "giv[ing] a new stamp to the currency," he believes that these new Cynics are mistaken in their practice of physical short-cuts to realize the properly philosophical life. While the community standards are to be ignored to some extent, the recipe for philosophic success is not ostentatious somatic deviance but, Julian says, contemplative asceticism and *paideia*.[72] Over the course of the oration, Julian's idealizing of the Cynic, as one who both stands apart from society and yet is somehow a decorous and obedient participant in it, generates considerable tension. While it was the case that the centuries had seen consistent efforts, especially by the Stoics, to idealize Cynics in general (and Diogenes in particular),[73] the more outrageously corporeal strategies of the Cynics were known to Julian[74] (and surely others), and, besides, these bad Cynics had to have learned how to behave badly from somewhere. In any case, this tension is mirrored in Julian's statements about his modes of speaking and in his self-presentation in the speech. One minute Julian embraces words of Bacchic abandon but then, elsewhere, praises speech of rational clarity. At one moment his persona derives power from the common sense of a soldier and, at the next, from *aretē* produced by *paideia*, and then, intensifying the sense of vertigo in the reader, from divine possession by Dionysus. The tension attending both Julian's modes of speaking and his persona increase his grandeur; his verbal effusiveness pours past any barrier, and who and what he is extends beyond all roles.[75]

---

72. 7.20/226B–C: asceticism and contemplation; 7.23/235C–D: *paideia*.

73. For the idealization of the Cynics and Diogenes, see Billerbeck 1996; Krueger 1996; Smith 1995: 53–55.

74. See *Or.* 9.19/202B–C, for example.

75. For more on *Against Heracleius*, see Elm's recent discussion (2012: 108–117). She gives welcome weight to Julian's concerns with both the construction of the philosophic *persona* and the paradoxical nature and use of myths. Prior appraisals of the oration have tended to see other things in it. Controversy has centered on whether the oration was meant to be an exposition of religious syncretism in support of a revival of pagan religious practice (e.g., Athanassiadi 1981: 134–37) or whether it was a display piece composed to impress intimates (Smith 1995: 90). For the purposes of the present argument, the ultimate goal of the seventh oration does not matter so much. Whatever its purpose, the discussion of the effect of myths features serious language and concepts typical of late antiquity in much the same way the ostensibly jocular *Caesares* does. Van Liefferinge's (1999: 227–33) and Clarke's (1998: 341–42) comments on the seventh oration and the connections between it and Iamblichus' conceptions are helpful (cf. Bouffartigue 1992: 337–45). Grasso (1996) on the incongruous (*apemphainon*/ἀπεμφαῖνον) spurring the late-ancient reader to interpretation is useful, as is Lamberton (1986) in general.

A major feature of the latter part of the speech is the allegorical *mythos* of Julian's own life (7.22/227C–234C), which, Julian says, is the sort of thing Heracleius should have said (7.21/227B). In this *mythos*, a rich man's sons fall to fighting when he dies because they were not taught to be virtuous. Impiety then takes over the land. This myth is transparently a representation of the struggles among Constantine's sons and of the coming of Christianity to the empire. Significantly, the *mythos* has an inconsistent focus. Now it is a depiction of problems on an estate somewhere, then it shows a crisis embroiling the empire. Zeus, in any case, pities the family and finds a nephew of the rich man (the stand-in for Julian) worth saving. The nephew acquires divine sponsors in Helios, Athene, and Hermes. Hermes guides the young man to a mountain to meet Helios, and Athene provides arms. Helios teaches the disconsolate and initially reluctant young man that the world needs his leadership. The young man, now instructed in virtue and ready to do what needs doing, returns to society to bring it to a better state.

As Julian tells the reader/hearer that this tale of his life is a *mythos*, its puzzling aspects, as will be seen shortly, suggest that probing is in order, for this is what Julian says should be done when incongruities in a *mythos* are noticed. The struggles of the Constantinian dynasty after the death of Constantine and momentous change in religion in the late-ancient empire don't fit well with the small-bore size of the *mythos* (and the latter, the invocation of religious transformation, all but breaks allegory's spell), and this poor fit creates changes in focus that are, arguably, puzzling and which pull the reader/hearer in to resolve ambiguities. The argument to come will be that ambiguities inviting readerly engagement are perceptible not only in the *mythos*, they also are in the *mythos*' ultimate object: Julian himself. Intertextuality with the story of the choice of Herakles (the hero, i.e., Julian, seems to choose the path of indolence) and with the *Iliad* (the hero is Helen, and taking up the duties of empire is allegorized as sleeping with Paris) adumbrate a complex masculine subjectivity that cannot be explained by reference to self-control and protocols of penetration alone. The excitement of carnal indulgence, i.e., Vice's road and sleeping with a prince of Troy, renders this subjectivity worthy to command an empire more lively, and its tarrying with the forbidden connects it to a scale of valuation greater than that of earthbound morals and standards. In sum, *Against Heracleius* offers both a theorization of the value of myths and an actual example of finding value in one.

A return to Julian's *mythos* of his life and consideration of the paradoxes surrounding Julian himself are to come. First, however, Julian's complaints about Heracleius' story and his reflections on myths:

Not for the first time are you hearing the gods blasphemed! We don't pursue our common interests so judiciously nor are we so temperate in private matters; indeed, we are not so lucky that we are able to keep our ears pure, or, in the final analysis, our eyes undefiled by the manifold impieties of this race of iron. In this moment, this dog [Heracleius the Cynic] has filled us, as though we had need of such evils, with impure words, depicting the best of the gods as he should never have, and as we should never have heard! (7.1/204D–205A)[76]

The portrayal of Zeus as the Cynic Heracleius and of Pan as Julian was, Julian says, impious, unclean, and evil. This was not the first time Julian has heard such things from these false Cynics, these epitomes of the irreligious ferrous age. Julian then speaks of the nature of myths and their proper use.

Placing myths in relation to philosophy, which he divides into three parts, natural philosophy, practical philosophy and logic, which are in turn divided into three sections each,[77] Julian states that *mythographia*/μυθογραφία, the written presentation of myths, is not appropriate to logic, physics, or mathematics, but is useful when philosophy turns to consideration of individuals, initiation, and mystery cults:

> Now of these branches [of philosophy], logic has no concern with *mythographia*; nor do physics and mathematics; but, if at all, the part of practical philosophy which deals with the individual man, and the part of theology which deals with initiation and the Mysteries do [have something to do with *mythographia*]. (7.11/216B)[78]

The myths with their often obscene contents (see below) are worthwhile because they tell people how to understand themselves as individuals and how to live and worship communally.

---

76. οὐ πρῶτον ἀκούεις τῶν θεῶν βλασφημουμένων, οὐχ οὕτω τὰ κοινὰ πράττομεν καλῶς, οὐχ οὕτω τῶν ἰδίων ἕνεκα σωφρονοῦμεν, οὐ μὴν οὐδὲ εὐτυχεῖς οὕτως ἐσμεν ὥστε τὰς ἀκοὰς καθαρὰς ἔχειν ἢ τελευταῖον γοῦν τὰ ὄμματα μὴ κεχράνθαι τοῖς παντοδαποῖς τουτουὶ τοῦ σιδηροῦ γένους ἀσεβήμασιν· ἐπεὶ δὲ ὥσπερ ἐνδεεῖς ἡμᾶς τῶν τοιούτων κακῶν ἀνέπλησεν οὐκ εὐαγῶν ὁ κύων ῥημάτων τὸν ἄριστον τῶν θεῶν ὀνομάσας, ὡς μήποτε ὤφελε μήτ' ἐκεῖνος εἰπεῖν μήτε ἡμεῖς ἀκοῦσαι.

77. 7.10/215C–216A. Julian divides natural philosophy into theology, mathematics, and concepts related to both things perishable and things eternal in their essential natures, i.e., "physics." Practical philosophy sees a division into individual ethics, the ethics of the household, and politics. Logic concerns itself with a) the truth of propositions (demonstrative logic), b) general opinions (polemical logic), and c) probabilities (eristic logic).

78. τούτων δὴ τῶν μερῶν οὔτε τῷ λογικῷ προσήκει τῆς μυθογραφίας οὔτε τῷ φυσικῷ οὔτε τῷ μαθηματικῷ, μόνον δέ, εἴπερ ἄρα, τοῦ πρακτικοῦ τῷ πρὸς ἕνα γινομένῳ καὶ τοῦ θεολογικοῦ τῷ τελεστικῷ καὶ μυστικῷ.

Continuing, Julian speaks about taking the measure of nature and the hidden quality of the divine, noting that both are elusive and that persons who are not pure (or discerning) will not be able to perceive them directly. All is not lost, though; the "unspeakable and unknown nature of *charaktēres*" and myths provide beneficent, if indirect, access:

> Nature (*physis*/φύσις) loves to hide itself, and the hidden-away essence of the gods does not allow itself to be flung in naked words into unpurified ears. With regards to this conundrum, the unspeakable and unknown nature of *charaktēres* was brought into being to help: it nourishes both souls and bodies and brings about the presence of the gods. Many times, I think, this comes about through the action of myths—whenever through riddles and in the company of the dramatic settings of myths, it (*sc.* this unspeakable nature of *charaktēres*) is insinuated into the ears of the multitude who cannot receive divine things in their pure form. (7.11/216C–D)[79]

Employing a tag from Heraclitus ("Nature loves to hide itself"[80]) and thereby importing a bit of Pre-Socratic glamour, Julian says that nature does not yield its secrets easily and that divinity's essence is likewise mysterious. Neither of them can be revealed as they truly are to most people; not initiated, the unworthy majority will not understand such communication. But it need not be the case that they learn nothing of nature or divine essence. "The unspeakable and unknown nature of *charaktēres*" (*tōn charaktērōn hē aporrētos physis . . . kai agnooumenē*/τῶν χαρακτήρων ἡ ἀπόρρητος φύσις . . . καὶ ἀγνοουμένη) provides a means of communication. It is fitting that Julian uses the word *charaktēr*: it is polysemous (and extraordinarily difficult to translate) and therefore appropriate in the present circumstance. In *LSJ* (χαρακτήρ II.2), "magical symbol" is suggested as the meaning for this precise passage and the suggestion does make a degree of sense. But the word is richer than that, and more meanings would have come to the mind of a fourth-century reader. *Charaktēr* can designate a letter of the alphabet, and Julian uses it with this meaning in his third oration (section 17/71D). *Charaktēr* can also mean "characteristic," "pattern," or even an "engraver" or a "mark engraved." In a letter to the Alexandrians written in 362, taking them to task for lynching their bishop, Julian

---

79. φιλεῖ . . . ἡ φύσις κρύπτεσθαι, καὶ τὸ ἀποκεκρυμμένον τῆς τῶν θεῶν οὐσίας οὐκ ἀνέχεται γυμνοῖς εἰς ἀκαθάρτους ἀκοὰς ῥίπτεσθαι ῥήμασιν. Ὅπερ δὲ δὴ τῶν χαρακτήρων ἡ ἀπόρρητος φύσις ὠφελεῖν πέφυκε καὶ ἀγνοουμένη· θεραπεύει γοῦν οὐ ψυχὰς μόνον, ἀλλὰ καὶ σώματα, καὶ θεῶν ποιεῖ παρουσίας· τοῦτ' οἶμαι πολλάκις γίγνεσθαι καὶ διὰ τῶν μύθων, ὅταν εἰς τὰς τῶν πολλῶν ἀκοὰς οὐ δυναμένας τὰ θεῖα καθαρῶς δέξασθαι δι' αἰνιγμάτων αὐτοῖς μετὰ τῆς μύθων σκηνοποιίας ἐγχέηται.

80. Frag. 123 (Diels): φύσις δὲ . . . κρύπτεσθαι φιλεῖ.

expresses the hope that their Greek heritage has put "a worthy and noble stamp (*charaktēr*) on [their] minds and habits."[81] As will be seen in discussion of the *Vita Antonii* in the next chapter, both Antony's life conceived as a whole and Athanasius' text itself provide a pattern, i.e., a *charaktēr*, that guides a potential or practicing ascetic in his vocation. Whatever the precise meaning of *charaktēres*, their "unspeakable and unknown nature" indicates in this passage from Julian's oration so great a surfeit of mystery around nature and "the hidden-away essence of the gods" (*to apokekrummenon tēs tōn theōn ousias*/τὸ ἀποκεκρυμμένον τῆς τῶν θεῶν οὐσίας) that it spreads to the mode of communication meant to convey an understanding of them. His choice of this word, with its profusion of possibilities, redoubles all by itself the effects of the adjectives, "unspeakable" and "unknown," making the surface of the valuable myths even more mysterious.

Having distinguished the surface of myths from their esteemed contents, Julian next tells how these myths with their riddling exteriors lead the hearer/reader to higher beneficent realizations. The incongruity between the surface of the myths and their asserted value spurs the mind to search for significance:

> The incongruous element in myths by its very self leads to the truth. For the more paradoxical and monstrous the riddle is, the more it seems to bear witness that we should not believe simply the things said in it, but that we should, rather, expend our efforts on the hidden things, and not cease until, under the guidance of the gods, those hidden things, having become plain, initiate or, better, perfect our mind—without us forgetting that there exists something more powerful than our mind: a certain small particle of the One and the Good which contains everything indivisibly, embracing both the soul's fulfillment [from the One] and comprehending in the One and the Good the whole of the soul itself through the prevailing, separate, and transcendent presence of It [i.e., the One]. (7.12/217C–D)[82]

---

81. Ep. 60 (Bidez 2004/1924) / 21 (Wright 1980b/1923), 380D: ἀξιόλογος καὶ γενναῖος ἐν τῇ διανοίᾳ καὶ τοῖς ἐπιτηδεύμασιν ὁ χαρακτήρ.

82. Τὸ γὰρ ἐν τοῖς μύθοις ἀπεμφαῖνον αὐτῷ τούτῳ προοδοποιεῖ πρὸς τὴν ἀλήθειαν. "Ὅσῳ γὰρ μᾶλλον παράδοξόν ἐστι καὶ τερατῶδες τὸ αἴνιγμα, τοσούτῳ μᾶλλον ἔοικε διαμαρτύρεσθαι, μὴ τοῖς αὐτόθεν λεγομένοις πιστεύειν, ἀλλὰ τὰ λεληθότα περιεργάζεσθαι καὶ μὴ πρότερον ἀφίστασθαι, πρὶν ἂν ὑπὸ θεοῖς ἡγεμόσιν ἐκφανῆ γενόμενα τὸν ἐν ἡμῖν τελέσῃ, μᾶλλον δὲ τελειώσῃ, νοῦν καὶ εἰ δή τι κρεῖττον ἡμῖν ὑπάρχει τοῦ νοῦ, αὐτοῦ τοῦ ἑνὸς καὶ τἀγαθοῦ μοῖρά τις ὀλίγη τὸ πᾶν ἀμερίστως ἔχουσα, τῆς ψυχῆς πλήρωμα καὶ ἐν τῷ ἑνὶ καὶ ἀγαθῷ συνέχουσα πᾶσαν αὐτὴν διὰ τῆς ὑπερχούσης καὶ χωριστῆς αὐτοῦ καὶ ἐξῃρημένης παρουσίας.

Inherently valuable through their relation to the gods and sacred truth, myths are also obscene things of mystery.[83] The wise man, however, will recognize that the more obscene and monstrous a riddle the myth presents, then all the harder he should work for revelation of what has been hidden. Interaction with myths leads to an understanding of the pervasive presence of the divine in the world. This achieved understanding also initiates the mind and puts it on the road to perfection.[84] The objectionable appearance offered by myths is valuable and what seems unworthy of welcome is to be welcomed. Enlivening corporeality—"monstrous" (*teratōdes*/τερατῶδες) and "incongruous" (*apemphainon*/ἀπεμφαῖνον), and what could be more "incongruous" with the singularity that is the One?—brings minds to enlightenment. But the wise one will also remember that mystery abides; he or she cannot understand everything. The embrace of the monstrous for the sake of divinity, of disorder for the sake of order, indicates a scale of value transcendent of earth-bound morals and logic; things exist prior to moral judgments and their liveliness, existent and indifferent to morals, lends mysterious, paradoxical, and frequently beneficent power to whatever they touch.

---

83. For more on the power of obscene/odd myths to compel the mind to realization of the sacred in Julian's seventh oration, see Elm 2012:111–14; Van Liefferinge 1999: 229–31; Clarke 1998: 341–42; Grasso 1996; Smith 1995: 122–23; Bouffartigue 1992: 616–25; Cosi 1986: 104–105.

84. A similar performative discourse appears elsewhere in Julian's works. In his eighth oration (*Hymn to the Mother of the Gods*), Julian sees the role of the reader as crucial whenever he or she is faced with the paradoxical contents of myths. Julian remarks that men of old "clothed" the truths of the universe "in paradoxical myths, so that through paradox and incongruity the fiction, detected, might turn us toward the search for truth" (8.10/170A–B: ἐσκέπασαν... μύθοις παραδόξοις, ἵνα διὰ τοῦ παραδόξου καὶ ἀπεμφαίνοντος τὸ πλάσμα φωραθὲν ἐπὶ τὴν ζήτησιν ἡμᾶς τῆς ἀληθείας προτρέψῃ). The great unwashed will accept the myths as they are, of course (8.10/170B), but those who are wiser, because they recognize that these myths are a riddling representation of a higher reality, will search for meaning beyond them (8.10/170B: διὰ μὲν τῶν αἰνιγμάτων ὑπομνησθεὶς ὅτι χρή τι περὶ αὐτῶν ζητεῖν). Saloustios' *De Deis et Mundo* also features this performative discourse. The puzzling aspects of myths engender respect in the uninformed and compel wise men to work to understand the mystery:

> [To] wish to teach all men the truth about the gods causes the foolish to despise, because they cannot learn, and the good to be slothful; whereas, to conceal the truth in myths prevents the former from despising philosophy and compels the latter to study it. (*De Deis et Mundo* 3.4)
>
> τὸ μὲν πάντας τὴν περὶ Θεῶν ἀλήθειαν διδάσκειν ἐθέλειν τοῖς μὲν ἀνοήτοις, διὰ τὸ μὴ δύνασθαι μανθάνειν, καταφρόνησιν, τοῖς δὲ σπουδαίοις ῥᾳθυμίαν ἐμποιεῖ· τὸ δὲ διὰ μύθων τἀληθὲς ἐπικρύπτειν τοὺς μὲν καταφρονεῖν οὐκ ἐᾷ, τοὺς δὲ φιλοσοφεῖν ἀναγκάζει.

Lamberton has helpful comments on similar dynamics to be found in Porphyry's and Proclus' understandings of Homer (1986: 113, 173).

THE MAKING OF JULIAN'S AUTHORITY IN *AGAINST HERACLEIUS*

As empowering paradox marks the valuation of myths in his seventh oration, so it marks Julian's characterization of proper modes of speech and of his own persona as authoritative. Julian speaks now in simple, direct, and calm language, and now in speech complex, allegorizing, Dionysian. His persona exhibits corollary contradictions. In one moment, he is the fearsomely educated philosopher, in another a rough-hewn soldier, and, in still one more, Bacchus' crazed thrall. As Julian disciplines Heracleius, speech and persona, constructed through paradox, accordingly have a connection to a scale of value greater than earth-bound logic: who and what he is are not able to be explained in a manner that will not leave an unexplained remainder.

Julian has praise for both possessed enigmatic speech and that which is direct and clear in the oration. As seen above, he finds much to like in the riddling and dramatic presentation of myths in the company of *charaktēres* (7.11/216C–D, cf. 7.17/222C–D). The One even appears through the kind offices of paradox. At other times, however, he will come right out and say that clear and direct speech—speech for a *mythos*—is the *desideratum:*

> It is said well by Euripides: "The *mythos* (μῦθος) of truth was born straightforward"[85]: He says that the liar and unjust man have need of "a writing of shadows." (7.9/214A–B)[86]

But not only does he say that both riddling *and* straightforward speech are to be preferred, leaving a contradiction to be sorted out, he also worries about being misunderstood no matter which kind of speech he uses.

At 7.16 (220D–221A), Julian straightforwardly rationalizes Semele's destruction by Zeus' thunderbolt. He says she, a hasty priestess, actually perished in a fire in a sacrificial rite undertaken before it should have been. It was not time for her son to be worshipped: Semele is impatient always and ever dies in flames, just prosaically this time. Julian then worries that this and other disambiguations of Dionysus' spectacular biography will not

---

85. This line, line 469 of Euripides' *Phoenissae,* is the first in a speech by Polynices to his brother who has just arrived on stage. Jocasta is present also. The dynamic of hatred among family members issuing from the intertext is able to be associated with the poisonous familial dynamics in the house of Constantine, for Julian's *mythos* of his life is coming up.

86. λέγεται . . . ὑπ' Εὐριπίδου καλῶς, "Ἁπλοῦς ὁ μῦθος τῆς ἀληθείας ἔφυ."· σκιαγραφίας γάρ φησι τὸν ψευδῆ καὶ ἄδικον δεῖσθαι.

be understood properly. Is it a matter of a certain lack of finesse owing to his own ignorance, he wonders, or does the difficulty stem from ambivalence about presenting such important material to an audience who will not understand it?

> [This explanatory activity of mine poses difficulties for me] perhaps because I still don't know all these things clearly, or perhaps I don't want to put this god at once hidden and evident on display, as though in a theater for non-discerning ears and minds turned to anything except philosophy. (7.16/221D)[87]

And as clear language causes anxiety, exuberantly "Bacchic" language does so too. Immediately after the passage on the power of the incongruous in myths to lead the mind to realization of the nature of the utterly transcendent One, Julian frets:

> Something, I know not what or how, impelled me to rave with his own sacred frenzy about the attributes of great Dionysus, "and now I set an ox on my tongue"[88]: it is necessary to say nothing about unspeakable things. However, may the gods grant their benefit to me and to many of you, as many as are still uninitiated. (7.12/217D–218A)[89]

The upshot of these contradictions, i.e., clear speech is both good and bad, as are Bacchic incongruities, is that Julian showcases the insufficiency of earthbound means to get at the thing Julian has in mind; whichever route he takes will always fail in one way or another. These inevitable failures show that divinity and truth are greater than earthbound language can lay hold of and communicate to an audience: there is always a remainder. The empowering paradox engendered by the collision of contrary valuations of language in the speech is mirrored by the contrary impressions seen previously in the matter of myths, and by the aspects of himself, in contradiction with one another, that Julian sports in this oration. If these

---

87. τυχὸν μὲν καὶ διὰ τὸ ἀγνοεῖν ἔτι περὶ αὐτῶν τὸ ἀκριβές, τυχὸν δὲ καὶ οὐκ ἐθέλοντι τὸν κρύφιον ἅμα καὶ φανερὸν θεὸν ὥσπερ ἐν θεάτρῳ προβάλλειν ἀκοαῖς ἀνεξετάστοις καὶ διανοίαις ἐπὶ πάντα μᾶλλον ἢ τὸ φιλοσοφεῖν τετραμμέναις.

88. Julian perhaps quotes from one (or more) of these sources: Theognis 1.815; Aeschylus, *Agamemnon* 36; Sophocles, *Oedipus at Colonus* 1051.

89. Ἀλλὰ ταῦτα μὲν ἀμφὶ τὸν μέγαν Διόνυσον οὐκ οἶδ' ὅπως ἐπῆλθέ μοι βακχεύοντι μανῆναι· τὸν βοῦν δὲ ἐπιτίθημι τῇ γλώττῃ· περὶ τῶν ἀρρήτων γὰρ οὐδὲν χρὴ λέγειν. Ἀλλά μοι θεοὶ μὲν ἐκείνων καὶ ὑμῶν δὲ τοῖς πολλοῖς, ὅσοι τέως ἐστὲ τούτων ἀμύητοι, τὴν ὄνησιν δοῖεν.

contradictions are read as paradox, and they should be, they suggest power and glamour that comes from beyond this earth.

Emergent in the oration is a portrait of Julian reminiscent of his idealized portraits of Diogenes and Crates. He has nothing but praise for them. As is Julian, they are pious. Diogenes' transgressions amount to refusing honors and pleasures, and there is little of the edgy behavior for which Cynics were famous, such as public masturbation.[90] The bad Cynics are liable to tell raunchy and blasphemous myths, like Heracleius did, or write tragedies of a similar quality, as Philiscus evidently and Oenomaus surely did (7.6/210D).[91] Julian also criticizes the current Cynics for thinking that virtue (*aretē*) can be acquired through a purely physical praxis:

> The staff, cloak, the (long) hair, and, from there, Voilà!, the ignorance, the effrontery, all that kind of stuff quite simply. They say they travel the short and intense path to virtue. You [Cynics] would do better to travel the long path. You would arrive with greater ease on that path in comparison to the one you are travelling now. Don't you know that shortcuts have great difficulties? (7.19/225B–C)[92]

Julian's point here is that these Cynics have neglected their minds, thinking only of their bodies; they have erroneously thought that they truly know themselves and that they can give a new stamp to the currency and thereby come to virtue (*aretē*) through physical means alone. In contrast, the road to virtue for Julian has been different. Unlike Heracleius, Julian was educated properly in the poets and in philosophy (7.23/235A–B), and through this course of study he acquired *aretē* and increased his piety to the gods (235B). Indeed, to be educated (235A: *paidotribeisthai*/παιδοτριβεῖσθαι) by his master (235A, C: *kathēgemōn*/καθηγεμών]), reading the books and attending the lectures he was told to, was tantamout to being initiated in a religious sense by a man (235A: *teleisthai* [*hyp' andri telesthēsomenos*]/

---

90. See, e.g., Diogenes Laertius 6.46: "Once when he [Diogenes] was working with his hands (i.e., masturbating) in the Agora, he said, 'if only I could rub my belly and in that way not be hungry'" (ἐπ' ἀγορᾶς ποτε χειρουργῶν, "εἴθε," ἔφη, "καὶ τὴν κοιλίαν ἦν παρατρίψαντα μὴ πεινῆν"). While such a thing is not mentioned in *Against Heracleius,* Julian is more forthcoming about Diogenes' public defecation, flatulence, and masturbation in the ninth oration at 19/202B–C.

91. Diogenes' supposed tragedies, which Julian prefers to attribute to some or other Cynic or to Philiscus, were notorious for cannibalism and incest and Oenomaus evidently continued in this vein and created even more outrageous plays (Dawson 1992: 249).

92. βακτηρία, τρίβων, κόμη, τὸ ἐντεῦθεν ἀμαθία, θράσος, <ἰταμό>της, <καὶ πάντα> ἁπλῶς τὰ τοιαῦτα. Τὴν σύντομον φασὶν ὁδὸν καὶ σύντονον ἐπὶ τὴν ἀρετὴν <πορεύεσθαι>· ὄφελον καὶ ὑμεῖς τὴν μακρὰν ἐπορεύεσθε· ῥᾷον ἂν δι' ἐκείνης <ἢ διὰ ταύτης> ἤλθετε. Οὐκ ἴστε ὅτι μεγάλας ἔχουσιν αἱ σύντομοι τὰς χαλεπότητας;

τελεῖσθαι [ὑπ' ἀνδρὶ τελεσθησόμενος]).⁹³ Throughout this process Julian says that his master "removed what was mad and overly bold (from me) and he tried to make me more temperate (*sōphronesteron*/σωφρονέστερον) than myself" (7.23/235B).⁹⁴ The making of the boy into a man by *paideia* is on display here, and it contrasts with the superficiality of adopting only a physical stance against the institutions of society, like the "bad" Cynics do. The educative scene in the manner of a dialogue of Plato (perhaps the *Charmides?*), with man and boy on a search for *sōphrosynē*, may occur to a sensitive reader.⁹⁵ Indeed, speaking from this place of investment in *paideia* and the product of it, Julian accuses these Cynics of simply "throwing expectations held in common about appropriate behavior into confusion . . . through bringing in a worse and more disgusting way of life for the *polis*/the citizenry (*politeia*)."⁹⁶ They thought they had found a shortcut to *aretē*, bypassing education and hard years of instruction, and, with their cheeky impudence posing as wisdom, they have merely offered degradation.

As was seen above, however, in the case of myths and in Julian's words about the desirability and limitations of riddling and clear language, the distinction Julian draws between himself and these Cynics is not as clear-cut as it might first appear. Once again Julian is holding positions on both sides of the question. Even as he insists on the necessity of *paideia*, elsewhere he indulges the notion that he is but a soldier who has come by what he knows via experiences not mediated by *paideia*:

> [It] is not a surprising thing if a soldier-man is not overly precise [about these philosophical matters] or if he does not have such things right at his fingertips, inasmuch as he does not speak on the basis of extended study of books [lit. from an *askēsis* of books] but from his way of coming upon them haphazardly. (7.10/216A)⁹⁷

---

93. For more on Julian's idea of education as ecstatic religious initiation, see Bouffartigue 1992: 633–34.
94. ἐξῄρει τὸ μανιῶδες καὶ θρασύ, καὶ ἐπειρᾶτό με ποιεῖν ἐμαυτοῦ σωφρονέστερον.
95. Indeed, a sensitive reader who knows the twelfth book of the *Anthologia Graeca* may recall that both the verb *paidotribeō*/παιδοτριβέω (to educate, to train a boy) and the noun *paidotribēs*/παιδοτρίβης (educator, trainer of boys) are liable to quite naughty *doubles-entendres* (see 12.34 and 12.222), i.e., the trainer "grinds into" the boy.
96. 7.5/210C: τὰ κοινὰ νόμιμα συγχέοντες . . . τῷ χείρονα καὶ βδελυρωτέραν ἐπεισάγειν πολιτείαν.
97. οὐδὲν θαυμαστὸν ἄνδρα στρατιώτην μὴ λίαν ἐξακριβοῦν μηδ' ἐξονυχίζειν τὰ τοιαῦτα, ἅτε οὐκ ἐκ βιβλίων ἀσκήσεως, ἀπὸ δὲ τῆς προστυχούσης αὐτὰ ἕξεως ἀποφθεγγόμενον.

Pretending that his fairly detailed description, just offered, of the parts of philosophy (three sections divided into three each [7.10/215C–216A], discussed above) is rather imprecise, Julian asserts that this is because he is a soldier man (*andra stratiōtēn*/ ἄνδρα στρατιώτην) who has learned philosophy not from books but through hearing of them in the context of experiences he has had. Not in the study, taming his boyish wild side, he is in the camps coming to manly understanding amid muscles flexing and weapons flashing (and the occasional book).[98]

Furthermore, in his praise of Bacchus, Julian prays that the god will excite his mind and that of Heracleius to a frenzy for true knowledge about the gods. Books seemingly are not enough, and neither is the rough-hewn attentiveness of a soldier-man; madness is needed for knowledge and peace in this life and the next. One must yield to Dionysus:

> I pray that my mind and yours may rage with Bacchic frenzy for true knowledge of the gods, lest, staying for a long time uninitiated by the god in Bacchic rites, we should suffer the things Pentheus did, perhaps while living and, at all events, when we have been freed from our bodies (in death). For in whomever the fullness of life has not been perfected by the singular and entirely indivisible and unmixed pre-existent substance of Dionysus through the divinely infused madness that exists all about the god, for this one there is the danger of life flowing in all directions, having been made to disperse and, torn apart, to be lost utterly. . . . (7.16/221D–222A)[99]

Complete with the possibility of salvation, a surrender to Bacchic madness enables knowledge of the gods and an ordered life. Lack of surrender, in contrast, means total loss. What to all appearances is abandon to disorder is an embrace of pre-existent substance embodied by Dionysus that enables an orderly life in this world. This looks very different from the picture that Julian draws elsewhere of himself as the obedient student whom his teacher endeavored to train to be more temperate than himself. It is different too

---

98. Julian speaks of himself in similar fashion in the *Misopogon* (*Or.* 12) at 30/359B–D. In the context of his depiction of himself as hard and masculine and the Antiochenes as soft and effeminate, he brandishes his formative experiences as a soldier man on hard campaign in Gaul.

99. προσεύχομαι τάς τε ἐμὰς καὶ τὰς ὑμετέρας ἐκβακχεῦσαι φρένας ἐπὶ τὴν ἀληθῆ τῶν θεῶν γνῶσιν, ὡς ἂν μὴ πολὺν ἀβάκχευτοι χρόνον τῷ θεῷ μένοντες ὁπόσα ὁ Πενθεὺς ἔπαθε πάθωμεν, ἴσως μὲν καὶ ζῶντες, πάντως δὲ καὶ ἀπαλλαγέντες τοῦ σώματος. Ὅτῳ γὰρ <ἂν> μὴ τὸ πεπληθυσμένον τῆς ζωῆς ὑπὸ τῆς ἑνοειδοῦς καὶ ἐν τῷ μεριστῷ παντελῶς ἀδιαιρέτου ὅλης τε ἐν πᾶσιν ἀμιγοῦς προϋπαρχούσης τοῦ Διονύσου οὐσίας τελεσιουργηθείη διὰ τῆς περὶ τὸν θεὸν ἐνθέου βακχείας, τούτῳ κίνδυνος ἐπὶ πολλὰ ῥυῆναι τὴν ζωήν, ῥυεῖσαν δὲ διεσπάσθαι καὶ διασπασθεῖσαν οἴχεσθαι. . . .

from the soldier-man who acquires his knowledge through practical experience and unsystematic study. Here, instead of suppressing parts of himself in the service of *askēseis* educative or martial, he is to let loose. In doing what he is not supposed to and giving the appearance of transcending the strictures of society that are often supported by him elsewhere,[100] he looks quite like the "good" Cynics, and even rather like the "bad" ones.[101]

In the context of a discussion of guidance Diogenes received from Apollo, Julian speaks of a close relationship he sees between the general philosophical maxim, "Know yourself," and the one particular to the Cynics, "Give a new stamp to the currency." At the conclusion of the following quotation, he comes to a strong statement about what he values and what anyone should value in this life:

> Do we know what the god said? [We know] that he ordered him (Diogenes) to disregard the opinions of the many and to give a new stamp not to truth but to the currency. How shall we understand the "Know yourself" in relation to this? Should we associate it with the currency? Or will we declare it to be the summation of truth and (at the same time) say that the way of "Give a new stamp to the currency" is an indirect way of saying "Know yourself"? For just as a man, placing no value in any way in conventional opinions and having come to truth itself, will manage himself not on the basis of conventional opinions about him but *on the basis of things as they really are* (*tois ontōs ousi*/τοῖς ὄντως οὖσι), so I think he who knows himself will know accurately *what he is* (*hoper estin*/ὅπερ ἔστιν) and not [only] what conventional opinion says he is. (7.7/211B–D, emphasis added)[102]

---

100. For more on Julian's decorous side, see Amm., *Res Gestae* 25.4.2–6 or see Julian contrasting his abstemious habits to the luxury of the Antiochenes in his *Misopogon* (*passim*). See, too, Barnes (1998: 156–57), Cosi (1986: 48–75), and Bowersock (1978: 12–20, 79–93). Smith (1995: 78) underscores Julian's discomfort with actual Cynicism. A letter, written in 362 from Antioch to an unknown non-Christian priest (see, especially, 300C–D [89B in Bidez and Cumont 1922 / Wright 1969/1913: 324]) provides further evidence of Julian's scolding tendencies (though note Smith's observation that Julian was in this case perhaps "prescribing a pious ideal for a restricted group" [1995: 14]).

101. Throughout a book on Julian's eighth oration (*Hymn to the Mother of the Gods*), Dario Cosi (1986) reveals and assesses the tension between these two aspects of Julian's thought and character. At the book's end, Cosi writes that for Julian "the ancient myth [of Attis and Cybele], vital and orgiastic, is all but turned on its head in a philosophic mystery that preaches sexual abstinence" (112: "L'antico mito vitalistico e orgiastico è ormai capovolto in un filosofico mistero che predica l'astensione sessuale"). At this moment Julian is close to Christian authors such as Victricius who are liable, say, to envision sobriety inebriated by denial seeking pardon for its excesses: "May sobriety drunk on vigils and fasts seek forgiveness for its sins" (Victric. 5: *Vigiliis et ieiuniis inebriata sobrietas ablutionem postulet peccatorum*).

102. Τί δὲ εἶπεν ὁ θεός, ἆρ' ἴσμεν; Ὅτι τῆς τῶν πολλῶν αὐτῷ δόξης ἐπέταξεν ὑπερορᾶν καὶ πα-

This quotation is key to Julian's effort to propose an idealized Cynicism as a foil to Heracleius' and other late-ancient Cynics' short-cut of physicality to philosophical *gravitas*. Julian writes the reflection embodied by *gnōthi sauton* into what he believes is a properly pursued Cynic activity of opposing societal norms: the proper Cynic "gives a new stamp to the currency," but only after searching reflection about who and what he is. After reflection, and only then, he acts. That this is an idealized version of Cynicism is beside the point, however; the point is that an ideal subjectivity should be tied to a standard that stretches beyond earthbound systems of morality. Not harnassed by the opinions of society, an admirable subjectivity takes existence as its guiding star, and Julian's suggestion, idealizing though it may be, turns out to have implications less tame than it might first appear to have.

Similarity between this proferred way of life and the attitude toward myths that Julian recommends elsewhere in the oration is manifest. The commandment for personal deportment—the man is supposed to privilege "things as they really are" in order to live in accordance with "what he is" in reality and "not on the basis of conventional opinions about him"—shares features with the approach to myths that finds value in the somatic and obscene as indicators of an order of existence more essential and important than things of this earth. The monstrosity and incongruity of myth draw the mind in and are signs of this greater order. What is unacceptable to society is to be accepted and contradiction is the sign of a transcendent, mysterious, and better order. To value myths and to live life well both involve disregarding society's judgments.

It is therefore of considerable interest that the major feature of the latter part of the oration is a *mythos*. On the present reading, the *mythos* Julian gives of his own life is in essence an embodiment of the two concerns of the oration: myth and how to live a life. In the scholarly literature, when this portion of the speech is engaged, the allegory has been read almost solely in terms of one of its indubitable meanings: the story of Julian and how his taking over the affairs of his family will turn the empire back to worship of the pagan gods.[103] This is sensible but does not exhaust the meaning able to

---

ραχαράττειν οὐ τὴν ἀλήθειαν, ἀλλὰ τὸ νόμισμα. Τὸ δὲ "Γνῶθι σαυτὸν" ἐν ποτέρᾳ θησόμεθα μοίρᾳ; Πότερον ἐν τῇ τοῦ νομίσματος; Ἢ τοῦτό γε αὐτὸ τῆς ἀληθείας εἶναι κεφάλαιον θήσομεν καὶ τρόπον εἰρῆσθαι τοῦ "Παραχάραξον τὸ νόμισμα" διὰ τῆς τοῦ "Γνῶθι σαυτὸν" ἀποφάσεως; "Ὥσπερ γὰρ ὁ τὰ νομιζόμενα παντάπασιν ἀτιμάσας, ἐπ' αὐτὴν δὲ ἥκων τὴν ἀλήθειαν οὔθ' ὑπὲρ ἑαυτοῦ τοῖς νομιζομένοις, ἀλλὰ τοῖς ὄντως οὖσι θήσεται, οὕτως οἶμαι καὶ ὁ γνοὺς ἑαυτὸν ὅπερ ἔστιν ἀκριβῶς εἴσεται καὶ οὐχ ὅπερ νομίζεται.

103. Referring to the *mythos* about to be discussed, Elm makes a fascinating suggestion whose logic is similar to that underlying the present argument: "the *paradoxon* of his [Julian's] association

be found in the *mythos*. As myths, on Julian's own testimony, solicit active engagement from a hearer/reader because of incongruities (*apemphainonta*/ ἀπεμφαίνοντα) to be seen in them, it seems sensible to take Julian at his word and read his own *mythos* as probingly as he would have all *mythoi* read. A commitment, emphatically appropriate in the present instance, to search out complexities and the powers provided by *paideia* lead the reader to the surprisingly complex man who *is* there.

IOULIANOS MYTHOUMENOS

Just prior to beginning his *mythos,* Julian mentions a *mythos* Demosthenes told the Athenians when Alexander the Great asked that the *rhetores* be sent to him (7.21/227B). Plutarch in his life of Demosthenes (23.4–6) relates a fuller version which gives an idea of the probable level of knowledge in Julian's audience about this historical event. After the destruction of Thebes, Plutarch says, Alexander summoned the leading *rhetores* (the text has *dēmagōgoi*). This was sinister. One of those on Alexander's list, Demosthenes, told a *logos* about how wolves persuaded the sheep to give up their guard dogs. The flock, dogless, was soon destroyed. Demosthenes and the other *rhetores,* of course, were the dogs, and Alexander the wolf.[104] Heracleius should have fashioned something like this (7.21/227B: ἐχρῆν οὖν τι τοιοῦτο πλάσαι), Julian says. Not having done this, Heracleius has forced Julian to become a mythmaker (*mythopoion genesthai*/μυθοποιὸν γενέσθαι) who tells a story allegorical of his life, a story with political dimensions—and in this regard certainly similar to Demosthenes' story— and with incongruities that invite interpretation. Julian offers a picture of a leader with *axiōma* for whom duty and work are luxuriating pleasures, i.e., he takes the easy road, and, after a possible schooling in masturbation, he appears as Helen of Troy, whose duty is to sleep with Paris. These incongruities suggest that this man is complicated, and they glamorize him with a hypertrophy of improprieties that employ carnalities of various kinds to infuse his imperial authority with life's vitality.

The *mythos* proper commences with a nameless wealthy man arranging his affairs poorly: after he died, his heirs quarreled among themselves.

---

with the dynasty of Constantine was a sacred symbol, or character, intended to activate the divine powers, to motivate the assiduous search for the truth, to heal men in body as well as soul, and 'to bring about the presence of the gods' (*theōn poiei parousias,* 216C) through Julian" (2012: 116).

104. Gert-Jan van Dijk (1997: 291–96) discusses various appearances of this tale of flock, wolves, and dogs in Greek literature.

Amid these struggles, the sons fostered impiety in the land by demolishing temples and not respecting ancestral usages (7.22/228C). A nephew of this irresponsible man, and the hero in the story, eventually comes into the inheritance. Much of the allegory works well enough. The sons of the rich man and the young man traumatized by the destruction of his relatives read neatly as the sons of Constantine I and Julian himself. The picture of the one son of the rich man left standing surrounded by mostly vicious shepherds (7.22/232B) draws the kind of unsympathetic portrait of Constantius II and his court that Ammianus Marcellinus will make familiar.

That said, the veil of allegory is rendered surpassingly thin by its inconsistent focus that whipsaws between the familial and ecumenical. How is it that troubles on this estate led to the profanation of temples, and why should faith in the country be transformed (7.22/228B–C)? Julian's wish to fold the Constantinian embrace of Christianity into the allegory stresses it a great deal. Furthermore, the picture of this young man, who is not even a direct heir of this curiously potent patrimony of an out-of-the-way estate, exciting divine interest stretches the allegory beyond the breaking point. Why should this no-account young man interest four gods (Zeus, Helios, Athene, and Hermes)? And why should they want the young man to take over this estate (7.22/232C)? That the *mythos* Demosthenes told the Athenians had no such excess of divine sponsorship is yet another incongruity summoning interpretation.

In any case, Helios takes over the education of the young man at the behest of Zeus. The sun god sees a spark of himself in the hero to be. Athene aids in raising him too. Disconsolate over what had happened to his relatives, the young man considers killing himself, but Helios and Athene throw him into a trance so that he does not do this. Eventually, he makes his way to the desert and, alone there, he worries about his sorry situation. Appearing to him, Hermes offers to guide him through the terrain to come:

> Then he [the young man], having found a rock, stopped there for a little while, and he was considering how he might make an escape from the enormity of such great troubles. Everything appeared wretched to him and there was nothing good anywhere at that moment. Then Hermes, for he was *simpatico* with him and appearing as an age-mate, greeted him with kindly intent and said, "Here, *I* will be a guide for you on a smooth and flatter path when you have gotten over this twisted and steep little patch, where you see all these ones tripping and making their way back away from here." (7.22/230C)[105]

---

105. Εἶτα ἐκεῖ λίθον τινὰ εὑρὼν μικρὸν ἀνεπαύσατο καὶ πρὸς αὐτὸν ἐσκόπει τίνα τρόπον ἐκφεύξεται τῶν τοσούτων κακῶν τὸ μέγεθος· ἤδη γὰρ αὐτῷ πάντα ἐφαίνετο μοχθηρά, καλὸν δὲ οὐδὲν

The appearance of Hermes at this point in the *mythos* is interesting and interpretable. It has often been assumed in the secondary literature that Heracleius' *mythos* of Zeus and Pan (i.e., of Heracleius and Julian) included the story that Hermes taught his son, the woodland god Pan, how to masturbate when the nymph Echo refused to have sex with him.[106] While such an assumption about what Heracleius said in his *mythos* can only be tentatively accepted because Julian only tells of the respective identifications of Heracleius and himself, it is plausible and doing so makes for the interesting prospect that this part of Julian's *mythos* responds directly to Heracleius'. It is also conceivable that this schooling in self-pleasure would have occurred to listeners without it appearing in Heracleius' oration, just as it has in the secondary literature which has no direct knowledge of Heracleius' oration. If we accept this story as plausibly in the minds of the audience at least, Julian depicts the young man, disconsolate over the death of his relatives, receiving Hermes' guidance to overcome his grief as a sort of antidote to Heracleius' Pan, disconsolate over the dearth of sexual opportunity, receiving Hermes' guidance on how to alleviate his feelings of sexual frustration through masturbation. But whether this posited confrontation between texts, with its carnality, can be accepted or not, there is still more that can be done with Julian's *mythos* at this point.

Hermes says that once the young man is done with the "twisted and steep little patch," he will then have an easier and smooth road to travel to, as it turns out, the foot of the mountain on which Zeus resides (7.22/230D). The mention of that patch that causes defeat to the many is a possible jibe against the short-cuts of the "bad" Cynics. The patch may also encode a reference either to the difficult goal of perfect self-mastery, or to the need for hard decisions about how to lead a worthy life. In addition, the prospect of paths difficult and easy is an (even hoary) intertextual crux; it recalls the famous Choice of Herakles, which has already appeared in the oration. Julian reported earlier that this famous moment from Herakles' biography, first presented by Prodikos, was a feature of Heracleius' oration (7.11/217A–B). As all educated people in late antiquity would have known, Herakles had to decide whether to follow Virtue on the long and difficult path, or Vice on the short, easy one (see, e.g., Xenophon, *Memo-*

οὐδαμοῦ τέως. Ἑρμῆς οὖν αὐτῷ, καὶ γὰρ εἶχεν οἰκείως πρὸς αὐτόν, ὥσπερ ἡλικιώτης νεανίσκος φανεὶς ἠσπάσατό τε φιλοφρόνως καί, "δεῦρο," εἶπεν, "ἡγεμὼν σοι ἐγὼ ἔσομαι λείας καὶ ὁμαλεστέρας ὁδοῦ τουτὶ [τὸ] μικρὸν ὑπερβάντι τὸ σκολιὸν καὶ ἀπότομον χωρίον, οὗ πάντας ὁρᾷς προσπταίοντας καὶ ἀπιόντας ἐντεῦθεν ὀπίσω."

106. This story is told by Dio Chrysostom at *Or.* 6.20. For more, see, e.g., Elm (2012: 109–111), though with one qualification: she thinks, incorrectly, that Pan invented masturbation. If anyone did, according to Dio at least, it was Hermes as teacher of it; cf. Branham 1996: 101.

rabilia 2.1.29[107]). While Julian's hero is certainly on his way to Virtue, the paths have incorrect shapes and qualities and, on top of that, the hero spends time on both of them. These are incongruities, *apemphainonta*, that invite even more interpretation, which will be forthcoming. But first, as the *mythos* continues, the young man makes his way on the longer and easier path:

> The young man, as he was departing, set off with great reverence, having in his possession sword, shield, and spear, though he was without helmet for the time being. Having persuaded him, Hermes led him forward along the smooth and untrod path which was pure and flourishing with many good flowers and fruits, as many as are the gods' own, and with trees too of ivy, laurel, and myrtle. (7.22/230C–D)[108]

With the naked head of the armed young man perhaps indicating the military commander and emperor Julian will become,[109] he makes his way along the easy path which, inexplicably, is untrodden and, in any case, is surrounded by plants belonging to the gods: ivy to Bacchus, laurel to Apollo, and myrtle to Aphrodite.

Whether or not these paths are considered in relation to the Choice of Herakles or not, though especially if they are, they pose questions. Is this easy path untrodden because so many persons are impious, as the ivy, laurel, and myrtle imply? But how can the path be untrodden, when it is easy? Related to this, why do "all these ones" choose the difficult path only to trip and leave in defeat? And if it is not a choice, because the easy path can only be taken after the hard work of the first path, then what to make of the practical inaccessibility of the easy path? It is, in any case, an unlikely *mythos* that starts with a rich man's inattention to succession and

---

107. Next, as Prodikos reports, Vice said in answer,

> "Herakles, are you considering how this woman here (i.e., Virtue) tells you of a hard and long path that is opposed to cheerfulness? I, on the other hand, will lead you along an easy and short path to happiness."

καὶ ἡ Κακία ὑπολαβοῦσα εἶπεν, ὥς φησι Πρόδικος·
"Ἐννοεῖς, ὦ Ἡράκλεις, ὡς χαλεπὴν καὶ μακρὰν ὁδὸν ἐπὶ τὰς εὐφροσύνας ἡ γυνή (sc. ἡ Ἀρετή) σοι αὕτη διηγεῖται; ἐγὼ δὲ ῥᾳδίαν καὶ βραχεῖαν ὁδὸν ἐπὶ τὴν εὐδαιμονίαν ἄξω σε."

108. Καὶ ὁ νεανίσκος ἀπιὼν ᾤχετο μετὰ πολλῆς εὐλαβείας ἔχων παρ' ἑαυτῷ ξίφος τε καὶ ἀσπίδα καὶ δόρυ, γυμνὰ δὲ αὐτῷ τέως ἦν τὰ περὶ τὴν κεφαλήν. Πεποιθὼς οὖν αὐτῷ προσῆγεν εἰς τὸ πρόσω διὰ λείας ὁδοῦ καὶ ἀτρίπτου καθαρᾶς τε πάνυ καὶ καρποῖς βριθούσης ἄνθεσί τε πολλοῖς καὶ ἀγαθοῖς, ὅσα ἐστὶ θεοῖς φίλα, καὶ δένδρεσι κιττοῦ καὶ δάφνης καὶ μυρρίνης.

109. Previous emperors received praise for being so informal around their soldiers that they would take off their helmets when they fraternized with them (see Campbell 1984: 48).

then comes to an armed young man making his way along the easeful path: shouldn't he be working hard?

This path to virtue and enlightenment and indeed to manhood (for this is a *mythos* of a young man's growing up) combines items that run athwart one another: precipice and plain, labor and ease. It is hard to get a read on this partially armed young man who has it tough and easy. There is rather more carnality here than is generally accorded to Julian in the secondary literature or in, for example, Ammianus Marcellinus (e.g., *Res Gestae* 25.4.2), especially if Hermes' lesson to Pan about self-pleasure is in the mind of listeners, and even more so if Vice's promise to Herakles is, when the text comes to the enchanting path leading to the foot of Zeus' mountain.

Somewhat later in the *mythos* there is another remarkable intertextual crux. When Helios is telling the young man that he must leave him and Athene, and fulfill his destiny on earth, the young man physically supplicates the god so that he will not have to do this. Having none of this, Helios quotes Homer to him:

> [At] this moment the young man clung (to Helios) and kept up with much supplication so that he could stay there. Helios said, "Don't you be so disobedient lest it ever be the case that 'I should hate you as much as I now so excessively love you.'" (7.22/232C)[110]

The quotation is nearly all of line 415 from book three of the *Iliad* (τὼς δέ σ' ἀπεχθήρω ὡς νῦν ἔκπαγλ' ἐφίλησα). It is from the famous scene where Helen is ordered by Aphrodite to bed Paris after Aphrodite has removed him from the aborted duel with Menelaus. Helen is reluctant to have sex with her hardly valiant husband at just that moment. In response Aphrodite issues the terrifying threat that should Helen not do as she is told she will incur Aphrodite's hate in precise proportion to the favor she currently enjoys. Therefore, the future leader of the empire is Helen herself, and Julian depicts the duties he is currently fulfilling as sexual relations with a famously luxuriating man. This intertextuality with the *Iliad*, though its simultaneous staging of dalliance and duty, recalls the suite of contrary effects the two paths to Zeus' mountain evoke.

What, then, to make of the incongruities (*apemphainonta*) in the *mythos*, for it is surely fair to evaluate them and the *mythos* according to Julian's prescription earlier in the oration (7.12/217C)?

---

110. ἐνταῦθα ὁ νεανίσκος ἀντείχετο καὶ πολλὰ ἱκέτευεν αὐτοῦ μένειν. Ὁ δέ, "Μὴ λίαν ἀπειθὴς ἔσο," φησί, "μή ποτέ 'σ' ἀπεχθήρω, ὡς νῦν ἔκπαγλ' ἐφίλησα.'"

The *mythos* offers *apemphainonta* along two axes. One axis is seen in elements, imperfectly allegorized and incongruous because of this imperfection, of the story of empire, succession, and religious change. The nameless estate groans under the weight of empire, and the stress on the allegory cues the reader/listener to keep at the story to find meaning. The other axis of incongruities can be seen in the attributes of the young man: who and what he is (and therefore who and what Julian is) raise questions and invite interpretation. The spectral presence of a schooling in self-pleasure haunts the text as this armed young man, who might be another Herakles and who is an emperor to be, has it easier than usual: the path the young man treads is unexpectedly smooth and enjoyable. The intertextuality with *Iliad* 3 makes Julian/the young man into Helen, the most beautiful woman in the world. It depicts the emperor as the object of insistent masculine desire and possessor of an acme of glamour. Duty is also luxuriating sexual activity.

Registering what had to come to mind for anyone in possession of *paideia* and allowing the incongruous elements to drive interpretation leads to a reading of the *mythos* that supplements the usual meanings asserted for it of biography and hopeful teleology. The *mythos* is also about "know[ing] accurately what [a man] is" (7.7/211D), about understanding what a man with *auctoritas* really is. There are veins of paradoxical carnality in the construction of manhood, and this oration constitutes a strong example of the way in which the erotic pervades the male homosocial field molded by *paideia* in late antiquity. Oration Seven as a whole also provides a theorized model of the operation, and then in the *mythos* an example of it, whereby the perceptible same-sex sexual charge of Marcus' *kallos amēchanon* could be an effective support to his *auctoritas* or *axiōma*/ἀξίωμα, even though "conventional opinion" would have it otherwise.

CONCLUSION

Discussion of Julian's *Caesares* and *Against Heracleius* has suggested how evocation of the forbidden could consolidate rather than dissipate masculine auctoritas/ἀξίωμα. In addition to giving an example of this consolidation, the seventh oration, through its discussion of the paradoxical valuation of the myths, provided a theorization and example of the workings of this counterintuitive operation. The claim, of course, is that the making of authority by counterintuitive means was a significant dynamic in elite male homosocial circles. The way *kallos amēchanon* glorifies *andria* in Iamblichus' *De Mysteriis* and Marcus Aurelius in Julian's *Caesares*, such that manhood's grandeur and admirability is metaphorized by same-sex sexual attractiveness, is able to be paralleled in other sources. The terrain of elite male homosociality in late antiquity was pervaded by same-sex desire that increased grandeur and marked status. This chapter and the introduction have already provided some examples. Here are a few more to conclude.

Kallos amēchanon appears in *Enneads* 5 of Plotinus, the famous late-Platonic philosopher.[111] Plotinus compares the advent of Mind (*Nous*) in the world to a gorgeous procession of elite men that precedes the arrival of the emperor:

> And so there is one nature itself for us; it is Mind, all things existent, the truth. And if this is so (and it is), it is a great god, but not just any, but one who thinks it right to be all these things at once [i.e., Mind, all things existent, and the truth]. And the god is nature itself, a god manifesting himself before we can see him. And he watches from above and sits, transcendent, upon a fair pediment, as it were. Nature depends on him, for it is certain that he will not make his way on something soulless nor have started his journey straightaway on Soul, but there is an irresistible/uncanny beauty (*kallos amēchanon*/κάλλος ἀμήχανον) going out before him. As before a great emperor there go first, in those preceding him, the lesser ranks, and the always more important ones and more lofty ones come after these. The ones near to the emperor are all the more imperial and, next come the honored ones with him and, suddenly the great emperor himself appears amid all these others. All utter prayers and bow down, as many as had not gone away, contented with the personages they had seen prior to the emperor. (Plot. 5.5.3.1–15)[112]

In general terms, this passage is best seen as a not too terribly clarifying allegorical explanation and simile of the unfolding of the universe from the One. In Plotinus' understanding of the universe, the One is the first hypostasis. The second hypostasis is Mind (*Nous*), and it is through the

---

111. Matthews (2000b: 445–46) drew my attention to this passage.
112. Μία τοίνυν φύσις αὕτη ἡμῖν, νοῦς, τὰ ὄντα πάντα, ἡ ἀλήθεια· εἰ δέ, θεός τις μέγας· μᾶλλον δὲ οὔ τις, ἀλλὰ πᾶς ἀξιοῖ ταῦτα εἶναι. Καὶ θεὸς αὕτη ἡ φύσις, καὶ θεὸς δεύτερος προφαίνων ἑαυτὸν πρὶν ὀρᾶν ἐκεῖνον· ὁ δὲ ὑπερκάθηται καὶ ὑπερίδρυται ἐπὶ καλῆς οὕτως οἷον κρηπῖδος, ἢ ἐξ αὐτοῦ ἐξήρτηται. Ἔδει γὰρ ἐκεῖνον βαίνοντα μὴ ἐπ' ἀψύχου τινὸς μηδ' αὖ ἐπὶ ψυχῆς εὐθὺς βεβηκέναι, ἀλλ' εἶναι αὐτῷ κάλλος ἀμήχανον πρὸ αὐτοῦ προϊόν, οἷον πρὸ μεγάλου βασιλέως πρόεισι μὲν πρῶτα ἐν ταῖς προόδοις τὰ ἐλάττω, ἀεὶ δὲ τὰ μείζω καὶ τὰ σεμνότερα ἐπ' αὐτοῖς, καὶ τὰ περὶ βασιλέα ἤδη μᾶλλον βασιλικώτερα, εἶτα τὰ μετ' αὐτὸν τίμια· ἐφ' ἅπασι δὲ τούτοις βασιλεὺς προφαίνεται ἐξαίφνης αὐτὸς ὁ μέγας, οἱ δ' εὔχονται καὶ προσκυνοῦσιν, ὅσοι μὴ προαπῆλθον ἀρκεσθέντες τοῖς πρὸ τοῦ βασιλέως ὀφθεῖσιν.

existence of Mind that the universe manifests and is even thinkable. Mind provides the needed context for the One, which is ineffability and existence *simplex*. Not surprisingly, Mind is a master term that encompasses nature, all things in existence, and the truth. Also, mentioned here is the third hypostasis, Soul (*Psyche*).[113] But the clarity or lack thereof of Plotinus' system in this passage is not important in the present moment; the contents of the simile and the heralding *kallos amēchanon* are the points of interest. Plotinus likens the majesty of the universe's unfolding after the acme of unspeakability that is the One to a procession of elite men that concludes with the arrival of the emperor. Just prior to the beginning of the simile, the now familiar "irresistible/uncanny beauty" appears. The simile of elites and emperor that follows tells more about this beauty. For readers versed in Plato, which describes to perfection his audience, Plotinus makes transcendent glamour, already associated with the One and Mind, coincident with same-sex sexual attractiveness in his description of elites and the emperor. A corporeal immediacy paradoxically glamorizes a masculine admirability that has transcendent ambitions.

The Missorium of Theodosius I (see frontispiece) provides another example of erotics in a scene of elite masculine homosociality and grandeur.[114] A large (74 centimeters / 29 inches in diameter), weighty (16.13 kilograms / 35.56 pounds), and elaborately engraved silver plate, the Missorium dates from 388 and commemorates the tenth anniversary of Theodosius' imperial rule. On the plate an imperial official receives his *codicilli* (documents of appointment in a case[115]) from Theodosius, as soldiers and Theodosius' co-emperors, Arcadius and Valentinian II, look on. A formalized scene with all but iconic emperors (and the very three whose names grace *Coll.* 5.3 / *CTh.* 9.7.6), the Missorium graphically shows the way members of the *sacra scrinia* or an official in the *sacrum palatium* "[share] something of [the] aura of sanctity which surrounded an emperor" (Kelly 2004: 188; cf. 1998b: 168–69).

This aura of otherworldly transcendence is paradoxically increased elsewhere on the plate by figures who, while divine, also embody corporeal desire and fertility. On the plate's lower third, the exurge, a mostly naked woman, appears. She is allegorical of Earth (Tellus) and reclines in a wheat field while three naked cupids flutter about. There are, in addition, two

---

113. For more, see, e.g., *Enneads* 5.2.1.1–24.
114. In composing these remarks on the Missorium of Theodosius I, I found Leader-Newby (2004: 11–14, 27–36, 47–49), Kelly (2004: 19–20), and Elsner (1997: 267–69) helpful.
115. Amm., *Res Gestae* 25.8.9; Valensi 1957: 93. Salzman (2002: 19) points out that these documents would have been displayed in the appointed man's house.

more cupids appearing toward the top of the plate in the arcaded pediment that overhangs the scene with the three emperors, soldiers, and official. Earth and cupids, comprising a ground that compromises the integrity of the representation (the cupids are both in the allegorical lower portion of the plate and in the representation of emperors and official), are incongruities (*apemphainonta*) that demand engagement: why is this homosocial scene of investiture graced with representations of love and desire?

Looking at the plate as a whole, both the representation of the men and the allegory of the Earth and cupids, and allowing Earth and cupids to drive interpretation—Earth is the ground of representation and the cupids are pervasive—, a viewer may conclude that the ceremony between men is productive of increase for the state and, further, a site of desire.[116] Earth and cupids directly embody "terrestrial" corporeal desire, even as they indicate celestialization and divinity. With the ground pervading the representation along a circuit of erotic desire (i.e., the cupids "in frame" and "in picture"), the plate generates a narrative of masculine grandeur whose productivities make the empire a richer place. The plate also offers a picture of relations between men whose closeness and genuineness has the liveliness of actual sexual release, as the depicted homosociality is associated with cupids.

Only a promotion is perhaps what a first glance will see, but the wise, reflecting on the *apemphainonta,* will see that the contours of life among the leaders of empire are being represented though a deployment of same-sex desire. Julian's remark, "he who knows himself will know accurately what he is and not [only] what conventional opinion says he is" (7.7/211D), encourages interpretation. Likewise, the plate speaks "to those able to know" (as Saloustios says at *De Deis et Mundo* 3.3), and the ceremony comes to gesture to realities and significance when the representation as a whole is engaged. Not only a career is here, erotics metaphorize relations between elite men. Erotics also heighten glamorous transcendence through a paradoxical invocation of forbidden desire.

---

116. Discussing the personification of Earth, or Tellus, Ruth Leader-Newby suggests that her presence on the plate was a classicizing touch that could have recalled the general *zeitgeist* of the reigns of much earlier emperors (Augustus and Hadrian in particular):

> Does Tellus simply represent abundance as guaranteed by Theodosius' reign and his dominion of the *oikoumene,* or does the image at the same time carry historic resonances which associate Theodosius with the peaceful prosperity of the earlier empire? (2004: 28–30)

As Leader-Newby knows and shows, the image is polysemous, and the present reading complements her persuasive ideas about the meaning of Tellus.

From this angle, then, the Missorium plate is of a piece with the amatory and celestializing modes of address that often accompany communication by emperors to inferiors in the legal documents. As discussed in the introduction to this book, an emperor finesses steep hierarchy and shows regard by calling his subordinates "most beloved" (*amantissime*), "most dear" (*carissime*), or "most delightful" (*iucundissime*). What perhaps will not seem so odd now is that these same inferiors are also addressed in abstract and lofty terms. Orientius, who is also "*iucundissime*," is called "Your Experience" in *Collatio* 5.3. Another common term of address in the *Codex* is *sublimitas:* "Your Sublimity" appears over seventy-five times.[117] *Experientia* and *sublimitas* are hardly the only such terms used. For example, "Your Acme" or "Your Loftiness" (employing the word *culmen*) also appears.[118] The elite terms of precedence, *clarissimus, spectabilis,* and *illustris* redouble this impression of otherworldly abstraction. Each of these designations calls to mind the sensation of light, extorts perception that takes the viewer beyond what is immediately before his or her eyes, and makes them think in celestial terms.[119] On this basis, these gradations of honor (*clarissimus, spectabilis,* and *illustris*) recall the descent of beauty from *ta theia* to its manifestation as *andria* in the excerpt from Iamblichus' *De Mysteriis* that began this chapter. They also recall "the light . . . most pure and stainless"[120] which Julian associates with Marcus Aurelius and his *kallos amēchanon*. In all these cases (i.e., Iamblichus, Julian, Plotinus, Missorium plate, imperial addresses), celestialization and same-sex desire inflect and interact with one another, and the corporeal liveliness of the latter makes the former shine more brightly through the power of paradox.

This operation whereby masculine glamour grows through paradox depends on accepting that a place exists prior to moral evaluation. The late-Platonists and others were accepting, and their positive recourse to

---

117. E.g.: Emperor Julian [sends the following words] to Mamertinus, the Praetorian Prefect: "May Your Sublimity call together the *rectores* of the Provinces . . . " (*CTh*.1.15.4 [362 Iun. 6]) [Imp. Iulianus a. ad Mamertinum praefectum praetorio. Rectores provinciarum Sublimitas Tua conveniat . . .]. See Gradenwitz (1970/1925: 240) for a list of occurences of *sublimitas* in the *Codex*.

118. *Culmen* occurs in the *Gesta Senatus* and in the following places in the *Codex*: 1.29.1 [364], 1.29.3 [late 360s or early 370s], 1.29.4 [368], 6.24.4 [387], 6.30.23 [422], 7.4.32 [412], 7.4.35 [423], 8.4.18 [394], 8.7.10 [369], 11.20.5pr. [424], 12.1.175 [412], 13.11.7 [396], 14.16.1 [409], 15.5.4 [424], 16.2.37 [404]. See Simon Corcoran's helpful presentation (1996: 324–334) of the wide variety of abstract terms that the emperors give to those they address. Corcoran's account focuses on the Tetrarchic period but looks ahead and many of his remarks are relevant to law-making and imperial address throughout the fourth century and into the fifth.

119. Christopher Kelly (1998a; 2004: 232–45) draws attention to a number of late-ancient works in which heaven was figured in terms that made God an emperor and the angels his bureaucrats.

120. 10.17/317D: τὸ καθαρώτατον καὶ εἰλικρινέστατον φῶς.

same-sex desire strips earthbound judgment from the corporeal excitement of same-sex desire and activity, and shows that it can be viewed as part of an existent order prior to the morals of society. Others in late antiquity did not accept that there was a place prior to earth's morals, and they wanted to see the other world morally responsive to this one. This was and is a live question and will more than likely remain so: can one let things be? Or is there a need to place order on them? This is the conundrum that the late-Platonists and those similar to them solved in the direction of choosing life in all its mystery. Others chose regulation and control and strict moral standards for life's messy indeterminacies. The next chapter, which focuses on Athanasius' *Vita Antonii*, shows what this choice looks like. When Athanasius creates a manhood for his hero, for the desert or *erēmos*, and, indeed, for eternity, he rejects and corporealizes same-sex desire and pleasure with an exactitude that indicates authority's all-discerning power. Athanasius also arguably puts the transcendent "in order," making it a logical, mystery-less place that reflects restrictive norms around same-sex desire and pleasure on earth. Athanasius' thorough policing of relations between men changes (the appearance of) the universe.

TWO

Athanasius' Antony

INTRODUCTION

This chapter continues the investigation of same-sex desire and homosociality among late-Roman elite men, and the connection of both to the making of masculine authority, centering on the *Vita Antonii* of Athanasius. Continuities between the masculinity proposed for Antony and that of elite men earlier in the book are considerable. As with other elites, a holy man such as Antony increases his *auctoritas* or ἀξίωμα though connection to things not of this world; defeat of demons, besting the Devil, and the omnipresent marks of God's favor indicate a transcendent source of power and recall the designation of "Your Sublimity" in the law codes. Which is appropriate here since Antony received letters from emperors (*Vita Antonii* 81.1). Athanasius also underscores Antony's status as a *vir* or *anēr*, presenting him as *patronus* to his clients and endowing him with virtual mastery of *paideia*.

While Antony's masculinity possesses these continuities with elite late-ancient manhood, there is discontinuity in the matter of same-sex desire and same-sex sexual attractiveness. If a reader has Julian's glamorization of Marcus Aurelius via Plato or the three emperors' address to Orientius as "most dear and delightful" in mind, he or she will note that the construction of Antony's masculine glamour proceeds with a relative absence of same-sex desire. The (nearly complete) embargo on desire between men in the *vita*—though there are complexities here—is explicable on the bases of the pronounced homosocial nature of ascetic withdrawal and Athanasius' interest in presenting Antony as unambiguously exemplary: same-sex desire would be exquisitely disruptive in an assertedly men-only space featuring complete sexual renunciation.

In the preface to the *vita*, Athanasius states directly that exemplarity is his goal, and the language he uses is similar to that just seen in the previous chapter. Addressing those in the West who are considering desert-style asceticism, he declares that he offers a *charaktēr* or pattern for *askēsis*:

> And I know that you, when you have heard, apart from your admiration for the man, will want to emulate his determination; seeing that for monks the life of Antony is a sufficient *charaktēr*/χαρακτήρ (i.e., pattern) for *askēsis*. (Praef. 3)[1]

Athanasius' *charaktēr* is to function as a model for mimesis. In this direct embrace of mimesis, Athanasius' use of *charaktēr* diverges significantly from Julian's polysemous use of it in his seventh oration. There, *charaktēr* plays an important role in the discussion of the value of myths; "the unspeakable and unknown nature of *charaktēres*" (7.11/216C) brings those reading/hearing myths to understanding amid a surfeit of mystery, understanding valuable to individual and community in matters of initiation and communal rites (7.11/216B). While the *vita* also exhibits concerns about the proper constitution of the individual, communal living, and initiation, *and* it is the word *charaktēr* being used, the distance from an "unspeakable and unknown nature of letters" that enjoins an embrace of opposites rendering even communication mysterious is considerable. Athanasius' *charaktēr* for imitation is not the thing of mystery seen in writings of Julian. Presenting, instead, a surfeit of rationality, Athanasius seemingly takes mystery out of his model masculine subjectivity, even when he is perhaps raising some questions. Although Athanasius' relative silence about desire between men indicates that Antony complies with, say, the *sacra generalitas* to be identified by Theodosius II's board, his admirable Antony departs in other ways from the accepted canons of elite manly deportment. But it is even more complicated than this.

As was seen in the introduction and previous chapter, in elite circles there is refusal of same-sex desire and, at the same time, an embrace of its

---

1. Οἶδα δέ, ὅτι καὶ ὑμεῖς ἀκούσαντες, μετὰ τοῦ θαυμάσαι τὸν ἄνθρωπον, θελήσετε καὶ ζηλῶσαι τὴν ἐκείνου πρόθεσιν. Ἔστι γὰρ μοναχοῖς ἱκανὸς χαρακτὴρ πρὸς ἄσκησιν ὁ Ἀντωνίου βίος.

liveliness to increase grandeur and authority. The address of *"amantissime"* in the legal documents or the often seen intertextuality with Plato indicates this embrace, to take some examples. In the *vita* the appearance of same-sex desire is different. Not obvious, either as thing explicitly forbidden or in use as a metaphor, it appears instead as an artifact of reception by an audience versed in the realities of the world.

When a reader who is aware of the realities attending homosocial environments[2] notes the absence of same-sex desire (though not of pederastic desire, which is a different thing of course) in the depiction of Antony, questions arise. Antony's perfect embodiment of earthbound moral ideals renders the *vita*'s asserted sufficiency (Athanasius says that it is a "sufficient" [*hikanos*/ἱκανός] *charaktēr* or pattern at Praef. 3) brittle and lacking at the point of readerly reception. As I have had occasion to argue elsewhere,[3] utopian accounts, such as the *Vita Antonii,* proliferate desire when readers in the real world have to make sense of them. The unreality of a utopian account causes the reader to jump to conclusions on the basis of his or her experience with non-utopian, i.e., real humanity. And so here, awareness of the reasonable assumption that homosocial environments, especially if sealed, will increase the incidence of same-sex desire and same-sex sexual behavior causes the surface of the *vita* to give way to reveal the presence of same-sex desire in a complex of physical symptoms. Same-sex desire emerges as an attribute of Antony's body and a same-sex sexual charge spreads to his wrestling match with the Devil (and to other things too). The emergence of same-sex desire in physical symptoms and entities is a function of the fact that, instead of the mystery in the transcendent seen, for example, in late-Platonism, Athanasius posits a transcendent colonized by earthly morals. Mystery denied the transcendent appears on earth as this world's reality. This conclusion gains considerable support when the contours of Athanasius' intellectual project are considered.

Athanasius is confident that earthly standards of behavior are reflective of the situation in the transcendent. In two of his treatises, written decades before he wrote the *vita* and showing the continuity of his thought across his life, he moralizes the transcendent and declares the material world as both non-existent and evil (see *Contra Gentes* 4.18[4] and *De Incarnatione* 4.23[5]). With some irony separating this world from the next (for he con-

---

2. The example of American prisons is suggestive in this regard (see, e.g., Bech 1997/1987: 20–25). See, too, the interesting work of Steven Zeeland (1999, 1996, 1995, 1993) on same-sex sexual behavior in various branches of the United States military.
3. Masterson 2006.
4. Ὄντα δέ ἐστι τὰ καλά, οὐκ ὄντα δὲ τὰ φαῦλα.
5. Οὐκ ὄντα γάρ ἐστι τὰ κακά, ὄντα δὲ τὰ καλά.

nects it quite strongly to man-made morals), Athanasius refuses to associate the transcendent with mystery and instead locates mystery, along with whatever he regards as immoral, in the physical world. In terms significant to this investigation of late-Roman manhood's relation to same-sex desire and pleasure, Athanasius twice (once in the *Contra Gentes*[6] and again in the *De Incarnatione*[7]) quotes Romans 1:26–27 as a summative explanation for mankind's refusal of God's law in order to favor things of this (treacherous) earth. As Romans 1:26–27 is Paul's famous denunciation of same-sex desire,[8] Athanasius makes male bodies by definition prone to this sin which is now a sin of sins. Same-sex desire on this basis becomes a corporeal inheritance for all men.[9] Given the exemplary power that Athanasius attributes to same-sex desire in his understanding of the nature of the universe, a reader of the *vita* will be thinking long and hard about the same-sex desire seemingly missing from Athanasius' Antony, same-sex desire that is then added because of things known about the dynamics of homosocial spaces, both closed and, indeed, not closed (as seen in the previous chapter and introduction to this book). An additional result of readerly engagement with the *vita* is that Athanasius starts to look like the three emperors who put their signatures to *Collatio* 5.3. He takes his place as a powerfully penetrating authority from whom no secrets of life can be kept, knowing, as he does, the forbidden nature of all men's bodies.

SOURCES AND ATHANASIUS' MÉTIER

The main sources for this chapter are the *Vita Antonii* of Athanasius[10] and a number of his other works, especially the *Contra Gentes* and *De Incarna-*

---

6. 26.7–13.
7. 5.16–34.
8. The literature on Romans 1:26–27 is vast and complex. Just what this important text that features same-sex desire between females (*thēleiai*/θήλειαι) and between males (*arrenes*/ἄρρενες) meant in Paul's context, and how this text is supposed to matter now, have been subjects of much debate. For more, a reader may start with Scroggs 1983, Brooten 1996, and Moore 2001.
9. Athanasius' making same-sex desire a concern for all men interestingly prefigures part of Eve Kosofsky Sedgwick's discussion (1990) of understandings of homosexuality since the late nineteenth century. Sedgwick suggests that there have been two modern discourses in conflict about homosexuality, the minoritizing and the universalizing. The minoritizing discourse regards homosexuality as a quality that only a minority of persons possesses in any meaningful way, while the universalizing one asserts that homosexuality is present in or a concern to all persons to a degree (small or large) (cf. Halperin 2002a: 10–13, 123). Athanasius' position on same-sex desire of course has similarities to Sedgwick's "universalizing" discourse.
10. There has been debate about whether Athanasius wrote the *vita* or not. Going along with most scholars, I think he did. For further discussion of the authorship question, start with Barnes 1986; Pettersen 1987: 238; Louth 1988; Bartelink 1994: 27–42; Cameron 1999; Bertrand 2005: 19–20.

tione. The *Vita Antonii* (written between 359 and 362) is one of the first texts to document withdrawal to the *erēmos*[11] (or "desert," on the understanding that desert will designate any place that is uninhabited).[12] The *vita* was enormously influential and Latin translations, one by Evagrius Antiochensis and the other anonymous, appeared within twenty years (both these Latin texts will be consulted later, as they provide valuable information on how Antony and the *vita* were understood in antiquity).[13] In words from the introduction, if accepted as genuine,[14] Athanasius states that he was writing his account "for monks in foreign parts,"[15] and he also makes reference to the existence of monasteries elsewhere in the empire and to "excellent competition in *askēsis* directed toward virtue"[16] between these monasteries and those in Egypt. Even without these words, however, it is clear that the *Vita Antonii* was intended to spread the word and to provide a *charaktēr* for ascetics everywhere. The treatises *Contra Gentes* and *De Incarnatione* will be discussed later in the chapter.

In addition to works by Athanasius and the two Latin translations of the *vita*, other works related to withdrawal to the *erēmos* round out the discussion: the anonymous *Apophthegmata Patrum* (second decade of the fifth century), the anonymous *Historia Monachorum* (circa 400), and Jerome's translation of Pachomius' rules for monastery living (*Interpretatio Regulae Sancti Pachomii*; circa 405). It is common practice to read these works (or a similar combination) together.[17] They all treat the fourth-century expe-

---

11. The word *erēmos* is to be preferred to desert because the word "desert" may be misleading, implying that ascetic withdrawal was always to the middle of nowhere. In fact, withdrawal to the *erēmos* [literally "the uninhabited zone"] could be to a location relatively proximate to inhabited land. That the middle of nowhere, i.e., the deep desert, could be a destination for a monk was certainly true. Indeed, it predominates in the historical record, but it certainly was not as common as the sources say it was. James Goehring (1993) convincingly argues that the predominance in the historical record of retreat to the deep desert does not reflect reality at all, but is, rather, a function of the desire to record the remarkable.

12. The amount of scholarship on asceticism and/or the *erēmos* is vast. Most any survey is going to be a partial one. Among the works consulted, treating one or both of these topics, were the following: Brakke 2006, 2001, 1995a, 1995b; Brown 1998, 1988; Burrus 2004, 2000; Cameron 2000, 1999; Caner 2009, 2000; Clark 1988; Elm 1994; Espejo-Muriel 1991; Finn 2009; Frank 2000; Goehring, 2005, 1999, 1993; Gould 1993; Kannengiesser 1995; Harpham 1998, 1987; Krawiec 2002; Krueger 2006; Layton 2007; Leyser 2000; Martin and Miller 2005; Miller 2001; Pettersen 1987; Rousseau 1985; Rousselle 1988/1983; Schroeder 2007, 2006; Shaw 1998; Vivian 1993; Wimbush and Valantasis 1998.

13. For discussion of these translations, see Bartelink (1994: 95–98) and Bertrand (2005: 27–28).

14. These words, translated, appear in Evagrius' version but not in the one by Anonymous. They appear in Bartelink's 1994 edition of the Greek *Vita Antonii*.

15. πρὸς τοὺς ἐν τῇ ξένῃ μοναχούς.

16. Praef.1: ἀγαθὴν ἅμιλλαν... τῇ κατ' ἀρετὴν... ἀσκήσει.

17. E.g., Brown 1988: 213–240; Frank 2000; Brakke 2006; also see Brakke (2006: 127–29 [esp.

rience of withdrawal from society to the *erēmos* in Egypt and were either written during the fourth century (Athanasius' *Vita Antonii*, the *Historia Monachorum*) or they are in retrospective mode: depiction in the early fifth century of fourth-century Egypt (the *Apophthegmata Patrum*, Jerome's translation of Pachomius' regulations). There are differences between them, but, on balance, these works are useful for teasing out what is said in compressed fashion in the *vita*.

An important qualification to arguments to come. A strong distinction will not be made between coenobitic and anachoretic/eremitical asceticisms: the former asceticism practiced in a monastery and the latter alone. There are distinctions to be made, of course. Coenobitic asceticism is an intensely social project that creates a new identity within the confines of a monastery, while anachoretic asceticism embraces a utopian solitude. One of the goals of the *coenobium* of monastery living is "world replacement," as Bentley Layton (2007) puts it. The monastery offers a new social world along with individual transformation in the process.[18] The anachoretic monk, in contrast, pointedly removes himself from the *saeculum* as an essential part of his personal transformation. The anachoretic monk also defines himself in opposition to society that remains as it was, and he and/or his publicizers have ambitions to change it through his glorious example. Since the goal of this discussion is to consider how asceticized manhood depicted in the *Vita Antonii* reflects, diverges from, and interacts with manhood and same-sex desire among elite men in general in the empire, it is not too much of a deformation of the evidence to allow these two types of withdrawal to run together somewhat, especially when the appreciable similarities between them are noted. In the case of both coenobitic and anachoretic asceticism, secular society, judged wanting, is rejected and there is concomitant personal transformation. Both modes also employ physical practices to secure a connection to things beyond this world. It is perhaps a question whether asceticism as a concept is able to be separated out and discussed separate from these two modes of its ancient social expression. The argument will proceed on the understanding that there is enough of an affirmative here to go forward.[19] With these qualifications in place, the *vita* will now be further contextualized through consideration of the circumstances of Athanasius' life.

129]) for reflections on the advantages and limitations of this common practice.

18. For more on coenobitic asceticism, see, in addition to Layton 2007, Schroeder 2007, Brown 1988, and Rousseau 1985.

19. Indeed, as will be seen below, the *vita* has the predominantly anachoretic Antony occasionally interacting with other monks in a communal setting.

While enduring the third of his five banishments from Alexandria, Athanasius wrote the *Vita Antonii*. Athanasius often ran afoul of emperors. He had to endure the displeasure of Constantine, Constantius II, Julian, and Valens. He was banished to the West twice (335–37 and 339–46). He was on the lam in the *erēmos* during the latter three banishments (356–62, 362–63, and 365–66). The world of the fourth-century bishop was characterized by high-stakes politics, and the penalties for the unsuccessful were severe. Athanasius occasionally had to use force to subdue his enemies.[20] Paul, the bishop of Constantinople, having declared for the usurper Magnentius, was strangled at the order of Constantius II in 350.[21] George of Cappadocia, one of Athanasius' replacements as head of the Alexandrian See, was lynched in 361. The bishop's life in the fourth century, then, was not only an abstracted realm in which devotion and theology reigned. Devotion and theology did matter, of course, and Athanasius wrote theological works (the *Contra Gentes* and *De Incarnatione* are examples), but politics were a concern too.

Given this mixture of religious devotion and his need to acquire and maintain power, it is reasonable to imagine that Athanasius would want to share the truth and further his political objectives in one and the same document.[22] Indeed, a coincidence of truth and policy is on display in the *Vita Antonii*, and it is clearly related to his efforts to win monks over to his side in the push to consolidate his power in Alexandria.[23] But this document that was part of a campaign to win allies among the monks and to (re)build support in Alexandria had to walk a fine line. Even as it offered an at times innovating *charaktēr* of a magnificent man for mimesis, there needed to be (and there was) much that would meet conservative expectations for men.[24] Had Athanasius not taken account of the conservative notions of his (often senatorial) readers in the *saeculum*, his *charaktēr* meant to further his objectives, via literary means, would have lost some of its persuasive power. In any case, this campaign, in which the *Vita Antonii* served, is best seen as part of Athanasius' long-lasting and multi-faceted crusade to bring elite laity and monks under more regular ecclesiastical authority.

Among the laity, Athanasius' strategy manifested itself in discourage-

---

20. Barnes 1993: 32.
21. Barnes 1993: 102.
22. The politics involved in Athanasius' long-term championing of asceticism and in his courting of the ascetics are well known. See, e.g., Brakke 1995a: 201–265; Cameron 2000 and 1999; Elm 1994: 361–72 (esp. 369–71); Burrus 2000: 68–78.
23. Burrus 2000: 70.
24. The remarks, here and later, on how Athanasius writes elements into his Antony so that the representation will speak to an elite male audience build on discussions by Burrus (2000: 68–78) and Brakke (1995a: 201–265 and 2006: 182–83).

ment of an academic, questioning Christianity.[25] Such questioning led to heresy.[26] To replace intellectualized Christianity, the *Vita Antonii* makes the proposition that a Christian life be realized through ascetic discipline.[27] Burrus sees Athanasius forging in the *vita* a modified manhood meant to travel from the *erēmos* back to the secular world to do needful work:

> ... *anachōrēsis,* or "withdrawal," as Athanasius represents it, constitutes not a simple rejection of the city in favor of an alternative but rather a strategy for refashioning the city, to which there is never, in Athanasius's mind, any alternative. (2000: 70)

While he had these recommendations for the laity, Athanasius was also concerned to bring the monastic movement into a more formal relationship with the See in Alexandria. The *erēmos* possessed great freedom from outside authority, and Athanasius, through the simple need, at least, for allies in the dangerous situations in which he often found himself, needed ties organizing the *erēmos* in relation to Alexandria—ties that would emphasize orthodoxy and secure the monks' support. To bring about this closer relationship between *erēmos* and himself as bishop, Athanasius did a number of things. He ordained monks as priests, some of whom were reluctant.[28] He emphasized Antony's obedience to the clergy (*Vita Antonii* 67). Also, bringing his authority into an intimate area of the *erēmos,* he ruled, in the *Letter to Amun,* on the relationship of nocturnal emissions to a monk's ascetic practice.[29] In the matter of church doctrine, Athanasius emphasized the need for orthodoxy among the monks. Accordingly, Athanasius depicted Antony as an implacable foe of heresy. Brakke notes that "the *Life of Antony* was the climactic weapon in Athanasius' campaign against monastic sympathy for the Arian cause and indifference about the controversy [of Arianism]" (1995a: 135).[30] Accordingly, Athanasius depicts Antony being critical of the Meletians and the Arians (*Vita Antonii* 68, 82), and even shows Antony making a special trip to Alexandria to denounce the Arians (*Vita Antonii* 69–70).[31]

---

25. See Brakke 1995a: 60–62.
26. Lim 1995: 138.
27. Brakke 1995a: 214; cf. Pettersen (1990: 5–34) on Athanasius' understanding of the body's importance as a tool to be used in service to God.
28. Brakke 1995a: 109.
29. See Vivian (1993) and Brakke (1995a: 90–99 and 1995b) for Athanasius' discussion of nocturnal emissions in the *erēmos.*
30. Cf. Brennan 1985: 218–19; Cameron 2000: 79–80; Bartelink 1994: 59–61.
31. See Burrus' (2000: 74–75) discussion of this passage; she remarks tellingly: "Antony appears oddly at home during this carefully scripted visit to the big city" (74).

Athanasius had a vision of an Egypt where there would be an association of lay semi-ascetics and ascetics. The laity would imitate the ascetics to the best of their ability and the ascetics would have their model in Antony:

> Athanasius is clearly attempting to present not one model among many, but *the* model of the Christian life. His goal is to freeze the flow of imitation and to create a single icon, one powerful enough to mirror a diverse set of virtues into a single civic life. (Brakke 1995a: 262 [emphasis in original]; cf. 13)

His life a *charaktēr*, Antony is at the crossing of chains of mimesis that extend through lay elites and, at the same time, through the monks: the *vita* speaks to both groups. Furthermore, the mimetic function of this account is not merely asserted in the *vita;* it is something that contemporaries recognized early on. Writing in 380, Gregory Nazianzenus calls the *Vita Antonii* "a codification of the monk's life in the form of a narrative."[32] The *vita* also features in Augustine's *Confessions* at 8.6.15: there, two friends who are serving the emperor (most likely Valentinian I) at Trier find a copy of the *vita*, and, having read it, are inspired to change their lives in imitation.

In writing the *Vita Antonii*, Athanasius wished to suggest the proper way to live a life, the proper way of belief, and what the proper abode of authority was. Antony modeled all of these, and did so in such a way that he advanced Athanasius' interests and—and this is key—as a man revolutionary in some ways and yet, ultimately, deeply conservative. Seemingly violating some of the canons of masculinity—he avoided cultivating the skills of elite manhood, claiming its privileges, or performing its duties—Antony uncannily possessed these seemingly rejected skills and easily commanded respect because Athanasius' portrait cleverly rendered Antony legible as an elite man.

ANTONY THE LEGIBLE

One of the first things Athanasius does to establish Antony's legibility as an elite man is to show that he is well-to-do, free, and of some standing in the community. Entering church one day, he hears Matthew 19:21 in a sermon.[33] In this passage, Christ implores the rich man to give away his

---

32. *Or.* 21.5.6–7: τοῦ μοναδικοῦ βίου νομοθεσίαν, ἐν πλάσματι διηγήσεως.
33. 2.3.

possessions. That, and another sermon with another tag, Matthew 6:34 ("Have no care for tomorrow"),[34] and Antony is on his way to the *erēmos:*

> And Antony, as though having come into possession of the mindfulness of the Saints through the agency of God, and as though the reading [Matthew 19:21] had been made with him in mind, after he had gone straight out of the church, made a gift of all the possessions he had from his forefathers (and there were 300 *arourai,* fertile and exceedingly choice) to those from the village so that they should not trouble at all for him and his sister. As regards all other things, the movable things they possessed, having sold it all and having gotten together sufficient money, he distributed it to the beggars, having preserved a little for his sister. (2.4–5)[35]

Clearly no longer a boy as he is able to exercise paternal authority, Antony starts off his career in sanctity by giving away nearly all his possessions to the villagers, which, as it provides for those with less, makes him seem the good *patronus*.[36] Furthermore, in spite of the fact that he has given up his household, he paradoxically remains a good *pater familias* because his female dependent is "properly" supervised. He entrusts her to local virgins who welcome her into their convent.[37]

Besides showing Antony's behavior as a proper head-of-household, Athanasius also surveys Antony's sexual interests. The Devil comes to Antony:

> For [the Devil] was thrusting[38] filthy thoughts [into Antony's mind] and [Antony] was overturning them with his prayers. [The Devil] was causing an itching, but he, while appearing to blush, through faith and fasts was walling off his body. The wretched Devil was even keeping at it to the extent that he took on the shape of a woman and in every way mimicked one during the night, only so he could deceive Antony. (5.4–5)[39]

---

34. 3.1.
35. Ὁ δὲ Ἀντώνιος, ὥσπερ θεόθεν ἐσχηκὼς τὴν τῶν ἁγίων μνήμην καὶ ὡς δι' αὐτὸν γενομένου τοῦ ἀναγνώσματος, ἐξελθὼν εὐθὺς ἐκ τοῦ κυριακοῦ τὰς μὲν κτήσεις ἃς εἶχεν ἐκ προγόνων (ἄρουραι δὲ ἦσαν τριακόσιαι εὔφοροι καὶ πάνυ καλαί), ταύτας ἐχαρίσατο τοῖς ἀπὸ τῆς κώμης, ἵνα εἰς μηδ' ὁτιοῦν ὀχλήσωσιν αὐτῷ τε καὶ τῇ ἀδελφῇ. (5) Τὰ δὲ ἄλλα ὅσα ἦν αὐτοῖς κινητά, πάντα πωλήσας καὶ συναγαγὼν ἱκανὸν ἀργύριον, διέδωκε τοῖς πτωχοῖς, τηρήσας ὀλίγα διὰ τὴν ἀδελφήν.
36. See Brown's highly influential presentation (1971/1982) of the notion of the holy man as a virtual patron. Also see his modifications to his idea (1987: 9; 1992: 62–63) and Cameron's presentation of the changes in his thinking (1999). Brakke (1995a: 248–53) discusses the presentation of Antony as a (reluctant) patron in the *vita* as a whole.
37. *Vita Antonii* 2–3; for more on Antony's sister, see Burrus 2000: 76.
38. For this translation of ὑπέβαλλε, see Lampe 1961: ὑποβάλλω 1.
39. Ὁ μὲν γὰρ ὑπέβαλλε λογισμοὺς ῥυπαρούς, ὁ δὲ ταῖς εὐχαῖς ἀνέτρεπε τούτους. Καὶ ὁ μὲν

The temptation in this section indicates a primary object of Antony's sexual desires. Both Athanasius and the Devil know that Antony's interests are directed at women. In the next section of the *vita,* as though to round out the shape of Antony's sexual desires with a proper Greco-Roman fullness, the Devil returns to Antony, this time in the shape of a black boy[40] who goes by the name "Spirit of Fornication":

> Finally then, as the serpent was not able to take Antony in this way [i.e., in the form of a woman], but rather saw himself thrust from his [Antony's] heart, gnashing his teeth, as it is written, and then, as though he were changing strategies, he subsequently appeared to Antony in a vision as a black boy, and this was a reflection of his [black] mind. (6.1)[41]

The boy announces that he is both the friend (*philos*/φίλος) and spirit (*pneuma*/πνεῦμα) of fornication (*porneias*/πορνείας). Thereupon, he and Antony debate for a while. As it is a wise man teaching a younger male, a Platonic encounter may come to mind. No sexual activity is present, but that is fitting, as sublimation is Platonic too. Besides, as the black boy goes by the titles of "Friend" and "Spirit of Fornication," sexual activity is here anyway.

And so, Athanasius establishes through these two encounters that Antony's sexual interests are normative, i.e., directed towards women and younger males. Antony behaves according to norms of the proposed readership of the *vita*. This is a situation of some paradox, however; Antony has sexual objects/activity choices, but does not have sex. Antony's sexual interests should not matter, but Athanasius clearly wants his readers to know that *if* Antony were going to be sexually active, his choice of activity would be penetration of a woman or a younger male.

Another significant element in Athanasius' depiction of Antony is the fact that he possesses the eloquence that is the possession of worthy men

---

ἐγαργάλιζεν, ὁ δέ, ὡς ἐρυθριᾶν δοκῶν, τῇ πίστει καὶ νηστείαις ἐτείχιζε τὸ σῶμα. (5) Καὶ ὁ μὲν διάβολος ὑπέμενεν ὁ ἄθλιος καὶ ὡς γυνὴ σχηματίζεσθαι νυκτὸς καὶ πάντα τρόπον μιμεῖσθαι, μόνον ἵνα τὸν Ἀντώνιον ἀπατήσῃ.

40. As nearly always when considering pederastic scenes, "boy" should be understood as referring to a male at some point in his maturation past the commencement of puberty and prior to the arrival of his heavy beard. Also see Brakke (2006: 157–81 and 2001) for discussion of the effect of Ethiopian ethnicity and blackness in the *erēmos*. I don't address this issue.

41. Τέλος γοῦν, ὡς οὐκ ἠδυνήθη τὸν Ἀντώνιον οὐδ' ἐν τούτῳ καταβαλεῖν ὁ δράκων, ἀλλὰ καὶ ἔβλεπεν ἑαυτὸν ἐξωθούμενον ἀπὸ τῆς καρδίας αὐτοῦ, τρίζων τοὺς ὀδόντας, κατὰ τὸ γεγραμμένον, καὶ ὥσπερ ἐξιστάμενος, οἷός ἐστι τὸν νοῦν, τοιοῦτος ὕστερον καὶ τῇ φαντασίᾳ μέλας αὐτῷ φαίνεται παῖς

(My thanks to Simon Perris for his aid on this translation.).

in antiquity. It is revealed early in the *vita* that Antony could not abide learning to read.[42] But for all the deficits this unwillingness to learn to read should have brought Antony's way, he nonetheless was able to speak with grace through divine intervention:

> He [God] also gave grace in speaking (*charin . . . en tōi lalein*/χάριν . . . ἐν τῷ λαλεῖν) to Antony. Thus he encouraged many of those who were in pain, and others in disputes [he encouraged] to change to friendship, saying to all that they should not place any of the things of the world before the love of Christ. (14.6)[43]

The ability to use words effectively was an essential mark of *paideia,* and through skillful use of words, elite men projected authority and built bonds with each other. Grace in speaking got things done and furthered careers.

But Antony has more than the ability to charm and achieve objectives through grace in speaking. He does not shy away from competition and presses home his arguments. Athanasius depicts Antony debating some "philosophers" when they come to visit him. Antony speaks, "that our faith is effective, observe then: we contend mightily with a faith that is Christ's, and you [do so] with sophistic word battles."[44] Antony sets the terms of argument, defining the philosophers' procedures as sophistry, against which he opposes his faith. Elsewhere, though, and in spite of his stated disdain for sophistic wizardry, Antony defeats them at their own game. Antony "astounds" them with a verbal coup complete with a New Testament tag: "If you come to a fool, then your effort is wasted. But if you suppose that I am wise, *become like me* [Galatians 4:12]."[45] In other words, swear off learning. It is short but it *is* sweet. Antony prevails through verbal mastery and the philosophers "withdrew impressed" (72.5: *thaumasantes anechōroun/* θαυμάσαντες ἀνεχώρουν). The verb used here for "withdraw" is *anachōreō/*

---

42. 1.2:

> But when he, having grown some, had become an [older] boy and was advancing in age, he could not endure to learn letters . . . .
>
> Ἐπειδὴ δὲ καὶ αὐξήσας ἐγένετο παῖς καὶ προέκοπτε τῇ ἡλικίᾳ, γράμματα μὲν μαθεῖν οὐκ ἠνέσχετο . . . .

43. Χάριν τε ἐν τῷ λαλεῖν ἐδίδου τῷ Ἀντωνίῳ· καὶ οὕτω πολλοὺς μὲν λυπουμένους παρεμυθεῖτο, ἄλλους δὲ μαχομένους διήλλαττεν εἰς φιλίαν, πᾶσιν ἐπιλέγων μηδὲν τῶν ἐν τῷ κόσμῳ προκρίνειν τῆς εἰς Χριστὸν ἀγάπης.

44. 78.2: ὅτι ἐνεργής ἐστιν ἡ πίστις ἡμῶν, ἰδοὺ νῦν ἡμεῖς ἐπερειδόμεθα τῇ πίστει τῇ εἰς τὸν Χριστόν, ὑμεῖς δὲ σοφιστικαῖς λογομαχίαις.

45. 72.4: Εἰ μὲν πρὸς μωρὸν ἤλθετε, περιττὸς ὑμῶν ὁ κάματος· εἰ δὲ νομίζετέ με φρόνιμον εἶναι, γίνεσθε ὡς ἐγώ.

ἀναχωρέω. As such, it is an instance of wordplay in the text and, hence, thematizes the verbal mastery Antony has just displayed, as this verb is used technically of monastic withdrawal from the secular world. Is Antony's victory so thorough that he has made anachoretic monks of the philosophers? In any case, Antony has just achieved domination in a competitive arena and acted as any man of his station would have hoped to.[46]

Antony's competitive spirit also spreads to his monastic bodily practice:

> Moreover, as he was accustomed, withdrawing by himself into his retreat, he extended his practice and daily he groaned, thinking of the dwellings in heaven, having his desire directed at them, while he was looking at this life of humans that was bound to pass. For on the point of eating, sleeping and [tending to himself] in the matter of other necessities of the body, he was ashamed while in contemplation of the intellection of the soul. Indeed, being about to eat in the presence of many of the other monks, having remembered the food of the spirit, he begged and went a great distance from them, knowing that he was ashamed to be seen eating by others. He did eat, however, because of the necessity of the body, both by himself and often too with the brothers, being ashamed before them on the one hand, but, on the other, freely offering [them] words of helpful encouragement. (45.1–4)[47]

He is ostentatious in his practice, even after spending twenty years in the deep desert. One can almost hear the other monks asking each other where Antony has gone when he has withdrawn to extend his practice. Anticipation mounts (for days?) and then, finally, he returns, more sanctified than before. When he is with the other monks, sometimes it is too much for him to be seen giving his body what it needs, and he makes an exit sure to be noted by all because he begged to be excused. Still other times, his behavior oscillates between shamed gratification of hunger and advice offered from a

---

46. Brakke (1995a: 253–54) remarks that these exchanges with the philosophers embody Athanasius' suspicion of academic Christianity and his preference for "unschooled wisdom" (254). This scene shows these things, but Antony's beating them at their own game also builds up the profile of Athanasius' hero.

47. Αὐτὸς μέντοι συνήθως καθ' ἑαυτὸν ἀναχωρῶν ἐν τῷ ἑαυτοῦ μοναστηρίῳ, ἐπέτεινε τὴν ἄσκησιν, καθ' ἡμέραν τε ἐστέναζεν, ἐνθυμούμενος τὰς ἐν οὐρανῷ μονάς, τόν τε πόθον ἔχων εἰς αὐτὰς καὶ σκοπῶν τὸν ἐφήμερον τῶν ἀνθρώπων βίον. (2) Καὶ γὰρ καὶ μέλλων ἐσθίειν καὶ κοιμᾶσθαι καὶ ἐπὶ ταῖς ἄλλαις ἀνάγκαις τοῦ σώματος ᾐσχύνετο λογιζόμενος τὸ τῆς ψυχῆς νοερόν. (3) Πολλάκις γοῦν μετὰ πολλῶν ἄλλων μοναχῶν μέλλων ἐσθίειν, ἀναμνησθεὶς τῆς πνευματικῆς τροφῆς, παρῃτήσατο καὶ μακρὰν ἀπ' αὐτῶν ἀπῆλθεν, νομίζων ἐρυθριᾶν, εἰ βλέποιτο παρ' ἑτέρων ἐσθίων. (4) Ἤσθιε μέντοι καθ' ἑαυτὸν διὰ τὴν τοῦ σώματος ἀνάγκην, πολλάκις δὲ καὶ μετὰ τῶν ἀδελφῶν, αἰδούμενος μὲν ἐπὶ τούτοις, παρρησιαζόμενος δὲ ἐπὶ τοῖς ὑπὲρ ὠφελείας λόγοις.

superior vantage-point. He has labored at his practice of denial, becoming the best practitioner among those around him.[48] Further, Antony not only performs his denial of sustenance in public, his sexual renunciation is at times played for an audience (5.3; to be discussed below).

In time, then, Antony secured a great reputation through his obvious excellence. Emperors accordingly wrote him:

> The renown of Antony made it even up to the emperors. For having heard of these things [i.e., Antony's deeds and admirable mode of life], Constantine Augustus and his sons Constantius [II] and Constans, both *augusti*, wrote to him as to a father, and they requested that they receive a response from him. (81.1)[49]

Antony realized these marks of imperial esteem through uncanny verbal excellence and public mortification of his body recoded as a winning performance in a competitive arena. And so, as remarked above, the net effect of Athanasius' representation is of a manhood for Antony that would have been recognizably that of a *vir* or *anēr*. Athanasius repeatedly brings out commonalities between Antony and elite Roman masculinity in terms of the duties he fulfills, the skills he displays, and the competitive situations in which he is seen. Indeed, the imperial recognition Antony enjoys recalls the end point of elite men's ambitions represented on the Missorium plate or textualized in the imperial addresses of *parens karissime atque amantissime* or *Experientia Tua* in the legal corpora.

As already noted, Athanasius emphasizes at the beginning of his account that Antony is free and elite. But Antony gives up the accoutrements of his class privilege, the surrender of which certainly could have brought his social identity close to that of a slave. Being a slave had ramifications for gender performance because a slave had no right to bodily integrity. It is significant, too, that his solitary practices of prayer and solitude were more than likely supported by slave labor on estates located near the places he lived as a monk. Most of the time Antony relied on the delivery of loaves to his hermitage every six months or so (12.5). Athanasius also reports

---

48. Cameron remarks that the holy man "needs an audience; doing good by stealth was not enough in itself, and many hagiographic tales turn precisely on recognition and revelation. The writing of a Life recognizes this explicitly by making his deeds known to the world, and to posterity" (1999: 37).

49. "Ἔφθασε δὲ καὶ μέχρι βασιλέων ἡ περὶ Ἀντωνίου φήμη. Ταῦτα γὰρ μαθόντες Κωνσταντῖνος ὁ Αὔγουστος καὶ οἱ υἱοὶ αὐτοῦ Κωνστάντιος καὶ Κώνστας οἱ Αὔγουστοι, ἔγραφον αὐτῷ ὡς πατρὶ καὶ ηὔχοντο λαμβάνειν ἀντίγραφα παρ' αὐτοῦ."

that Antony's understanding of his relationship to his body is such that it replays the subjugation of slave to master in Roman society:

> And he [Antony] said that it was necessary to give all attention to the soul instead of the body. [He also counseled] to concede a little space of time to the body through necessity, but to devote the whole of one's time to the soul and to seek help for it so that it [the soul] would not be dragged down by the pleasures of the body but rather that the body be enslaved by it [the soul]. (45.5–6)[50]

Athanasius mostly leaves servility out of Antony's identity. His sense of himself works from a spot defined oppositionally to that of a slave. Indeed, the definition of Antony's subjectivity in opposition to that of a slave is of a piece with the formation of elite male subjectivity at large in the rest of the empire. The contours of elite Roman manhood seen in Athanasius' portrait of Antony occur elsewhere in the literature of the *erēmos*.

Abba Sisoes is getting on in years and is surely entitled to a reduced helping of bitter *askēsis*. Perhaps, as he is older, it would be advisable. When his disciple suggests that he come in closer to settled land, he is appalled by the idea that he may encounter a woman:

> Abba Sisoes' disciple said to him, "Father, you have become old, let's go back nearer to the inhabited area for the remaining time [you will be alive]." The old man says to him, "To the place where there are no women, let's go back to there." His disciple says to him, "What place does not have women except for the *erēmos*?" The old man says accordingly, "Take me to the *erēmos*." (*Apophth. Patr.*, Sisoes 4 [PG 65 392D])[51]

Even amid old age's exhaustion, the temptation that women provide to the monk seemingly remains overpowering. This disavowal remains a key proof of the monk's serious attitude to his practice. Another example makes this point in an even balder manner. Arsenius has been fooled into looking

---

50. Καὶ ἔλεγε χρῆναι τὴν πᾶσαν σχολὴν διδόναι τῇ ψυχῇ μᾶλλον ἢ τῷ σώματι καὶ συγχωρεῖν μὲν διὰ τὴν ἀνάγκην ὀλίγον καιρὸν τῷ σώματι, τὸ δὲ ὅλον σχολάζειν τῇ ψυχῇ καὶ τὴν ταύτης ὠφέλειαν ζητεῖν, (6) ἵνα μὴ αὕτη καθέλκηται ὑπὸ τῶν ἡδονῶν τοῦ σώματος, ἀλλὰ μᾶλλον τὸ σῶμα παρ' αὐτῆς δουλαγωγῆται.

51. Ἔλεγεν ὁ μαθητὴς τοῦ ἀββᾶ Σισόη πρὸς αὐτόν· "Πάτερ, ἐγήρασας, ἀπέλθωμεν ἐγγὺς τῆς οἰκουμένης, λοιπόν." Λέγει αὐτῷ ὁ γέρων· "Ὅπου οὐκ ἔνι γυνή, ἐκεῖ ἀπέλθωμεν." Λέγει αὐτῷ μαθητὴς αὐτοῦ· "Καὶ ποῦ ἔστι τόπος ὁ μὴ ἔχων γυναῖκα, εἰ μὴ ἡ ἔρημος;" Λέγει οὖν ὁ γέρων· "Εἰς τὴν ἔρημον ἆρόν με."

upon a virtuous virgin of senatorial rank from Rome. She wanted to meet him to ask him to pray for her. Appalled by seeing her, he says, "I pray to God that he erase the memory of you from my heart."[52] Disconsolate over the way everything turned out, the virgin returns to Alexandria and becomes ill. Bishop Theophilus visits her and explains Arsenius' reaction. He says that women are the way the Devil battles against the monks: "Don't you know that you are a woman and that through women the enemy wages war against the holy ones?"[53] In the face of this dismaying news, however, Theophilus reassures her that Arsenius will pray for her. This reassurance comforts her: having recovered her health, she returns to Rome joyfully.

What should be noted from this story and the others is that depictions of the *erēmos* featured nearly total separation of the sexes and a concomitant hysterical heightening of men's desire for women, such that an old man could be expected to take his (probably) arthritic frame out into the *erēmos*, or that a monk would pray to forget the sight of a woman, or that, even at ninety years old, John of Lycopolis, who had not seen a woman for forty years, would absolutely refuse to allow a woman into his sight.[54]

On the other side of this hysteria, and in impeccably logical counterpoint, monks are sometimes accused of impregnating women in the neighborhood[55] or of bringing women into their cells. In the *Apophthegmata Patrum*, there is an example of this latter story-line; Ammonas keeps monks who are searching a monk's cell from finding a woman by sitting on the wine jar that conceals her.[56] Stories such as these strengthen the sense of continuity between masculinity in the *erēmos* and that extant back in the cities. Both the hystericized separation *and* the suspicion or clear evidence of desire consummated depict the presence of normative sexual desire among the monks in much the same way the Devil coming as a woman to Antony does.

Furthermore, similar to the Devil's appearance as a boy to Antony, younger males appear as objects of desire in other literature of the *erēmos*. Isaac of Kellia cautioned against boys: "Don't allow boys to remain here in this way, for four churches at Scetis have become deserted because of

---

52. *Apophth. Patr.*, Arsenius 28 (*PG* 65 97A): Εὔχομαι τῷ Θεῷ, ἵνα ἐξαλείψει τὸ μνημόσυνόν σου ἐκ τῆς καρδίας μου.
53. *Apophth. Patr.*, Arsenius 28 (*PG* 65 97B): Οὐκ οἶδας ὅτι γυνὴ εἶ, καὶ διὰ τῶν γυναικῶν ὁ ἐχθρὸς πολεμεῖ τοὺς ἁγίους;
54. Anonymous, *Historia Monachorum* 1.4; for more on male monks' hysteria when faced with women, see Brakke (2006: 199–206) or Brown (1988: 242–44).
55. See, e.g., *Apophth. Patr.*, Nicon (*PG* 65 309A-C).
56. Ammonas 10 (*PG* 65 121D–124A).

boys."⁵⁷ Eudaemon, evidently too attractive when he was younger, summed up both approved sexual objects in his person⁵⁸:

> Abba Eudaemon said [this] about Paphnutius the father of Scetis: "I went there when I was younger and he did not allow me to stay there, saying about me, 'I will not allow the face of a woman to stay at Scetis on account of my struggle with the enemy.'" (*Apophth. Patr.*, Eudaemon [*PG* 65 176B])⁵⁹

As competition in the *Vita Antonii* reveals a continuity between masculine life in the *erēmos* and that found in the cities, so in other works that document withdrawal to the *erēmos*. The anonymous author of the *Historia Monachorum* sees in competition a salient characteristic of *anachōrēsis* as a whole:

> And some in the caves in the uninhabited places and others in the most remote places, all in every way most desirous of competition with each other display their marvelous *askēsis*. The ones further out making the effort so that no other in his disciplinary practices should surpass them, and those nearer [making the effort] so that not one [of them], since sin was burdening them from all sides, should be esteemed less than those further out. (Praef.11)⁶⁰

The *erēmos* is the site of individual competition too:

> "I [Ammoun is speaking] have greater travail [in discipline] than you, and how is it that your name is made greater among men over and beyond me?" Abba Antony says to him, "I love God more than you do." (*Apophth. Patr.*, Ammoun of Nitria [*PG* 65 128B])⁶¹

---

57. *Apophth. Patr.*, Isaac of Kellia 5 (*PG* 65 225A–B): Μὴ φέρετε ὧδε παιδία. Τέσσαρες γὰρ ἐκκλησίαι εἰς Σκῆτιν ἔρημοι γεγόνασι διὰ τὰ παιδία.
58. See Gould (1993: 125) for more instances of boys as objects of sexual desire in the *erēmos*.
59. Εἶπεν ὁ ἀββᾶς Εὐδαίμων περὶ τοῦ ἀββᾶ Παφνουτίου τοῦ Πατρὸς τῆς Σκήτεως, ὅτι "Κατῆλθον ἐκεῖ νεώτερος, καὶ οὐκ ἀφῆκέ με μεῖναι ἐκεῖ, λέγων ἐπὶ ἐμοῦ, '"Οψιν γυναικὸς οὐκ ἀφιῶ μεῖναι εἰς Σκῆτιν, διὰ τὸν πόλεμον τοῦ ἐχθροῦ.'"
60. Καὶ οἱ μὲν ἐν τοῖς σπηλαίοις τοῖς ἐν ἐρήμοις, οἱ δὲ ἐν τοῖς ἀπωτάτοις, πάντες πανταχοῦ φιλονικότατον ἀλλήλων τὴν ἑαυτῶν ἄσκησιν θαυμαστὴν ἐπιδείκνυνται, οἱ μὲν πόρρωθεν σπουδάζοντες μὴ τις ἕτερος ἐν τοῖς κατορθώμασιν αὐτοὺς ὑπερβάλοι, οἱ δὲ ἔγγυθεν μὴ τις κακίας αὐτοῖς πανταχόθεν ὀχλούσης ἧττον τῶν πορρωτάτω εὐδοκιμήσωσιν.
61. "Ἐγὼ πλείονα σου κόπον ἔχω, καὶ πῶς τὸ ὄνομά σου ἐμεγαλύνθη ἐν τοῖς ἀνθρώποις ὑπὲρ ἐμέ;" Λέγει αὐτῷ ὁ ἀββᾶς Ἀντώνιος· "Ἐπειδὴ ἐγὼ ἀγαπῶ τὸν Θεὸν ὑπὲρ σέ."

In another instance of competition from the *Apophthegmata Patrum* (Antony 17 [*PG* 65 80D]), Joseph proposes some scripture (not specified) to a group of monks for interpretation. Each monk offers an interpretation and each time Joseph pronounces the attempt wrong. When it is Antony's turn, he says he has no idea how to interpret the passage. This is the answer Joseph has been looking for and Antony wins.

Also in much the way the *Vita Antonii* does, other literature from the *erēmos* shows monks identifying with the master and not with the slave. Pityrion, one of Antony's disciples, spoke of the passions needing enslavement:

"Accordingly, my children," he says to us, "whoever wishes to drive out demons, first he must enslave the passions. For whichever passion one overcomes, he also drives out its demon. It is necessary that you conquer the passions little by little, so that you may drive out their demons." (*Hist. Monach.* 15.2–3)[62]

In a mildly humorous example, Arsenius addresses sleep as though it were a slave:

Abba Daniel said about Abba Arsenius that he used to spend the whole night sleepless. And when around dawn he came to sleep because of the requirements of nature, he used to say to sleep, "Come here, you wretched slave." And he seized it, sleeping a little, and then straightaway he would awaken. (*Apophth. Patr.*, Arsenius 14 [*PG* 65 92A])[63]

In sum, then, the various authors of literature of the *erēmos* complect the actions of their ascetic heroes so that continuities between them and men who have not withdrawn to the *erēmos*—and who are an important part of the reading audience—are visible. That said, though, it is important to underscore that the reading audience of non-monks is getting back a simplified version of their manhood. The complexities around finessing hierarchy and depicting friendship through metaphors of same-sex desire are not much in evidence. In reference to the *vita* and this simplified version of manhood, one might say that the *charaktēr* is something of a carica-

---

62. "'Ὅστις οὖν, ὦ τέκνα," πρὸς ἡμᾶς φησίν, "βούλεται τοὺς δαίμονας ἀπελαύνειν, πρότερον τὰ πάθη δουλώσῃ. (3) Οἵου γὰρ ἂν πάθους τις περιγένηται, τούτου καὶ τὸν δαίμονα ἀπελαύνει. Καὶ δεῖ κατὰ μικρὸν ὑμᾶς νικῆσαι τὰ πάθη, ἵνα τούτων τοὺς δαίμονας ἀπελάσητε."

63. Ἔλεγεν ὁ ἀββᾶς Δανιὴλ περὶ τοῦ ἀββᾶ Ἀρσενίου, ὅτι ὅλην τὴν νύκτα διετέλει ἀγρυπνῶν· καὶ ὅτε ἦλθε περὶ τὸ πρωῒ διὰ τὴν φύσιν καθευδῆσαι, ἔλεγε τῷ ὕπνῳ· "Δεῦρο, κακὲ δοῦλε" καὶ ἥρπαζε μικρὸν καθεζόμενος, καὶ εὐθέως ἠγείρετο.

ture. All the same, though, these continuities build a bridge and make the transgressive nature of Antony's and other monks' actions more palatable to a reading public in the *saeculum* that has had its self-image supported to a large degree. But the *vita* and other literature from the *erēmos* don't merely give back a simplified reflection of the canons of elite masculinity. This literature means to be an intervention; there is a brief for transformation, and aspects of monastic withdrawal depicted in these works depart from expectations for elite men in the empire. Visible here are men who figure themselves as slaves, avoid competition, and are submissive. The models are Christ and the martyrs. The literature from the *erēmos* is one of the ways the deadly ideals embodied by the savior and those who died for their faith were domesticated for use in a life to be lived. On the basis of the masochism evident in these models, it is arguable that the ascetics subvert their identities as men.[64] But such a perception is attenuated in the first place by the countervailing details, discussed above, that associate the ascetics with elite men of the *saeculum*. Secondly, and no less importantly, the association with Christ and the martyrs (and with holy scripture) that "biblicize[s]"[65] the ascetics connects their actions to a higher power, i.e., God, which resignifies their actions as holy and therefore as suitably and masculinely attached to something beyond this world. The address of *Tua Sublimitas* or the title, *illustris,* may come to mind at this moment.

The *Vita Antonii* contains moments of undeniable submissiveness in Antony that contrast with his masculine assertion elsewhere. For example, while he rejects the persona of the slave at one point (45.5–6), he embraces it at another. Here, Antony compares his devotion to *askēsis* to what a slave has to do:

> Just as the slave would not dare to say, "Since I worked yesterday, I'm not working today," [so] will he [sc. the ideal ascetic] not, in consideration of time gone by, leave off [working] during the days to come, but daily, as it is written in the gospels, he shows the same eagerness so that he may please his master, and not incur risk. . . . (18.2)[66]

On another occasion he declares that he will not avoid any beating that the Devil may care to give him (9.2). Slaves are the ones who receive beat-

---

64. Harpham 1987: 81; Burrus 2004: 11.
65. Frank 2000: 160.
66. "Ὥσπερ οὖν ὁ δοῦλος οὐκ ἂν τολμήσῃ λέγειν· "Ἐπειδὴ χθὲς εἰργασάμην, οὐκ ἐργάζομαι σήμερον," οὐδὲ τὸν παρελθόντα χρόνον μετρῶν, παύσεται τῶν ἑξῆς ἡμερῶν, ἀλλὰ καθ' ἡμέραν, ὡς ἐν τῷ εὐαγγελίῳ γέγραπται, τὴν αὐτὴν προθυμίαν δείκνυσιν, ἵνα τῷ κυρίῳ αὐτοῦ ἀρέσῃ καὶ μὴ κινδυνεύσῃ. . . .

ings, of course. Antony also demonstrates his submissiveness in the context of his relationship to the clergy:

> How forbearing was his character and how humble he was in his soul! For being of this sort [i.e., forbearing and humble], he both emphatically honored the rule of the church and he preferred that all clergy be placed ahead of him in honor. For he was not ashamed to bend his head to bishops and presbyters. (67.1–2)[67]

Antony's self-effacement here contrasts with his aggressive questioning of the philosophers at 72.4–5 (discussed earlier). Elsewhere, in a further example of submissiveness, Antony characterizes his behavior through reference to 2 Corinthians 12:10:

> He would not anoint himself with oil, saying it suited young men to be earnest in training and not to seek what would soften the body; but they must accustom it to labor, mindful of the Apostle's words, "when I am weak, then I am strong." (7.8)[68]

The proximate reference, encapsulated by the New Testament quotation, is to the body that has been disciplined and weakened by *askēsis* so that the soul will be stronger (7.9). But the quotation also designates the submissiveness that marks the holy man in whom authority and power reside on account of his resemblance to Christ and the martyrs (which in turn connects him to God).

A survey of the literature of the *erēmos* uncovers other examples of activity that can be understood via 2 Corinthians 12:10. There is, for example, Agathon:

> They said about Abba Agathon that he held a rock in his mouth for three years until he mastered silence. (*Apophth. Patr.*, Agathon 15 [*PG* 65 113C])[69]

Such silence is not the grace in speaking that served Antony well (14.6) and most assuredly is not Demosthenes practicing declamation with pebbles

---

67. Πῶς δὲ καὶ τὸ ἦθος ἀνεξίκακος ἦν καὶ τῇ ψυχῇ ταπεινόφρων. Τοιοῦτος γὰρ ὤν, τόν τε κανόνα τῆς ἐκκλησίας ὑπερφυῶς ἐτίμα καὶ πάντα κληρικὸν τῇ τιμῇ προηγεῖσθαι ἤθελεν ἑαυτοῦ. (2) Τοῖς μὲν γὰρ ἐπισκόποις καὶ πρεσβυτέροις οὐκ ᾐδεῖτο κλῖναι τὴν κεφαλήν.

68. Ἀλείφεσθαι δὲ ἐλαίῳ παρῃτεῖτο, λέγων μᾶλλον πρέπειν τοὺς νεωτέρους ἐκ προθυμίας ἔχειν τὴν ἄσκησιν καὶ μὴ ζητεῖν τὰ χαυνοῦντα τὸ σῶμα, ἀλλὰ καὶ ἐθίζειν αὐτὸ τοῖς πόνοις λογιζομένους τὸ τοῦ ἀποστόλου ῥητόν· "Ὅταν ἀσθενῶ, τότε δυνατός εἰμι."

69. Ἔλεγον περὶ τοῦ ἀββᾶ Ἀγάθωνος, ὅτι τρία ἔτη ἐποίησεν, ἔχων λίθον εἰς τὸ στόμα αὐτοῦ, ἕως οὗ κατώρθωσε τὸ σιωπᾶν.

in his mouth.⁷⁰ This cultivation of silence is an abrogation of *paideia* that trained men to communicate and compete with figured words. In another example, Father Achilles does not challenge one of the brothers who said something that bothered him; he bleeds from his mouth instead:

> One of the old men came to Abba Achilles and he saw him spitting blood from his mouth. He asked him, "What is this, father?" The old man said to him, "a brother's word pained me, and I have fought mightily against telling him, and I begged God that he remove [it] from me. The word became blood in my mouth, I spat it out, I have obtained rest, and I have forgotten my pain." (*Apophth. Patr.*, Achilles 4 [*PG* 65 125A])⁷¹

When I suffer in silence I have won. *When I am weak, then I am strong.* Is this behavior less than manly? To the extent that the mouth may be metaphorized as any other bodily opening, male or female, this particular story suggests a passivity and femininity, or effeminacy, in Abba Achilles. But in the end, the insult that this story may impart merely marks a moment of weakness underwriting greater strength in the future as this man is made more worthy of respect through his forbearance.⁷²

The story of Paul the Simple from the *Historia Monachorum* provides another example of empowering weakness. He is practically an anti-type to the assertive *vir* or *anēr* who has mastered *paideia*. His wife—note the wife—commits adultery, and he, when he discovers that she has been unfaithful, just packs up and leaves the home they shared. Adultery was a serious matter and complete acquiescence in the face of it was a scandal:

> Having apprehended his wife in the very act of adultery, saying nothing to anybody, he headed out to the *erēmos* to Antony. (*Hist. Monach.* 24.1)⁷³

In the *erēmos*, Paul becomes Antony's disciple. Antony, as his abba, demands amazing amounts of discipline from him. On Antony's orders, Paul stands in a sunny place for a week (24.2), gathers up spilled honey from the ground

---

70. a common story, e.g., Plutarch, *Demosthenes* 11.1.

71. Παρέβαλέ τις τῶν γερόντων τῷ ἀββᾷ Ἀχιλᾷ, καὶ θεωρεῖ αὐτὸν ῥίψαντα αἷμα ἐκ τοῦ στόματος αὐτοῦ· καὶ ἠρώτησεν αὐτόν· "Τί ἐστι τοῦτο, Πάτερ;" Καὶ εἶπεν ὁ γέρων· ὅτι "Λόγος ἐστὶν ἀδελφοῦ λελυπηκότος με, καὶ ἠγωνισάμην τοῦ μὴ ἀναγγεῖλαι αὐτῷ, καὶ ἐδεήθην Θεοῦ ἵνα ἀρθῇ ἀπ' ἐμοῦ· καὶ γέγονεν ὁ λόγος ὡς αἷμα ἐν τῷ στόματί μου, καὶ ἔπτυσα αὐτόν, καὶ ἀνεπάην, καὶ τὴν λύπην ἐπελαθόμην."

72. For more on the role of silence among the ascetics in the *erēmos*, see Gould (1993: 116–17, 162–66).

73. Οὗτος τὴν ἑαυτοῦ γαμετὴν ἐπ' αὐτοφώρῳ καταλαβὼν μοιχευομένην μηδενὶ μηδὲν εἰπὼν ἐπὶ τὴν ἔρημον πρὸς Ἀντώνιον ὥρμησεν.

without bringing any dirt up with it (24.8), weaves and unweaves baskets, and sews and unsews Antony's cloak (24.9). Graham Gould (1993: 52–58) argues that absolute obedience (*hypakoē*/ὑπακοή) was required in the relationship between abba and disciple. This was how the disciple would learn humility and endurance. In the *Apophthegmata Patrum,* Hyperechius compares the perfected obedience of the monk to the acquiescence of Christ to his sad destiny, which underscores the high regard accorded this quality.[74] And a scenario like the one between Antony and Paul was a hyperbolic representation that clarified roles decisively because of its extreme nature. What is of interest here, however, is the submission of Paul, this "when I am weak, then I am strong" type of abasement that yields rewards later. He submits in service to a greater goal:

> And to so great an extent did the man [sc. Paul the Simple] possess obedience (*hypakoēn*/ὑπακοήν), that a grace from God (*charin . . . theothen*/ χάριν . . . θεόθεν), the power to drive out demons, was bestowed on him. The demons that the blessed Antony was not able to drive out, these he sent to Paul and they were cast out immediately. (*Hist. Monach.* 24.10)[75]

In one respect, and not a trivial one, given the high value placed on the ability to drive out demons in the *erēmos*, Paul tops his tyrannical former master, and the contradictions inherent in Paul's identity are harmonized away through God's grace. Paul comes to possess an enviable accrual of *auctoritas* or ἀξίωμα courtesy of God himself.[76]

The literature from the *erēmos* avoids the metaphorization of *auctoritas* or ἀξίωμα by metaphors of same-sex desire and attractiveness. Whereas Julian, for example, conjures with same-sex desire and attractiveness in order to metaphorize admiration and excellence, the *vita* and related literature from the *erēmos* do not feature discussion of same-sex desire and behavior between adults, and in the *vita* there is no explicit mention of them at all. This elision produces tension at the point of reception of these texts. Those who know of the realities of homosociality and/or have experience of elite late-ancient homosociality's at times close relationship to same-sex desire—these readers will find they have questions and will start reading more closely.

---

74. Cited in Gould 1993: 53 (Hyperechius 8 432.3–7).
75. Καὶ τοσαύτην ὁ ἀνὴρ ἐκτήσατο ὑπακοήν, ὥστε καὶ χάριν αὐτῷ δεδόσθαι θεόθεν τὴν κατὰ τῶν δαιμόνων ἐλασίαν. Οὓς γὰρ οὐκ ἠδύνατο ὁ μακάριος Ἀντώνιος ἐκβάλλειν δαίμονας, τούτους πρὸς Παῦλον ἀπέστελλεν καὶ αὔθωρον ἐξεβάλλοντο.
76. For more on Paul the Simple, see Brakke (2006: 236–37) and Masterson (2006).

In the first place, the *erēmos* is a homosocial space, and, as such, there is the reasonable expectation that it will be a place of heightened levels of same-sex desire. A reader cognizant of realities sooner or later will be driven to ponder such things, especially if the author opts for a utopian sheen for his account (and this precisely describes the complexion of the *Vita Antonii*). Athanasius proposes a *charaktēr* for *askēsis* whose utopian inaccessibility makes a reader who is concerned with mimesis read with ever increasing engagement because reality demands what utopia elides.[77]

The relentless idealization that characterizes Athanasius' account proposes Antony as a man who will be the one least likely to feel same-sex desire or pleasure. His relation to them is that he seemingly has none. All the same, though, recreation of a reception of this text that takes into account the text of the *vita* as a whole, its intertextuality with the Septuagint and Plato, and the dynamics of homosociality—in short, the recreation of an *engaged* late-ancient reception of this text—reveals that same-sex desire is perceptible in the *vita* and that its author, Athanasius, is an authority as knowledgeable about forbidden matters as the authors of *Collatio* 5.3.

The coming interpretation may well be the very *charaktēr* of a "wayward" reception. Indeed, I hear that "Athanasius surely did not mean this!" I hope I am not setting up a straw man, but at this point I encourage readers to consider whether approaches to the *vita* should be restricted to ones based on perceived authorial intention, especially when readers who want such a restriction will have their position tested when this chapter concludes with discussion of the *Contra Gentes* and the *De Incarnatione*. The more that is known about Athanasius' intellectual project, especially as it relates to the body (and this is where, according to the argument to come, he places same-sex desire and pleasure in the *Vita Antonii*), the stronger the reading about to commence becomes.

FIGURING ANTONY

The Devil sexually tempts Antony as a woman and then as a boy. A backstory establishes the existence of a wife for Paul the Simple. These details can be understood as part of knowledgeable authority's staging of the exemplary contours of desire. The more transgressive possibility that a monk will

---

[77]. For an example of a utopian account of life in the *erēmos* that drives the reader into engaged interpretation, see my "Impossible Translation" (2006), where I discuss the story of Paul the Simple in the *Historia Monachorum*.

desire or be desired by another adult male, and the chaos that would cause in the *erēmos*, don't emerge into explicit representation. Readers mindful of realities attending the pronounced homosociality depicted in the *vita* and other literature will have questions: the explicit encounters don't cover all likely permutations of desire and activity.

The argument to come will be that Antony's encounter in section five of the *vita* with the Devil features, in addition to the Devil's assumption of the tempting form of a woman, a highly obscene anal intrusion that addresses, in corporeal fashion, the possibility of sexual activity between monks in the *erēmos*. Readers encounter an itching interior to Antony's body whose obscenity comes into view when the passage's *mise-en-scène* of a wrestling match (*palē*), which recalls for educated readers the *palaestra* of the Platonic dialogues, takes its place in an interpretation that encompasses the passage's intertextuality with both Plato and the Septuagint. If readers assume, reasonably, that Athanasius is an authority as knowledgeable as the consistory that will write *Collatio* 5.3 in about thirty years, they will not overlook this feature of the text that a close reading reveals.

Before proceeding to discussion of *Vita Antonii* 5, however, it is best to take note of some moments from the literature of the *erēmos* in which same-sex desire and behavior are approached. In this literature, there is occasional direct mention of same-sex desire, but more common is a practice of not addressing it directly. All the same, when its handling is indirect, imaginative pressure often is able to bring into evidence that which lacks explicit mention.

Shenoute of Atripe (late fourth to early fifth century) considered same-sex sexual activity a serious transgression in the White Monastery. David Brakke (2006: 101–102) and Caroline Schroeder (2006, 2007) both discuss his often articulated concern over same-sex sexual behavior. Indeed, Shenoute's recourse to sexualized imagery to name and denounce sins of all kinds leaves little doubt about how serious a transgression same-sex sexual behavior would have been in his establishment (Schroeder 2007: 37–39). Brakke, e.g., notes that "homoerotic activity . . . became for Shenoute the archetypal sin" (2006: 101). In addition to the rhetorical use of homoeroticism, Shenoute frankly discusses varieties of sexual sin, including, in *Canon* 1, "fornication in general and homoerotic encounters, pederasty, and masturbation" (Schroeder 2007: 36 [cf. 2006: 87–88]). Schroeder elsewhere remarks: "Shenoute's frequent admonitions against sexual desire seek to purge sexual expression from the community, yet ironically they also serve to position sexuality as one of the foremost markers of monastic identity" (2007: 56). In Pachomius' monastery, same-sex sexual encounters were not tolerated either; they apparently were grounds for expulsion.[78]

In a translation of Pachomius' regulations for proper coenobitic living, and moving in the direction of less explicit mention of same-sex desire, Jerome presents a number of rules that seem dedicated to keeping same-sex desire from emerging.[79] Prevention of intimacy was a *desiderandum:*

> No one should look at another while he is making a rope, or praying; he should be intent on his work with his gaze averted. (Jerome, *Reg. Pachom.* 7 [*PL* 23 69A])[80]

> No one will wash another or rub oil on [another's body], unless he has been ordered to do so. (Jerome, *Reg. Pachom.* 93 [*PL* 23 78A])[81]

> No one should speak to another after lights out. No one should sleep with another on a rush mat. No one should hold another's hand; but whether they stand, walk, or sit, let [each] be separated from the other by one cubit. (Jerome, *Reg. Pachom.* 94 [*PL* 23 78A–B])[82]

> No one will dare to remove a thorn from the foot of another, with the exception of the head of the house, or in the second place, another who has been ordered to do so. (Jerome, *Reg. Pachom.* 95 [*PL* 23 78B])[83]

Rather than outlawing sexual behavior directly, these rules limit social and physical contact, closing off opportunities. It is clear enough what is at issue, however. Corollary to these prohibitions is a poignant (and likewise indirect) saying of Abba Agathon:

> If someone is dear to me beyond bounds, and I know that he brings me to a fault, I cut him off from me. (*Apophth. Patr.*, Agathon 23 [*PG* 65 116B])[84]

---

78. Rousseau (1985: 95–97); for still more on sexual behavior between adult males addressed in the literature dedicated to providing rules for coenobitic living, see discussions and evidence in Layton 2007 and Espejo-Muriel 1991.

79. Aline Rousselle (1988/1983: 155) first drew my attention to these rules (cf. Vivian 1993: 92).

80. VII: Nemo aspiciat alterum torquentem funiculum, vel orantem; sed in suo defixis luminibus opere sit intentus.

81. XCIII: Nullus lavare alterum poterit, aut unguere, nisi ei fuerit imperatum.

82. XCIV: Nemo alteri loquatur in tenebris: nullus in psiathio cum altero dormiat: manum alterius nemo teneat; sed sive steterit, sive ambulaverit, sive sederit, uno cubito distet ab altero.

83. XCV: Spinam de pede alterius, excepto domus praeposito, et secundo, et alio cui iussum fuerit, nemo audebit evellere.

84. Ἀγαπητός μού τις ἐὰν ᾖ καθ' ὑπερβολήν, καὶ γνῶ ὅτι κατάγει με εἰς ἐλάττωμα, ἀποκόπτω αὐτὸν ἀπ' ἐμοῦ.

While Agathon says nothing specific about present actions, the future, minus prevention now, could be full of desire, and even physical consummation.

It is with this amount of pressure that *Vita Antonii* 5 should be read, or perhaps with even more, for the *vita* is cagier on this subject than either the rules Jerome translated or Agathon's *apophthegma*. The utopian *vita* extorts hyperbolic awareness from the reader at the point of the text's reception. It compels this awareness not only because of readerly knowledge about the realities of homosocial spaces: both *paideia* and knowledge of the Septuagint also play crucial roles. Here is the entirety of section five of the *vita*, printed here for convenience:

> But the Devil, who hates what is beautiful and is envious, could not endure to see such resolution in a younger one (*neōteroi*/νεωτέρῳ) and he endeavored to carry out against him too the sorts of things he was accustomed to work [against others]. (2) First of all, he tried to lead him away from *askēsis,* thrusting [into his mind] memory of his wealth, care for his sister, claims of kindred, love of money, love of glory, the various pleasures of the table and the other relaxations of life, and at last the difficulty of virtue (*aretēs*/ἀρετῆς) and how the labor for it is a great undertaking. He suggested also the body's weakness and the length of the time. (3) In a word, he raised in his mind a great dust storm (*polyn . . . koniorton*/πολὺν . . . κονιορτόν) of thoughts, wishing to cut him off from his righteous intention. But the enemy [the Devil] saw that he had little power in the face of Antony's resolve, and that rather he was outwrestled (*katapalaiomenon*/καταπαλαιόμενον) because of Antony's strength (*strerrotētos*/στερρότητος); that he was flipped over by his faith and was taking a fall by means of Antony's constant prayers—then indeed feeling confident in the weapons of "the belly's navel" [Job 40:16] and glorying in them (for these are the first innermost things [*ta prōta . . . enedra*/τὰ πρῶτα . . . ἔνεδρα] to attack when battling against the younger ones), he proceeds against this younger one (*neōterou*/νεωτέρου), harassing him by night and harrying him during the day, such that even those watching were perceiving a great grappling/wrestling (*palēn*/πάλην) between them. (4) For [the Devil] was thrusting filthy thoughts (*logismous rhuparous*/ λογισμοὺς ῥυπαρούς) [into Antony's mind] and [Antony] was overturning them with his prayers. [The Devil] was causing an itching (*egargalizein*/ἐγαργάλιζεν), but he, while appearing to blush, through faith and fasts was walling off his body (*eteichize to sōma*/ἐτείχιζε τὸ σῶμα). (5) The wretched Devil was even keeping at it to the extent that he took on the shape of a woman and in every way mimicked one during the night,

only so he could deceive Antony. But he, directing his mind to Christ and contemplating both nobility through him and the intellectual part of his soul, was quenching the coal (*apesbennue ton anthraka*/ἀπεσβέννυε τὸν ἄνθρακα) of that one's lie. (6) Again the enemy was thrusting [into Antony's mind] the ease of pleasure. But he, similar to one raging and grieving, was contemplating the threat of the flames and the labor of the worm. Setting these [thoughts] in opposition, he was passing through, unharmed by these [designs of the Devil]. All these things were happening to the shame (*aischunēn*/αἰσχύνην) of the Enemy. (7) He who supposed himself to be the equal of God was now being made a plaything by a young man (*hypo neaniskou . . . epaizeto*/ὑπὸ νεανίσκου . . . ἐπαίζετο). The one vaunting himself as the victor over flesh and blood was being flipped over by a flesh and blood mortal. Christ was working with him—he who took on flesh for our sake and who gave victory over the Devil to the body [through the resurrection] with the result that each of those who are struggling in reality might say, "not I but the grace of God which was with me." [1 Corinthians 15:10][85]

At about the mid-point of section 5, the Devil makes a play for Antony:

For [the Devil] was thrusting filthy thoughts (*logismous rhuparous*/λογισμοὺς ῥυπαρούς) [into Antony's mind] and [Antony] was overturning

---

85. (5.1)Ὁ δὲ μισόκαλος καὶ φθονερὸς διάβολος οὐκ ἤνεγκεν ὁρῶν ἐν νεωτέρῳ τοιαύτην πρόθεσιν, ἀλλ' οἷα μεμελέτηκε ποιεῖν, ἐπιχειρεῖ καὶ κατὰ τούτου πράττειν. (2) Καὶ τὸ μὲν πρῶτον ἐπείραζεν αὐτὸν ἀπὸ τῆς ἀσκήσεως καταγαγεῖν, ὑποβάλλων μνήμην τῶν κτημάτων, τῆς ἀδελφῆς τὴν κηδεμονίαν, τοῦ γένους τὴν οἰκειότητα, φιλαργυρίαν, φιλοδοξίαν, τροφῆς τὴν ποικίλην ἡδονήν, καὶ τὰς ἄλλας ἀνέσεις τοῦ βίου, καὶ τέλος τὸ τραχὺ τῆς ἀρετῆς, καὶ ὡς πολὺς αὐτῆς ἐστιν ὁ πόνος. Τοῦ τε σώματος τὴν ἀσθένειαν ὑπετίθετο, καὶ τοῦ χρόνου τὸ μῆκος. (3) Καὶ ὅλως πολὺν ἤγειρεν αὐτῷ κονιορτὸν λογισμῶν ἐν τῇ διανοίᾳ, θέλων αὐτὸν ἀποσχοινίσαι τῆς ὀρθῆς προαιρέσεως. Ὡς δὲ εἶδεν ἑαυτὸν ὁ ἐχθρὸς ἀσθενοῦντα πρὸς τὴν τοῦ Ἀντωνίου πρόθεσιν καὶ μᾶλλον ἑαυτὸν καταπαλαιόμενον ὑπὸ τῆς ἐκείνου στερρότητος, ἀνατρεπόμενόν τε τῇ πίστει καὶ πίπτοντα ταῖς συνεχέσιν Ἀντωνίου προσευχαῖς, τότε δὴ τοῖς ἐπ' ὀμφαλοῦ γαστρὸς ὅπλοις ἑαυτοῦ θαρρῶν καὶ καυχώμενος ἐπὶ τούτοις (ταῦτα γάρ ἐστιν αὐτοῦ τὰ πρῶτα κατὰ τῶν νεωτέρων ἔνεδρα), προσέρχεται κατὰ τοῦ νεωτέρου, νυκτὸς μὲν αὐτὸν θορυβῶν, μεθ' ἡμέραν δὲ οὕτως ἐνοχλῶν ὡς καὶ τοὺς ὁρῶντας αἰσθέσθαι τὴν γινομένην ἀμφοτέρων πάλην. (4) Ὁ μὲν γὰρ ὑπέβαλλε λογισμοὺς ῥυπαρούς, ὁ δὲ ταῖς εὐχαῖς ἀνέτρεπε τούτους. Καὶ ὁ μὲν ἐγαργάλιζεν, ὁ δέ, ὡς ἐρυθριᾶν δοκῶν, τῇ πίστει καὶ νηστείαις ἐτείχιζε τὸ σῶμα. (5) Καὶ ὁ μὲν διάβολος ὑπέμενεν ὁ ἄθλιος καὶ ὡς γυνὴ σχηματίζεσθαι νυκτὸς καὶ πάντα τρόπον μιμεῖσθαι, μόνον ἵνα τὸν Ἀντώνιον ἀπατήσῃ. Ὁ δὲ τὸν Χριστὸν ἐνθυμούμενος, καὶ δι' αὐτὸν τὴν εὐγένειαν, καὶ τὸ νοερὸν τῆς ψυχῆς λογιζόμενος, ἀπεσβέννυε τὸν ἄνθρακα τῆς πλάνης ἐκείνου. (6) Πάλιν τε ὁ μὲν ἐχθρὸς ὑπέβαλλε τὸ λεῖον τῆς ἡδονῆς. Ὁ δέ, ὀργιζομένῳ καὶ λυπουμένῳ ἐοικώς, τὴν ἀπειλὴν τοῦ πυρὸς καὶ τοῦ σκώληκος τὸν πόνον ἐνεθυμεῖτο· καὶ ἀντιτιθεὶς ταῦτα διέβαινε τούτους ἀβλαβής. Ἦν δὲ ταῦτα πάντα πρὸς αἰσχύνην γινόμενα τοῦ ἐχθροῦ. (7)Ὁ γὰρ νομίσας ὅμοιος γενέσθαι Θεῷ ὑπὸ νεανίσκου νῦν ἐπαίζετο· καὶ ὁ σαρκὸς καὶ αἵματος κατακαυχώμενος ὑπὸ ἀνθρώπου σαρκοφοροῦντος ἀνετρέπετο. Συνήργει γὰρ ὁ Κύριος αὐτῷ, ὁ σάρκα δι' ἡμᾶς φορέσας, καὶ τῷ σώματι δοὺς τὴν κατὰ τοῦ διαβόλου νίκην, ὥστε τῶν ὄντως ἀγωνιζομένων ἕκαστον λέγειν· "Οὐκ ἐγὼ δέ, ἀλλ' ἡ χάρις τοῦ Θεοῦ ἡ σὺν ἐμοί."

them with his prayers. [The Devil] was causing an itching (*egargalizen/* ἐγαργάλιζεν).... (5.4)[86]

Just what does the Devil have in mind? Readers familiar with the *Philebus* (47A–B[87])—and the *Philebus* had an honored place in *paideia*[88]—will note that *gargalizō*/γαργαλίζω, the verb that designates the itching, appears in this text of Plato where it indicates a pain that, when it accompanies pleasure, creates an all-around delightful sensation:

> SOCRATES: Surely then, whenever there is more of pleasure mixed throughout all these things, the less prevalent element of pain causes an itching (*gargalizei*/γαργαλίζει) and makes for gentle irritation. Yet, again, the large element of pleasure, the element pouring in the more, makes one strain and sometimes throb. Does it not bring about all manner of colors to your face, all manner of bodily postures, all kinds of changes in your breathing, while it causes astonishment and shouting with madness?
> PROTARCHUS: Absolutely!
> SOCRATES: Furthermore, my friend, it makes one say about himself (and another say about him) that he is being charmed by these pleasures as though to die from them. And he most assuredly pursues these pleasures closely by all means possible, and this is in proportion to how undisciplined and thoughtless he happens to be. He will call them, too, the greatest of things and he will number the one living always amidst these pleasures absolutely the most blessed. (*Phlb.* 47A–B)[89]

Coming on the heels of remarks on how too much discomfort can cancel the effect of pleasure present at the same time, this passage asserts that if the level of discomfort is lower than that of the concomitant pleasure, there may be a (quite possibly delirious) intensification of this pleasure.

---

86. Ὁ μὲν γὰρ ὑπέβαλλε λογισμοὺς ῥυπαρούς, ὁ δὲ ταῖς εὐχαῖς ἀνέτρεπε τούτους. Καὶ ὁ μὲν ἐγαργάλιζεν....
87. My thanks to Steven Smith for drawing my attention to this passage from the *Philebus*.
88. Lamberton 2001: 444–45.
89. ΣΩ. Οὐκοῦν ὁπόταν αὖ πλείων ἡδονὴ κατὰ <τὰ> τοιαῦτα πάντα συμμειχθῇ, τὸ μὲν ὑπομεμειγμένον τῆς λύπης γαργαλίζει τε καὶ ἠρέμα ἀγανακτεῖν ποιεῖ, τὸ δ' αὖ τῆς ἡδονῆς πολὺ πλέον ἐγκεχυμένον συντείνει τε καὶ ἐνίοτε πηδᾶν ποιεῖ, καὶ παντοῖα μὲν χρώματα, παντοῖα δὲ σχήματα, παντοῖα δὲ πνεύματα ἀπεργαζόμενον πᾶσαν ἔκπληξιν καὶ βοὰς μετὰ ἀφροσύνης ἐνεργάζεται;
ΠΡΩ. Μάλα γε.
ΣΩ. Καὶ λέγειν τε, ὦ ἑταῖρε, αὐτόν τε περὶ ἑαυτοῦ ποιεῖ καὶ ἄλλον ὡς ταύταις ταῖς ἡδοναῖς τερπόμενος οἷον ἀποθνήσκει· καὶ ταύτας γε δὴ παντάπασιν ἀεὶ μεταδιώκει τοσούτῳ μᾶλλον ὅσῳ ἂν ἀκολαστότερός τε καὶ ἀφρονέστερος ὢν τυγχάνῃ, καὶ καλεῖ δὴ μεγίστας ταύτας, καὶ τὸν ἐν αὐταῖς ὅτι μάλιστ' ἀεὶ ζῶντα εὐδαιμονέστατον καταριθμεῖται.

Putting the *vita* together with the *Philebus* (and other instances from Plato[90]) because of this verb, *gargalizō,* and indeed because the reference to filthy thoughts (*logismous rhuparous*/λογισμοὺς ῥυπαρούς) suggests some manner of sexual activity, is tantamount to importing scandal to this context, for anal penetration generally has some measure of discomfort associated with it until relaxation sets in.

In a move that suggests "better safe than sorry" and supports the idea that anal penetration is at issue, Antony closes up his body—seemingly to avoid a painful intrusion, the pain of which may give way to an all-around delightful sensation (why else the blush?):

> ... but he [Antony], while seeming to blush, through faith and fasts was walling off his body. (5.4)[91]

He renders himself impenetrable, walled-off, and safe. The Devil is not going to get in, though he keeps trying.[92]

At length giving up, the Devil will try to entice Antony to come out:

> The wretched Devil was even keeping at it to the extent that he took on the shape of a woman and in every way mimicked one during the night, only so he could deceive Antony. (5.5)[93]

---

90. The related noun, *gargalismos*/γαργαλισμός, appears in the *Symposium* (188E) where it refers to the tickling that Aristophanes, using some object or other (185D: τι τοιοῦτον), caused to induce a sneeze to end his hiccups. The verb and noun also occur in the *Phaedrus* (251C and 253E) where they refer to the itching of the wings growing in the charioteer's soul because of his desire for his beloved (*paidika* [251A], *pais* [251E], *erōmenos* [252C]).

91. ... ὁ δέ, ὡς ἐρυθριᾶν δοκῶν, τῇ πίστει καὶ νηστείαις ἐτείχιζε τὸ σῶμα.

92. Besides the scenarios with Satan, Antony's body is sealed and rendered impenetrable later in the *vita:*

> Taking heart, thereupon, he [Antony] answered back, "If you [he is addressing demons] have the ability and a power against me in your possession, then come on!; but if you don't, why do you stir yourselves up to no purpose? For my faith in Christ is a seal and wall of safety for me." (9.10)

> Θαρρῶν γοῦν πάλιν ἔλεγεν· "Εἰ δύνασθε καὶ ἐξουσίαν ἐλάβετε κατ' ἐμοῦ, μὴ μέλλετε, ἀλλ' ἐπίβητε· εἰ δὲ μὴ δύνασθε, τί μάτην ταράσσεσθε; Σφραγὶς γὰρ ἡμῖν καὶ τεῖχος εἰς ἀσφάλειαν ἡ εἰς τὸν Κύριον ἡμῶν πίστις."

This passage is not overtly sexual, but can be interpreted as a covert instance as it recalls Antony's prophylactic sealing up of his body (especially the reference to a wall) when he is confronted by the Devil at 5.4.

93. Καὶ ὁ μὲν διάβολος ὑπέμενεν ὁ ἄθλιος καὶ ὡς γυνὴ σχηματίζεσθαι νυκτὸς καὶ πάντα τρόπον μιμεῖσθαι, μόνον ἵνα τὸν Ἀντώνιον ἀπατήσῃ.

The Devil encourages Antony to penetrate him. There had been danger of the Devil getting in, but Antony has parried diabolic provocation, and it is the Devil who faces the charge of passivity. Antony's sexuality appears to be directed properly. But the situation is more complicated than this, as the itching indicates.

There are two desires (for women and boys), on the one hand, that Antony refuses overtly, while, on the other hand, there is something stowed away in "filthy thoughts" and in the verb "to cause to itch" whose refusal Athanasius stages in an occult manner. But this does not mean that the refusal and desire are invisible. In order to carry forward the argument that anal penetration is at issue and that this is the writing of an authority knowledgeable about life, the passage will be contextualized further with its surroundings in the *vita* (particularly the intertextuality with the Septuagint and references to wrestling). Following this will be consideration of the way the Latin translators understood this passage, for they provide valuable early evidence of the way it was received. In sum, the vitality imported by reading the *vita* with the *Philebus* finds confirmation.

Just before the Devil provokes filthy thoughts and Antony walls off his body, the Devil, frustrated with his lack of progress against Antony's resolve, decides to put his faith "in the weapons of the 'belly's navel'" which he has found to be effective against the younger ones (5.3). The "belly's navel" is a quotation from Job (40:16). It appears in God's words to Job, where he describes the strength the great beast, the Behemoth, has in its belly. G. Bartelink (1994: 143) points to a number of interpretations that have been offered to explain this moment of intertextuality with the Septuagint.

In the first place, it has been suggested that the Devil is trusting in Antony's stomach, which can mean he is relying on Antony's appetite (understood as sexual, for the *logismoi rhuparoi* are right around the corner) to bring the saintly young man down. At times, exegesis of the Septuagint has provided an additional allegory of the navel of Behemoth; it is first allegorized as the stomach and then, presumably because the stomach is a cavity, it is re-allegorized as female genitalia (*morion thēlykon*/μόριον θηλυκόν). The double allegorization looks forward to the appearance of the Devil as a woman, that is, unless it could be the penetrable anus of Antony, which cannot be ruled out on account of the grappling to come and the fact he is still a young man. This quotation from Job has also been understood to refer to male genitalia (*morion andros*/μόριον ἀνδρός), which in turn could have a referent in Antony's penis or, interestingly, in the Devil's (for the reference in Job is to the strength of a beast). Ultimately it is undecidable what the precise referent is, and interpreters are best off viewing the "belly's navel" as an instance of intertextuality that is polysemous and polymorphously sexualizing.[94]

In any case, and moving on, there follows grappling or wrestling (5.3: *palēn*/πάλην; cf. "outwrestled" [*kata*palaio*menon*/καταπαλαιόμενον], also at 5.3]) between the Devil and Antony, which is something that the younger ones do together—and the wrestling grounds or *palaestra* (the place where *palē* takes place) was the site of much same-sex eroticism in classical Greece, and is the setting of Plato's *Charmides*. Athanasius also mentions Antony's younger age three times in the passage. Twice he is a younger one (*neōterōi*/νεωτέρῳ at 5.1, *neōterou*/νεωτέρου at 5.3), and once he is called a young man (*neaniskou*/νεανίσκου at 5.7). While ages are always difficult to determine, it is safe to say that he is younger but not a boy;[95] it is his strength (5.3: *strerrotētos*/στερρότητος) that is "flipping over" the Devil, after all, and he was, as previously noted, competent to dispose of his father's estate and put his sister in a convent. This approach by the Devil, therefore, is not an encoded version of an invitation that would be given to a boy. It is, rather, a competition that will produce a humiliated loser; when the Devil is defeated, Athanasius remarks that "all these things were happening to the shame of The Enemy."[96] The word for shame, *aischunēn*/αἰσχύνην, is redolent of the sexual humiliation of someone who should be impenetrable being penetrated. And this point is brought home when Athanasius immediately adds the following: "he who supposed himself to be the equal of God was now being made a plaything by a young man (*hypo neaniskou . . . epaizeto*/ὑπὸ νεανίσκου . . . ἐπαίζετο)" (5.7). The Greek word for "was made a plaything" (*epaizeto*) is from the same root as boy (*pais*); so the Greek says in addition that the Devil is playing the role of a boy, a penetrable *pais*, and this becomes a reality in the very next section when the Devil arrives as the black boy (6.1: *melas . . . pais*/μέλας . . . παῖς). Continuing into this section of the *vita* is worthwhile in the present moment.

At this point in Athanasius' text, the verb *gargalizō* (and the noun related to it) appears again. The Devil as a black boy speaks to Antony:

---

94. Cf. Shanzer's discussion (2006: 191–92) of the capability of the belly's navel in the Job story to be both male and female genitalia in Jerome and other late-ancient Latin sources.

95. The Latin translations of the *vita* diverge on this point. Calling Antony a *iuvenis* (young man) and *iunior* (younger one) in his translation of the *vita,* the anonymous Latin translator certainly does not see him as a boy and hence quite directly supports my assertion. Indeed, men are called *iuvenes* up to the age of forty in Latin. Consistently calling Antony an *adolescens* throughout the passage, Evagrius Antiochensis in his translation places him on the cusp between boyhood and manhood. Evagrius and I don't appear to be seeing eye to eye.

96. 5.6: Ἦν δὲ ταῦτα πάντα πρὸς αἰσχύνην γινόμενα τοῦ ἐχθροῦ.

I am the Friend of Fornication! I take upon myself the innermost things (*ta enedra*/τὰ ... ἔνεδρα) of it and the itchings (*tous ... gargalismous*/ τοὺς ... γαργαλισμούς) [it causes] in the younger ones. I am called the Spirit of the Fornication. How many wanting to be temperate I deceived! How many fakers I persuaded through causing that itching (*gargalizōn*/ γαργαλίζων)! (6.2)[97]

The noun *gargalismos*/γαργαλισμός appears here for the first time in the *vita*, while *gargalizō* and "the innermost things" (*ta ... enedra*/ τὰ ... ἔνεδρα) are repeated from section five. These verbal repetitions put sections five and six in a close relationship, and the sexualized nature of the itching is now undeniable. Indeed, "the innermost things" (*ta ... enedra*/ τὰ ... ἔνεδρα), surely now activated with sexual meanings (if they were not before), have become quite interesting in this regard. *LSJ* ἔνεδρος II shows an adjective used by the fourth-century C.E. medical writer Oribasios: *enedros-a-on*/ἔνεδρος-α-ον. When this adjective appears with the noun *syringes*/σύριγγες (in plural) to create the phrase, *enedrai syringes*/ ἔνεδραι σύριγγες, it is translated as "anal passages." Following *LSJ*, then, the phrase, "the innermost things of it" (*ta eis tautēn enedra*/τὰ εἰς ταύτην ἔνεδρα), is able to be translated as "the things anal about it." Indeed, any reasonable reading of section six will see that the boy is trying to tempt Antony into penetrating him. Reading sections five and six together accordingly shows that there was an association of things anal with the verb *gargalizō*. And this association supports the assertion that Antony walling off his body is a refusal of penetration.

Two Latin translations, one anonymous and the other by Evagrius Antiochensis, appeared within twenty years of Athanasius' original. The one by Anonymous was most likely the earlier of the two.[98] These translations provide evidence of late-ancient understandings of Athanasius' text that support the reading just offered of the feeling that itches, the walling off of the body, and, too, the seeming blush. Here are Anonymous' and Evagrius' renditions of Athanasius' Greek:

Et ille quidem ad inmunditiam voluntatem provocabat, hic vero quasi verecundiam passus, fide et ieiuniis ut muro circumvallabat corpus suum. (Anonymous, *Vita Antonii* 5)

---

97. Ἐγὼ τῆς πορνείας εἰμὶ φίλος· ἐγὼ τὰ εἰς ταύτην ἔνεδρα καὶ τοὺς ταύτης γαργαλισμοὺς κατὰ τῶν νεωτέρων ἀνεδεξάμην καὶ πνεῦμα πορνείας κέκλημαι. Πόσους θέλοντας σωφρονεῖν ἠπάτησα! Πόσους ὑποκρινομένους μετέπεισα γαργαλίζων!

98. Hoppenbrouwers 1960.

And that one [the Devil] indeed was provoking his will to uncleanliness, but he, just as if he had endured the shame, by faith and fasts, as though they were a wall, was putting up a rampart around his body.

Nam et ille cogitationes sordidas conabatur inserere et hic eas oratu submovebat assiduo. Ille titillabat sensus naturali carnis ardore, hic fide, ac ieiuniis corpus omne vallabat. (Evagrius Antiochensis, *Vita Antonii* 5)

For that one [the Devil] was also trying to thrust/graft[99] filthy thoughts [into/onto Antony's mind], but he was removing them by constant prayer. That one was thrilling his senses with the natural heat of his flesh, while he through faith and fasts was fortifying his entire body.

In all three versions (the two translations and Athanasius' original), Antony takes measures so that the Devil does not gain access to his body. The Latin versions also give details about how this itching, which demands these measures, was understood in antiquity. In Anonymous' version, the Devil tries to provoke Antony's will so that he desires something unclean, while Evagrius understands the Devil to be using the body's natural warmth to create compelling sensations. There are further contrasts to observe between the Latin texts and Athanasius'. Athanasius portrays Antony walling off his body by means of his belief and discipline and, as he does so, he seems to blush. Seemingly reflecting to some extent Athanasius' phrasing with its mention of a blush, Anonymous says that it was "just as if he had endured the shame." Evagrius in contrast leaves Athanasius' blush and Anonymous' shame out of his translation. The introduction of shame by Anonymous raises questions that Evagrius, if he had been aware of this translation, perhaps opted to avoid through translating Athanasius' Greek differently.

When Anonymous renders Athanasius' "while seeming to blush" (*hōs eruthrian dokōn*/ὡς ἐρυθριᾶν δοκῶν) with "just as if he had endured the shame" (*quasi verecundiam passus*), he underscores the sexual subtext perceptible in Athanasius' text (again: why else the blush?). The word for "endured," *passus*, is the perfect participle of the verb *patior*. This verb, among its various uses, is used in a phrase that designates what a man experiences when he allows another man to penetrate him anally: *pati muliebria* (*lit.* "to endure womanly things"). This idiom, as previously noted, is alive

---

99. The present infinitive Evagrius uses, *inserere,* can be from either of these two Latin verbs: *insero-inserere-inserui-insertum* ("to thrust into") and *insero-inserere-insevi-insitum* ("to graft onto"). For reasons detailed below, it is best that a reader keep both meanings in mind.

in late antiquity, and is likely to occur to a reader, especially in a context detailing proper objects for sexual activities and the body's walling off that concretizes a fear of penetration.

The hypothesis coursing through both versions (Anonymous' "*just as if* he had endured the shame" representing Athanasius' "while *seeming* to blush") provides an additional opportunity for interpretation. One way to see the hypothetical nature of these statements is that they are a strategy through which Antony's penetration is rendered impossible in the homosocial space of the *erēmos*. Both phrases' embrace of unreality (they *are* hypothetical) underlines the greatness of Antony: facing down the Prince of Darkness, he could never be defeated. There certainly seems to be no need for, e.g., Pachomian rules that indirectly address the issue of disallowed desire between adult males. However, Athanasian hyperbole, i.e., Antony is more than enough for Satan!, raises questions at the point of reception. Faith in the knowingness of Athanasius' authority and readerly expectations about the realities of homosociality power a search for this desire's address. Anonymous' use of *passus* to explain Athanasian hypothesis and hyperbole provides evidence of one such search, as he converts a seeming blush into imagined submission.

Anonymous' word for shame, *verecundia,* is worth consideration too. In a discussion of one of the words for shame in Latin, *pudor*—a word which is synonymous with *verecundia* in the literature from the *erēmos* and often elsewhere, and a derivative of which, *pudicus,* occurs nearby in Anonymous' translation of the episode with the black boy[100]—Carlin Barton writes the following:

> [A]lthough shame [*pudor*] provided the restraint necessary for the preservation of all contracts and bonds, no Roman was credited with a sense of shame unless he or she was also credited with the desire and means to transgress those same contracts and bonds. In the words of Publilius Syrus: "The highest praise that one can give a man is that he is capable of doing harm but chooses not to" (397). "The good man wishes it to be remembered that he spared when he could have destroyed" (Cicero, *Pro Quinct.* 16.51). (2001: 217)

For a Roman to convey the impression that his or her sense of shame was operative, it had to be clear that they had the interest (successfully resisted)

---

100. In this passage, the Devil (as the black boy) exclaims, "I am called the Spirit of Fornication. How many I have seduced who wanted to be *chaste* [=to be in possession of *pudor/shame*]!" (Anonymous, *Vita Antonii* 6: [S]piritus fornicationis appellor. Quantos volentes esse *pudicos* seduxi!).

and the wherewithal (not employed) to do what was forbidden. This particular quotation is not concerned with sexual matters, but Barton later connects this notion to the maintenance of chastity, noting that the chaste man or woman "in ancient Rome could never feel purely chaste. At the very least (or most), they always felt shame before themselves" (2001: 241), for they knew just what they were capable of should they allow themselves to do it.

Barton makes a distinction between *pudor* and *verecundia*. She sees the latter superseding the former over time, because of what she posits as the more purely inhibiting nature of *verecundia*; *verecundia*, she says, tends toward denying that the desire for the forbidden thing even exists, while *pudor* acknowledges and then refuses such desire (2001: 282). It is not clear that this distinction between *pudor* and *verecundia* holds. It is easy enough to read them as synonyms at almost any time in the Roman Empire.[101] In fact, they appear to be synonymous in Anonymous' text, *verecundia* appearing in section five and a derivative of *pudor* (the adjective, *pudicus*) in section six.[102] Even if Barton's distinction between the *pudor* and *verecundia*

---

101. At the end of the first century C.E., e.g., Quintilian uses both words in the same passage:

> Greater disturbance will be present when someone lodges a complaint about things that must cause shame (*pudenda*), as in the case of *stuprum* [unlawful sexual penetration of a free person], especially in males, or over a debauched mouth . . . this sort of injury is more shameful (*verecundius*) for those who are have endured it (*passis*) to confess than it is for those who have dared to do it. (*Institutio Oratoria* 11.84–85)

> illic maior aestus ubi quis pudenda queritur, ut stuprum, praecipue in maribus, aut os profanatum . . . hoc iniuriae genus verecundius est <fateri> passis quam ausis.

102. Citing lines from one of Gregory Nazianzenus' many poems, Barton (2001: 226) in any case does allow for shame, such as she defines it for earlier in the empire, to persist into the later empire. In this poem shame that knows what it wants and a blush that would not be out of place on a Roman face from centuries earlier is visible:

> Heroic renown fell to the most dishonorable and dishonor to the best, and they were exchanging places with no justice. But plotting Evil did not escape the notice of God, the Lord; late to avenge, he spoke these words: "It is not right that there be the same glory for good and bad men; in this way evil will only become more widespread. I will therefore give to them a most excellent sign, so you may know well who is evil and who is good." Having finished speaking, he reddened the cheeks of the good, making the blood flow beneath their skin when *shame* (*aischeos*/αἴσχεος) was provoked; especially for women he suffused more within, since they are weak in form and tender at heart. And he stiffened an inflexible something or other and placed this thing within evil persons, and that is why they are not in the least affected by shameful things (*aischesi*/αἴσχεσι). (Gregory Nazianzenus, *Poematia Moralia*, PG 37.3 898–99)

> Κῦδος ἀτιμοτάτοισιν, ἀτιμίη δέ τ' ἀρίστοις
> ἔσπετο, οὔτι δίκῃ τῶν δ' ἐπαμειβομένων.
> Ἀλλ' οὐ λῆθεν ἄνακτα Θεὸν κακίη μεδέουσα
> ὀψὲ δ' ἀλαστήσας τοῖον ἔειπεν ἔπος·

is able to be contested for late antiquity, her idea on the nature of *pudor* is useful indeed. It enables perception of how the interpreting translators understand and change Athanasius' meaning; in Athanasius' text there seems to be no same-sex desire in the mind of Antony (his body is another matter), while in the translations, possibilities for such desire exist in mind *and* body.

Athanasius' "while seeming to blush" may leave the impression that he sees Antony transcendent of the economy of *pudor* proposed by Barton. If he only seems to blush, then his ownership of this desire is denied: the blush is a lie, a mere seeming. From this angle, then, his seeming lack of relation to same-sex desire makes him fit well with the developing definition of *verecundia* that Barton sees coming with Christianity—except for the fact that he does have a vulnerability. For Athanasius, weakness resides in the body and the superhuman saint, though only seeming to blush, still has work to do. His body would betray him if his mind were not so excellent. It is here that Athanasius and the Latin authors part company.

Anonymous attenuates Antony's hyperbolic mental mastery and depicts weakness in both body and mind. Anonymous has the provocation to uncleanliness from the Devil affect Antony's mind as though it were a shameful act. The invocation of shame (*verecundia* [=Barton's *pudor*]), which indicates the presence of a desire (if only to be refused), points to susceptibility in Antony's mind as well as his body. In contrast, deciding what Evagrius' position on Antony's mind might be is more challenging and may be best regarded as indeterminable. Depending on how his Latin is read, it is possible to see him positing either a total mental mastery in Antony of the kind Athanasius proposes or the attenuated mastery Anonymous suggests. Much depends on what the reader makes of the present infinitive that Evagrius uses in his translation. When Evagrius translates Athanasius' *hyperballe logismous rhuparous*/ὑπέβαλλε λογισμοὺς ῥυπαρούς ("[he] was thrusting filthy thoughts [into Antony's mind]") with *cogitationes sordidas conabatur inserere* ("[he] was trying to thrust/graft filthy thoughts [into/

"οὐ θέμις ἔστ' ἀγαθοῖσιν ὁμὸν κλέος ἠδὲ κακοῖσιν
ἔμμεναι, ὧδ' ἂν ἔοι πλειοτέρη κακίη.
Τοὔνεκα τοῖσιν ἐγὼ σημήιον ἐσθλὸν ὀπάσσω,
ὄφρ' εὖ γινώσκῃς, ὃς κακός, ὅς τ' ἀγαθός."
Ὥς εἰπὼν ἐρύθηνε παρήια τοῖς ἀγαθοῖσιν,
αἷμ' ὑπὸ δέρμα χέας, αἴσχεος ὀρνυμένου·
θηλυτέραις δὲ μάλιστα, ἐπεὶ καὶ εἶδος ἀραιαὶ
καὶ κραδίην ἁπαλαί, πλεῖον ὑπεσκέδασε·
τοῖς δὲ κακοῖσιν ἔπηξε, καὶ ἄτροπον ἔνδον ἔθηκε
τοὔνεκεν οὐδ' ὀλίγον αἴσχεσι συμφέρεται.

onto Antony's mind]), *inserere* is rich in possibilities, as *inserere* is a present infinitive shared by two different verbs: *insero-inserere-inserui-insertum* ("to thrust into") and *insero-inserere-insevi-insitum* ("to graft onto"). For the reader who knows the Greek text, the meaning of the first ("thrusting") will perhaps make the meaning of the second ("grafting") come a distant second. But in the absence of the Greek translation, the second meaning of "grafting" is eminently possible, especially as this verb (in the perfect passive participle form) has a highly influential appearance in Virgil:

> et saepe alterius ramos impune videmus
> vertere in alterius, mutatamque *insita* mala
> ferre pirum et prunis lapidosa rubescere corna. (Virgil, *Georgics* 2.32–34)

> And often we see the branches of one (tree) harmlessly turn into the branches of another, and the transformed pear bears apples *that have been grafted onto it* and the stony cornelcherries blush on the plum trees.

Awareness of the glamorous Virgil at the point of reception of Evagrius' text makes the meaning of grafting a likely one, especially in the presence of *paideia*. The end result of these divergent meanings is that a reader who reads the Latin text as "thrust into" will be conceiving of Antony's mind in substantially the terms (imperturbable, inviolate: the Devil's efforts are successfully resisted) Athanasius envisions. Entertaining the notion of grafting suggests for Evagrius' text a meaning closer to that of Anonymous': the filthy thoughts the Devil introduces have something already there they can work and grow with.

All three versions of the life present the possibility of same-sex desire and pleasure with indirection (with Athanasius' version the most indirect of all). But indirection at the point of the texts' various receptions is consumed by knowledge of reality and faith in the knowingness of authority until temptation housed in mind *and* body (Anonymous), mind perhaps and body certainly (Evagrius), and body alone (Athanasius) is what remains. The Latin authors, and especially Anonymous through his invocation of shame, underline the status of this approach of the Devil as a temptation which can affect mind and body. Evagrius speaks of filthy thoughts (that may or may not have "grafted" purchase on Antony's mind) and thrilling bodily sensations. Stereotypically Hellenic, Athanasius sees the danger as a function only of the body. The blush that only seems to be there suggests a mental incapability in Antony to submit in his mind. His body would be another matter, however (and hence temptation is present). Athanasius burdens the body, evidently "born to be passive" (*pati natum*) and shifty, as the certain source of man's desire for man in the *erēmos*.

Before moving on to discussion of the *Contra Gentes* and *De Incarnatione*, a final point. Within the small space of *Vita Antonii* 5, the pressure of not addressing same-sex desire and pleasure with at least a Pachomian indirectness arguably precipitates a complex of physical symptoms that are compensatory for same-sex desire and pleasure gone missing. The physicalities of itching, walls around a body, a dust storm, a coal that needs quenching, and a wrestling match (complete with shameful submission) make the case, *in bodily form,* that readers expect from omniscient authority. The late-ancient record has parallels for these physical phenomena that play a part in an argument: an *illustris* shines with light; Rome in *Collatio* 5.3 is the "mother of all virtues/manly excellences" (*virtutum omnium matrem*). A man whose *auctoritas* gleams and the eternal city giving birth to goodness and brave manhood have much in common with a manly itch whose scratching would be a diabolical triumph.

Making Antony's body the source of same-sex desire is similar to what is seen in the *Contra Gentes* and *De Incarnatione*. In these two theological treatises from much earlier in his career, but conceptually of a piece with his thoughts on the body in the *vita,* Athanasius makes stark distinctions between the mind and the body and between the *logos* (rationality) and materiality. The place of sin is the body, and Athanasius forcefully associates the surrender to materiality, sin, and body with same-sex desire.

TWO TREATISES

Athanasius wrote the theological treatises *Contra Gentes* (*Gent.*) and *De Incarnatione* (*Inc.*) in 335 or 336 (Thomson 1971: xxiii).[103] They consider respectively the false beliefs of the pagans and the nature of the embodiment of Christ (the *Logos*). The relation of the soul to the body and material world is a central concern in both. In these treatises, Athanasius sees same-sex desire as a signal material failing and something as far as can be from the *Logos* and the transcendent. This understanding of same-sex desire as an expression of corporeal nature is clearly related to Athanasius' vision of Antony's body as a site of danger that needs a rampart. This conception of same-sex desire also presupposes a transcendent that is the perfect expres-

---

[103]. Virginia Burrus' presentation (2000: 40–47) of the *De Incarnatione* (and of Athanasius' thought in general [36–79]) was most helpful in formulating these comments. Alvyn Pettersen's (1990) and David Brakke's (1995a: 145–61) discussions were consulted with profit too.

sion of moralizing impulses on earth. Athanasius' transcendent is therefore at odds with the late-Platonic one, which, as seen in the first chapter and introduction of this book, is a thing mysteriously existent, and precedent to and beyond earthbound logic and morals.

In the *Contra Gentes*, contemplation of God is the proper role of the mind and transcendence of the body is the goal:

> For when the mind (*nous*/νοῦς) of men does not consort with bodies and does not possess anything of desire from them from outside, but, whole, is above in communion with itself, as it was made in the beginning—then at that time transcending all sensations and mortal things, above, it is aloft, and, seeing, it perceives the *Logos* and the Father of the *Logos* in the *Logos*, being pleased in contemplation of him and enflamed by desire for him [i.e., the Father of the *Logos*]. (*Gent.* 2.21–27)[104]

As Athanasius has occasion to say often in both treatises, the upper world, the place of God, is the eternal "existent entities" (*ta onta*/τὰ ὄντα), and the material realm is the non-eternal "non-existent entities" (*ta ouk onta*/τὰ οὐκ ὄντα), and it is most decidedly below. Along with the relative altitudes, Athanasius assigns moral value to these two realms, stating that "existent entities" are good and that "non-existent entities" are evil (*Gent.* 4.18[105]; *Inc.* 4.23[106]). The material world, because it was created from nothing, is corruptible and therefore not perfect and hence evil.[107] The eternal *ta onta*, which by Athanasius' definition are transcendent of this world, are comparable *to an extent* to, say, Iamblichus' *ta theia*. But unlike the philosopher's *ta theia*, Athanasius' *ta onta* function as a perfect expression of earthbound moralizing impulses and do not have the mystery of Iamblichus' "things divine."

The *De Incarnatione* features a similar formulation. Mankind, provided it does not "look down" and away from the "eternal things" (*ta aiōnia*/τὰ αἰώνια [=*ta onta*/τὰ ὄντα]), will through the grace of God transcend its materiality:

---

104. Ὅτε γὰρ οὐ συνομιλεῖ τοῖς σώμασιν ὁ νοῦς ὁ τῶν ἀνθρώπων, οὐδέ τι τῆς ἐκ τούτων ἐπιθυμίας μεμιγμένον ἔξωθεν ἔχει, ἀλλ' ὅλος ἐστὶν ἄνω ἑαυτῷ συνὼν ὡς γέγονεν ἐξ ἀρχῆς· τότε δή, τὰ αἰσθητὰ καὶ πάντα τὰ ἀνθρώπινα διαβάς, ἄνω μετάρσιος γίνεται, καὶ τὸν Λόγον ἰδών, ὁρᾷ ἐν αὐτῷ καὶ τὸν τοῦ Λόγου Πατέρα, ἡδόμενος ἐπὶ τῇ τούτου θεωρίᾳ, καὶ ἀνακαινούμενος ἐπὶ τῷ πρὸς τοῦτον πόθῳ.

105. Ὄντα δέ ἐστι τὰ καλά, οὐκ ὄντα δὲ τὰ φαῦλα.

106. Οὐκ ὄντα γάρ ἐστι τὰ κακά, ὄντα δὲ τὰ καλά.

107. Alvyn Pettersen (1990) points out that Athanasius also says that God is incapable of making a universe or body that is not good (5, 7) and that both are sustained by his grace (3, 8). Athanasius' thought on these topics across his works does not make things easy for his exegetes.

For God not only made us out of what does not exist but he made us a gift of living according to God through the grace of the *Logos*. But men turning away from eternal things and, through the counsel of the Devil, turning to the things of corruption became responsible through themselves for corruption in death, being as I said before corruptible by nature, but fleeing away from that which is their nature through the grace of communion with the *Logos*, if they remained good. (*Inc.* 5.1–7)¹⁰⁸

Turning away from the eternal and preferring to look to the material and perishable world is the practice of a sort of somatology instead of a theology or envisioning of God. Alvyn Pettersen argues that Athanasius locates the origin of evil in the perverse exercise of free will; paying ruinous attention to embodied life here on earth, mankind "fail[s] to live *theocentrically*" and chooses instead to "liv[e] *anthropocentrically*" (1990: 22). Pettersen's distinction is compelling to the extent that the decision to do evil is often presented in antiquity as a perverse investment in earthly things. The enormously influential Plato says this in a myriad of ways. Still, according to Athanasius, it is not just the will; the body is a key component in this regrettable sequence. When a man or woman does not look where they are supposed to, doing things with their body they should not, it is not a matter of an evil use of an intrinsically good creation; the materiality of the body, corruptible and bound to return to nothing, is morally suspect too. In a discussion of the *De Incarnatione,* Burrus notes that "Athanasius's creator . . . fight[s] a losing battle in [his] repeated attempts to stabilize a fundamentally and indeed fatally shifty creation" (2000: 45). When all matter was created *ex nihilo,* at that moment a divide between God's divinity and matter was created. Matter ever wants to grow corrupt and return to nothing. Hence, the scandal of God "barely" able to "keep his handiwork from unraveling" and "the good cosmos seem[ingly] destined for a bad end" (Burrus 2000: 44). Indeed, elsewhere, Pettersen notes that Athanasius "ascrib[es] *all* Christ's incarnate passions," psychological and otherwise, "first and foremost to his assumed body" (1990: 27 [emphasis in original]). The body is not merely a tool to be used, it is the place from where evil comes.¹⁰⁹ Indeed, it is such in the *Vita Antonii* as far as the sainted Antony,

---

108. Ὁ μὲν γὰρ Θεὸς οὐ μόνον ἐξ οὐκ ὄντων ἡμᾶς πεποίηκεν, ἀλλὰ καὶ τὸ κατὰ Θεὸν ζῆν ἡμῖν ἐχαρίσατο τῇ τοῦ Λόγου χάριτι. Οἱ δὲ ἄνθρωποι, ἀποστραφέντες τὰ αἰώνια, καὶ συμβουλίᾳ τοῦ διαβόλου εἰς τὰ τῆς φθορᾶς ἐπιστραφέντες, ἑαυτοῖς αἴτιοι τῆς ἐν τῷ θανάτῳ φθορᾶς γεγόνασιν, ὄντες μὲν ὡς προεῖπον κατὰ φύσιν φθαρτοί, χάριτι δὲ τῆς τοῦ Λόγου μετουσίας τοῦ κατὰ φύσιν ἐκφυγόντες, εἰ μεμενήκεισαν καλοί.

109. Pettersen's representation of Athanasius' view of the body as an entity to be used either for good or bad (1990: 23) disregards the status of materiality and, hence, the body as problematic entities in Athanasius' thought.

whose will is so much more virtuous than the average person's, is concerned; he cannot help but exercise his will for good, and it is his body that poses danger. His will must wall off his body as an itch promises perhaps only partially painful pleasure.

And so, as Athanasius continues, those who cease to gaze upon the deity allow their senses to tell them what is real and worthwhile. As these benighted people live *anthropocentrically*, things productive of pleasure take divinity's place in misguided imaginations. Bodily desire (*sarkikē epithumia*/σαρκικὴ ἐπιθυμία) rules their souls:

> [N]o longer does the soul see what is necessary for the soul to contemplate, but it is carried off in every direction, and it sees only those things that strike against it in sensation. Thereupon filled with all manner of bodily desire and in the opinions of them confused, it fashioned for itself God, whom it had forgotten in its own mind, through bodily and sensible things, applying the name of God to things that are visible and thinking reasonable only those things that it liked and what it saw as pleasurable. (*Gent.* 8.12–18)[110]

This turning away enmeshes the soul in sensation and desire and, in short order, realizes idolatry. Athanasius elsewhere elaborates this idea of making God out of sensible things. In the following quotation about idolatry, Athanasius also anticipates his Antony of perfect will with an absolutizing claim about holy men (*hagioi*) lacking sin altogether:

> Sin was not present in the beginning. For it is not now present among the holy men (*en tois hagiois*/ἐν τοῖς ἁγίοις), and it is completely non-existent according to their example. But men began to think of it and to model it for themselves from themselves. Thereupon they fashioned for themselves the contrivance of idols, supposing that the non-existent was existent. (*Gent.* 2.1–6)[111]

And so, a false notion about the universe is formed as the soul allows itself to become utterly involved in the body:

---

110. οὐκέτι μὲν ὁρᾷ ἃ δεῖ ψυχὴν νοεῖν· παντὶ δὲ περιφέρεται, καὶ μόνα ἐκεῖνα ὁρᾷ τὰ τῇ αἰσθήσει προσπίπτοντα. Ὅθεν δὴ πάσης σαρκικῆς ἐπιθυμίας γέμουσα, καὶ ἐν ταῖς τούτων δόξαις ταραττομένη, λοιπόν, ὃν ἐπελάθετο τῇ διανοίᾳ Θεόν, τοῦτον ἐν σωματικοῖς καὶ αἰσθητοῖς ἀναπλάττεται, τοῖς φαινομένοις τὴν Θεοῦ προσηγορίαν ἀνατιθεῖσα, καὶ μόνα ταῦτα δοξάζουσα ἅπερ αὐτὴ βούλεται, καὶ ὡς ἡδέα ὁρᾷ.

111. Ἐξ ἀρχῆς μὲν οὐκ ἦν κακία· οὐδὲ γὰρ οὐδὲ νῦν ἐν τοῖς ἁγίοις ἐστίν, οὐδ' ὅλως κατ' αὐτοὺς ὑπάρχει αὕτη· ἄνθρωποι δὲ ταύτην ὕστερον ἐπινοεῖν ἤρξαντο, καὶ καθ' ἑαυτῶν ἀνατυποῦσθαι· ὅθεν δὴ καὶ τὴν τῶν εἰδώλων ἐπίνοιαν ἑαυτοῖς ἀνεπλάσαντο, τὰ οὐκ ὄντα ὡς ὄντα λογιζόμενοι.

Having turned away from contemplation of things intelligible/celestial (*tōn noētōn*/τῶν νοητῶν) and misusing the faculties of individual parts of the body and taking pleasure in the contemplation of the body and perceiving its own pleasure to be the good, having erred, it [the soul] misused the name of the good and supposed that pleasure (*hēdonēn*/ἡδονήν) was the real/eternal good. (*Gent.* 4.1–5)[112]

Besottedness with the body, and there is strong implication of the sexual here, creates false values. People imprisoned their souls in pleasures and their souls, disoriented, were fouled by desires (*Gent.* 3.11–12). Idolatry, the practice that comes out of these false values and directs attention away from God and the transcendent, mightily exercises Athanasius in the *Contra Gentes*.

At *Contra Gentes* 9, people continued to such an extent in impiety that they made gods of the things which caused this separation from God in the first place: pleasure and desire (*tēn hēdonēn kai tēn epithumian*/τὴν ἡδονὴν καὶ τὴν ἐπιθυμίαν).[113] From this primal error come the gods Eros and Aphrodite (*Gent.* 9.31–34). Section nine concludes revealingly when he speaks of a more recent deification that occurred on account of pleasure and desire, the deification of Hadrian's beloved, Antinous:

[A]nd now the Roman emperor Hadrian's boy-love (*paidikos*/παιδικός), Antinous [compels worship]. Although they know he was a mortal and not honorable but filled with lewdness (*aselgeias*/ἀσελγείας), they give him worship on account of their fear of the one ordering it. For when Hadrian was staying in Egypt, Antinous the servant of his (sexual) pleasure (*hēdonēn*/ἡδονήν) died, and he decreed that he should be worshipped, for he loved the boy (*paidos*/παιδός) even after his death. Nevertheless, he offered up condemnation for himself and proof as regards all idolatry that it was invented by men for no other reason than the desire (*epithumian*/ἐπιθυμίαν) of those who made (the idols), just as the Wisdom of God has previously witnessed, saying: "The devising of idols was the beginning of fornication" [Wisd. 14:12]. (*Gent.* 9.39–48)[114]

---

112. Ἀποστᾶσα τῆς τῶν νοητῶν θεωρίας, καὶ ταῖς κατὰ μέρος τοῦ σώματος ἐνεργείαις καταχρωμένη, καὶ ἡσθεῖσα τῇ τοῦ σώματος θεωρίᾳ καὶ ἰδοῦσα καλὸν ἑαυτῇ εἶναι τὴν ἡδονήν, πλανηθεῖσα κατεχρήσατο τῷ τοῦ καλοῦ ὀνόματι, καὶ ἐνόμισεν εἶναι τὴν ἡδονὴν αὐτὸ τὸ ὄντως καλόν.

113. And others have extended their impiety to the point of deifying and worshipping the excuse for their inventions and wickedness—pleasure and desire. (*Gent.* 9.31–33)

ἐπιτείνοντες δὲ τὴν ἀσέβειαν ἕτεροι, τὴν πρόφασιν τῆς τούτων εὑρέσεως καὶ τῆς ἑαυτῶν κακίας τὴν ἡδονὴν καὶ τὴν ἐπιθυμίαν θεοποιήσαντες προσκυνοῦσιν.

114. καὶ ὁ νῦν Ἀδριανοῦ τοῦ Ῥωμαίων βασιλέως παιδικὸς Ἀντίνοος, ὃν καίπερ εἰδότες ἄνθρωπον, καὶ ἄνθρωπον οὐ σεμνόν, ἀλλ' ἀσελγείας ἔμπλεων, διὰ φόβον τοῦ προστάξαντος σέβου-

In this particular case it surely is a matter of fornication bringing about an idol (and Athanasius is at odds with his tag from Wisdom), but insistence on proper sequence is probably misguided as he wants to burden the idols with as much "disgusting" sexual sin as possible, and, hence, is more concerned with invective than consistent logic. Speaking more generally of idolatry elsewhere, Athanasius observes the sequence from Wisdom. Idols will be worshipped, the actual material images as well as the perverse gods for which they stand. These are idols of gods who are adulterers, murderers, lovers of boys, and castrators of their fathers, and they become exemplars to be imitated:

> [F]rom Zeus they learned the ruin of boys and adultery, from Aphrodite fornication, from Rhea lewdness, from Ares murder, and from other gods similar things, which the law punishes and which every temperate man avoids. (*Gent.* 26.15–19)[115]

Sexual sins are tied up in the long depressing history of mankind's turn away from God toward the worship of false gods. Same-sex desire (and in particular a desire in a man to be penetrated) makes an appearance, though, and corollary to its representation in the *vita*, its portrayal in the *Contra Gentes* is indirect.

The *Galli*, the self-castrating priests of Magna Mater or Rhea—and she, just mentioned, is the one who teaches lewdness/*aselgeia*/ἀσέλγεια, which was the abiding sin of Antinous—honor her through cultivating the *mores* of women:

> And the men, refusing their nature and no longer wishing to be men, fashion for themselves the nature of women, making out of these activities sweet gifts and honor for the one whom they call the Mother of the Gods. (*Gent.* 26.4–7)[116]

σιν. ἐπιδημήσας γὰρ Ἀδριανὸς τῇ χώρᾳ τῶν Αἰγυπτίων, τελευτήσαντα τὸν τῆς ἡδονῆς αὐτοῦ ὑπηρέτην Ἀντίνοον ἐκέλευσε θρησκεύεσθαι, αὐτὸς μὲν καὶ μετὰ θάνατον ἐρῶν τοῦ παιδός, ἔλεγχον δὲ ὅμως καθ' ἑαυτοῦ, καὶ γνώρισμα κατὰ πάσης εἰδωλολατρείας παρέχων, ὅτι οὐκ ἄλλως ἐφευρέθη παρὰ τοῖς ἀνθρώποις αὕτη ἢ δι' ἐπιθυμίαν τῶν πλασαμένων, καθὼς καὶ ἡ σοφία τοῦ Θεοῦ προμαρτύρεται λέγουσα· "'Ἀρχὴ πορνείας ἐπίνοια εἰδώλων."

115. ἐκ μὲν . . . Διὸς τὴν παιδοφθορίαν καὶ τὴν μοιχείαν, ἐκ δὲ Ἀφροδίτης τὴν πορνείαν, καὶ ἐκ μὲν Ῥέας τὴν ἀσέλγειαν, ἐκ δὲ Ἄρεος τοὺς φόνους, καὶ ἐξ ἄλλων ἄλλα τοιαῦτα μεμαθήκασιν, ἃ οἱ νόμοι μὲν κολάζουσι, πᾶς δὲ σώφρων ἀνὴρ ἀποστρέφεται.

116. "Ἄνδρες δέ, τὴν φύσιν ἀρνούμενοι καὶ μηκέτι εἶναι θέλοντες ἄρρενες, τὴν γυναικῶν πλάττονται φύσιν, ὡς ἐκ τούτων καταθύμια καὶ τιμὴν τῇ μητρὶ τῶν παρ' αὐτοῖς λεγομένων θεῶν ποιοῦντες.

The perception surely was that these activities included allowing penetration (and not only effeminate dress/mannerisms and castration) because in words immediately after these, Athanasius quotes Romans 1:26–27:

> And all together live in the basest ways and compete with each other in ever more evil activities; and as the holy servant of Christ, Paul, said, "For their women changed the natural use of the female to one that was against nature. Likewise did the men, leaving behind the natural use of women, burn in their desire for each other, men practicing shamelessness in men." (*Gent.* 26.7–13)[117]

A key point about the genesis of same-sex desire is its indirection. Other sins arise through clear mimesis of gods by men. Child sacrifice, violence against fathers, pederasty, adultery, found on Olympus, are imported to earth. Same-sex desire/pleasure that is age-consonant, i.e., non-pederastic, is different. Mimesis is displaced by an ideal of men's homage to a goddess.[118] It of course did not have to be this way. There was a minor tradition of a god who, as an adult male, was sexually passive: Bacchus.[119] But that is not how Athanasius presents it. For him, this desire issues from inside the men, and the desire to be sexually penetrated is part of a personal transformation meant to honor a goddess. The actual penetration, initially unspoken and veiled by cross-dressing and transgender behavior, is eventually unveiled by the quotation from Romans. It also is not a simple sin: connected to traditional religious rites, it is a direct turning away from God.

This desire and pleasure also play an important role in remarks on the evil of involvement in corporeal things in the *De Incarnatione*. The appearance of same-sex desire (again the passage from Romans [1:26–27]) consti-

---

117. Πάντες δὲ ὁμοῦ τοῖς αἰσχίστοις βιοῦσι, καὶ τοῖς χείροσιν ἑαυτοῖς ἁμιλλῶνται· καὶ ὡς εἶπεν ὁ ἅγιος τοῦ Χριστοῦ διάκονος Παῦλος· "Αἵ τε γὰρ θήλειαι αὐτῶν μετήλλαξαν τὴν φυσικὴν χρῆσιν εἰς τὴν παρὰ φύσιν. Ὁμοίως δὲ καὶ οἱ ἄρρενες, ἀφέντες τὴν φυσικὴν χρῆσιν τῆς θηλείας, ἐξεκαύθησαν ἐν τῇ ὀρέξει αὐτῶν εἰς ἀλλήλους, ἄρρενες ἐν ἄρσεσι τὴν ἀσχημοσύνην κατεργαζόμενοι."

118. The emphasis on indirection complicates Brakke's thesis that male worshippers of a goddess become more like the object of their devotion (1995a: 168, cf. 2006: 207). To be sure, the cross-dressing and passive sexuality Athanasius imagines among the male worshippers do show some similarities to the supposed life and sexual activities of a goddess. But the mimesis is less direct than when a man takes up adultery or pederasty in imitation of Zeus/Jove. The persona of the *Gallus* also has a greater degree of complexity than his exemplar, Rhea.

119. Clement of Alexandria, *Protrepticus* 2.34.3–5 (late second-century); Arnobius, *Adversus Gentes* 5.28 (late third- /early fourth-century); Firmicus Maternus, *De Errore Profanarum Religionum* 12.4 (mid-fourth-century); Gregory Nazianzenus, *Or.* 5 (at 32) and "To Nemesios" 1572.12–1573.13 (in *Carmina quae spectant ad alios [TLG]*) (mid-fourth-century).

tutes a climax to man's fall into excessive involvement in the material world, a fall which begins with excessive focus on the self. Humans embrace death and corruption "to their own measure" (*kath' heautōn*/καθ' ἑαυτῶν), and it goes downhill from there:

> [T]hey advanced into excess, from the beginning having become the discoverers of sin and to their own measure (*kath' heautōn*/καθ' ἑαυτῶν) having called to themselves death and corruption. And later, having turned to unrighteousness and exceeding all lawlessness and not stopping at one evil but devising all manner of new ones through novel activities, they became insatiable as regards sinning. For there were adulterers and thieves everywhere, and the whole world was full of murders and depredations and, amid corruption and unrighteousness, there was no thought of law. But all sins individual and communal were perpetrated by all—cities warred against cities, peoples were mustered against peoples and the whole world was demolished by revolutions and battles, with each [person] loving to compete in doing wrong. That those things that are against nature be a great distance from them—this was not the case, but as the witness of Christ, the apostle, said, "For their women changed the natural use of the female to one that was against nature. Likewise did the men, leaving behind the natural use of women, burn in their desire for each other, men practicing shamelessness in men and receiving in themselves the recompense that was due for this error." (Inc. 5.16–34)[120]

Involved in the activities of earth, people are not looking where they are supposed to. The things on which the mind (*nous*/νοῦς) ought to focus its attention are apart from and above the material world. In a passage from the *Contra Gentes* previously discussed, Athanasius states this directly:

> [A]bove it is aloft, and, seeing, it perceives the *Logos* and the Father of the

---

120. εἰς ἄμετρον ἐληλύθασιν, ἐξ ἀρχῆς μὲν εὑρεταὶ τῆς κακίας γενόμενοι, καὶ καθ' ἑαυτῶν τὸν θάνατον προκαλεσάμενοι καὶ τὴν φθοράν· ὕστερον δὲ εἰς ἀδικίαν ἐκτραπέντες καὶ παρανομίαν πᾶσαν ὑπερβαλόντες, καὶ μὴ ἑνὶ κακῷ ἱστάμενοι, ἀλλὰ πάντα καινὰ καινοῖς ἐπινοοῦντες, ἀκόρεστοι περὶ τὸ ἁμαρτάνειν γεγόνασι. Μοιχεῖαι μὲν γὰρ ἦσαν καὶ κλοπαὶ πανταχοῦ, φόνων δὲ καὶ ἁρπαγῶν πλήρης ἦν ἡ σύμπασα γῆ. Καὶ νόμου μὲν οὐκ ἦν φροντὶς περὶ φθορᾶς καὶ ἀδικίας· πάντα δὲ τὰ κακὰ καθ' ἕνα καὶ κοινῇ παρὰ πᾶσιν ἐπράττετο. Πόλεις μὲν κατὰ πόλεων ἐπολέμουν, καὶ ἔθνη κατὰ ἐθνῶν ἠγείρετο· διῄρητο δὲ πᾶσα ἡ οἰκουμένη στάσεσι καὶ μάχαις, ἑκάστου φιλονεικοῦντος ἐν τῷ παρανομεῖν. Οὐκ ἦν δὲ τούτων μακρὰν οὐδὲ τὰ παρὰ φύσιν, ἀλλ' ὡς εἶπεν ὁ τοῦ Χριστοῦ μάρτυς Ἀπόστολος· "Αἵ τε γὰρ θήλειαι αὐτῶν μετήλλαξαν τὴν φυσικὴν χρῆσιν εἰς τὴν παρὰ φύσιν. Ὁμοίως δὲ καὶ οἱ ἄρρενες, ἀφέντες τὴν φυσικὴν χρῆσιν τῆς θηλείας, ἐξεκαύθησαν ἐν τῇ ὀρέξει αὐτῶν εἰς ἀλλήλους, ἄρρενες ἐν ἄρσεσι τὴν ἀσχημοσύνην κατεργαζόμενοι, καὶ τὴν ἀντιμισθίαν ἣν ἔδει τῆς πλάνης αὐτῶν ἐν ἑαυτοῖς ἀπολαμβάνοντες."

Logos in [the *Logos*], being pleased in contemplation of him and enflamed by desire for him [the Father of the *Logos*]. (2.24–27)

In a motion that recalls the focus fostered by sexual desire, but whose objects could hardly be more different, the mind should make its way to Christ in his guise as the *Logos* and toward God himself. As did many Christian theologians, Athanasius Platonizes here and he changes the objective of Plato's sublimating "ladder of love" from "The Good" to God and the *Logos*. So, in the context of this prescription for the mind, what could be a more perfectly perverse valuing of the material than to desire, in a solipsistic downward-looking gape (vid. *Inc.* 5.17–18: *kath' heautōn*/καθ' ἑαυτῶν), physical copulation with a body that mirrors one's own? And all the more when it is recalled how different Athanasius' transcendent is from the mysterious existent one proposed by the late Platonists. Mystery is not present in his celestial cosmos; his heaven is taken up utterly by the *Logos* and the Father of the *Logos*, whose connection to the moral order on earth is never in doubt. According to Athanasius, mystery is here on earth instead. He packs the body with mysteries that are the objects of celestial solicitude, even though body and its demonic puzzlements are destined to pass away, created *ex nihilo*.

So then, man's desire for man appears in *Contra Gentes* as an indicative failure to value the transcendent over the material—a failure that replays in the here and now the primal failure of humanity to "look" where it was supposed to and the consequent development of idolatry. In the *De Incarnatione*, same-sex desire and pleasure function as a metaphor for the origin of sin and a symbol of the worst things that sin can be. In addition, the stigmatization of the body that occurs when Antony has to wall off his body is seen in these earlier treatises too. Composed of fascinating matter, the surrender to which same-sex eroticism provides a one-stop archaeology and summation, the body possesses an indicative relationship to same-sex eroticism because the body is a material thing. The sheer force of Athanasius' argumentation against same-sex eroticism, which makes it a yielding of great significance to matter, renders the body itself uniquely connected to such desire, a condition to which Antony's wall attests.

CONCLUSION

A vision of late-Roman manhood in which same-sex desire and pleasure played important roles in the portrayal and penetrative power of masculine authority was presented in the introduction and chapter one of this book. A man's admirability could be emphasized via a metaphor that made him an object of sexual regard; the corporeal intensity of such a metaphor made it a favored mode to portray a man's worthiness. An important friendship between men could also be depicted via carnal metaphors, whose immediacy told all that this friendship was special. Knowledge of same-sex desire and pleasure also made masculine authority more powerful. Demonstration of this knowledge was an authorizing demonstration of power's reach. There was nowhere that this authority could not go, even if the possession of such knowledge was possibly a dubious thing for a manly man to possess.

A reader of the *vita* would have every reason to believe that the authoritative Athanasius would be well-versed enough in the realities of this world to account for same-sex desire. Indeed, a major portion of this chapter was dedicated to showing how the reader's faith in Athanasius' powers of perception brings an accounting for this desire into focus. Where the *vita* and literature of the *erēmos* part company from much of the evidence in the introduction and first chapter of this book is in their avoidance of same-sex sexual attractiveness as a way to metaphorize masculine grandeur. This demurral was partially on account of the homosocial nature of withdrawal to the *erēmos*. But it also had a basis, at least in the case of Athanasius, in larger thoughts about the nature of this world and the next. Athanasius' thoughts about matter and divinity and body and soul entailed a decisive separation of things of this earth from the transcendent. At the same time, however, Athanasius understood the next world (with some irony) in terms that made it a perfect reflection and realization of earthbound norms. Athanasius saw the propensity to "misbehave" as a function of material bodies. Indeed, rather than a possible metaphor for masculine authority, same-sex desire and pleasure were instead examples of the worst thing sin could be. Athanasius did not have dispassion about things that exist and indicted the world as a fatally flawed entity.

The next chapter leaves the *erēmos* for the center of the imperial court and the person of the emperor as he appears in Ammianus Marcellinus' *Res Gestae*. Although Ammianus wants his emperor to be awesomely transcendent of the world, he is concerned about the autocratic excess which the grand Constantius II displays. This concern causes the old discourse of tyrannical effeminacy to attach to Constantius, while, in contrast, emperor Julian's civility is praised as moral *and* faulted for not being grand enough. Ammianus is also conflicted about same-sex sexual attractiveness. It emerges as a positive attribute of Julian, while Constantius is slandered as effeminate and passive in his sexual desires. This conflict also plays out in Ammianus' depiction of the transcendent: he both wants it grandly different from this world (as embodied by Constantius II) and, yet, responsive to this world and looking rather Athanasian.

THREE

Ammianus' Emperors

INTRODUCTION

The emperors had a pervasive presence in late-Roman society. Triumphal arches commemorating their victories are found all over the empire; the Codex Calendar of 354 is replete with dates dedicated to anniversaries associated with various imperial houses[1]; board games[2] and even molds for cakes[3] speak of imperial victories; coins hardly need be mentioned. A personage of awesome power, the emperor's will was an ultimate source of physical benefit or torment.[4] Coexisting with this physical presence, however, was a claim to transcendence of the world. Emperors throughout the history of the empire had claimed association with the divine to varying degrees, and pagan emperors had often been deified upon their demise.[5]

---

1. Rees 2002: 18.
2. McCormick 1986: 34.
3. McCormick 1986: 32–33.
4. See Valensi (1957: 84–86) for both an economical description of various late-ancient imperial abilities/powers and arguments for the exemplarity of Constantius II (a major figure in this chapter) in this regard.
5. MacCormack (1981: 170) notes, for example, that Maximian (286–305 C.E.) and Diocletian (284–305 C.E.) associated themselves with Hercules and Jove respectively, while Constantine (307–337 C.E.) chose Helios/Apollo (1981: 36). Indeed, Diocletian was known as "the/an evident and present Jove" (*conspicuus et praesens Iuppiter*) while he was still alive (MacCormack 1981: 107). With the coming of Christian emperors, the scene grows considerably more complicated, but it is still the case that they claim association with the divine. The divinization of the emperor and/or the associa-

While Christian emperors would not claim divine honors in the way pagan emperors had, in the legal *corpora* they were assiduous about claiming an association with things divine for themselves. The board of men tasked by Theodosius II edited the utterances of various emperors with the goal of revealing these utterances' "sacred generality" (*CTh.* 1.1.5: *sacra generalitas*). It was an emperor's *manus divina*[6] which authored *epistulae* and other documents presented in a proprietary script: the "heavenly letters" (*caelestes litterae*).[7] Though they were Christian, emperors in the *Codex* speak of godhead (*numen*) as a term of self reference.[8] In sum, the emperor in late antiquity hyperbolically exemplified the recourse to the transcendent to secure *auctoritas* or ἀξίωμα.

All the same, even as he constituted an utter zenith, the emperor shared characteristics with other elite men in the late empire. The exemplary Antony and the *clarissimi, spectabiles,* and *illustres,* to take some examples, likewise had ambitions to transcendence. The emperor also was to have mastery of *paideia,* and "rustic" military emperors' pretensions to learning and the provision of education to their sons show they understood its value.[9] Emperors also had to function within the homosocial contexts of late-Roman manhood. There was an expectation that the emperor would consent to be bound by laws and display *civilitas*. As has already been seen, the emperor employed amatory language when addressing subordinates to show regard and ameliorate hierarchy's asperity. And his own glamour, in

---

tion of him with the divine are widely discussed in primary and secondary literature. In an analysis of evidence that stretches back into the Republic, Alföldi (1980/1935: *passim,* but 25–74, 213–57) provides a history of the treatment of the emperor as though he were divine in the centuries prior to late antiquity (with occasional discussion of late antiquity too) (cf. Nock 1930, 1947, 1957). For late antiquity, see Corcoran 1996: 63–69 (esp. 63–65); Dvornik 1955: 72; Kelly 1998a, 1998b: 138–45; 2004: 232–45; Matthews 1989: 243–49; Valensi 1957: 74–79, 87–88.

    6. In the *Gesta Senatus* [439 C.E.], *Novellae Valentini* (1.3 [450 C.E.], 9 [440 C.E.], 16 [445 C.E.], 17 [445 C.E.], 19 [445 C.E.]); see Matthews 2000a: 51; Vessey 2003: 356.

    7. In *CTh.* 9.19.3 (originally from 367 C.E.), Valentinian I and Valens tell the proconsul Festus to cease using the *caelestes litterae* in his pronouncements. These letters are to be employed only by "the bureaux of our everlastingness" (*scrinia nostrae perennitatis*) (see Kelly 2004: 31; Matthews 2000a: 188). The actual pronouncements themselves were also worthy of worship. A rescript of Constantine from 340 was described as "a law divine and worthy to be bowed down before" (θεῖον καὶ προσκυνητὸν νόμον) (Corcoran 1996: 49, cf. 176, 184, 186). For more on this effect of imperial pronouncements in hard copy, as it were, see Vessey 2003: 347; Matthews 2000a: 181–82; Kelly 1998b: 143.

    8. For *numen* in the *Codex,* see, e.g., 1.2.12 [413 C.E.], 1.9.2 [386 C.E.], 2.23.1 [423 C.E.], 2.33.4 [405 C.E.], 5.12.3 [434 C.E.], 6.4.29 [396 C.E.], 6.4.32 [397 C.E.], 6.14.3 [413 C.E.], 6.23.3 [432 C.E.], 6.30.15 [399 C.E.], 7.7.4 [415 C.E.], 7.8.3 [384 C.E.], 8.1.13 [382 C.E.], 8.5.40 [382 C.E.], 8.5.62 [401 C.E.], 9.40.11 [360s C.E.], 10.26.1 [426 C.E.], 11.1.33 [424 C.E.], 11.21.3 [424 C.E.], 11.28.15 [434 C.E.], 11.30.49 [389 C.E.], 12.12.7 [380 C.E.], 15.4.1 [425 C.E.], 15.5.5 [425 C.E.], 16.4.4 [404 C.E.], 16.8.13 [397 C.E.].

    9. E.g., Valentinian I and Valens (Lenski 2002: 95).

140 · CHAPTER THREE

turn, could be metaphorized as same-sex sexual attractiveness. Indeed, the emperor's place at the apex of power made for an at times piquant relation with same-sex desire; the more forbidding and absolute the emperor was thought to be, the more vulnerable he was to discourse critical of tyrants, a feature of which was the attribution of effeminacy and enjoyment of passive same-sex sexual pleasure; admiring amatory metaphor could metamorphose into invasive and garishly sexualizing invective.

The frequent touchstone in this chapter dedicated to investigating the connections between same-sex desire, homosociality, and the making of imperial authority will be Ammianus Marcellinus' *Res Gestae*. The focus of this late fourth-century work of historiography on the emperors Constantius II, Julian, Jovian, Valentinian I, Valens, and Gratian, as well as on *caesar* Gallus, and Ammianus' manifest sensitivity to their place *vis-à-vis* Roman society make his narrative an obvious main-player in an investigation into ideas about late-Roman emperors. The famous scene of arrival or *adventus* of Constantius II to Rome in 357 in book 16 is considered first. This passage from the *Res Gestae* has assumed iconic status as the *locus classicus* to be canvassed if discussion of the fourth-century emperors is undertaken. In this scene, Ammianus recreates (and thereby endorses) the glamour of the emperor as transcendent of this world. Next follows discussion of a passage from book 15 in which Ammianus presents Constantius being flattered, signing his letters with the words "My Eternity," and then having the temerity, in Ammianus' opinion, to claim that he was equivalent to one of the "civil" emperors of the second-century C.E. Dismissing Constantius' self-styling as a civil emperor and focusing on his absolute claims, Ammianus finds that Constantius goes too far in his assertion of transcendence when he signs his letters with this subscription. Ammianus' depiction of Constantius' behavior is compared throughout to his representation of Julian and to late-Roman society in general. It turns out that Constantius' claim to eternity is typical imperial behavior and that Ammianus' criticism is out of the mainstream. Ammianus' view, however, is nonetheless informative in spite of its minority status: the conclusion to which Ammianus leads the reader shows an end-point to thinking oneself beyond captation by earthbound systems of morality, and it also serves a purpose within the *Res Gestae* of putting the moral virtues of his hero, Julian, into relief.[10] As has been recognized over the years with dismay at times, the

---

10. The following works were helpful for comments (here and later) on the dynamic of Ammianus' complementary shaping of Constantius and Julian: Neri 1984 (most of all); Kelly 2005; Barnes 1998: 17–18, 132–38, 143–55; Matthews 1989: 33–39, 231–52; Roberts 1988; de Bonfils 1986: 86–89; Sabbah 1978: 437–39, 442–45; Camus 1967: 110–15, 239–46; Tassi 1967; Thompson 1947: 72–86.

contrasting portraits bear the marks of Ammianus' special interest in praising his hero Julian; Constantius comes off badly so Julian can look good, and it is surely the case that the interests of History are not served.[11] For present purposes, however, Ammianus' prejudice is not an impediment but provides, instead, an opportunity.

Imperial authority's complex relation to homosociality is in the interstices of this moralizing comparison of emperors. The imperial *personae* are radically different: Constantius' is remote, otherworldly, while Julian's is more approachable. Constantius jealously insists on hierarchal distinctions and does not wish to break them down amid warm homosociality of the kind Julian favors. In Ammianus' opinion, Constantius' behavior is an appropriate aspect of imperial deportment, and Julian would have done well to remember it. However, as Ammianus also asserts, Constantius is thoughtless of the people over whom he towers. He lacks *civilitas,* or a concern to remember that he is an emperor of men. There is obvious tension in Ammianus' thought. The glamour emanating from association with the transcendent is desirable, but it also is praiseworthy to consider the society of other men and achieve accreditation through interaction with them. Ammianus wants otherworldly and transcendent glamour for his emperor (Constantius), while at the same time (and with contradiction) wanting the transcendent filled with civility, the provenance of which is earth: coming down from the heavens after starting on earth, civility graces Julian. Similar to Athanasius, Ammianus wants to fill the transcendent with earthly morals.

There is similar complexity in Ammianus' use of and attitude toward same-sex desire and attractiveness in the *Res Gestae*. On the one hand, and recalling the glamorization of Marcus Aurelius by Julian himself, he metaphorizes the glamour of his civil paradigm, Julian, as a *venustas* that attracts the eyes of the soldiers. On the other hand, and similar to the writers of *Collatio* 5.3 and Athanasius, he is the knowing authority who can see through the manly transcendence of his grand emperor to a shameful covert relation to sexual passivity. Close examination of the language Ammianus uses to describe Constantius reveals the presence of a subtle discourse that attributes obscene desire to him.

Before proceeding to the argument, it is time to speak in general about the appropriateness of using Ammianus' text in this study. In the first place, the broad learning on display in the *Res Gestae* strongly suggests its

---

11. See Barnes (1998: 11–19) for discussion of how Ammianus shapes his account in ways that a documentary historian wouldn't (cf., e.g., Blockley 1975: 100; Thompson 1947: 48).

relevance.¹² The *Res Gestae* was clearly meant for the elite culture of late antiquity that valued *paideia* and the performative excellence it bestowed on men who mastered it. Positing knowledgeable and engaged contemporary reception is eminently reasonable. Also, as is likely, the *Res Gestae* would have been revealed to the world in recitations (*recitationes*)¹³ in Rome (where Ammianus lived in the 380s and 390s). While hard proof is not available, it seems this work was part of the intellectual scene in Rome at about the same time the *epistula* that is *Collatio* 5.3 was issued.¹⁴ It is intriguing that the forceful and knowing rejection of passive male sexual desire and pleasure that is part of the performative effect of *Collatio* 5.3 is contemporary with Ammianus' imputation of this desire to Constantius II. It also is of interest that Theodosius I, one the signing emperors of *Collatio* 5.3, had his own *adventus* to Rome in 389.¹⁵ Ammianus' historiography was therefore part of an intensely educated and homosocial milieu in which legislation concerning same-sex desire was written. The coming investigation, premised on the near certainty of the text's educated reception and putting issues of homosociality and same-sex desire front and center, is consonant with likely societal dynamics in play at the place and time of the first hearing and reading of the *Res Gestae*.

ADVENTUS

In the year 357, Constantius II made a ceremonial arrival, or *adventus*, to Rome. In Ammianus' depiction of it, Constantius is grand and impassive as he makes his splendid entrance into the eternal city.¹⁶ Ammianus

---

12. For Ammianus' broad learning, see now Kelly 2008: *passim*, but esp. 161–221. See also, e.g., Blockley 1996; Fornara 1992; Rosen 1982: 92–98; Sabbah 1978: *passim*, but 65–111; Camus 1967: 33–47, 61–73; Fletcher 1937.

13. Frakes 2000; Blockley 1996: 458; Thompson 1947: 17.

14. Frakes (2000) persuasively suggests that the audience for the *Res Gestae* was first and foremost elites who served in the imperial government. Some of them, at least, would have heard this work in *recitationes* in Rome. There is no need, of course, to manufacture a circle presided over by Symmachus, which Alan Cameron cautioned against in 1964 (cf. Kelly 2008: 110).

15. Valerio Neri (1984: 54) and Guy Sabbah (1978: 329–32) see Ammianus' written *adventus* of Constantius possibly making a comment on this *adventus* of Theodosius I. From here, then, a plausible contemporary reception of the *Res Gestae* will associate the entire portrait of Constantius with Theodosius for differences *and* similarities. It has occasionally been suggested that Theodosius himself could have heard sections of the *Res Gestae* in its probable *recitationes* (see discussion with bibliography in Frakes 2000: 397–98).

16. As noted above, this is a *locus classicus*. See, e.g., the following discussions: Kelly 1998b: 142–43; Matthews 1989: 231–35; Roberts 1988; McCormick 1986: 84–91; Neri 1984: 45–60; MacCormack 1981: 39–45; MacMullen 1964 (=1990: 78–106, esp. 85–90). For discussion of the imperial *adventus* ceremony in general, see Kolb 2001: 44–46, 121–23; MacCormack 1981: 17–61.

renders the scene's grandeur and thereby gives his approval to at least this action of Constantius. He does carp a little around the edges, complaining, for example, that this *adventus,* practically a triumph, lacked a compelling victory for an occasion, and, instead, was put on because Constantius wanted to display his troops (16.10.2). And later, when Constantius has ambitions to leave a magnificent memorial of himself in Rome, he is overawed by the Forum of Trajan, and has to scale back his ambitions. At first, he thinks to make a copy of Trajan's horse (16.10.15). He abandons that plan, however, and settles for the erection of an obelisk in the Circus Maximus (16.10.17). These relatively modest plans do cut Constantius down to size. Still, Ammianus' lavish treatment of his appearance as he makes his way into the city indicates that the historiographer thinks that display of otherworldly grandeur is essential for an emperor, though asserting this bucks a trend in the scholarly literature that sees Ammianus predominantly critical of Constantius.[17] Be that as it may, this impression of Ammianus' approval is strengthened later when he criticizes Julian for being too informal. It is also good to remember that the *adventus* possessed such a feeling of divine epiphany that Victricius could trope the arrival of relics to Rotomagus as an imperial arrival.[18]

The inhabitants of Rome line the path the procession is taking. When the emperor appears in the procession, he is surrounded by purple woven dragons attached to golden jeweled spears and these dragons, with the wind coursing through them, hiss, seeming to seethe in anger (16.10.7: *velut ira perciti sibilantes*). On either side of the emperor march two columns of warriors with occasional armored horsemen, whose mail-armor was form-fitting to such an extent that the observer would think them statues polished by the hand of the famous sculptor Praxiteles (16.10.8: *ut Praxitelis manu polita crederes simulacra*). Ammianus then shifts attention from the inanimate, and yet oddly animate, dragons hissing and soldiers marching to statue-like horsemen and, thence, to the heart of the matter, the emperor:

> The *augustus*, named in auspicious cheers, did not shrink from the thundering roar of the hills and banks, showing himself as, and as immobile

---

17. Much of the secondary literature prefers to focus on the ways in which Ammianus undercuts the impression Constantius makes in his *adventus*. See, e.g., Roberts 1988: 184; Neri 1984: 53; Rosen 1982: 40. I see the point, but prefer to see Ammianus, conflicted, preserving the emperor's glamour (e.g., Kelly 1998b: 142–43; McCormick 1986: 84–91; MacCormack 1981: 39–45; MacMullen 1964 [=1990: 78–106, esp. 85–90]), even as he has some criticisms to make.

18. Victric. 3 (pp. 379–80 in G. Clark 1999); Brown 1981: 98–101; Miller 2005b: 49 and 2005c: 29–30; Hunter 1999: 424. See too Kelly's discussion (1998a) of a variety of late-ancient sources in which God and the heavenly host are metaphors for the emperor and his administration, and vice-versa.

as he was usually seen in his provinces. He even bent his quite short body as he was making his way under the high gates. Holding his line of sight straight, as though his neck were chained, he did not turn his face either right or left. As though a statue of a man, he was never seen nodding when a wheel jolted, neither spitting nor rubbing his face, nor scratching his nose, nor moving a hand. Although he was affecting all these things, they, and other things in his life hidden from view, were proof of a not middling forbearance belonging to him alone, as was generally thought. (16.10.9–11)[19]

The performance that is the emperor is placed before the eyes in Ammianus' virtuosic writing. This representation of the icon-like emperor who seems almost inhuman when on display goes all the way back to Xenophon's *Cyropaedia* (8.1.40–42)[20] and also seems a reasonable portrayal when such *realia* as the Arch of Constantine are considered. Surrounded in the first instance by his soldiery and attendant pageantry and, in the second, by all of Rome in an uproar (for the crowd is calling out his name[21]), Constantius is the nearly still, and impassive in any case, eye of a hurricane of movement and sound. It is as though he were more a divine epiphany than a human being. The enlivening of the material (the woven dragons seem alive) and iconization of the alive (the emperor seems a statue) are suggestive of the interpenetration of this world with the next, and both can be seen as allegories of the late-Platonic notion of the enlivening power of the transcendent suffusing this world. There is more than a little here that recalls Plotinus' metaphorization of the emanation of the transcendent into the world as an imperial *adventus* (*Enneads* 5.5.3.1–15; discussed in chapter one).

In spite of occasional critique accompanying the passage, Ammianus in general approves of this grandeur. Ammianus' summation of the good

---

19. Augustus itaque faustis vocibus appellatus non montium litorumque intonante fragore cohorruit talem se tamque immobilem, qualis in provinciis suis visebatur, ostendens. nam et corpus perhumile curvabat portas ingrediens celsas et velut collo munito rectam aciem luminum tendens nec dextra vultum nec laeva flectebat tamquam figmentum hominis nec, cum rota concuteret, nutans nec spuens aut os aut nasum tergens vel fricans manumve agitans visus est umquam. quae licet affectabat, erant tamen haec et alia quaedam in citeriore vita patientiae non mediocris indicia, ut existimari dabatur, uni illi concessae.

(Note: Although I wished to signal the endings of Ammianus' *clausulae* by means of spaces, I decided that the difficulties in doing so were too great to justify the effort, especially as argument does not turn to them specifically.)

20. See Charlesworth (1947) and Matthews (1989: 233) for discussion.

21. As both de Jonge (1972b: 120) and Matthews (1989: 234) underscore, citing depiction of another *adventus* in Claudian (6H 616–17): "A single echo on the seven citadels [of Rome] thunders 'Augustus'" (unaque totis / intonat Augustum septenis arcibus echo).

and bad qualities of Constantius on the occasion of his death confirms it. He praises Constantius' ability to embody the grandeur appropriate to an emperor:

> Therefore, with distinction between his [*sc.* Constantius'] good qualities and faults truly preserved, it will suit that his special virtues be enumerated first. Always making the haughty glory of imperial power (*imperatoriae auctoritatis coturnum*) his concern, he, with a lofty and great spirit, counted at nothing the favor of the people. He was exceedingly frugal in the matter of conferring the higher dignities, having allowed no innovations (with a couple of exceptions) as far as adding to the bureaucracies was concerned, and never raising up the horns of the military men. (21.16.1)[22]

Chary with promotions and innovation, Constantius never allowed the impression of his loftiness to be compromised. Constantius (and Ammianus) had an understanding that imperial *auctoritas* had to be complected properly; it needed to be staged.[23] Hence, the word *coturnus,* translated here by the phrase "haughty glory" (for which, see *TLL* 4.1088.43–45), refers first and foremost to the boot (*kothornos*/κόθορνος) worn by actors in tragedies (*TLL* 4.1087.26–1088.6). It shows up elsewhere in the *Res Gestae* where it designates someone acting in an outsized manner. For example, *coturnus* appears in Ammianus' unflattering description of Probus, praetorian prefect at Rome in 368 (and evidently a blowhard):

> When he felt confident, he rumbled *from atop the tragic boot* (*de coturno . . . tragico*), but when he was afraid, he was lower than the slipper the comic actors wear. (27.11.2)[24]

There are other instances of this word[25] (and an adjective and adverb derived from it[26]) that all refer to the exaggerated emotions of the stage. *Coturnus* could be regarded as part of Ammianus' criticism of the emperor, but that would be a mistake. The emperor, for all his faults, did occupy the apex of power and therefore had the position to back up dramatic entrances

---

22. Bonorum igitur vitiorumque eius differentia vere servata praecipua prima conveniet expediri. imperatoriae auctoritatis coturnum ubique custodiens popularitatem elato animo contemnebat et magno erga tribuendas celsiores dignitates impendio parcus nihil circa administrationum augmenta praeter pauca novari perpessus numquam erigens cornua militarium.
23. Valensi 1957: 86–87.
24. cum sibi fideret, de coturno strepere tragico et, ubi paveret, omni humilior socco.
25. 20.1.2, 28.6.29.
26. 28.1.4, 28.4.27.

and reactions (and non-reactions, say, in an *adventus*). Indeed, Julian, who is Ammianus' ideal most of the time, receives a rare moment of criticism from the historiographer on this score:

> Amidst these events, he spent much time in the senate in order to settle various matters, which cleverly resourceful factions were bringing to his attention. One day, as he was observing cases there [in the senate], when it had been announced to him that the philosopher Maximus had come from Asia, he leapt up in an unseemly manner, and having forgotten who he was, and having, at a full run, made his way far from the forecourt, he led him (Maximus), thoroughly kissed and reverently received, in with himself. He appeared, through this inappropriate performance to be an overzealous pursuer of empty glory and unmindful of that quite famous saying, criticizing such ones, of Cicero, which goes like this: "Those same philosophers write their own names in the very books which they write on the necessity of despising glory. The result of this is that in the very moment in which they despise renown and rank, they wish to be talked about and to be named."[27] (22.7.3–4)[28]

Ostentatiously rushing out to greet an inferior, Julian, the emperor, adds nothing to his stature because there is no way to increase it. He is already the greatest. What need could showing obvious favor to an inferior meet? Indeed this gesture can only diminish the emperor, pull him down to earth. In Ammianus' opinion, an emperor should not look to develop relations with others like this as he has no peers among his subjects.

Ammianus is critical of similar behavior on two other occasions. At one point in 362 in Constantinople, Julian attended, on foot (and not riding, as Ammianus clearly believes he should have been doing), a ceremony honoring the consuls Mamertinus and Nevitta. This was thought by some to be cheap affectation (22.7.1: *affectatum et vile*), and on another occasion he fined himself ten pounds of gold for speaking out of turn at a ceremonial freeing of slaves at the circus (22.7.2). While Ammianus does not put down

---

27. den Boeft et al. (1995: 77) point out that words close to these are found in Cicero at *Tusc.* 1.34 and *Arch.* 26.

28. Frequentabat inter haec curiam agendo diversa, quae divisiones multiplices ingerebant. et cum die quodam ei causas ibi spectanti venisse nuntiatus esset ex Asia philosophus Maximus, exsiluit indecore et, qui esset, oblitus effuso cursu a vestibulo longe progressus exosculatum susceptumque reverenter secum induxit per ostentationem intempestivam, nimius captator inanis gloriae visus praeclarique illius dicti immemor Tulliani, quo tales notando ita relatum: "ipsi illi philosophi etiam in his libris, quos de contemnenda gloria scribunt, nomen suum scribunt, ut in eo ipso, quo praedicationem nobilitatemque despiciunt, praedicari de se ac se nominari velint."

his, or anyone else's, reaction to this self-fining, it is fair to conclude that he found this affectation too, especially in light of the following comments from the summation of Julian's life in book 25:

> Pleased by the applause of the common people, he was an excessive pursuer of praise for the smallest things, through desire for popular favor often affecting to speak with unworthy persons. (25.4.18)[29]

An abiding sin of Julian was that he did not keep the throne as grand as it should have been: rushing to Maximus at a full run (*effuso cursu*); Maximus not just kissed, *thoroughly* kissed (ex*osculatum*). As John Matthews puts it, Ammianus' view was that "an emperor ought in his public appearances to set a certain standard of dignified behavior, to do otherwise being a perverse ostentation" (1989: 236[30]). In contrast, Valerio Neri sees in these refusals of imperial protocol evidence of Julian's *civilitas* (1984: 52) and Guy Sabbah judges them manifestations of his lively humanity and free will (1978: 444). These latter points are true in a way, but the first point predominates. Ammianus criticizes Julian for not understanding that he, as emperor, needed to be seen as awe-inspiring. Ammianus notes that both Julian and Constantius in their own ways were engaging in affectation (22.7.1, 25.4.18 [Julian] and 16.10.11 [Constantius], all discussed above), but only approves of it in the case of the latter, and it is because of the need for an emperor to be grand.

But even as he reproduces and at times endorses the effect Constantius aimed at and no doubt made, Ammianus nonetheless resists the spell. Praise and blame so far have been allotted on the bases of one emperor making himself appropriately grand and beyond regular men and the other for being too down to earth. Now it is time for the reverse. Showing ambivalence about the office and ambitions of the emperor, Ammianus elsewhere reprehends Constantius' reach beyond this world.

IMPERIAL SIGNATURE

In book fifteen, Ammianus depicts the situation in Constantius' court after he hears the news of the "fall" of *caesar* Gallus. The year is 355. Gallus was a cousin (and Julian's half-brother) whom Constantius had been groom-

---

29. Volgi plausibus laetus, laudum etiam ex minimis rebus intemperans appetitor, popularitatis cupiditate cum indignis loqui saepe affectans.
30. Cf. Kolb 2001: 20, 135; Smith 1995: 44; Blockley 1975: 77–78; Thompson 1947: 79–83.

ing to become *augustus*. He turned out to be unsatisfactory as a sharer in the rule. Constantius became suspicious of him and, stripped of office, he was executed. Prone to giving flattery, Constantius' ministers attribute this welcome event to the emperor's manly excellence/bravery/virtue (*virtus*) and good fortune, exalting both of them to heaven.[31] And so, according to Ammianus, in a fever brought on by his sudden freedom from the threat Gallus posed, Constantius takes the manipulative words of his ministers to heart and sees himself in the proffered panegyrical terms. He claims to be beyond this world, assigning to himself in subscription the appellation, "My Eternity":

> Raised up by the well-wrought zeal of [his ministers'] flattery and confidently supposing that he would be untouchable by every discomfort of mortality, he forthwith swerved from justice (*a iustitia declinavit*) so rashly that during dictation he sometimes would sign "My Eternity" below, and, while writing in his own hand, he would often call himself master of the entire world. If others were saying this, he surely would have had to have taken it badly—he who labored, with all due diligence expended, to model his life and *mores* in emulation of the emperors who valued civility (*civilium principum*), as he kept on declaring. For even if he were ruling Democritus' infinity of worlds, of which Alexander the Great dreamed with Anaxarchus' encouragement, yet reading or listening he should have reflected upon the fact that, as the astronomers in universal agreement teach, the circuit of the entire earth, which seems immeasurable to us, next to the greatness of the universe has the image of a tiny point. (15.1.3–4)[32]

As one of his abiding sins is susceptibility to flattery (according to Ammianus), Constantius believes the unrelievedly affirming words of his advisors and comes to think himself untouchable. Thereupon behaving "unjustly" (literally "swerving from Justice," which, as will be seen, indicates a lack of civility [*civilitas*]), he signs his correspondence with the title "My Eternity"

---

31. 15.1.2: virtutem felicitatemque imperatoris extollebant in caelum.

32. quo ille studio blanditiarum exquisito sublatus immunemque se deinde fore ab omni mortalitatis incommodo fidenter existimans confestim a iustitia declinavit ita intemperanter, ut "Aeternitatem meam" aliquotiens subsereret ipse dictando scribendoque propria manu orbis totius se dominum appellaret; quod dicentibus aliis indignanter admodum ferre deberet is, qui ad aemulationem civilium principum formare vitam moresque suos, ut praedicabat, diligentia laborabat enixa. namque etiam si mundorum infinitates Democriti regeret, quos Anaxarcho incitante Magnus somniabat Alexander, id reputasset legens vel audiens, quod, ut docent mathematici concinentes, ambitus terrae totius, quae nobis videtur immensa, ad magnitudinem universitatis instar brevis obtinet puncti.

and calls himself master of the entire world. Attracting Ammianus' particular disapproval is the claim to transcendence that Constantius makes, and that his ministers also make, as they exalt the emperor's manly excellence or *virtus* to heaven.

This claim to transcendence is false in a number of ways: the emperor is mortal; the world of which he falsely claims mastery (the Sassanid empire exists), and of which he is inescapably a part, is material and subject to decay. Ammianus also finds unpersuasive Constantius' evidently oft-repeated claim that he was like one of the good/civil emperors, i.e., Nerva, Trajan, Hadrian, Antoninus Pius, or Marcus Aurelius. This passage benefits from exegesis that, taking its cue from the passage itself, considers the dichotomization of eternity (*aeternitas*) to civility (*civilitas*) both in the *Res Gestae* and outside of it.[33] This investigation reveals that Constantius, though more than capable of a good show, does not succeed to his claimed transcendence, and this failure is the result of his lack of *civilitas:* for Ammianus, devotion to *civilitas* and *iustitia* bring about a desirable and true transcendence, as his hero Julian demonstrates. Ammianus has also placed in the interstices of his depiction of the uncivil Constantius details that suggest an interest in masculine same-sex sexual passivity. The ease with which he crafts his portrait along these scandalous lines and its ready legibility to an educated readership (in the present moment and at the time of the writing of the *Res Gestae*) suggest that an emperor who removes himself from association with other men and has uncanny connection with things beyond this world is uniquely susceptible to such a hostile reading precisely because he is embracing things that are beyond this world. As practiced by Ammianus' Constantius, transcendence is recourse to things beyond morals and it compromises his identity as a *vir.* Rejecting homosociality leavened with civility, Constantius comes to seem a sexualized passive man instead. Rejecting civility, the tyrant is prey to desire.

AETERNITAS IN THE *RES GESTAE* AND BEYOND

In addition to being a self-chosen title for Constantius, the noun *aeternitas* appears on two other occasions in the *Res Gestae*. At 14.6.8, in a digression

---

33. *Civilitas* of course does not appear in this passage. Present instead is the adjective derived from it, *civilis*. For ease of discussion the noun is used, and it does, in any case, appear elsewhere in the *Res Gestae* (25.4.7, 28.4.17, 30.4.3), as does its antonym, *incivilitas* (18.2.7, 29.5.6). Matthews (1989: 235–36) and Neri (1984: 3–34, but, esp., 12, 24–27 and n. 52 on pp. 24–25) were helpful in formulating comments on Constantius' failed claim to *civilitas*.

on the city of Rome, Ammianus remarks that the rich Romans make statues of themselves in the belief that they can secure immortality in this way:

> Of these some, thinking that they can be recommended to eternity (*aeternitati*) by means of statues, strongly desire them as though they would acquire more benefit from bronze images that lack all feeling than from the knowledge of deeds done honestly and morally. (14.6.8)[34]

Having these statues made is similar to Constantius' subscription since these men claim eternity for themselves too. Ammianus also prefigures the distinction he makes in the passage about the signature: these men think only of eternity and not of moral deeds. Their failing is similar to the one with which Ammianus charges Constantius when he refuses to credit his claim to be similar to the civil emperors. A short time later in the *Res Gestae*, the daughter of Justice, the goddess of just-vengeance (more or less), Nemesis or Adrastia, who oversees mortal affairs "from a certain hidden *eternity*" (14.11.25: *ex abdita quadam* aeternitate), brings an end to both the tyrannical Gallus and those who, although Gallus needed to be stopped, used underhanded methods to bring him down. Ammianus anticipates Constantius' self-styling to come in the next book and lays the groundwork for its skeptical reception; justice comes from a hidden eternity and not from a visible emperor claiming to be an eternity.

The adjective *aeternus* is a word often used in the *Res Gestae* (appearing 22 times). Fifteen of these references are to Rome, calling it "the eternal city" (*urbs aeterna*), which is an exceedingly common name for Rome.[35] Ammianus uses the word twice to describe the fires of the sun as eternal[36] and once to portray the shadows in the Underworld as likewise everlasting.[37] *Aeternus* also appears in the periphrasis *in aeternum*, which means, more or less, "eternally," and Ammianus uses this phrase to designate the way in which the magnificent Capitoline hill through its temple makes Rome eternally venerable.[38] Conquered by Caesar so long ago, Gaul is joined to Rome "by means of an eternal treaty."[39] "Manly Excellence/Bravery/

---

34. ex his quidam aeternitati se commendari posse per statuas aestimantes eas ardenter affectant quasi plus praemii de figmentis aereis sensu carentibus adepturi quam ex conscientia honeste recteque factorum.

35. 14.6.1, 15.7.1, 15.7.10, 16.10.14, 19.10.1, 21.12.24, 22.9.3, 23.1.4, 23.3.3, 25.10.5, 26.3.1, 28.1.1, 28.1.36, 28.1.56, 29.6.17.

36. 20.3.6, 25.10.3.

37. 17.7.13.

38. 22.16.12.

39. 15.12.6: foederibus . . . aeternis.

Virtue and Fortune came together in a treaty of *eternal* peace" (14.6.3: *foedere pacis* aeternae *Virtus convenit atque Fortuna*) and enabled magnificent Rome to conquer nearly the whole world.

If the ways Ammianus uses *aeternitas* and *aeternus* are considered closely, it will be seen that he uses them, naturally enough, to describe divinity and entities that last beyond the span of an individual human life and don't suffer the effects of time. As regards emperors in general and Constantius in particular, the infinity and freedom from limit that are the marks of eternity are things that Ammianus is reluctant to grant them, while, at the same time, he wants emperors to be grand. Indeed, the association between Rome and eternity, which is found everywhere in writings from late antiquity—Rome is the eternal city, after all—, makes this maneuver of the emperor an effort to secure the glamour of Rome for himself. Of course, Ammianus is more than happy to recognize that there is a special relationship between the emperors and Rome, as is seen here in his depiction of eternal Rome in its old age putting itself into the caretaking hands of the emperors:

> Therefore, the venerable city, as though a thrifty, careful and wealthy parent, afterwards entrusted the proud necks of the savage nations that had been crushed and the laws, the foundations and eternal halters of freedom that had been set in place, [these] she entrusted to the *caesares,* as though these things were the terms of an inheritance to be managed. (14.6.5)[40]

At this point in its life, which implies that the eternal city is less than eternal—but no matter that—Rome, as the venerable parent, is in the custodianship of the emperors. The emperors are but the current authorities and the thing eternal, according to Ammianus, is Rome. But Ammianus' skepticism of imperial eternity is not the only view taken of it. In other sources, emperors (and other men) frequently claim eternity. Although Ammianus disapproves, the hyperbolic self-styling evident in the self-appellation of "My Eternity" is something seen often in other sources.

On a plaque at the base of an equestrian statue of Constantius II, perhaps dedicated at the time of his visit to Rome in 357, there is an inscription of thanksgiving to the emperor for putting down the usurpation of Magnentius in 352. He is "restorer of the city of Rome and the world and extinguisher of the pestiferous tyranny, Our Lord Flavius Julius Constan-

---

40. ideo urbs venerabilis post superbas efferatarum gentium cervices oppressas latasque leges fundamenta libertatis et retinacula sempiterna velut frugi parens et prudens et dives Caesaribus tamquam liberis suis regenda patrimonii iura permisit.

tius, Victor and Triumphator, *perpetual* (semper) *augustus*."[41] He has always been *augustus* and always will be, and Constantius' subscribing hand is not alone in saying that he is unbounded in time. Indeed, in spite of what Ammianus says, the claim of *Mea Aeternitas* was not merely something that emerged from a fog of flattery-induced bad judgment on Constantius' part. In the *Codex Theodosianus,* for example, other emperors claim eternity as an imperial attribute, and are also liable to insist that their judgments have force that will/should never lose potency.

"We affirm the dignity of the equestrian order bestowed upon you by the divine Constantine and Julian, the Eternal emperors. . . ."[42] With these words whose original version dates from 380 (this of course is the *sacra generalitas* that Theodosius' board crafted to come into effect in 439), in legislation meant to benefit this class of Roman society, the emperors Gratian, Valentinian II, and Theodosius I associate their predecessors Constantine and Julian with eternity. From 390, the addressee in the law "will be revering the eternity" of the three emperors then ruling.[43] The brother emperors, Arcadius and Honorius, speak of their deceased father, Theodosius I, on his birthday as the/an "eternal emperor" (*CTh.* 6.4.30: *aeterni principis* [probably originally from 396]) and Arcadius, a few year later in 398, refers to himself as *Mea Aeternitas*.[44] A little further along in time, the year 408 sees three emperors making reference to the way in which their predecessor (and father/grandfather) in death "has now changed his human eternity into a celestial one."[45] Also, emperors did not only call themselves and their co-emperors eternal (or welcome this appellation coming from others), they often figured their actions as having eternal force. Eternity and

---

41. *ILS* 731; *CIL* 6.1158: Restitvtori vrbis Romae a<d>qve or[bis] et extinctor(i) [p]estiferae tyrannidis Fl(avio) Ivl(io) Constanti[o] victori [ac] trivm<f>atori semper Avgvsto . . . ; see McCormick 1986: 40. It is worth noting that Ammianus has Constantius claiming eternity elsewhere in the terms seen on this plaque. In book 17, Constantius begins a letter to Sapor, king of the Parthians, in this way: "I, Constantius, victor on land and sea, *perpetual* Augustus, do heartily greet my brother, king Sapor . . . " (17.5.10) ("Victor terra marique Constantius *semper* Augustus fratri meo Sapori regi salutem plurimam dico . . . ").

42. *CTh.* 13.5.16: Delatam vobis a divo Constantino et Iuliano principibus aeternis equestris ordinis dignitatem nos firmamus. . . .

43. *CTh.* 10.22.3: adoraturus aeternitatem nostram; Valentinian II, Theodosius I, and Arcadius are the emperors in question. See MacCormack (1981:61) for more.

44. *CTh.* 12.1.160: " . . . in the fourth consulship of our master, the *augustus* Honorius, brother of My Eternity . . . (. . . cons[ulatu] d[omini] n[ostri] Hon[orii] Aug[us]ti fratris aeternitatis meae IIII . . .).

45. *CTh.* 5.16.31: . . . pater iam humanam in caelest<em a>eternitatem mutavit; Arcadius, Honorius, and Theodosius II are the signees and Theodosius I is the object of this reverence. See Matthews 1989: 235. For further examples of emperors associated with eternity, see the *Gesta Senatus* (four occurrences), *CTh.* 1.12.5, the first *novella* of Theodosius II, and the first *novella* of Valentinian III.

perpetuity also can be seen associated with the force of emperors' law in the *Codex*[46] and in the *novellae* of Theodosius II[47] and Valentinian III.[48] Ammianus is also at variance with evidence of previous centuries,[49] which needs no discussion in the present instance.

Ammianus' criticism of Constantius for calling himself *Aeternitas Mea* is taking him to task, then, for behavior in the mainstream of imperial behavior and exemplary of a developing situation. Be that as it may, this criticism of his claim is connected to Ammianus' rejection of Constantius' claim that he is one of the civil emperors. Having swerved from justice, the emperor is no longer civil, and this disallows the absolute claim. Canvassing *civilis* and *civilitas* in the *Res Gestae* reveals that Ammianus believes that an emperor could only be truly admirable, and not just properly awe-inspiring, if he were "civil." This, however, is a site of conflict in Ammianus' thought: as far as Ammianus is concerned, a claim to the absolute can only be underwritten by a commitment to civility and homosociality, both of which are non-absolute.

An eternity claimed with justice is one that is responsive to earthly standards of moral behavior and this is a contradiction in terms, for eternity, by definition, is transcendent of this world. As does Athanasius, Ammianus moralizes the transcendent, fills it with earthly morals. Also similar to Athanasius' depiction of Antony, the pressure of filling the transcendent with earthly morals leads to physical manifestations on earth. Earth is where mysteries are and faults emerge. Similar to what happens with Antony's body and other physical phenomena in *Vita Antonii* 5, e.g., the intimate itching, the wrestling match, or the dust storm, Constantius "swerves" like a most material atom, and the world over which he claims dominion is but a material point. Furthermore, amid the demonstration of incivility and materiality, Ammianus' language also reveals that Constantius vitiates his masculinity when he is not civil. Authority made in despite of homosociality causes scandalous same-sex desire, the desire to be penetrated, to emerge. When Constantius puts himself over and beyond other men, it is at this moment that a connection to passive male sexuality emerges at the fine lexical level in a way similar to what happens in the *Vita Antonii*. Furthermore, instead of Antony's tacit "no" to a material and scandal-

---

46. E.g., 4.22.2, 6.24.6, 8.4.23, 10.10.22, 10.20.11, 13.3.14, 13.10.8, 14.4.4, 14.5.1, 16.1.4, 16.2.47, 16.5.5, 16.10.20.

47. Nos. 5, 6, 7, 8, 9, 10, 11, 13, 15, 17, 19, 20, 21, 22, 26.

48. Nos. 2, 7, 16, 18, 21, 22, 23, 32, 35.

49. For eternity as an attribute claimed by emperors and elite men in previous centuries, see *TLL* 1.1139.45–1141.71, Alföldi (1980/1935: 208–209 [*aeternus*], 209 [*perpetuus*]), and Charlesworth (1936).

ous reality, a tacit "yes" to same-sex desire and pleasure is perceptible in Constantius.

NOT A CIVIL EMPEROR

Going all the way back to the earliest days of the Roman polity, *civilis* denotes behavior of rulers respectful of laws and limits on their power[50] and even graciously bound by a sense of identification with those over whom they have authority.[51] When the emperor claims to be *civilis,* he is portraying himself as having some manner of position within the polity and rejecting the notion that he towers over it.[52] Valerio Neri (1984: 33) suggests that the *genius publicus* which Julian saw when he was acclaimed emperor in the Gauls (20.5.10) is an instantiation of the Roman people and traditions who watch over him as he, with *civilitas,* watches over them. As he lay dying, Constantius said that a certain being which he could only see dimly (not Julian's being of clarity) no longer came to him (21.14.2; Neri 1984: 23–24). The matter of the *genius publicus* shows that both Julian and Constantius have connections to the transcendent, but Julian's *civilitas* makes for a stronger link.

As the paragon of what an emperor is supposed to be much of the time in the *Res Gestae* in matters of moral consistency, Julian exhibits civil behavior. For example, when he presides at a trial in which the prosecutor, who seemingly lacks the means to make his case, attempts to change the terms of his argument to impugning the obviously and unavoidably interested motive of the defendant to beat the charge, Julian advocates for the downtrodden:

> "Will anyone ever be found guilty, most flourishing *caesar,* if to deny the charge will be sufficient?" Against this one and impelled wisely in just that moment, Julian said, "And who will ever be found innocent if to have brought the charge will be sufficient?" These words indeed and many

---

50. Camus 1967: 114; Seager 1986: 22, cf. 36–39.

51. J. den Boeft et al. (1991: 258–59) note that *civilitas* is a central imperial virtue and that it can even tend toward synonymity with *clementia.* Ammianus idealized a notion of an empire in which

> [strong] emperors had inherited the protection of law and settled life from the senatorial government of the Republic. Their function was to defend men of good will ... there were properly instituted courts and regular procedures, and in the observance of these was the essence of what Ammianus, in just this context, called a "civil and rightful empire" [*civile iustumque imperium*]. (Matthews 1989: 252)

52. For these claims about *civilis* and also its profound and long-lasting implication with law/*ius* (and hence *iustitia*), see *TLL* 3.1213.58–1215.47.

(others) of this kind were proofs of his civil behavior (*huius modi multa civilia*). (18.1.4)[53]

Constantius, by contrast, fails at being *civilis,* and it is a failure that stems from his ambition to be transcendent and his insistence that he is not bound by things of this earth.[54] Indeed, "His Eternity" lacks all sense of *civilitas* or *iustitia* when he feels that his majesty has been lessened. He becomes predatory and looks to extend the misery of his enemies by torture, behaving "more fiercely than civilly," if he judges that their constitutions can handle it:

> His bitterness (and rage and suspicions swollen against all things of this sort) was added to miseries of those poor ones who were denounced in the matter of diminishing or slighting his majesty. If something of this kind had made a peep, he, rising up into investigations more fiercely than civilly (*acrius . . . quam civiliter*), placed savage judges in charge of these trials and, in case of some of those being punished—and more fierce than even [the third-century emperor] Gallienus in some cases of this kind—, he used to try to have their deaths extended, if nature would permit it. (21.16.9)[55]

Constantius was so unreliable when it came to matters of *iustitia* that Silvanus (an infantry commander on the northern frontier) felt that he had no hope, and so had himself acclaimed emperor:

> [K]nowing the pliant/soft mind of the fickle emperor and fearing that he would be butchered without being heard and with no process of condemnation . . . through the means of purple insignia taken on the spur of the moment from the standards of the dragons and *vexilla,* Silvanus rose to imperial loftiness. (15.5.15–16)[56]

---

53. "ecquis, florentissime Caesar, nocens esse poterit usquam si negare sufficiet?" contra quem Iulianus prudenter motus ex tempore,"et quis," ait, "innocens esse poterit si accusasse sufficiet?" et haec quidem et huius modi multa civilia.

54. Ammianus' presentation of Constantius as not civil is frequently noted in the secondary literature. See, e.g., the following: Kelly 2005; Barnes 1998: 132–38; Matthews 1989: 33–39; Neri 1984: 10–12 and *passim*; Sabbah 1978: 437–39; Tassi 1967.

55. addebatur miserorum aerumnis, qui rei maiestatis imminutae vel laesae deferebantur, acerbitas eius et iracundia suspicionesque in huiusmodi cuncta distentae. Et si quid tale increpuisset, in quaestiones acrius exsurgens quam civiliter spectatores apponebat his litibus truces mortemque longius in puniendis quibusdam, si natura permitteret, conabatur extendi in eiusmodi controversiarum partibus etiam Gallieno ferocior.

56. sciens animum tenerum versabilis principis timensque, ne trucidaretur absens et indemnatus . . . cultu purpureo a draconum et vexillorum insignibus ad tempus abstracto ad culmen imperiale surrexit.

Driven by fear of Constantius' eagerness to destroy those whom he viewed as a threat—and note that he fears being tortured (probably at length) and executed without a trial—Silvanus rationally decided that, as he had nothing to lose, he might as well go into revolt. Indeed, on Constantius' watch, as it were, the *caesar* Gallus displayed decidedly uncivil behavior. Through his penchant for preying on elites and abuse of authority, confiscations and executions occurred with abandon and "a civil and just empire (*civile iustumque imperium*) had been converted to bloody caprice."[57]

DECLINATIO AND EMPEROR

Ammianus intimately connects the failure of civility in Constantius with physical manifestations that pull him down to earth and eventually lead to a reader's perception of a desire in the emperor to be sexually penetrated. The springboard of the discussion that reveals this connection is Ammianus' remark that Constantius "has swerved from justice" (15.1.3: *a iustitia declinavit*) when he claims the title "My Eternity" and evidently feels free of mortality and, as his behavior elsewhere suggests, of morality. Constantius' *declinatio* from justice to claim eternity creates an initial impression that his claims are "unjustified" because he is mortal, and if he is going to claim the mantle of civil emperor, he should hardly be embracing a strategy of justicial declension. Indeed, given that the emperor was the premiere source of *ius* on account of the simple fact that he was emperor, this passage is bitterly ironic.

Subsequent to Ammianus' mention of Constantius' assertion that he makes it his business to imitate the civil emperors, the historiographer places His Eternity, the self-naming supposed master of the world, into a much larger frame (quoted again for convenience):

> For even if he were ruling Democritus' infinity of worlds, of which Alexander the Great dreamed with Anaxarchus' encouragement, yet reading or listening he should have reflected upon the fact that, as the astronomers in universal agreement teach, the circuit of the entire earth, which seems immeasurable to us, next to the greatness of the universe has the image of a tiny point. (15.1.4)

In the first place, the mention of the fifth-century B.C.E. philosopher Democritus attracts attention. One of his beliefs, to which Ammianus refers,

---

[57]. 14.1.4: civili iustoque imperio ad voluntatem converso cruentam.

was that this world was one of an infinite number of worlds composed out of random motions of atoms.[58] This larger prospect cuts Constantius' claim to being master of the world down to size: it is "unjust" of him to pretend to grandeur when so great a scheme of things renders him so small. Cognizance too of the well-known fact that Democritus was an exponent of atomism suggests that interpretation of this imperial swerve is not complete. Indeed, the mention of atomism presages the dissipation of Constantius' transcendence into physical symptoms.

Locating ultimate reality in the interplay of atoms and the void, atomism is a doctrine quite precisely *not* transcendent. And it is the physicality of this doctrine that sheds light on the phrase characterizing Constantius' claim of mastery of the world as a swerve from justice (*a iustitia declinavit*). *Declinare* (and the related noun *declinatio*) are words used to describe the movement of atoms in atomic theory.[59] A critical Cicero, for example, reports Epicurus' belief that the necessity of fate could be rendered irrelevant through the swerving of an atom (*declinatione atomi*).[60] Employing *declinare*, Lucretius connects the swerve of atoms to impulses leading people to act in various ways.[61] Ammianus' use of *declinare* accordingly physicalizes Constantius' embrace of eternity and mastery of the world, pulling him from the transcendental register that he claims for himself. Indeed the impression of physicalization is reinforced by Ammianus' use of *declinare* in a haughty letter the Persian king of kings, Sapor II, writes to Constantius in book seventeen:

> At no place swerving (*declinans*) from his inborn arrogance, he gave a letter for Constantius to a certain legate Narseus, who had been sent with gifts. I have been given to understand that this is the sense of the letter: "I, Sapor, king of kings, partner of the stars, brother of the sun and moon, wish to my brother, the *caesar* Constantius, health to the greatest degree. . . . " (17.5.2–3)[62]

Sapor claims to be transcendent of this world in a letter which, contentwise, could have come from Constantius himself. Noting that Sapor is "at no place *swerving* from his inborn arrogance," Ammianus employs with

---

58. de Jonge 1972a: 11.
59. *TLL* 5.1 191.72–73; 75–6 (*declinare*); *TLL* 5.1 188.63–65 (*declinatio*).
60. *Fat.* 22: Epicurus declinatione atomi vitari necessitatem fati putat.
61. Lucr. 2.249–60.
62. missoque cum muneribus Narseo quodam legato litteras ad Constantium dedit nusquam a genuino fastu declinans, quarum hunc fuisse accepimus sensum: "Rex regum Sapor, particeps siderum, frater Solis et Lunae, Constantio Caesari fratri meo salutem plurimam dico. . . . "

irony the same verb he used earlier of Constantius. Also, in calling this arrogance of Sapor inborn, he identifies a material basis for it. Both born into imperial houses, Constantius and Sapor accordingly come by their arrogance because of their enmeshment in the physical world. The implication is that they will be true to material things and not to the abstract values to which the truly virtuous ruler should hew.

These characterizations of Sapor and Constantius anticipate what Claudian will soon write in 398, when he depicts (with irony) emperor Theodosius I saying to his son Honorius (destined to be emperor—and his brother Arcadius is already one) that it is through virtue and worthiness of deeds that he will deserve the throne and not, as is the case always with the Persian kings, through lineage:

> If fortune had given you the throne of the Persians,
> my dear boy, the barbarian tiara (a thing to be worshipped from afar
> by eastern lands) would rise above [your] Arsacid face.
> Sublime lineage would suffice and nobility alone
> would be able to protect you as you idly fell into luxury.
> Very much other is the condition for the rulers of Roman
> royal power. It is right that it [Roman royal power] is
> supported through *virtus* and not through blood. (4H 214–220)[63]

While the absolute monarch may claim transcendent dessert and status, if there are no good works and civility, it will be mere physical assertion with no warrant beyond its evanescent existence here on earth. Indeed, ruling without a connection to transcendent values, as Ammianus says Constantius does, associates Constantius with emperors in the past whose behavior was a poisonous mixture of sexual deviance and tyrannical incivility. Nero, Commodus, and especially Elegabalus come to mind.[64] While the known facts of Constantius' life don't report him straying from being the impen-

---

63. Si tibi Parthorum solium Fortuna dedisset,
care puer, terrisque procul venerandus Eois
barbarus Arsacio consugeret ore tiaras:
sufficeret sublime genus luxuque fluentem
deside nobilitas posset te sola tueri.
Altera Romanae longe rectoribus aulae
condicio. Virtute decet, non sanguine niti.

64. For more on connections between sexual deviance and absolute imperial power, see Mathew Kuefler's discussions (2001: 56–61, 88–90) of both the retrospective portrait of the early third-century emperor Elegabalus in the late fourth-century *Historia Augusta* and similar notions in Claudian and Pacatus.

etrable penetrator in his sexual practice, his absolutist *mores* as ruler make him susceptible to critique on this basis. The argument now turns specifically to how Ammianus creates the impression that Constantius is open to playing the passive role in same-sex sexual activity.

A short time after the swerve and in the midst of a narrative of the activities of informants and subsequent betrayals after the deposition and execution of *caesar* Gallus, Ammianus characterizes Constantius most interestingly when he is led to believe, as he could be so easily, that conspirators were plotting against him. Africanus (the governor of Lower Pannonia) gave a dinner party in Illyricum where the guests, in their cups, criticized the current regime. Unfortunately for the participants, Gaudentius, a member of the secret service (*agens in rebus*), was in attendance and he reported back:

> One of those present, Gaudentius, an *agens in rebus,* a stupid man with an impetuous mind, had denounced the matter as a serious one to Rufinus, who was at that time chief of staff of the praetorian prefecture, and a man always greedy for extreme things and notorious for his ingrained evil. And this one (Rufinus) flew without delay as if raised aloft on wings to the court of the emperor, and inflamed him (the emperor), who was soft and penetrable (*mollem et penetrabilem*) in the matter of suspicions of this kind—[he inflamed him] so sharply that, without any thought, Africanus and all the guests at the fatal banquet were ordered to be snatched up and away. (15.3.8–9)[65]

In a significant choice of vocabulary, Ammianus terms Constantius "soft and penetrable" to those who use words that play to his ever-ready paranoia. The two words, *mollis* and *penetrabilis,* are well-known for their reference to gender dissidence (*mollis*) and to passive male sexuality (both *mollis* and *penetrabilis*). Indeed, Constantius' well-known openness to hear and believe such things is characterized by the verb *pateo* ("to lie open") a little before the passage just now presented:

> Because of this and going forward, Constantius, as though he would tear out the already decreed order of the fates, *was lying open (patebat)* with

---

65. E quorum numero Gaudentius agens in rebus mente praecipiti stolidus rem ut seriam detulerat ad Rufinum apparitionis praefecturae praetorianae tunc principem, ultimorum semper avidum hominem et coalita pravitate famosum. qui confestim quasi pinnis elatus ad comitatum principis advolavit eumque ad suspiciones huiusmodi mollem et penetrabilem ita acriter inflammavit, ut sine deliberatione ulla Africanus et omnes letalis mensae participes iuberentur rapi sublimes.

heart disclosed all the more powerfully to the many who were planning treachery. (15.3.3)[66]

The verb *pateo* is obscene when applied to a person: legs are spread.[67] *Pateo* will appear in 399 in Claudian's first invective against the eunuch consul Eutropius, where the sexualized nature of this word is evident. This excerpt from a passage full of *doubles-entendres* (IE 1.358–70[68]) shows this side to *pateo:* "He fears nothing from the back. With his concern everywhere vigilant he lies open (*patet*) night and day" (362–63: *Nil timet a tergo; vigilantibus undique curis / nocte dieque patet*). Although there is perhaps enough evidence that Ammianus is mounting a challenge to Constantius' impenetrable manhood when he speaks of him as *mollis* and *penetrabilis* with

---

66. vehementius hinc et deinde Constantius quasi praescriptum fatorum ordinem convulsurus recluso pectore *patebat* insidiantibus multis.

67. In the *TLL* (10.1 659.58–660.16, cf. 667.15–16), *pateo* often refers to bodily openings and sexualized meanings are frequent.

68. Claudian puts a speech full of sexual *doubles-entendres* in the mouth of one of three men in conversation about the marvelously distressing fact that a eunuch is consul:

> Another one more playful chimes in with a healthy amount of salty language: "Do you marvel? There is nothing great which Eutropius does not conceive in his heart. Always new things, big things always he loves and he gives a taste to every single one of them with a swift sense. He fears nothing from the back. With his concern everywhere vigilant, he lies open night and day. Gentle and easy to be moved by entreaties, yet most yielding in the midst of anger, he says no to nothing and offers himself even to those who are not demanding. What pleases the mind, he handles and serves it up to be enjoyed. Whatever you like, that hand will give it. He performs every duty in common and his power loves to be turned aside. He has given birth to this [position of his] through his "consultations" and the merit of his exertions. He receives the consul's robes as a reward for a skillful right hand." (Claud., IE 1.358–70)

> Subicit et mixtis salibus lascivior alter:
> "Miraris? Nihil est, quod non in pectore magnum
> concipit Eutropius. Semper nova, grandia semper
> diligit et celeri degustat singula sensu.
> Nil timet a tergo; vigilantibus undique curis
> nocte dieque patet; lenis facilisque moveri
> supplicibus mediaque tamen mollissimus ira
> nil negat et sese vel non poscentibus offert.
> Quidlibet ingenio subigit traditque fruendum;
> quidquid amas, dabit illa manus; communiter omni
> fungitur officio gaudetque potentia flecti.
> Hoc quoque conciliis peperit meritoque laborum
> accipit et trabeas argutae praemia dextrae."

Tasting implies fellatio. That "he fears nothing from the back" and that "he lies open night and day" refers to his availability for anal intercourse. Claudian's designation of Eutropius as "most yielding" (*mollissimus*) further confirms this availability. The reference to hands suggests willingness to give a hand-job. For more, see Long (1996: 142–43).

his mind lying open, the case becomes even stronger if Ammianus' use of another word is considered: *tener* ("pliant, soft").

Tener historically had a valence of effeminacy[69] and was similar to *mollis* in this regard. *Tener* designates the opposite of tough masculinity, and is often applied to the beloved object in love/erotic poetry.[70] Ammianus twice describes Constantius' mind as *tener*. The usurper Silvanus was driven into revolution partially because he feared the "*pliant/soft* mind of the fickle princeps" (15.5.15: *animum* tenerum *versabilis princeps*). And, at 14.5.2, Ammianus describes Constantius' mind as narrow and *soft* (*angustus et* tener):

> As an ill body is accustomed to be shattered by even light illnesses, so his narrow and *soft* (*tener*) mind, thinking that whatever made a peep was a thing done or contemplated with a view toward making him unsafe—[so his soft mind] made his victory [over Magnentius] a thing full of grief through the slaughter of innocent persons. (14.5.2)[71]

At a moment when the emperor is acting in a manner not at all civil, Ammianus again uses language that casts aspersions on Constantius' manhood.

Tener elsewhere suggested effeminacy in contemporary literature concerned with political figures. In an oration for Theodosius I given in 389, Pacatus develops a fanciful comparison between Theodosius' manly Gothic troops and the unmanly troops from Egypt that Octavian/Augustus defeated when he bested Mark Antony in the first century B.C.E. These troops were "shining in their *soft* costume" (tenero *perlucentes amictu*), and they are, significantly, depicted as coming from "*effeminate* Canopus" (mollis *Canopus*) (Pacat., *Pan. Lat.* 2 [12] 33.4). Claudian uses *tener* in his first invective against Eutropius when he wishes for an eclipse to the political power eunuchs have come to possess in the eastern part of the empire:

> Let them [the eunuchs] recede from the brow of Power. Public majesty knows nothing of being wielded by a soft (*tenero*) heart. (IE 1.422–24)[72]

---

69. *OLD* 7.
70. *OLD* 6b; see, e.g., Tibullus 1.4.9, 1.6.33; Propertius 2.25.41; Ovid, *Amores* 2.1.33, 3.4.1; Martial 1.109.16.
71. utque aegrum corpus quassari etiam levibus solet offensis, ita animus eius angustus et tener, quicquid increpuisset, ad salutis suae dispendium existimans factum aut cogitatum, insontium caedibus fecit victoriam luctuosam.
72. . . . a fronte recedant
    imperii. Tenero tractari pectore nescit
    publica maiestas.

The other four appearances of *tener* in the *Res Gestae* also support the notion that *tener* imputes an unmanly softness to whatever or whomever it describes.

The peach fuzz just coming out onto *caesar* Gallus' face is described as *soft* (14.11.28: *emergente lanugine* tenera), and the children enslaved by the Persians and immature males castrated by the mythical Queen Semiramis are both described as *soft* (18.10.2: tenerioris *aetatis;* 14.6.17: teneros *mares*). The Chinese make silk that has the *softest* sort of subtlety to it (23.6.67: *subtilitatem* tenerrimam). And so, for Ammianus *tener* designates luxury items, children, and immature males who historically were objects of sexual desire for older males. It is telling, then, that the one who signs his name *Mea Aeternitas* should also have his mind described in this way. Furthermore, these four instances, when added to the two times *tener* is applied to Constantius' mind, exhaust the number of times *tener* appears in the *Res Gestae*.

A return now to *declinare*. When Constantius has swerved from justice, which means he is leaving behind civility and strongly suggests a surrender to materiality, and when the present reading of *tener, mollis, penetrabilis,* and *pateo* as descriptive of Constantius is kept in mind, the anonymous fourth-century Latin physiognomy (a work mentioned in the introduction to this book which features the sneeze telling Cleanthes that the man before him is no man) provides a relevant intertext. In this work, the verb *declinare* and the related noun, *declinatio,* describe the way unmanly *cinaedi* turn their heads and necks:

> The neck leaning (*declinata*) to the left side signifies to some extent a stupid man and even more a *cinaedus*. Aristotle even attributes leaning (*declinationem*) of the head to the right side to *cinaedi*. (*Anon. Lat.* 55)[73]

If this intertext is added to the preceding evidence, is there much to choose between a swerve from justice and a come-hither lean of the head? With this question in mind, it is of great interest that Ammianus' paragon of civility, Julian, is quite precisely not about to swerve; he is, rather, "unswervable" (*indeclinabilis*).

Where Constantius is all materializing swerves and transcendent insistence which make him uncivil and raise questions about his sexual desires, Julian engineers his transcendence through being unswervable (*indeclinabilis*) in the matter of justice and civility:

---

73. Cervix in sinistram partem declinata stultum aliquatenus ac cinaedum magis significat. Aristoteles etiam ad dexteram partem declinationem capitis cinaedis attribuit.

[H]aving great enthusiasm for civility (*civilitati admodum studens*), claiming only so much for himself as he imagined would keep a space between being worthy of scorn and insolence . . . he was enthusiastic in all judicial investigations and was sometimes an unswervable (*indeclinabilis*) judge. The fiercest censor in the matter of regulating *mores*, a calm despiser of riches, looking down on all mortal affairs, in summation he used to say that it was shameful for a wise man to seek to obtain praise for his body when he had a mind. (25.4.7)[74]

Julian set great store by civil behavior and this, consistently enough, led to a passion for legality and to seeing himself within a regularized legal context. He cultivated a limited majesty that contrasts sharply with the grand claims that Constantius made for himself. There is mild censure present when Ammianus identifies occasional inflexibility in Julian, but clearly this is better than the pliant paranoia of Constantius. The passage continues with an economical nod in the direction of transcendence: Julian knows that true value lies in the mind and not in the body. Julian's thoughtful and just engagement with the world is the way to a transcendence of which Ammianus would approve. This engagement is tantamount to an immortality, indeed an eternity, secured through "the knowledge of deeds done honestly and morally."[75] On another occasion, an entirely approving Ammianus again terms Julian *indeclinabilis* in his capacity as judge. When it was possible that important personages could trample on the rights of the less powerful, "he was an *unswervable* judge of the just and the unjust" (18.1.2: *erat* indeclinabilis *iustorum iniustorumque distinctor*). The contrast between Julian and Constantius could not be balder, as the one will not swerve from justice while the other makes a practice of doing so. Further observation of Ammianus' use of this adjective supports the idea that Julian's civil behavior eases his access to the transcendent. At 29.1.34, *indeclinabilis* describes the power of fate, and, at 19.8.2, a stalemate of two valiant armies in battle is broken "by an *unavoidable* accident" (*eventu* . . . indeclinabili). This adjective marks things as being beyond mortal control; Julian's being *indeclinabilis* is perhaps something superhuman (cf. *TLL* 7.1 2573–7).

---

74. civilitati admodum studens, tantum sibi arrogans, quantum a contemptu et insolentia distare existimabat . . . studiosus cognitionum omnium et indeclinabilis aliquotiens iudex; censor in moribus regendis acerrimus, placidus opum contemptor, mortalia cuncta despiciens, postremo id praedicabat, turpe esse sapienti, cum habeat animum, captare laudes ex corpore.

75. 14.6.8: ex conscientia honeste recteque factorum (from the passage on the inhabitants of Rome thinking they can secure immortality from statues).

CONCLUSION

Embodied in the contrasting portraits of Julian and Constantius, Ammianus' thoughts on the emperor speak to the panorama of late-ancient manhood's homosociality, same-sex desire and the construction of authority elaborated in this book so far. The emperor, apex though he be of *auctoritas* or ἀξίωμα, is in some respects typical.

The ambitions of late-ancient manhood to grandeur depend on homosociality and yet, connecting *auctoritas* to things greater than the approval of other men is a *desiderandum*. His writing reflecting this dynamic outside the *Res Gestae*, Ammianus both wants and does not want transcendence for the emperor, or, put differently, he both enjoins and devalues connection to things of this world: he is conflicted over Constantius' grandeur *and* Julian's approachability. There is also conflict around same-sex desire and pleasure. Being desirous of another male's penetrative sexuality is shameful for a man in Ammianus' world (as it is elsewhere in late antiquity), but knowledge of this desire as a real possibility allows Ammianus to sharpen his critique of Constantius. Ammianus' pulling Constantius to earth through deployment of forbidden knowledge makes him as authoritative as the contemporary consistory of Theodosius I who wrote *Collatio* 5.3. In this vein, then, a return to the take-down of Constantius that, at the same time, shows Ammianus' penetrating powers of criticism.

In a passage previously discussed, Ammianus scandalously figures Constantius' susceptibility to those telling him about talk against his *maiestas* as a sort of lying open:

> Because of this and going forward, Constantius, as though he would tear out the already decreed order of the fates (*quasi praescriptum fatorum ordinem convulsurus*), was lying open with heart disclosed all the more powerfully to the many who were planning treachery. (15.3.3)

Earlier analysis pointed out the sexual subtext that the verb *pateo* ("to lie open") imports. It is time to build on this observation. At this moment, Constantius would do nothing less than overwhelm fate ("*as though he would tear out the already decreed order of the fates*"). About as forceful an assertion of transcendence as can be imagined—Constantius is aiming to place himself beyond the power of fate—, what is he doing to get to this absolute place? Constantius renders fate immaterial through throwing his gates wide open. The authoritative and knowledgable Ammianus presents an embodiment of tyrannical power's obscenity.

There are further points to be made. As outrageous as this revelation of imperial obscenity is, it is of a piece with the figuration of same-sex attractiveness as a metaphor for masculine admirability and power in late antiquity. Just as it is possible to go up and down the "ladder of love" from the *Symposium,* so the sublimation of sexual desire inherent in its use as a metaphor for masculine grandeur can be desublimated or undone, and unacceptable desire is suddenly rampant. Julian himself figures the imperial glamour of Marcus Aurelius as a *kallos amēchanon,* which has its lineage of same-sex desire commencing with Plato, and the immediacy of desire brings a compelling liveliness to the portrait. In the case of Ammianus' Constantius, same-sex desire, not adding liveliness via metaphor this time, appears sans metaphor to besmirch Constantius' reputation and render his grandeur obscenely vital.

Furthermore, while Ammianus is no fan of same-sex desire, he is a man of the ancient world and his knowledgeable and negative use of it in Constantius' case is not the whole story of it in the *Res Gestae.* As did many men in late antiquity, he appreciates beauty in younger males (see, e.g., 14.11.28 on the beauty of *caesar* Gallus), but he is of a school of "look, but don't touch" (as his condemnation of initiatory pederasty among the Taifali at 31.9.5 shows). Where *viri* are concerned, Ammianus generally, though not always (see below), avoids a glamorization of masculine authority via same-sex sexual attractiveness. As has been seen, same-sex sexual attractiveness and desire lurk as obscene dimensions to absolutist authority, manifesting in the texture of Ammianus' language and in a series of images and vocabulary that slander. But, interestingly, the charm of celestialized manly authority, metaphorized as same-sex sexual attractiveness, nonetheless proves irresistible to Ammianus in the case of Julian.

In book fifteen Constantius ennobles Julian, a full-grown man of twenty-four years, with the title of *caesar.* The dramatic date is 355 and Constantius presents Julian to the soldiery in Milan:

> "We stand before you, best defenders of the empire, in order to champion our cause with one shared spirit, one almost of all humanity. How I will do this, I will tell you briefly as though before impartial judges. After the destruction of those rebellious tyrants whom savagery and fury compelled to those gambits they tried, the barbarians, as though sacrificing with Roman blood to their evil Manes, dance through the Gauls as the peace of the boundaries has been shattered; they are heartened by the belief that difficult necessities hold us fast throughout our provinces so exceedingly far from one another. If, while time permits, the opinion of you and us, both

consulted, should meet this evil already slithering beyond bounds, the necks of the proud tribes will sag and the boundaries of our empire will be inviolate. It remains for you to make strong with favoring action the hope for future affairs which I have. This Julian, this brother, my cousin, as you have known, one rightly known (*lit.* "seen" [*spectatum*]) for his modesty (on account of which he dear to us, as much as for the fact he is a relative) and already a young man of gleaming purpose (*elucentis industriae*), [this Julian] I wish to bring into the rank of *caesar*, with this action, if it seems good to you, confirmed by your agreement." (15.8.5–8)[76]

Looking for help after Gallus disappointed him and proposing Julian as the new *caesar*, Constantius uses revealing words. Constantius describes Julian's good character as something visible (*spectatum*) and his sense of purpose (*industria*) is likewise able to be seen: it shines (*elucens*). This admirable man has about him a play of light, and this calls to mind the *clarissimi, spectabiles, illustres,* and Julian's Marcus Aurelius. As Ammianus continues, the soldiers cannot remain still and they disrupt the ceremony:

> Interrupting, the gathering (*contio*) was gently was keeping him [Constantius] from saying more about these things, even as he was trying to continue. As though knowing beforehand what was to come, the gathering was proclaiming that [this elevation of Julian] was the work of highest godhead (*summi numinis*) and not of mortal mind. (15.8.9)[77]

While Constantius' final words certainly primed the soldiery to make their interruption, the interruption becomes an occasion for Ammianus to portray Julian's progress into higher office as the work of providential and transcendent divinity (*summum numen*). As he continues, Constantius speaks more of Julian, and develops the connection to the divine further:

---

76. "Assistimus apud vos, optimi rei publicae defensores, causae communi uno paene omnium spiritu vindicandae, quam acturus tamquam apud aequos iudices succinctius edocebo. Post interitum rebellium tyrannorum, quos ad haec temptanda, quae moverunt, rabies egit et furor, velut impiis eorum manibus Romano sanguine parentantes persultant barbari Gallias rupta limitum pace hac animati fiducia, quod nos per disiunctissimas terras arduae necessitates adstringunt. Huic igitur malo ultra apposita iam proserpenti, si dum patitur tempus occurrerit nostri vestrique consulti suffragium, et colla superbarum gentium detumescent et imperii fines erunt intacti. Restat ut venturorum spem, quam gero, secundo roboretis effectu. Iulianum, hunc fratrem meum patruelem, ut nostis, verecundia, qua nobis ita ut necessitudine carus est, recte spectatum iamque elucentis industriae iuvenem, in Caesaris adhibere potestatem exopto coeptis, si videntur utilia, etiam vestra consensione firmandis."

77. Dicere super his plura conantem interpellans contio lenius prohibebat arbitrium summi numinis id esse non mentis humanae velut praescia venturi praedicamans.

Standing still until they were silent, the emperor finished his speech more confidently: "Because your happy roar shows your assent present with us now, let this young man of steady vigor whose tempered *mores* are more to be imitated than talked about, [let this young man] rise up to this almost expected honor, [this young man] whose most excellent natural talents (*praeclaram indolem*), schooled in an excellent education (*bonis artibus institutam*), I believe I have made fully evident because I have chosen him (for this office). Therefore, with the present approval of God in heaven (*praesente nutu dei caelestis*), I will put the imperial robe on him." (15.8.9–10)[78]

Constantius points out the various excellences of Julian. Light gleams again with the shining of his excellent natural talents (*praeclara indoles*). He is in possession of *paideia,* his natural talents "schooled in an excellent education" (*bonis artibus instituta*). It also is significant that the investiture occurs both within the homosocial space of a gathering of men (15.8.9: *contio*) and with the approval of heaven (*praesens nutus dei caelestis*): civility and absolute grandeur are both represented.

Somewhat later in book fifteen and after Julian makes his remarks to the *contio,* Ammianus metaphorizes his grandeur as same-sex sexual attractiveness. The mode and effect of this evocation of same-sex sexual attractiveness contrasts markedly with the graphic desire Ammianus imputes to Constantius. Instead of calling penetration to mind (e.g., *pateo* or *penetrabilis*), Ammianus offers loveliness (*venustas*) as a metaphor for the admirability of this well-educated, virtuous young man whose *auctoritas* has been approved by other men and who has been touched by heaven itself. The soldiers gaze upon him and they see in him an awe-inspiring beauty that is tantamount to the *kallos amēchanon* that Julian himself attributed to Marcus Aurelius: "Looking for a long time and intently on his eyes were terrible with loveliness (*venustate terribiles*) and on his countenance rather animatedly pleasing, the soldiers could tell who he was going to be . . . " (15.8.16).[79] The mechanics of sex between men are not present in the way they are in the depiction of Constantius, but desire's affect and power, and perhaps even the goddess of love herself, nonethe-

---

78. stansque imperator immobilis, dum silerent, residua fidentius explicavit: "quia igitur vestrum quoque favorem adesse fremitus indicat laetus, adolescens vigoris tranquilli, cuius temperati mores imitandi sunt potius quam praedicandi, ad honorem prope speratum exsurgat: cuius praeclaram indolem bonis artibus institutam hoc ipso plene videor exposuisse, quod elegi. ergo eum praesente nutu dei caelestis amictu principali velabo."

79. cuius oculos cum venustate terribiles vultumque excitatius gratum diu multumque contuentes, qui futurus sit, colligebant . . .

less provide a metaphor for the glamour of Julian's present and future *auctoritas* that Ammianus connects to corporeal arousal.

Consideration of ideas found in the sources surveyed in the first chapter and the contrast they have with those of Ammianus and Athanasius bring this chapter well and truly to an end. Discourses discussed in chapter one (late-Platonic philosophy and theorizing concerned with myths) feature an embrace of paradox and an accompanying belief in the diffusion of transcendent powers into the material world. This diffusion exceeds the power of logic to describe it definitively and a broader ontological order contextualizes this world of human laws and morals; the power of earthbound morals is only sufficient for this world and more exists than can be accounted for according to them. Hence, same-sex desire can be invoked to metaphorize masculine admirability, even though it is officially frowned upon: the forbidden indicates distinction. In contrast, when Ammianus describes Julian's admirable connection to the transcendent, he projects men's morals and laws into the transcendent and Julian's connection to the transcendent is, in the end, accomplished through playing by the rules and being civil.[80] Ammianus' association of the transcendent with earthbound *civilitas* resembles Athanasius' moralization of it. In Athanasius' case, the need for his Antony to exemplify earthly morals with no remainder (even as his *auctoritas* or ἀξίωμα assertively emanates from transcendent sources) leads, ultimately, to an association of all men's bodies with same-sex desire. It is arguable that something similar happens with Ammianus' Constantius. When Ammianus packs the transcendent with civility, the failure of Constantius on this score short-circuits his connection to absolute grandeur and the emergent human fault is all too corporeal same-sex desire. Does it "itch" (*gargalizei*/γαργαλίζει)? Unlike Athanasius, though, Ammianus is conflicted. Even though he reviles what he characterizes as Constantius' tyrannical ways, he nonetheless finds steep hierarchical distinctions praiseworthy and necessary, for he faults Julian for not remembering this. Ammianus also, and again at variance with Athanasius, takes a page from the late-Platonic playbook and metaphorizes the admirability of Julian as a thing capable of inspiring desire: the liveliness of erotic regard electrifies the respect Julian commands.

Ammianus holds, therefore, multiply contradictory viewpoints on imperial *auctoritas* or ἀξίωμα, and his important historiography has insolubilities at its heart on this score. He envisions appropriate imperial grandeur,

---

80. For more on Ammianus' moralization of things beyond this world, see de Bonfils' interesting discussion of transcendent *fas* guaranteeing *ius* (1986: 109–111).

otherworldly, as ultimately something obscene, while, at the same time, proposing a moralized transcendent embodied by earthbound morals. Still, this moralizing effort is countered by his desire for mystery and something greater than this world. This world disappoints him over and over again, as is well-known; all one has to do is read the *Res Gestae:* humanity is feral all too often.[81] And though he wants mysteriously remote imperial grandeur, he ultimately must refuse it; Constantius' fearlessness must be perverted, and what good can be salvaged from men and their institutions must flood heaven instead.

---

81. Auerbach 1953.

CONCLUSION

In 376 or 377, when emperor Gratian was approaching his twentieth birthday (he was born in 359 and had been emperor since 367), Themistius, a major intellectual and political figure in the empire, delivered an oration, his thirteenth,[1] at Rome in the emperor's praise. Gratian was not present, but the senate at Rome was (177D, 178B, 178D). The speech is entitled, significantly in the context of this book, "A Discourse on Love/Desire or Concerning the Emperor's Beauty" (*Erōtikos [logos] ē peri kallous basilikou* / Ἐρωτικὸς [λόγος] ἢ περὶ κάλλους βασιλικοῦ).[2] Throughout the oration, Gratian's beauty, a potent and chameleon-like entity, transfixes all who behold it with love and desire.

Themistius confesses that he loves, saying that he has come to Rome not as a philosopher but as a sort of rhetorical or poetical lover.[3] In language recalling Plato and studded with Homer, Themistius says that his encounter with Gratian's stunning beauty of soul and body makes him give birth to love of philosophical beauty, and this, in turn, has caused him to write the speech:

---

1. For dating, context, and discussion of Themistius' thirteenth oration, see Vanderspoel (1995: 179–84). I thank Amy Richlin for directing my attention back to this work.

2. As the most cursory glance at Menander Rhetor will show, adding *logos*/λόγος to the title merely makes explicit the noun that would have been tacitly understood.

3. *Or.* 13.171B: ἀντὶ φιλοσόφου ῥητορικός τις ἢ ποιητικὸς ἐραστής.

[B]eing in travail (*ōdinōn*/ὠδίνων)⁴ with that love, which philosophy had written in me, for the beauty of a beautiful and lovable young man, who mixes both beauties, that of the soul and that of the body, gleaming with friendliness and steadiness in a manliness of luxury—"a young man whose beard is just coming out, one whose youth is at its most attractive"⁵—being in travail with love of such beauty, and dreaming and hoping on the one hand, and finding, on the other, its like nowhere on earth or on the sea, I was experiencing wondrous things, as I was just saying, and I was thinking there ought to be some kind of account of his beauty.... (*Or.* 13.164C–165A)⁶

Themistius is deeply affected by the sight of this young man whose journey into manhood is well underway. The unparalleled beauty of soul and body awakens vague dreams and inchoate hopes. A welcoming demeanour wondrously steady "in a manliness of luxury"—and this phrase, "in a manliness of luxury" (*en andreiai hēdupatheias*/ἐν ἀνδρείᾳ ἡδυπαθείας), exemplifies the late-ancient penchant for securing glamour through paradox—this demeanor has put pen in hand and stiffened resolve to write under *erōs*' orders.

Themistius is not the only one who should or will be moved by *erōs* for the emperor. He hopes that the senate will love Gratian as he does. At the very end of the oration, and again using Platonic language, i.e., *Phdr.* 255D–E,⁷ Themistius asks Zeus, Athena, and Quirinus to inspire *erōs* in Gratian for Rome and an *anterōs* in Rome for Gratian: "may all of you grant to my boyfriend that he *love* (*eran*/ἐρᾶν) Rome and that he *be loved in return* (*anterasthai*/ἀντερᾶσθαι) by Rome."⁸ Preferring to avoid force and have his handsome and civilized soul win them over, Gratian makes the barbarians love him also:

---

4. Plato famously uses the noun for the travail of childbirth to refer to males, e.g., *Phdr.* 251E (ὠδίνων) or *Smp.* 206E (ὠδῖνος), and Themistius uses here the related verb, *ōdinein*/ὠδίνειν (to be in travail [of childbirth]), to refer to himself.

5. This is a mild misquotation (ὑπηνήτην instead of ὑπηνήτῃ) of a line (πρῶτον ὑπηνήτῃ, τοῦ περ χαριεστάτη ἥβη) that occurs twice in Homer: *Il.* 24.348 and *Od.* 10.279. Both times the reference is to Hermes.

6. ὠδίνων μὲν τὸν ἔρωτα ἐκείνου τοῦ κάλλους, ὃν φιλοσοφία μοι ὑπεγράψατο, νέου καλοῦ καὶ ἐρασμίου, τὰ κάλλη ἄμφω κερασαμένου, τῆς τε ψυχῆς καὶ τοῦ σώματος, λάμποντος φιλοφροσύνῃ καὶ εὐσταθείᾳ ἐν ἀνδρείᾳ ἡδυπαθείας "πρῶτον ὑπηνήτην, τοῦ περ χαριεστάτη ἥβη," τοιούτου κάλλους ὠδίνων ἔρωτα καὶ ὀνειροπολῶν μὲν καὶ ἐλπίζων, εὑρίσκων δὲ οὐδαμοῦ οὔτε ἐν γῇ οὔτε ἐν θαλάσσῃ, θαυμαστὰ ἔπασχον, ὥσπερ ἔφην, καὶ ᾤμην δεῖν τὸν περὶ τοῦ κάλλους λόγον τοιοῦτον εἶναι....

7. εἴδωλον ἔρωτος ἀντέρωτα ἔχων.

8. 13.180A–B: διδοίητε τοῖς ἐμοῖς παιδικοῖς ἐρᾶν μὲν Ῥώμης, ἀντερᾶσθαι δὲ ὑπὸ Ῥώμης.

Ares . . . is not a god for our good emperor by choice but through necessity. Our emperor is blessed in that he considers how it might be possible to make the barbarians obedient not through the sword but through the beauty and cultivation of his soul. Not only do philosophers love the splendor of Gratian, it seems, but the barbarians do as well, and willingly they yield and go under the yoke, defeated by his intention. (*Or.* 13.176B)[9]

To some extent metaphorizing Gratian's power and *auctoritas/axiōma* as sexual attractiveness—the philosophers and barbarians, compelled by the beauty (*kallonēi*/καλλονῇ) of his soul, come to love or have *erōs* (*erōsi*/ἐρῶσι) for his splendor—, Themistius uses the corporeal reality of erotic yearning to make his praise more lively. In this regard, the intertextuality of the speech with works of Plato, mention of which has already been made above, rewards more detailed consideration. For the hearer or reader in possession of knowledge of Plato, the pederastic and, as will be shown, same-sex sexual investments of this oration delivered in the homosocial environs of the senate are considerable. Giving due weight to these intertextualities further intensifies the perception that this oration is saturated with same-sex desire.

The conclusion of the speech with *erōs* for emperor and *anterōs* for Rome and senators calls the *Phaedrus* to mind. This intertextuality with the *Phaedrus* renders the oration as a whole a specimen of ring composition, for there is undeniable reference to the dialogue at its beginning. The beginning of the oration's title, *Erōtikos [logos]*, and the fact that the first word of the speech is "Socrates" (161B) bring the *Phaedrus* immediately to mind. Perhaps the most famous *erōtikos logos*, or discourse on love/desire, in history is the one that appears shortly after the beginning of Plato's dialogue (Phaedrus speaks):

> This matter surely is appropriate for you to hear, Socrates. There was indeed a *logos*, engaging us [Lysias and Phaedrus] for some time, that was *erōtikos* in some kind of way. Lysias wrote of one of the beautiful ones being courted, not by the one who desired/loved him and—and this very thing you will agree is so very clever—he says that the beautiful one must give in to the one who does not love him, instead of to the one who does. (*Phdr.* 227C)[10]

---

9. Ἄρης . . . ἀγαθῷ βασιλεῖ θεὸς οὐχ αἱρετός, ἀλλ' ἀναγκαῖος. καὶ εὐδαίμων ὅτῳ μὴ ἐξείη μηδὲ τοὺς βαρβάρους σιδήρῳ εὐηνίους ποιεῖν, ἀλλὰ τῇ τῆς ψυχῆς καλλονῇ καὶ εὐμουσίᾳ. τῆς δὲ Γρατιανοῦ ἀγλαΐας οὐχ οἱ φιλόσοφοι μόνον, ὡς ἔοικεν, ἀλλὰ καὶ οἱ βάρβαροι ἤδη ἐρῶσι καὶ ἑκόντες εἴκουσι καὶ ὑποκύπτουσι, τῇ γνώμῃ αὐτοῦ ἡττώμενοι.

10. Καὶ μήν, ὦ Σώκρατες, προσήκουσα γέ σοι ἡ ἀκοή· ὁ γάρ τοι λόγος ἦν, περὶ ὃν διετρίβομεν,

Shortly after these words, Phaedrus reads out Lysias' carnal and evidently engaging *logos erōtikos*, which then is followed by not one, but two more *logoi erōtikoi* from Socrates: one ironic and the other sincere. While there is further intertextuality with the *Phaedrus*,[11] the pederastic investments of Themistius' oration through its intertextuality with Plato don't stop here. The *Symposium* frequently lends vocabulary and verbal jingles to Themistius' text.[12] Significant in the context of the argument of this book are mentions of Charmides and Alcibiades.[13] And it is not just Plato. At a particularly swooning moment in which he says he can no longer look at Gratian, Themistius senses himself "being breathed on . . . and being inspired" (165D: *empneomenou . . . kai enthousiōntos*/ἐμπνεομένου . . . καὶ ἐνθουσιῶντος). This new sensory register for Themistius that takes the place of refused sight recalls Theocritus' famous pederastic *Idyll* 12 (lines 10–16). Readers or listeners who know this poem will associate Themistius, as he is in this state, with the figure of the *erōmenos* in the *Idyll*. There the "listener" (line 14: *aïtēn*/ἀίτην, i.e., the *erōmenos*) is breathed upon by the "inspirer" or "the one who breathes upon" (line 13: *eispnēlos*/εἴσπνηλος, i.e, the *erastēs*). Interestingly, in this moment of the sensory overload, Themistius allows the tables to be turned and becomes the boy to Gratian's man.[14]

There is, then, a hypertrophy of intertextual pederasty at the point of educated reception of Themistius' oration. But even though Themistius is often presenting in Gratian a golden vision of a desired and beautiful young man who is at the upper age limit to be a beloved boy, that is not all that is going on in the oration. As has already started to be evident, i.e., Gratian is also a man who "inspires" Themistius, Gratian is more than a boy and the roles assumed in pederasty are not adhered to. Indeed, elsewhere in the oration, Themistius presents Gratian as a soldier-man and holder of adult authority, which again takes the metaphorization of Gratian's admirability by desire out of pederasty's asymmetries and into the realm of same-sex desire between men:

οὐκ οἶδ' ὅντινα τρόπον ἐρωτικός. γέγραφε γὰρ δὴ ὁ Λυσίας πειρώμενόν τινα τῶν καλῶν, οὐχ ὑπ' ἐραστοῦ δέ, ἀλλ' αὐτὸ δὴ τοῦτο καὶ κεκόμψευται· λέγει γὰρ ὡς χαριστέον μὴ ἐρῶντι μᾶλλον ἢ ἐρῶντι.

11. In addition to the moments of intertextuality already mentioned, Themistius' oration is arguably intertextual with the dialogue at 165A–B (cf. *Phdr.* 252C [note: the *TLG* text of Themistius' oration here has reference to the *Phaedo* (Φαίδωνι), which is incorrect]), 166A (cf. *Phdr.* 228D), and 168D, which has βλάστην ἐρασμιωτέραν (cf. βλάστην at *Phdr.* 251D).

12. See 161D–163A, 164A, 164C–165A, 165D, 166A, 168C–D, 177B–178A, 178B; 164A, with its νέα ἐν νέῳ, ἀνθοῦσα ἐν ἀνθοῦντι recalling *Smp.* 195A–C (youth) and 196A (blooming), is typical.

13. 13.177B.

14. Emperor Julian's fourth oration also has a notable moment of intertextuality with Theocritus' *Idyll* 12. See my discussion in Masterson 2010: 91–93.

I am the exegete and prophet of my boyfriend: indeed, he has so much beauty that he makes the barbarian beautiful, the Goth gentle, the Persian tame, the Armenian already Roman, the Iberian Greek, and the nomad a householder: each changing from his former shame to the opposing beauty. I am the praiser and lover of both the soldier's belt and emperors, especially if I see the belt pulled tight with Justice, but I should wish more to praise and love the head and eyes, where the place and dwelling of thought and mind are. (*Or.* 13.166C–D)[15]

The pederastic aspect to Themistius' regard for Gratian is certainly reinforced when Themistius calls him his boyfriend (*ta paidika*/τὰ παιδικά), as he does a number of times in the speech.[16] But other details from the passage argue that Themistius is ultimately talking about same-sex desire between men, and the pederastic language, as so often in late antiquity, is a means to this end. This desire, in turn, metaphorizes the admiration of a magnificent man by another man.

Themistius provides a clear example of this metaphorical use of same-sex desire in the passage when he says that he is the lover (*erastēs*) of emperors. A little later in the oration, at 177C, he says that "his desire (*erōs*) is for two emperors,"[17] and the referents are Gratian and his uncle, emperor Valens, who is nearly fifty years old. Themistius also metaphorizes Gratian's exercise of power to police the others on the border of empire in terms of sexual attractiveness. Through a sort of sympathetic reaction, Gratian's beauty makes the barbarian himself beautiful, and causes changes, salutary from a Roman point of view, in Goth, Persian, Armenian, Iberian, and nomad. The welcome alterations that make the others more attractive, easier to handle, and even Roman and Greek are metaphors for military subjugation, a point which is driven home when Themistius says he is not just the lover (and praiser) of emperors, he is the lover too of the soldier's belt, the *cingulum*, rendered in the passage by the word *zōnē* (ζώνη).[18]

---

15. τῶν ἐμῶν δὲ παιδικῶν ὁ ἐξηγητὴς καὶ προφήτης, τοσοῦτον ἄρα αὐτῷ κάλλος περίεστιν ὥστε καὶ βάρβαρον ποιεῖν καλόν, καὶ τὸν Γέτην ἥμερον καὶ τὸν Πέρσην ἐπιεικῆ καὶ τὸν Ἀρμένιον ἤδη Ῥωμαῖον καὶ τὸν Ἴβηρα Ἕλληνα, καὶ τὸν σκηνητὴν οἰκουρόν· καὶ ἕκαστον ἐκ τοῦ πρόσθεν αἴσχους εἰς τὸ ἐναντίον κάλλος μεταμορφοῦν. Ἐγὼ δὲ εἰμὶ μὲν καὶ τῆς ζώνης καὶ τῶν βασιλέων ἐπαινέτης καὶ ἐραστής, καὶ μάλιστα εἰ καὶ ξὺν δίκῃ ζωννυμένην αὐτὴν καθορῴην, πολὺ δὲ μᾶλλον ἐπαινοίην ἂν καὶ ἐρῴην τῆς κεφαλῆς καὶ τῶν ὀμμάτων, ἵνα τὸ τῆς γνώμης καὶ νοῦ χωρίον καὶ οἰκητήριον.

16. 166C, 168C, 175D, 179A, 180B.

17. ὁ δὲ ἐμὸς ἔρως δυοῖν βασιλέοιν ἐστίν.

18. For *cingulum* as *zōnē*, see *LSJ* ζώνη II.3 or Lampe ζώνη 1C.

Themistius uses *zōnē* metaphorically twice, and then, following these uses, *zōnē* designates non-metaphorically the actual soldier's belt (*cingulum*) cinched tight on Gratian's body. First, *zōnē* refers in a general way to soldierly endeavor: "I am the . . . lover of . . . the soldier's belt. . . ." His love for the *zōnē* expresses his esteem for the military. *Figura Etymologica*, not easy to reproduce in English and embodied in the pairing of *zōnēs*/ ζώνης ("belt") with *zōnnumenēn xun dikēi*/ζωννυμένην ξὺν δίκῃ ("pulled tight [i.e., belted] with Justice"), reveals the second metaphorical meaning *zōnē* can have, that of imperial *axioma*/ἀξίωμα.[19] Themistius praises and loves the belt, now understood as imperial authority, when it is graciously restrained by legality (which of course it *always* is, as this is panegyric, and this declaration of love functions as hopeful recommendation). And then, in the next phrases, "but more should I wish to praise and love the head and eyes, where the place and dwelling of thought and mind are," the *zōnē*/ *cingulum*, no longer a metaphor for things military or gubernatorial, is made to appear literally on Gratian's body, as the reader's eyes, having had their long look, are raised up from the manly belt to the eyes. There has also been a correction from thinking of things below and corporeal (the crotch) to things above and sublimatory (the head and eyes). A "ladder of love" has been scaled.

In this short passage and, indeed, throughout the speech, Themistius shows the implication of same-sex desire in the making of authority amid homosociality among late-Roman men. Themistius delivers the oration in the homosocial space of the Roman senate, trusting in *paideia* to make his audience understand what he is saying (and the speech lives on in written format, available for multiple educated receptions, late-ancient and later). Exemplified in the passage, but recurring throughout the oration, is the glamorization of masculine authority through associating its admirability with same-sex desire. This is the use of corporeal excitement to give liveliness to admiration, and, furthermore, the forbidden nature of the desire increases the stature of the grand emperor through the empowering effects of paradox (e.g., Gratian's "manliness of luxury"; the use of the forbidden and illicit, i.e., same-sex desire, to increase the stature of that which is emphatically licit, i.e., imperial *axiōma*). In addition, Themistius' gentle correcting movement of the reader's gaze up from the belt to the head and eyes recalls the empowered knowingness that disciplining authorities have of the desire that they interdict: Themistius knows of same-sex desire and is one to incite, direct, and control it.

---

19. For *zōnē* as *axiōma*, see *LSJ* ζώνη II.3.

The goal of this book has been to reveal the ways in which same-sex desire and pleasure were visible within elite late-Roman manhood. In late antiquity there were a suite of visibilities of same-sex desire that recent accounts of this period have often missed due to scholars' excessive deference both to the sources' frequent protrepic goals and to perceived authorial intention. The corporeality of actual encounters remembered, intellectually known, and/or feared, left its mark on late-ancient discourse beyond the enunciation of prohibition in norms and law. As a constituent part of late-ancient manhood and an ever-present possibility, same-sex desire provoked rejection, enjoyed acceptance as a vehicle to express admiration or portray friendship, and increased authority's power through demonstrations of penetrating observation and knowing discipline. Discourses that had (relative) dispassion about the fact of same-sex desire in masculine life found this desire useful rhetorically. The corporeal intensity of desire achieving its objective made for a powerful metaphor, and the obscene and material, through a paradoxical logic much favored in late antiquity, were choice vehicles for expressing their ostensible opposites: the sacred and transcendent. Asserting that inexplicable connections exist between this world and the next, late-Platonic philosophy played a part in making such metaphors and paradoxes effective too.

But this was not the whole story. The exemplary Athanasius presented a manhood whose glamour and admirability could not be metaphorized as same-sex sexual attractiveness. While Athanasius did show a scrutinizing and uncompromising authority's knowledge of same-sex sexual activity, he separated same-sex desire and pleasure from the transcendent and relentlessly corporealized them. Athanasius' stance was a logical result of his envisioning the transcendent as a perfect reflection of terrestrial norms and not the thing of inscrutability and mystery proposed by late Platonists such as Iamblichus. Ammianus' presentation of the emperor fell between the late-Platonists' (and others') use of same-sex desire as a positive metaphor and Athanasius' rejection of it. While wanting at times an Athanasian transcendent responsive to earthbound morals (civility), and yet, at other times, embracing one that was mysterious (Constantius' imperial grandeur), Ammianus delivered respective blame and praise to his emperors, Constantius and Julian, via the medium of same-sex desire.

In a recent high-profile publication that considers changes to the family in late antiquity, the following is offered as part of a summative comment on late-Roman manhood:

> To be survived by a hearty son, able to consolidate and perhaps extend one's dominance, was the crown of male military achievement. That this depended on factors beyond a man's own control, such as longevity and the right reproductive partner, made it all the more potent a sign of divine favor.[20]

In these remarks, the domestic scene is important. There is much of the *domus* or *oikos* here, and fair enough; the piece is, in the first instance, about changes to the family in late antiquity and the household is important to consider if gender broadly construed is the topic. What deserve question are the claims implicit in the evocative phrases, "extend one's dominance" and "the crown of male military achievement." The family has been left behind when we speak of dominance and an acme of soldierly accomplishment. It is no longer the *oikos* or *domus;* this is the *polis,* empire, the political. However the notion of "military achievement" in relation to the vast majority of elite households in the late-ancient empire is to be understood—and that must surely count as an open question, inasmuch as late antiquity saw a controversial barbarization of the army—, it is overreach to pronounce the birth of a son key to securing dominance in a political sense. Marriage strategies were important to elites and the secondary literature coruscates with mention of the advantageous marriages men would make,[21] but fathering a son is not a political accomplishment comparable to achieving success in the homosocial environs of, say, service to the emperor. For example, the plaque the province of Asia set up for Nummius Aemilianus Dexter mentions no son, and it is surely the case that his political career was substantially a function of friendly relations with other officials and the hardly pro-marriage Jerome.

Restricting the view of late-ancient men in the matter of desire to that for women obscures important dynamics in the male homosocial spheres that characterized the expanding senate and the growing classes of elites serving the emperor. Same-sex desire was productive of powerful positive and negative passions in this homosocial world. The reality of (knowledge

---

20. Cooper 2009, 192.
21. Cooper 2007; Evans-Grubbs 2009; Lenski 2002: 58, 65, 276; Marcone 1998: 366; Matthews 1975: 74, 83; Sivan 1993: 49–66, 88, 143; Sogno 2010.

of) this desire and pleasure constituted a dimension to late-ancient men's experience that will be always be missed if it is imagined that erotic and emotional needs could (and can) be met without remainder in all cases by the licit pleasures and joys of marriage to a woman and the satisfactions of family. The reality was more complicated. It is my hope that this book will lead to a more balanced appraisal of late-Roman manhood and the undeniable presence of same-sex desire within it.

BIBLIOGRAPHY

PRIMARY SOURCES

Ammianus Marcellinus, *Res Gestae* (Seyfarth 1978).
Anthologia Graeca (*TLG*).
Apophthegmata Patrum [Alphabetic] (*PG* and *TLG*).
Arnobius, *Adversus Gentes* (Marchesi 1953).
Athanasius, *Contra Gentes* (Thomson 1971).
———, *De Incarnatione* (Thomson 1971).
———, *Epistula ad Amunem* (Joannou 1963).
———, *Vita Antoni* (Bartelink 1994).
Ausonius, *Opera* (Green 1991).
Claudian, *Opera Omnia* (J. B. Hall 1985).
Codex Theodosianus (Mommsen, Meyer, and Sirmond 1905).
Collatio [*Mosaicarum et Romanarum Legum Collatio*] (Riccobono and Arangio-Ruiz 1968).
Eunapius, Fragments of the *Chronicle after Dexippus* (Blockley 1983).
———, *Lives of the Philosophers* (*Sophists*) (Civiletti 2007).
Evagrius Antiochensis, *Vita Antonii* (Bertrand 2005).
Firmicus Maternus, *De Errore Profanorum Religionum* (Turcan 1982).
Historia Monachorum in Aegypto (Festugière 1961).
Iamblichus, *De Mysteriis* (*Réponse à Porphyre*) (Saffrey and Segonds 2013).
Jerome, *Interpretatio Regulae Sancti Pachomii* (*PL*).
———, *Vita Sancti Pauli, Primi Eremita* (Leclerc et al. 2007).

Julian, emperor, *Orations 1–5* (Bidez 2003).
———, *Orations 6–9* (Rochefort 2003).
———, *Oration 7* (Guido 2000).
———, *Orations 10–12* (Lacombrade 2003).
———, *Letter and Fragments* (Bidez 2004 and Bidez and Cumont 1922).
Macrobius, *Commentaria in Somnium Scipionis* (Eyssenhardt 1893).
Menander Rhetor (Russell and Wilson 1981).
Pacatus, *Panegyricus Dictus Theodosio* (*Panegyrici Latini* 12 [2]) (Mynors 1964).
Panegyrici Latini (Mynors 1964).
Paulinus of Nola, *Carmina* (Hartel and Kamptner 1999).
De Physiognomonia Liber, Anonymi (*Anon. Lat.*) (André 1981).
Plotinus, *Enneads* (*TLG*).
Saloustios, *De Deis et Mundo* (Rochefort 2003).
Themistius, *Oration 13* (*TLG*).
Theocritus (Gow 1950).
Victricius, *De Laude Sanctorum* (Mulders and Demeulenaere 1985).
Vita Antonii (Latina), Anonymi (Hoppenbrouwers 1960).
Xenophon. *Memorabilia* (*TLG*).
Zonaras, *Epitome Historiarum* (*TLG*).

SECONDARY SOURCES

Adams, J. N. 1982. *The Latin Sexual Vocabulary.* Baltimore: The Johns Hopkins University Press.

Adams, Rachel and David Savran, eds. 2002. *The Masculinity Studies Reader.* Malden, MA: Blackwell.

Alföldi, Andreas. 1980 (1935). *Die monarchische Repräsentation im römischen Kaiserreiche.* Darmstadt: Wissenschaftliche Buchgesellschaft.

Alonso-Nuñez, J. M. 1978. "El César Juliano y el Filósofo Salustio." *Helmantica* 29: 399–402.

———. 1974. "Política y Filosofia en *Los Césares* de Juliano." *Hispania Antigua* 4: 315–20.

Amerise, Marilena. 2002. "La Figura di Costantino nei *Caesares* di Giuliano l'Apostata." *Rivista Storica dell'Antichita* 32: 141–49.

André, Jacques. 1981. *Traite de Physiognomie.* Paris: Société d'Édition "Les Belles Lettres."

Arjava, Antti. 1998. "Paternal Power in Late Antiquity." *The Journal of Roman Studies* 88: 147–65.

———. 1996. *Women and Law in Late Antiquity.* Oxford: Oxford University Press.

Arnold, John H. and Sean Brady, eds. 2011. *What Is Masculinity?: Historical Dynamics from Antiquity to the Contemporary World.* New York: Palgrave-Macmillan.

Ast, Friedrich. 1835. *Lexicon Platonicum sive Vocum Platonicarum Index.* Leipzig: In Libraria Weidmanniana.

Athanassiadi (-Fowden), Polymnia. 2002. "The Creation of Orthodoxy in Neoplatonism." *Philosophy and Power in the Graeco-Roman World*. G. Clark and T. Rajak, eds. New York: Oxford University Press. 271–291.

———. 1981. *Julian and Hellenism: An Intellectual Biography*. Oxford: Clarendon Press.

Athanassiadi, P. and M. Frede, eds. 1999. *Pagan Monotheism in Late Antiquity*. Oxford: Clarendon Press.

Auerbach, Erich. 1953. *Mimesis: The Representation of Reality in Western Literature*. Williard R. Trask, trans. Princeton: Princeton University Press.

Avery, William. T. 1940. "The *Adoratio Purpurae* and the Importance of the Imperial Purple in the Fourth Century of the Christian Era." *Memoirs of the American Academy in Rome* 17: 66–80.

Baker-Brian, Nicholas, and Shaun Tougher, eds. 2012. *Emperor and Author: The Writings of Julian the Apostate*. Swansea: The Classical Press of Wales.

Baldwin B. 1978. "The *Caesares* of Julian." *Klio* 60: 449–66.

Barnes, Timothy David. 1998. *Ammianus Marcellinus and the Representation of Historical Reality*. Ithaca, NY: Cornell University Press.

———. 1996. "Oppressor, Persecutor, Usurper: The Meaning of 'Tyrannus' in the Fourth Century." Giorgio Bonamente and Marc Mayer, eds. *Historiae Augustae Colloquium Barcinonense*. Bari: Edipuglia. 55–65.

———. 1993. *Athanasius and Constantius: Theology and Politics in the Constantinian Empire*. Cambridge, MA: Harvard University Press.

———. 1990. "Literary Convention, Nostaglia, and Reality in Ammianus Marcellinus." *Reading the Past in Late Antiquity*. G. W. Clarke et al., eds. Rushcutters Bay, New South Wales, Australia: Australian National University Press. 59–92.

———. 1986. "Angel of Light or Mystic Initiate? The Problem of the *Life of Antony*." *Journal of Theological Studies* 37: 353–68.

———. 1978. "A Correspondent of Iamblichus." *Greek, Roman and Byzantine Studies* 19.1: 99–106.

Bartelink, G. J. M. 1994. *Athanase d'Alexandrie: Vie d'Antoine*. Sources Chrétiennes 400. Paris: Les Éditions du Cerf.

Barton, Carlin A. 2001. *Roman Honor: The Fire in the Bones*. Berkeley: University of California Press.

Bassi, Karen. 1988. *Acting like Men: Gender, Drama, and Nostalgia in Ancient Greece*. Ann Arbor: University of Michigan Press.

Bech, Henning. 1997 (1987). *When Men Meet: Homosexuality and Modernity*. Teresa Mesquit and Tim Davies, trans. Chicago: University of Chicago Press.

Bertrand, Pascal, 2005. "Die Evagriusübersetzung der *Vita Antonii*: Rezeption—Überlieferung—Edition, unter besonderer Berücksichtigung der *Vitas Patrum* Tradition." PhD diss., Proefschrift Universiteit Utrecht.

Bidez, J. 2004 (1924). *L'Empereur Julien: Œuvres Complètes, Lettres et Fragments*. Paris: l'Association Guillaume Budé.

———. 2003 (1932). *L'Empereur Julien: Œuvres Complètes, Discours de Julien César (I–V)*. Paris: l'Association Guillaume Budé.

———. 1930. *La Vie de l'Empereur Julien*. Paris: Société d'Édition "Les Belles lettres."

Bidez, J. and F. Cumont. 1922. *Imp. Caesaris Flavii Claudii Iuliani Epistulae, Leges, Poematia, Fragmenta Varia.* Paris: Belles Lettres.

Billerbeck, M. 1996. "The Ideal Cynic from Epictetus to Julian." *The Cynics: The Cynic Movement in Antiquity and Its Legacy.* R. Bracht Branham and Marie-Odile Goulet Cazé, eds. Berkeley: University of California Press. 203–21.

Blockley, R. C. 1996. "Ammianus Marcellinus and his Classical Background—Changing Perspectives." *International Journal of the Classical Tradition* 2.4: 455–66.

———.1983. *The Fragmentary Classicising Historians of the Later Roman Empire.* Liverpool: Francis Cairns.

———. 1975. *Ammianus Marcellinus: A Study of his Historiography and Political Thought.* Bruxelles: Latomus.

Bloomer, W. Martin. 1997. "Schooling in Persona: Imagination and Subordination in Roman Education." *Classical Antiquity* 16.1: 57–78.

Blumenthal, H. J. and E. G. Clark, eds. 1993. *The Divine Iamblichus: Philosopher and Man of Gods.* London: Bristol Classical Press.

Born, Lester K. 1934. "The Perfect Prince According to the Latin Panegyrists." *The American Journal of Philology* 55.1: 20–35.

Børtnes, Jostein. 2000. "Eros Transformed: Same-Sex Love and Divine Desire. Reflections on the Erotic Vocabulary in St. Gregory of Nazianzus's Speech on St. Basil the Great." *Greek Biography and Panegyric in Late Antiquity.* Tomas Hägg and Philip Rousseau, eds. Berkeley: University of California Press. 180–93.

Boswell, John. 1994. *Same-Sex Unions in Premodern Europe.* New York: Villard Books.

———. 1980. *Christianity, Social Tolerance, and Homosexuality.* Chicago: University of Chicago Press.

Bouffartigue, Jean. 1992. *L'Empereur Julien et la Culture de son Temps.* Paris: Institut d'Études Augustiniennes.

Bowersock, G. W. 1990. *Hellenism in Late Antiquity.* Ann Arbor: University of Michigan Press.

———. 1982. "The Emperor Julian on his Predecessors." *Later Greek Literature.* John J. Winkler and Gordon Willis Williams, eds. Cambridge: Cambridge University Press. 159–72.

———. 1978. *Julian the Apostate.* Cambridge, MA: Harvard University Press.

Boyarin, Daniel. 2006. "What do We Talk about When We Talk about Platonic Love?" *Toward a Theology of Eros: Transfiguring Passion at the Limits of Discipline.* Virginia Burrus and Catherine Keller, eds. New York: Fordham University Press. 3–22.

Boys-Stones, George. 2007. "Physiognomy and Ancient Psychological Theory." *Seeing the Face, Seeing the Soul: Polemon's Physiognomy from Classical Antiquity to Medieval Islam.* Simon Swain, ed. Oxford: Oxford University Press. 19–124.

Brakke, David. 2006. *Demons and the Making of the Monk: Spiritual Combat in Early Christianity.* Cambridge, MA: Harvard University Press.

———. 2001. "Ethiopian Demons: Male Sexuality, the Black-Skinned Other, and the Monastic Self." *Journal of the History of Sexuality* 10.3/4: 501–35.

———. 1995a. *Athanasius and the Politics of Asceticism.* Oxford: Oxford University Press.

———. 1995b. "The Problematization of Nocturnal Emissions in Early Christian Syria, Egypt, and Gaul." *Journal of Early Christian Studies* 3.4: 419–460.

Brandt, Axel. 1999. *Moralische Werte in den "Res Gestae" des Ammianus Marcellinus.* Göttingen: Vandenhoeck & Ruprecht.

Branham, R. Bracht. 1996. "Defacing the Currency: Diogenes' Rhetoric and the Invention of Cynicism." *The Cynics: The Cynic Movement in Antiquity and Its Legacy.* R. Bracht Branham and Marie-Odile Goulet Cazé, eds. Berkeley: University of California Press. 81–104.

Branham, R. Bracht and Marie-Odile Goulet Cazé, eds. 1996. *The Cynics: The Cynic Movement in Antiquity and Its Legacy.* Berkeley: University of California Press.

Bray, Alan. 2003. *The Friend.* Chicago: University of Chicago Press.

Brennan, Brian. 1985. "Athanasius' *Vita Antonii:* A Sociological Interpretation." *Vigiliae Christianae* 39: 209–27.

Bringmann. Klaus. 2004. *Kaiser Julian.* Darmstadt: Primus.

Brisson, Luc. 2009. "Salustius." *Brill's New Pauly* (http://www.brillonline.nl/subscriber/uid=1773/entry?entry=bnp_e1028720)

———. 2004. *How Philosophers Saved Myths: Allegorical Interpretation and Classical Mythology.* Chicago: University of Chicago Press.

———. 1998. *Plato the Myth Maker.* Chicago: University of Chicago Press.

Brooten, Bernadette J. 1996. *Love Between Women: Early Christian Responses to Female Homoeroticism.* Chicago: Chicago University Press.

Brown, Peter. 2000. "The Study of Elites in Late Antiquity."*Arethusa* 33.3: 321–46.

———. 1998. "Asceticism: Pagan and Christian." *The Cambridge Ancient History 13: The Late Empire* A.D. *337–425.* Averil Cameron and Peter Garnsey, eds. Cambridge: Cambridge University Press. 601–31.

———. 1995. *Authority and the Sacred: Aspects of the Christianisation of the Roman World.* Cambridge: Cambridge University Press.

———. 1992. *Power and Persuasion in Late Antiquity: Towards a Christian Empire.* Madison, WI: University of Wisconsin Press.

———. 1988. *The Body and Society: Men, Women, and Sexual Renunciation in Early Christianity.* New York: Columbia University Press.

———. 1987. "The Saint as Exemplar in Late Antiquity." *Saints and Virtues.* J. S. Hawley, ed. Berkeley: University of California Press. 3–14.

———. 1982 (1971). "The Rise and Function of the Holy Man in Late Antiquity." *Society and the Holy in Late Antiquity.* Berkeley: University of California Press. 103–52.

———. 1981. *The Cult of the Saints: Its Rise and Function in Latin Christianity.* Chicago: University of Chicago Press.

———. 1978. *The Making of Late Antiquity.* Cambridge, MA: Harvard University Press.

———. 1971. See 1982.

Burger, Glenn and Steven F. Kruger. 2001. "Introduction." *Queering the Middle Ages.* Glenn Burger and Steven F. Kruger, eds. Minneapolis: University of Minnesota Press. xi–xxiii.

Burrus, Virginia. 2004. *The Sex Lives of Saints: An Erotics of Ancient Hagiography.* Philadelphia: University of Pennsylvania Press.

———. 2001. "Queer Lives of Saints: Jerome's Hagiography." *Journal of the History of Sexuality* 10.3/4: 442–79.

———. 2000. *"Begotten, not Made": Conceiving Manhood in Late Antiquity.* Stanford: Stanford University Press.

———. 1996. "'Equipped for Victory': Ambrose and the Gendering of Orthodoxy." *Journal of Early Christian Studies* 4.4: 461–75.

Burrus, Virginia and Catherine Keller. 2006. *Toward a Theology of Eros: Transfiguring Passion at the Limits of Discipline.* New York: Fordham University Press.

Burton-Christie, Douglas. 1993. *The Word in the Desert: Scripture and the Quest for Holiness in Early Christian Monasticism.* Oxford: Oxford University Press.

Cairns, Francis. 1972. *Generic Composition in Greek and Roman Poetry.* Edinburgh: Edinburgh University Press.

Cameron, Alan. 2011. *The Last Pagans of Rome.* New York: Oxford University Press.

———. 1970. *Claudian: Poetry and Propaganda at the Court of Honorius.* Oxford: Clarendon Press.

———. 1964. "The Roman Friends of Ammianus." *The Journal of Roman Studies* 54: 15–28.

Cameron, Alan and Jacqueline Long. 1993. *Barbarians and Politics at the Court of Arcadius.* Berkeley: University of California Press.

Cameron, Averil. 2002. "The 'Long' Late Antiquity: A Late Twentieth-Century Model." *Classics in Progress: Essays on Ancient Greece and Rome.* T. P. Wiseman, ed. Oxford: Published for the British Academy by Oxford University Press. 165–92.

———. 2000. "Form and Meaning: The *Vita Constantini* and the *Vita Antonii.*" *Greek Biography and Panegyric in Late Antiquity.* Tomas Hägg and Philip Rousseau, eds. Berkeley: University of California Press. 72–88.

———. 1999. "On Defining the Holy Man." *The Cult of Saints in Late Antiquity and the Middle Ages: Essays on the Contribution of Peter Brown.* Paul Antony Hayward and James Howard-Johnston, eds. New York: Oxford University Press. 27–43.

———. 1998. "Education and Literary Culture." *The Cambridge Ancient History 13: The Late Empire A.D. 337–425.* Averil Cameron and Peter Garnsey, eds. Cambridge: Cambridge University Press. 665–707.

———. 1991. *Christianity and the Rhetoric of Empire: The Development of Christian Discourse.* Berkeley: University of California Press.

Cameron, Averil and Peter Garnsey, eds. 1998. *The Cambridge Ancient History 13: The Late Empire, A.D. 337–425.* Cambridge: Cambridge University Press.

Campbell, J. B. 1984. *The Emperor and the Roman Army: 31 B.C.–A.D. 235.* Oxford: Oxford University Press.

Camus, P. M. 1967. *Ammien Marcellin: Témoin des Courants Culturels et Religieux à la Fin du IVe Siècle.* Paris: Société d'Édition "Les Belles Lettres."

Caner, Daniel. 2009. "'Not of This World': The Invention of Monasticism." *A Companion to Late Antiquity.* Philip Rousseau and Jutta Raithel, eds. Malden, MA: Wiley-Blackwell. 588–600.

———. 2000. "Nilus of Ancyra and the Promotion of a Monastic Elite." *Arethusa* 33.3: 401–10.

Cantarella, Eva. 1992. *Bisexuality in the Ancient World.* New Haven: Yale University Press.

Castelli, Elizabeth A. 1998. "Gender, Theory, and the 'Rise of Christianity': A Response to Rodney Stark." *Journal of Early Christian Studies* 6.2: 227–57.

———. 1991a. *Imitating Paul: A Discourse of Power.* Louisville: Westminster/John Knox Press.

———. 1991b. "'I Will Make Mary Male': Pieties of the Body and Gender Transformation of Christian Women in Late Antiquity." *Body Guards: The Cultural Politics of Gender Ambiguity.* Julia Epstein and Kristina Straub, eds. New York: Routledge. 29–49.

Civiletti, Maurizio, trans. and comm. 2007. *Eunapio di Sardi: Vite di Filosofi e Sofisti.* Milan: Bompiani.

Charlet, J.-L. 1988. "Aesthetic Trends in Late Latin Poetry (325–410)." *Philologus* 132: 74–85.

Charlesworth, M. P. 1947. "Imperial Deportment: Two Texts and Some Questions." *The Journal of Roman Studies* 37: 34–38.

———. 1936. "Providentia and Aeternitas." *Harvard Theological Review* 29.2: 107–32.

Chastagnol, André. 1992. *Le Sénat Romain à l'Époque Impériale: Recherches sur la Composition de l'Assemblée et le Statut de ses Membres*. Paris: Les Belles Lettres.

———. 1982a. *L'Évolution Politique, Sociale et Économique du Monde Romain de Dioclétien à Julien*. Paris: Société d'Éd. d'Enseignement Supérieur.

———. 1982b. "La Carrière Sénatoriale du Bas-Empire (depuis Dioclétien)." *Colloquio Internazionale AIEGL su Epigrafia e Ordine Senatorio, Roma, 14–20 maggio 1981*, vol. 1, tituli 4. Rome. 167–93.

———. 1960. *La Préfecture Urbaine à Rome sous le Bas-Empire*. Paris: Presses Universitaires de France.

Chauncey, George. 1994. *Gay New York: Gender, Urban Culture, and the Making of the Gay Male World, 1890–1940*. New York: HarperCollins.

Chauvot, Alain. 1998. *Opinions Romaines face aux Barbares au IVe Siècle Ap. J.-C*. Paris: De Boccard.

Chiabò, Maria. 1983. *Index Verborum Ammiani Marcellini*. New York: Olms.

Clark, Elizabeth A. 1999. *Reading Renunciation: Asceticism and Scripture in Early Christianity*. Princeton, NJ: Princeton University Press.

———. 1992. *The Origenist Controversy: The Cultural Construction of an Early Christian Debate*. Princeton: Princeton University Press.

———. 1988. "Foucault, the Fathers, and Sex." *Journal of the American Academy of Religion* 56 (Winter): 619–41.

Clark, Gillian. 2005. "'In the Foreskin of their Flesh': The Pure Male Body in Late Antiquity." *Roman Bodies: Antiquity to the Eighteenth Century*. Andrew Hopkins and Maria Wyke, eds. London: British School at Rome. 43–53.

———. 2004. *Christianity and Roman Society*. Cambridge: Cambridge University Press.

———. 2000. "Philosophic Lives and the Philosophic Life: Pophyry and Iamblichus." *Greek Biography and Panegyric in Late Antiquity*. Tomas Hägg and Philip Rousseau, eds. Berkeley: University of California Press. 29–51.

———. 1999. "Victricius of Rouen: Praising the Saints." *Journal of Early Christian Studies* 7.3: 365–99.

———.1998. "The Old Adam: The Fathers and the Unmaking of Masculinity." *Thinking Men: Masculinity and its Self-Representation in the Classical Tradition*. Lin Foxhall and J. B. Salmon, eds. New York: Routledge. 170–82.

———. 1996. "'The Bright Frontier of Friendship': Augustine and the Christian Body as Frontier." *Shifting Frontiers in Late Antiquity*. R. W. Mathisen and H. S. Sivan, eds. Aldershot: Ashgate. 217–29.

Clark, G. and T. Rajak, eds. 2002. *Philosophy and Power in the Graeco-Roman World*. New York: Oxford University Press.

Clarke, Emma C. 2001. *Iamblichus' De Mysteriis: A Manifesto of the Miraculous*. Aldershot: Ashgate.

———. 1998. "Communication, Human and Divine: Saloustios Reconsidered." *Phronesis* 43.4: 326–50.

Clarke, Emma C., John M. Dillon, and Jackson P. Hershbell, trans. and comm. 2003. *Iamblichus: On the Mysteries*. Atlanta: Society for the Study of Biblical Literature.

Coleiro, E. 1957. "St. Jerome's Lives of the Hermits." *Vigiliae Christianae* 11.3: 161–78.

Collobert, Catherine, Pierre Destrée, and Francisco J. Gonzalez. 2012. *Plato and Myth: Studies on the Use and Status of Platonic Myths*. Leiden: Brill.

Connell, R. W. 2000. *The Men and the Boys*. Berkeley: University of California Press.

———. 1995. *Masculinities*. Berkeley: University of California Press.

———. 1987. *Gender and Power: Society, the Person and Sexual Politics*. Stanford: Stanford University Press.

Connolly, Joy. 2003. "Like the Labors of Heracles: *Andreia* and *Paideia* in Greek Culture under Rome." *Andreia: Studies in Manliness and Courage in Classical Antiquity*. Ralph M. Rosen and Ineke Sluiter, eds. Leiden: Brill. 287–317.

Conte, G. 1986. *The Rhetoric of Imitation: Genre and Poetic Memory in Virgil and Other Latin Poets*. Ithaca: Cornell University Press.

Conybeare, Catherine. 2002. "The Ambiguous Laughter of Saint Laurence." *Journal of Early Christian Studies* 10.2: 175–202.

———. 2000. *Paulinus Noster: Self and Symbols in the Letters of Paulinus of Nola*. Oxford: Oxford University Press.

Cooper, Kate. 2009. "Gender and the Fall of Rome." *A Companion to Late Antiquity*. Philip Rousseau and Jutta Raithel, eds. Malden, MA: Wiley-Blackwell. 187–200.

———. 2007. *The Fall of the Roman Household*. Cambridge: Cambridge University Press.

———. 1996. *The Virgin and the Bride*. Cambridge, MA: Harvard University Press.

———. 1992. "Insinuations of Womanly Influence: An Aspect of the Christianization of the Roman Aristocracy." *The Journal of Roman Studies* 82: 150–64.

Cooper, Kate and Conrad Leyser. 2000. "The Gender of Grace: Impotence, Servitude, and Manliness in the Fifth-Century West." *Gender and History* 12: 536–51.

Copjec, Joan. 1994. *Read My Desire: Lacan against the Historicists*. Cambridge: MIT Press.

Corbeill, Anthony. 1996. *Controlling Laughter: Political Humor in the Late Roman Republic*. Princeton: Princeton University Press.

Corcoran, Simon. 1996. *The Empire of the Tetrarchs: Imperial Pronouncements and Government, A.D. 284–324*. Oxford Classical Monographs. Oxford: Clarendon Press.

Corpus Inscriptionum Latinarum. 1968. Berlin: De Gruyter

Cosi, Dario M. 1986. *Casta Mater Idaea: Giuliano l'Apostata e l'Etica della Sessualità*. Venezia: Marsilio.

Coulter, James A. 1976. *The Literary Microcosm: Theories of Interpretation of the Later Neoplatonists*. Leiden: E. J. Brill.

Cox, Patricia. 1983. *Biography in Late Antiquity: A Quest for the Holy Man*. Berkeley: University of California Press.

Cremer, F. W. 1969. *Die chaldäischen Orakel und Jamblichs de Mysteriis*. Meisenheim am Glan: A. Hain.

Cribiore, Raffaella. 2009. "The Value of a Good Education: Libanius and Public Authority." *A Companion to Late Antiquity*. Philip Rousseau and Jutta Raithel, eds. Malden, MA: Wiley-Blackwell. 233–45.

———. 2001. *Gymnastics of the Mind: Greek Education in Hellenistic and Roman Egypt.* Princeton, NJ: Princeton University Press.

Crook, John. 1967. *Law and Life of Rome.* Ithaca, New York: Cornell University Press.

Dagron, Gilbert. 2003. *Emperor and Priest: The Imperial Office in Byzantium.* Cambridge: Cambridge University Press.

———. 1974. *Naissance d'une Capitale: Constantinople et ses Institutions de 330 à 451.* Paris: Presses Universitaires de France.

Dalla, Danilo. 1987. *"Ubi Venus Mutatur": Omosessualità e Diritto nel Mondo Romano.* Seminario Giuridico della Università di Bologna, 119. Milan: Giuffrè.

Davidson, James. 2007. *The Greeks and Greek Love: A Radical Reappraisal of Homosexuality in Ancient Greece.* London: Weidenfeld & Nicolson.

———. 2001. "Dover, Foucault, and Greek Homosexuality: Penetration and the Truth of Sex." *Past and Present:* 3–51.

Davis, Stephen J. 2002. "Crossed Texts, Crossed Sex: Intertextuality and Gender in Early Christian Legends of Holy Women Disguised as Men." *Journal of Early Christian Studies* 10.1: 1–36.

Dawson, Doyne. 1992. *Cities of the Gods: Communist Utopias in Greek Thought.* New York: Oxford University Press.

Dean, Tim. 2000. *Beyond Sexuality.* Chicago: University of Chicago Press.

de Bonfils, G. 1986. *Ammiano Marcellino e l'Imperatore.* Bari: Edizioni Fratelli Laterza.

de Jonge, P. 1977. *Philological and Historical Commentary on Ammianus Marcellinus XVII.* Groningen: Bouma.

———. 1972a. *Philological and Historical Commentary on Ammianus Marcellinus XV.1–5.* Groningen: Bouma.

———. 1972b. *Philological and Historical Commentary on Ammianus Marcellinus XVI.* Groningen: Bouma.

den Boeft, J., et al. 1995. *Philological and Historical Commentary on Ammianus Marcellinus 22.* Groningen: Egbert Forsten.

———. 1991. *Philological and Historical Commentary on Ammianus Marcellinus 21.* Groningen: Egbert Forsten.

Desmond, William D. 2008. *Cynics.* Berkeley: University of California Press.

Dessau, Hermann. 1892. *Inscriptiones Latinae Selectae.* Berolini: apud Weidmannos.

Deutscher, Penelope. 1997. *Yielding Gender: Feminism, Deconstruction and the History of Philosophy.* New York: Routledge.

Dijk, Gert-Jan van. 1997. *Ainoi, Logoi, Mythoi: Fables in Archaic, Classical, and Hellenistic Greek Literature: With a Study of the Theory and Terminology of the Genre.* Leiden: Brill.

Dillon, John. M. 1998. "Rejecting the Body, Refining the Body: Some Remarks on the Development of Platonist Asceticism." *Asceticism.* Vincent L. Wimbush and Richard Valantasis, eds. New York: Oxford University Press. 80–87.

———. 1987. "Iamblichus of Chalcis (c. 240–325)." *Aufstieg und Niedergang der römischen Welt* II 36.2: 862–909.

———. 1977 (1996). *The Middle Platonists, 80 B.C. to A.D. 220.* Ithaca: Cornell University Press.

———. 1975. "Image, Symbol and Analogy: Three Basic Concepts in Neoplatonic Exegesis."

The Significance of Neoplatonism. Studies in Neoplatonism, v. 1. R. Blaine Harris, ed. Norfolk, VA: International Society for Neoplatonic Studies, Old Dominion University. 247–62.

Dillon, John and Jackson Hershbell, eds. and trans. 1991. *Iamblichus: On the Pythagorean Life*. Atlanta: Scholars Press.

Dodds, E. R. 1965. *Pagan and Christian in an Age of Anxiety: Some Aspects of Religious Experience from Marcus Aurelius to Constantine*. Cambridge: Cambridge University Press.

———. 1951. *The Greeks and the Irrational*. Berkeley: University of California Press.

Dover, K. J. 1978. *Greek Homosexuality*. Cambridge, MA: Harvard University Press.

duBois, Page. 1988. *Sowing the Body: Psychoanalysis and Ancient Representations of Women*. Chicago: University of Chicago Press.

Dudink, Stefan. 1998. "The Trouble with Men: Problems in the History of 'Masculinity.'" *European Journal of Cultural Studies* 1: 419–31.

Dvornik, F. 1955. "The Emperor Julian's 'Reactionary' Ideas on Kingship." *Late Classical and Mediaeval Studies in Honor of Albert Mathias Friend, Jr.* K. Weitzmann, ed. Princeton, NJ: Princeton University Press. 71–81.

Ebbeler, Jennifer. 2009. "Tradition, Innovation, and Epistolary *Mores*." *A Companion to Late Antiquity*. Philip Rousseau and Jutta Raithel, eds. Malden, MA: Wiley-Blackwell. 270–84.

Edmunds, Lowell. 2001. *Intertextuality and the Reading of Roman Poetry*. Baltimore: Johns Hopkins.

Edwards, Catharine. 1993. *The Politics of Immorality in Ancient Rome*. Cambridge: Cambridge University Press.

Edwards, Mark J. 2004. "Pagan and Christian Monotheism in the Age of Constantine." *Approaching Late Antiquity: The Transformation from Early to Late Empire*. Simon Swain and Mark Edwards, eds. Oxford: Oxford University Press. 211–34.

———, trans. 2000. *Neoplatonic Saints: The Lives of Plotinus and Proclus by Their Students*. Liverpool: Liverpool University Press.

———. 1993. "Two Images of Pythagoras: Iamblichus and Porphyry." *The Divine Iamblichus: Philosopher and Man of Gods*. H. J. Blumenthal and E. G. Clark, eds. London: Bristol Classical Press. 159–72.

Elm, Susanna. 2012. *Sons of Hellenism, Fathers of the Church: Emperor Julian, Gregory of Nazianzus, and the Vision of Rome*. Berkeley: University of California Press.

———. 2000. "A Programmatic Life: Gregory of Nazianzus' Orations 42 and 43 and the Constantinopolitan Elites." *Arethusa* 33.3: 411–27.

———. 1994. *"Virgins of God": The Making of Asceticism in Late Antiquity*. Oxford: Oxford University Press.

Elsner, Jaś. 1997. *Art and the Roman Viewer: The Tranformation of Art from the Pagan World to Christianity*. Cambridge: Cambridge University Press.

Espejo-Muriel, Carlos. 1991. *El Deseo Negado: Aspectos de la Problemática Homosexual en la Vida Monástica (Siglos III–VI D. C.)*. Granada: Universidad de Granada.

Evans, Elizabeth C. 1969. "Physiognomics in the Ancient World." *Transactions of the American Philosophical Society*. Vol. 59, Pt. 5. Philadelphia: The American Philosophical Society.

Evans-Grubbs, Judith. 2009. "Marriage and Family Relationships in the Late Roman West." *A Companion to Late Antiquity*. Philip Rousseau and Jutta Raithel, eds. Malden, MA: Wiley-Blackwell. 201–19.

———. 1995. *Law and Family in Late Antiquity: The Emperor Constantine's Marriage Legislation.* Oxford: Clarendon Press.

Eyssenhardt, Franz. 1893. *Ambrosius Aurelius Theodosius Macrobius: Macrobius.* Lipsiae: in Aedibus B. G. Teubneri.

Feeney, D. C. 1991. *The Gods in Epic: Poets and Critics of the Classical Tradition.* Oxford: Clarendon Press.

Festugière, A. J., ed. 1961. *Historia Monachorum in Aegypto.* Bruxelles: Société des Bollandistes.

———. 1959. *Antioche Païenne et Chrétienne.* Paris: E. de Boccard.

———. 1931. "'Υπομονή dans la Tradition Grecque." *Recherches de Science Religieuse* 21: 477–86.

Finamore, John F. 1993. "Iamblichus on Light and the Transparent." *The Divine Iamblichus: Philosopher and Man of Gods.* H. J. Blumenthal and E. G. Clark, eds. London: Bristol Classical Press. 55–64.

———. 1985. *Iamblichus and the Theory of the Vehicle of the Soul.* Chico, CA: Scholars Press.

Finamore, John F. and John M. Dillon. 2002. *Iamblichus:* De Anima. Leiden: Brill.

Finn, Richard. 2009. *Asceticism in the Graeco-Roman World.* Cambridge: Cambridge University Press.

Fischler, Susan. 1998. "Imperial Cult: Engendering the Cosmos" (in Foxhall and Salmon, *When Men Were Men:* 165–83).

Fitzgerald, John T. 1997. *Greco-Roman Perspectives on Friendship.* Atlanta: Scholars Press.

Flemming, Rebecca. 2000. *Medicine and the Making of Roman Women: Gender, Nature, and Authority from Celsus to Galen.* Oxford: Oxford University Press.

Fletcher, G. B. A. 1937. "Stylistic Borrowings and Parallels in Ammianus Marcellinus." *Revue de Philologie* 63: 377–95.

Fornara, Charles W. 1992. "Studies in Ammianus II." *Historia* 41.1: 420–38.

Förster, R. 1893. *Scriptores Physiognomonici Graeci et Latini.* Leipzig: Teubner.

Foucault, Michel. 1986. *The Care of the Self (The History of Sexuality, Vol. 3).* Robert Hurley, trans. New York: Vintage.

———. 1985. *The Use of Pleasure (The History of Sexuality, Vol. 2).* Robert Hurley, trans. New York: Vintage.

———. 1978. *The History of Sexuality.* Robert Hurley, trans. New York: Pantheon Books.

Fowden, G. 2005. "Sages, Cities and Temples: Aspects of Late Antique Pythagorism." *The Philosopher and Society in Late Antiquity: Essays in Honour of Peter Brown.* A Smith, ed. Swansea: Classical Press of Wales. 145–70.

———. 1986. *The Egyptian Hermes: A Historical Approach to the Late-Pagan Mind.* Cambridge: Cambridge University Press.

———. 1982. "The Pagan Holy Man in Late Antique Society." *Journal of Hellenic Studies* 102: 33–59.

Fowler, Don. 2000. *Roman Constructions: Readings in Postmodern Latin.* Oxford. Oxford University Press.

Fox, M. 1998. "The Constrained Man." *Thinking Men: Masculinity and Its Self-Representation in the Classical Tradition.* L. Foxhall and J. B. Salmon, eds. London: Routledge. 6–22.

Foxhall, Lin. 1998. "Introduction" (in Foxhall and Salmon, *When Men Were Men:* 1–9).

Foxhall, Lin and J. B. Salmon, eds. 1998. *When Men Were Men: Masculinity, Power and Identity in Classical Antiquity.* New York: Routledge.

Frakes, Robert M. 2011. *Compiling the Collatio Legum Mosaicarum et Romanarum in Late Antiquity.* Oxford: Oxford University Press.

———. 2006. "The Religious Identity and Purpose of the Compiler of the *Collatio Legum Mosaicarum et Romanarum* or *Lex Dei.*" *Religious Identity in Late Antiquity.* Elizabeth DePalma Digeser and Robert M. Frakes, eds. Toronto: Edgar Kent, Inc., Publishers. 126–47.

———. 2002. "Item Theodosianus? (Observations on Coll. V.3.1)." *Quaderni Urbinati di Cultura Classica* 71.2: 163–68.

———. 2000. "Ammianus Marcellinus and his Intended Audience." *Studies in Latin Literature and Roman History X.* C. Deroux, ed. Collection Latomus 254. Brussels. 392–442.

Frank, Georgia. 2000. *The Memory of the Eyes: Pilgrims to Living Saints in Christian Late Antiquity.* Berkeley: University of California Press.

Gardner, Jane F. 1998. "Sexing a Roman: Imperfect Men in Roman Law" (in Foxhall and Salmon, *When Men Were Men:* 136–52).

———. 1991. *Women in Roman Law and Society.* Bloomington: Indiana University Press.

Garnsey, P. and C. Humfress. 2001. *The Evolution of the Late Antique World.* Cambridge: Orchard Academic.

Gerson, Lloyd P. 2003. "Neoplatonism." *The Blackwell Guide to Ancient Philosophy.* Christopher Shields, ed. Malden, MA: Blackwell Pub. 303–22.

Gilliam, J. F. 1967. "Titus in Julian's *Caesares.*" *American Journal of Philology* 88.2: 203–208.

Gizewski, Christian. 2012. "Illustris vir." *Brill's New Pauly.* Antiquity volumes edited by: Hubert Cancik and Helmuth Schneider. Brill, 2012. *Brill Online.*

Gleason, Maud W. 1995. *Making Men: Sophists and Self-Presentation in Ancient Rome.* Princeton: Princeton University Press.

———. 1986. "Festive Satire: Julian's *Misopogon* and the New Year at Antioch." *The Journal of Roman Studies* 76: 106–19.

Goehring, James E. 2005. "The Dark Side of the Landscape: Ideology and Power in the Christian Myth of the Desert." *The Cultural Turn in Late Ancient Studies: Gender, Asceticism, and Historiography.* Dale B. Martin and Patricia Cox Miller, eds. Durham: Duke University Press. 138–49.

———. 1999. *Ascetics, Society, and the Desert: Studies in Early Egyptian Monasticism.* Harrisburg, PA: Trinity Press International.

———. 1993. "The Encroaching Desert: Literary Production and Ascetic Space in Early Christian Egypt." *Journal of Early Christian Studies* 1: 281–96.

Goldhill, Simon. 1995. *Foucault's Virginity: Ancient Erotic Fiction and the History of Sexuality.* Cambridge: Cambridge University Press.

Gould, Graham. 1993. *The Desert Fathers on Monastic Community.* Oxford: Clarendon Press.

Goulet, Richard. 2001. *Études sur les Vies de Philosophes dans l'Antiquité Tardive: Diogène Laërce, Porphyre de Tyr, Eunape de Sardes.* Paris: Vrin.

Gow, A. S. F. 1952. *Theocritus.* Cambridge: Cambridge University Press.

Gradenwitz, Otto. 1925 (1970). *Heidelberger Index zum Theodosianus.* Berlin: Weidmann.

Grasso, Fabio. 1996. "L'Interpretazione Allegorica in Giuliano Imperatore: Il Concetto di *Apemphainon* e la Funzione del Mito Teologico." *Rudiae* 8: 31–40.

Green, R. P. H. 1991. *The Works of Ausonius*. Oxford: Clarendon Press.

Groß-Albenhausen, Kirsten. 2012a "Spectabilis." *Brill's New Pauly.* Antiquity volumes edited by: Hubert Cancik and Helmuth Schneider. Brill, 2012. *Brill Online.*

———. 2012b. "Vir clarissimus." *Brill's New Pauly.* Antiquity volumes edited by: Hubert Cancik and Helmuth Schneider. Brill, 2012. *Brill Online.*

Guido, Rosanna. 2000. *Al cinico Eraclio*. Galatina (Lecce): M. Congedo.

———. 1998. "La Nozione di Φιλία in Giuliano Imperatore." *Rudiae* 10: 113–44.

———. 1991. "Μύθους Πλάττειν: Un'Eco Platonica in Iul. Or.7?" *Rudiae* 3: 89–103.

Gunderson, Erik. 2003. *Declamation, Paternity, and Roman Identity: Authority and the Rhetorical Self.* Cambridge: Cambridge University Press.

———. 2000. *Staging Masculinity: The Rhetoric of Performance in the Roman World.* Ann Arbor: University of Michigan Press.

Gutman, Matthew C. 1997. "Trafficking in Men: The Anthropology of Masculinity." *Annual Review of Anthropology* 26: 385–409.

Hall, John Barrie. 1985. *Claudii Claudiani Carmina*. Leipzig: Teubner.

Halperin, David. M. 2002a. *How to Do the History of Homosexuality.* Chicago: University of Chicago Press.

———. 2002b. "Forgetting Foucault: Acts, Identities, and the History of Sexuality." *The Sleep of Reason: Erotic Experience and Sexual Ethics in Ancient Greece and Rome*. Martha C. Nussbaum and Juha Sihvola, eds. Chicago: The University of Chicago Press. 21–54.

———. 1990. *One Hundred Years of Homosexuality and Other Essays on Greek Love*. New York: Routledge.

Halsall, Guy. 2004. "Gender and the End of Empire." *Journal of Medieval and Early Modern Studies* 34.1: 17–39.

Hamilton, Edith and Huntington Cairns. 1971. *The Collected Dialogues of Plato*. Princeton: Princeton University Press.

Hamilton, Walter, trans. 1986. *Ammianus Marcellinus: The Later Roman Empire (A.D. 354–378)*. Harmondsworth: Penguin Books.

Harper, Kyle. 2013. *From Shame to Sin: The Christian Transformation of Sexual Morality in Late Antiquity.* Cambridge, MA: Harvard University Press.

Harpham, Geoffrey Galt. 1998. "Asceticism and the Compensations of Art." *Asceticism.* Vincent L. Wimbush and Richard Valantasis, eds. New York: Oxford University Press. 357–68.

———. 1987. *The Ascetic Imperative in Culture and Criticism*. Chicago: The University of Chicago Press.

Harries, Jill. 1999. *Law and Empire in Late Antiquity.* Cambridge, UK: Cambridge University Press.

———. 1998. "How to Make a Law-Code." *Modus Operandi: Essays in Honour of Geoffrey Rickman*. M. Austin, J. D. Harries, and C. Smith, eds. *Bulletin of the Institute of Classical Studies* 71. London: 63–78.

———. 1988. "The Roman Imperial Quaestor from Constantine to Theodosius II." *The Journal of Roman Studies* 78: 148–72.

Hartel, Wilhelm August, and Margit Kamptner. 1999. *Sancti Pontii Meropii Paulini Nolani.* 2 vols. Vindobonae [Vienna]: Verlag der österreichischen Akademie der Wissenschaften.

Harvey, Paul B. 1998. "Saints and Satyrs: Jerome the Scholar at Work." *Athenaeum* 86.1: 35–56.

Hauck, F. 1975 (1967). "Μένω." *The Dictionary of the New Testament* 4: 574–88.

Heath, Malcolm. 2004. *Menander: A Rhetor in Context.* Oxford: Oxford University Press.

Heather, P. J. 1998. "Senators and Senates." *The Cambridge Ancient History 13: The Late Empire, A.D. 337–425.* A. Cameron and P. Garnsey, eds. Cambridge. 184–210.

———. 1994a. "Literacy and Power in the Migration Period." *Literacy and Power in the Ancient World.* Alan K. Bowman and Greg Woolf, eds. Cambridge: Cambridge University Press. 177–97.

———. 1994b. "New Men for New Constantines? Creating an Imperial Elite in the Eastern Mediterranean." *New Constantines: The Rhythm of Imperial Renewal in Byzantium, 4th–13th Centuries.* P. Magdalino, ed. Aldershot, UK. 11–33.

Heim, François. 1991. *Virtus: Idéologie Politique et Croyances Religieuses au IVe Siècle.* Berne: Peter Lang.

Henderson, Jeffrey. 1991. *The Maculate Muse: Obscene Language in Attic Comedy.* New York: Oxford University Press.

Hinds, Stephen. 1998. *Allusion and Intertext: Dynamics of Appropriation in Roman Poetry.* Cambridge: Cambridge University Press.

Hine, Daryl. 2001. *Puerilities: Erotic Epigrams of* The Greek Anthology. Princeton: Princeton University Press.

Hirschfeld, Otto. 1901. *Die Rangtitel der römischen Kaiserzeit.* Berlin: K. Akademie der Wissenschaften.

Honoré, Tony. 1998. *Law in the Crisis of Empire, 379–455 A.D.: The Theodosian Dynasty and its Quaestors.* Oxford: Clarendon Press.

Hopkins, Andrew and Maria Wyke. 2005. *Roman Bodies: Antiquity to the Eighteenth Century.* London: British School at Rome.

Hopkins, Keith. 1978. *Conquerors and Slaves.* Cambridge: Cambridge University Press.

Hoppenbrouwers, H. 1960 *La plus Ancienne Version Latine de la Vie de S. Antoine par S. Athanase; Étude de Critique Textuelle.* Nijmegen: Dekker & van de Vegt.

Hubbard, Thomas K. 2003. *Homosexuality in Greece and Rome: A Sourcebook of Basic Documents.* Berkeley: University of California Press.

Humfress, Caroline. 2009. "Law in Practice." *A Companion to Late Antiquity.* Philip Rousseau and Jutta Raithel, eds. Malden, MA: Wiley-Blackwell. 377–91.

Humphries, Mark. 2009. "The Shapes and Shaping of the Late Antique World: Global and Local Perspectives." *A Companion to Late Antiquity.* Philip Rousseau and Jutta Raithel, eds. Malden, MA: Wiley-Blackwell. 97–109.

Hunt, D. 1998. "Julian." *The Cambridge Ancient History,* vol. 13, *The Late Empire,* A.D. 337–425. Averil Cameron and P. Garnsey, eds. Cambridge: Cambridge University Press. 44–77.

———. 1995. "Julian and Marcus Aurelius." *Ethics and Rhetoric: Classical Essays for Donald Russell on his Seventy-Fifth Birthday.* D. A. Russell, et al. eds. Oxford: Clarendon Press. 287–98.

Hunter, David G. 1999. "Vigilantius of Calagurris and Victricius of Rouen: Ascetics, Relics, and Clerics in Late Roman Gaul." *Journal of Early Christian Studies* 7.3: 401–30.

Hunter, Richard. 1996. *Theocritus and the Archaeology of Greek Poetry.* Cambridge, Cambridge University Press.

Irigaray, Luce. 1985 (1974). *Speculum of the Other Woman*. Gillian C. Gill, trans. Ithaca: Cornell University Press.

Jacobs, Andrew S. 2006. "'Papian Commands One Thing, Our Paul Another': Roman Christians and Jewish Law in the *Collatio Legum Mosaicarum et Romanarum*." *Religion and Law in Classical and Christian Rome*. Clifford Ando and Jörg Rüpke, eds. Stuttgart: Franz Steiner Verlag. 85–99.

Jagose, Annamarie Rustom. 1996. *Queer Theory: An Introduction*. New York: New York University Press.

Joannou, P.-P. 1963. *Fonti. Fasciolo ix. Discipline Générale Antique (ii–ix s.). Les Canons des Pères Grecs*. Vol. II. Rome: Tipographia Italo-Orientale "S. Nilo."

Johnston, S. I. 1997. "Rising to the Occasion: Theurgic Ascent in Its Cultural Milieu." *Envisioning Magic: A Princeton Seminar and Symposium*. P. Schäfer and H. G. Kippenberg, eds. Leiden: Brill. 165–94.

Jones, A. H. M. 1971. *The Prosopography of the Later Roman Empire 1. A.D. 260—395*. Cambridge: Cambridge University Press.

———. 1964. *The Later Roman Empire, 284–602: A Social, Economic, and Administrative Survey*. Baltimore: The Johns Hopkins University Press.

Jordan, Mark D. 2006. "Flesh in Confession: Alcibiades beside Augustine." *Toward a Theology of Eros: Transfiguring Passion at the Limits of Discipline*. Virginia Burrus and Catherine Keller, eds. New York: Fordham University Press. 23–37.

Kaldellis, Anthony. 2007. *Hellenism in Byzantium: The Transformations of Greek Identity and the Reception of the Classical Tradition*. Cambridge, UK: Cambridge University Press.

Kannengiesser, Charles. 1998. "Athanasius of Alexandria and the Ascetic Movement of his Time." *Asceticism*. Vincent L. Wimbush and Richard Valantasis, eds. New York: Oxford University Press. 479–92.

Kaster, Robert A. 1988. *Guardians of Language: The Grammarian and Society in Late Antiquity*. Berkeley: University of California Press.

Kelly, Christopher. 2004. *Ruling the Later Roman Empire*. Cambridge, MA: Belknap Press of Harvard University Press.

———. 1998a. "Emperors as Gods, Angels as Bureaucrats: The Representation of Imperial Power in Late Antquity." *Antigüedad, Religiones y Sociedades* 1: 301–26.

———. 1998b. "Emperors, Government and Bureaucracy." *The Cambridge Ancient History 13: The Late Empire A.D. 337–425*. Averil Cameron and Peter Garnsey, eds. Cambridge: Cambridge University Press. 138–83.

———. 1994. "Later Roman Bureaucracy: Going through the Files." *Literacy and Power in the Ancient World*. Alan K. Bowman and Greg Woolf, eds. Cambridge: Cambridge University Press. 161–76.

Kelly, Gavin. 2008. *Ammianus Marcellinus: The Allusive Historian*. Cambridge: Cambridge University Press.

———. 2005. "Constantius II, Julian, and the Example of Marcus Aurelius: Ammianus Marcellinus XXI, 16, 11–12." *Latomus* 64: 409–16.

Kelly, J. N. D. 1995. *Golden Mouth: The Story of John Chrysostom—Ascetic, Preacher, Bishop*. Ithaca, New York: Cornell University Press.

Kennedy, George Alexander. 2000. *Progymnasmata: Greek Textbooks of Prose Composition Introductory to the Study of Rhetoric*. Fort Collins: Chez l'auteur.

———. 1994. *A New History of Classical Rhetoric*. Princeton, NJ: Princeton University Press.

———. 1983. *Greek Rhetoric under Christian Emperors*. Princeton, NJ: Princeton University Press.

King, Richard J. 2006. *Desiring Rome: Male Subjectivity and Reading Ovid's Fasti*. Columbus: The Ohio State University Press.

———. 2004. "Male Homosocial Readership and the Dedication of Ovid's Fasti." *Arethusa* 37.2: 197–223.

Knight, Gillian. 2005. "Friendship and Erotics in the Late Antique Verse-Epistle: Ausonius to Paulinus Revisited." *Rheinisches Museum für Philologie* 148.3/4: 361–403.

Kolb, F. 2001. *Herrscherideologie in der Spätantike*. Berlin: Akademie Verlag.

Konstan, David. 1996a. "Friendship, Frankness, and Flattery." *Friendship, Flattery, and Frankness of Speech: Studies on Friendship in the New Testament World*. John T. Fitzgerald, ed. Leiden: E. J. Brill. 7–19.

———. 1996b. *Friendship in the Classical World*. Cambridge: Cambridge University Press.

———. 1996c. "Greek Friendship." *American Journal of Philology* 117: 71–94.

———. 1996d. "Problems in the History of Christian Friendship." *Journal of Early Christian Studies* 4.1: 87–113.

Krawiec, Rebecca. 2002. *Shenoute and the Women of the White Monastery: Egyptian Monasticism in Late Antiquity*. New York: Oxford University Press.

Krueger, Derek. 2006. "Homoerotic Spectacle and the Monastic Body in Symeon the New Theologian." *Toward a Theology of Eros: Transfiguring Passion at the Limits of Discipline*. Virginia Burrus and Catherine Keller, eds. New York: Fordham University Press. 99–118.

———. 1996. "The Bawdy and Society: The Shamelessness of Diogenes in Roman Imperial Culture." *The Cynics: The Cynic Movement in Antiquity and Its Legacy*. R. Bracht Branham and Marie-Odile Goulet Cazé, eds. Berkeley: University of California Press. 222–39.

Kuefler, Mathew. 2006. "The Boswell Thesis." *The Boswell Thesis: Essays on Christianity, Social Tolerance, and Homosexuality*. Mathew Kuefler, ed. Chicago: University of Chicago Press. 1–31.

———. 2001. *The Manly Eunuch: Masculinity, Gender Ambiguity, and Christian Ideology in Late Antiquity*. Chicago: The University of Chicago Press.

Lacombrade, C. 2003 (1965). *L'Empereur Julien: Œuvres Complètes, Discours de Julien Empereur (X–XII)*. Paris: l'Association Guillaume Budé.

———. 1967. "L'Empereur Julien, Émule de Marc-Aurèle." *Pallas* 14: 9–22.

Lamberton, Robert. 2001. "The Schools of Platonic Philosophy of the Roman Empire: The Evidence of the Biographies." *Education in Greek and Roman Antiquity*. Y. L. Too, ed. Leiden: Brill. 433–58.

———. 1999. "Sweet Honey in the Rock: Pleasure, Embodiment, and Metaphor in Late-Antique Platonism." *Constructions of the Classical Body*. James I. Porter, ed. Ann Arbor: University of Michigan Press. 314–26.

———. 1986. *Homer the Theologian: Neoplatonist Allegorical Reading and the Growth of the Epic Tradition*. Berkeley: University of California Press.

Lampe, G. W. H. and Henry George Liddell. 1961. *A Patristic Greek Lexicon*. Oxford: Clarendon.

Lanzi, Silvia. 2004. "Sosipatra, La Teurga: Una "Holy Woman" Iniziata ai Misteri Caldaici." *Studi e Materiali di Storia delle Religioni.* 70/2, n. 28: 275–94.

Laqueur, Thomas. 1990. *Making Sex: Body and Gender from the Greeks to Freud.* Cambridge, MA: Harvard University Press.

Layton, Bentley. 2007. "Rules, Patterns, and the Exercise of Power in Shenoute's Monastery: The Problem of World Replacement and Identity Maintenance." *Journal of Early Christian Studies* 15.1: 45–73.

Leader-Newby, Ruth E. 2004. *Silver and Society in Late Antiquity: Functions and Meanings of Silver Plate in the Fourth to Seventh Centuries.* Aldershot, Hants, England: Ashgate.

Leclerc, Pierre, Edgardo Martín Morales, and Adalbert de Vogüé. 2007. *Jerome: Trois Vies de Moines: Paul, Malchus, Hilarion.* Paris: Cerf.

Lee, A. D. 1998. "The Army." *The Cambridge Ancient History 13: The Late Empire, A.D. 337–425.* Averil Cameron and Peter Garnsey, eds. Cambridge: Cambridge University Press. 211–37.

Lendon, J. E. 1997. *Empire of Honour: The Art of Government in the Roman World.* Oxford: Oxford University Press.

Lenski, Noel Emmanuel. 2004. "Valens and the Monks: Cudgeling and Conscription as a Means of Social Control." *Dumbarton Oaks Papers* 58: 93–117.

———. 2002. *Failure of Empire: Valens and the Roman State in the Fourth Century A.D.* Berkeley: University of California Press.

Lesher, J. H., Debra Nails, and Frisbee C. C. Sheffield, eds. 2006. *Plato's Symposium: Issues in Interpretation and Reception.* Cambridge, MA: Center for Hellenic Studies.

Leyser, Conrad. 2000. *Authority and Asceticism from Augustine to Gregory the Great.* Oxford: Clarendon Press.

———. 1999. "'This Sainted Isle': Panegyric, Nostalgia, and the Invention of 'Lerinian Monasticism.'" *The Limits of Ancient Christianity: Essays on Late Antique Thought and Culture in Honor of R. A. Markus.* William Klingshirn and Mark Vessey, eds. Ann Arbor: University of Michigan Press. 188–206.

Levine, N. A. S. 1968. "The *Caesares* of Julian. An Historical Study." PhD. diss., Columbia University.

Lewy, Yochanan and Michel Tardieu. 1978 (1956). *Chaldaean Oracles and Theurgy: Mysticism, Magic, and Platonism and the Later Roman Empire.* Paris: Institut d'Études Augustiniennes.

Leyerle, Blake. 2005. "Monks and Other Animals." *The Cultural Turn in Late Ancient Studies: Gender, Asceticism, and Historiography.* Dale B. Martin and Patricia Cox Miller, eds. Durham: Duke University Press. 150–71.

Liddell, Henry George, Robert Scott, Henry Stuart Jones, and Roderick McKenzie. 1996. *A Greek-English lexicon.* Oxford: Clarendon Press.

Liebeschuetz, J. H. W. G. 2012. "Julian's *Hymn to the Mother of the Gods:* The Revival and Justification of Traditional Religion." *Emperor and Author: The Writings of Julian the Apostate.* Nicholas Baker-Brian and Shaun Tougher, eds. Swansea: The Classical Press of Wales. 213–27.

———. 1990. *Barbarians and Bishops: Army, Church, and State in the Age of Arcadius and Chrysostom.* Oxford: Clarendon Press.

Liebs, Detlef. 1987. *Die Jurisprudenz im spätantiken Italien (260–640 n. Chr.).* Berlin: Duncker & Humblot.

Lilla, S. 1992. "Neoplatonism." *Encyclopedia of the Early Church*. Angelo di Berardino, ed. New York: Oxford University Press. 585B–593A.

Lim, Richard. 1995. *Public Disputation, Power and Social Order in Late Antiquity*. Berkeley: University of California Press.

Lloyd, A. C. 1990. *The Anatomy of Neoplatonism*. Oxford: Clarendon Press.

———. 1967. "The Later Neoplatonists." *The Cambridge History of Later Greek and Early Medieval Philosophy*. A. H. Armstrong, ed. London: Cambridge University Press. 269–325.

Lloyd, Genevieve. 1993. *The Man of Reason: "Male" and "Female" in Western Philosophy*. 2nd ed. Minneapolis: University of Minnesota Press.

Lobel, E. and D. L. Page, ed. 1955. *Poetarum Lesbiorum Fragmenta*. Oxford: Clarendon Press.

Löhken, Henrik. 1982. *Ordines Dignitatum: Untersuchungen zur formalen Konstituierung der spätantiken Führungsschicht*. Köln: Böhlau.

Long, Jacqueline. 1996. *Claudian's In Eutropium; Or, How, When, and Why to Slander a Eunuch*. Chapel Hill: University of North Carolina Press.

Louth, Andrew. 1988. "St. Athanasius and the Greek *Life of Antony*." *The Journal of Theological Studies* 39.2: 504–509.

Luck, Georg. 1989. "Theurgy and Forms of Worship in Neoplatonism." *Religion, Science, and Magic: In Concert and in Conflict*. Jacob Neusner, Ernest S. Frerichs, and Paul Virgil McCracken Flesher, eds. New York: Oxford University Press. 185–228.

MacCormack, Sabine G. 1998. *Shadows of Poetry: Vergil in the Mind of Augustine*. Berkeley: University of California Press.

———. 1981. *Art and Ceremony in Late Antiquity*. Berkeley: University of California Press.

———. 1975. "Late Latin Panegyrics." *Empire and Aftermath: Silver Latin II*. T. A. Dorey, ed.: London: Routledge & Kegan Paul. 143–205.

MacMullen, Ramsay. 1990. *Changes in the Roman Empire: Essays in the Ordinary*. Princeton: Princeton University Press.

———. 1962. "Roman Bureaucratese." *Traditio* 18: 364–78.

Marchesi, Concetto, ed. 1953. *Arnobii Adversus Nationes: Libri VII*. Aug. Taurinorum: I. B. Paravia et Socii.

Marcone, Arnaldo. 2012. "The Forging of an Hellenic Orthodoxy: Julian's Speeches Against the Cynics." *Emperor and Author: The Writings of Julian the Apostate*. Nicholas Baker-Brian and Shaun Tougher, eds. Swansea: The Classical Press of Wales. 239–50.

———. 1998. "Late Roman Social Relations." *The Cambridge Ancient History 13: The Late Empire, A.D. 337–425*. Averil Cameron and Peter Garnsey, eds. Cambridge: Cambridge University Press. 338–70.

Markus, R. A. 1996. *Signs and Meanings: World and Text in Ancient Christianity*. Liverpool: Liverpool University Press.

Marrou, H. I. 1956. *A History of Education in Antiquity*. George Lamb, trans. Madison: The University of Wisconsin Press.

Martin, Dale B. and Patricia Cox Miller. 2005. *The Cultural Turn in Late Ancient Studies: Gender, Asceticism, and Historiography*. Durham: Duke University Press.

Mason, H. J. 1974. *Greek Terms for Roman Institutions; A Lexicon and Analysis*. Toronto: Hakkert.

———. 1970. "The Roman Government in Greek Sources: The Effect of Literary Theory on the Translation of Official Titles." *Phoenix* 24: 150–59.

Masterson, Mark. Forthcoming. "Authoritative Obscenity in Iamblichus and Arnobius." *Journal of Early Christian Studies* 22.3.

———. 2013. "Studies of Ancient Masculinity." *Blackwell Guide to Ancient Sexuality*. Thomas K. Hubbard, ed. Malden, MA: Wiley-Blackwell. 17-30.

———. 2010. "Erotics and Friendship in Emperor Julian's Fourth Oration." *Scholia* 19: 79–110.

———. 2006. "Impossible Translation: Antony and Paul the Simple in the *Historia Monachorum*." *The Boswell Thesis: Essays on* Christianity, Social Tolerance, and Homosexuality. Mathew Kuefler, ed. Chicago: University of Chicago Press. 215–35.

Mastrangelo, Marc. 2008. *The Roman Self in Late Antiquity: Prudentius and the Poetics of the Soul*. Baltimore: Johns Hopkins University Press.

Matthews, John F. 2000a. *Laying Down the Law: A Study of the Theodosian Code*. New Haven: Yale University Press.

———. 2000b. "The Roman Empire and the Proliferation of Elites." *Arethusa* 33.3: 429–46.

———. 1989. *The Roman Empire of Ammianus*. London: Duckworth.

———. 1975. *Western Aristocracies and Imperial Court A.D. 364–425*. Oxford: Clarendon Press.

Mayer, Wendy. 2009. "Approaching Late Antiquity." *A Companion to Late Antiquity*. Philip Rousseau and Jutta Raithel, eds. Malden, MA: Wiley-Blackwell. 1–13.

McCormick, Michael. 1986. *Eternal Victory: Triumphal Rulership in Late Antiquity, Byzantium, and the Early Medieval West*. Cambridge: Cambridge University Press.

McDonnell, Myles Anthony. 2006. *Roman Manliness: Virtus and the Roman Republic*. Cambridge: Cambridge University Press.

McGinn, Thomas A. J. 1998. *Prostitution, Sexuality, and the Law in Ancient Rome*. New York: Oxford University Press.

Merrill, Robert V. 1944. "Eros and Anteros." *Speculum* 19.3: 265–84.

Middleton, Peter. 1992. *The Inward Gaze: Masculinity and Subjectivity in Modern Culture*. New York: Routledge.

Miles, Richard. 1999. *Constructing Identities in Late Antiquity*. London: Routledge.

Millar, Fergus. 1986. "Review: A New Approach to the Roman Jurists." *The Journal of Roman Studies* 76: 272–80.

———. 1983. "Empire and City, Augustus to Julian: Obligations, Excuses and Status." *The Journal of Roman Studies* 73: 76–96.

———. 1977. *The Emperor in the Roman World, 31 B.C.–A.D. 337*. Ithaca, NY: Cornell University Press.

Miller, D. A. 1991. "Anal *Rope*." *Inside/Out: Lesbian Theories, Gay Theories*. Diana Fuss, ed. New York: Routledge. 118–41.

Miller, Patricia Cox. 2005a. "Is There a Harlot in This Text?: Hagiography and the Grotesque." *The Cultural Turn in Late Ancient Studies: Gender, Asceticism, and Historiography*. Martin, Dale B. and Patricia Cox Miller, eds. Durham: Duke University Press. 87–102.

———. 2005b. "Relics, Rhetoric, and Mental Spectacles." *Seeing the Invisible in Late Antiquity and the Early Middle Ages*. Utrecht Studies in Medieval Literacy 14. Giselle de Nie, Karl F. Morrison, and Marco Mostert, eds. Turnhout: Brepols Publishers. 25–52.

———. 2005c. "Shifting Selves in Late Antiquity." *Religion and the Self in Antiquity.* David Brakke, Michael Satlow, and Stephen Weitzman, eds. Bloomington: Indiana University Press. 15–39.

———. 2004. "Visceral Seeing: The Holy Body in Late Ancient Christianity." *Journal of Early Christian Studies* 12.4: 391–411.

———. 2001. *The Poetry of Thought in Late Antiquity: Essays in Imagination and Religion.* Burlington, VT: Ashgate Publishing Limited.

———. 2000a. "Strategies of Representation in Collective Biography: Constructing the Subject as Holy." *Greek Biography and Panegyric in Late Antiquity.* Tomas Hägg and Philip Rousseau, eds. Berkeley: University of California Press. 209–54.

———. 2000b. "'The Little Blue Flower is Red': Relics and the Poetizing of the Body." *Journal of Early Christian Studies* 8.2: 213–36.

———. 1998a. "'Differential Networks': Relics and Other Fragments in Late Antiquity." *Journal of Early Christian Studies* 6.1: 113–38.

———. 1998b. "Dreaming the Body: An Aesthetics of Asceticism." *Asceticism.* Vincent L. Wimbush and Richard Valantasis, eds. New York: Oxford University Press. 281–300.

———. 1996. "Jerome's Centaur: A Hyper-Icon of the Desert." *Journal of Early Christian Studies* 4.2: 209–33. (=2001, 75–99)

———. 1994a. "Desert Asceticism and 'The Body from Nowhere.'" *Journal of Early Christian Studies* 2: 137–53. (=2001, 159–79)

———. 1994b. *Dreams in Late Antiquity: Studies in the Imagination of a Culture.* Princeton: Princeton University Press.

———. 1993. "The Blazing Body: Ascetic Desire in Jerome's Letter to Eustochium." *Journal of Early Christian Studies* 1.1: 21–45. (=2001, 135–58)

Mommsen, Theodor, Paul M. Meyer, and Jacques Sirmond. 1905. *Theodosiani Libri XVI: cum Constivtionibvs Sirmondianis et Leges Novellae ad Theodosianvm Pertinentes; Consilio et Avctoritate Academiae Litterarvm Regiae Borvssicae Edidervnt Th.* Berolini: apvd Weismannos.

Montserrat, Dominic. 1998. "Experiencing the Male Body in Roman Egypt" (in Foxhall and Salmon, *When Men Were Men:* 153–64).

Moore, Stephen. D. 2001. *God's Beauty Parlor and Other Queer Spaces in and around the Bible.* Stanford: Stanford University Press.

Mulders, I. and R. Demeulenaere. 1985. *Victricii Rotomagensis De laude Sanctorum.* Turnholt: Brepols.

Müller, Friedhelm L. 1998. *Die beiden Satiren des Kaisers Julianus Apostata: Symposion oder Caesares, und Antiochikos oder Misopogon.* Stuttgart: Franz Steiner.

Müller, Guido, S. J. 1952. *Lexicon Athanasianum.* Berlin: Walter de Gruyter & Co.

Mynors, R. A. B. 1964. *XII Panegyrici Latini.* Oxonii: E Typographeo Clarendoniano.

Näf, Beat. 1995. *Senatorisches Standesbewusstsein in spätrömischer Zeit.* Freiburg: Universitätsverlag.

Neri, Valerio. 1984. *Costanzo, Giuliano e l'Ideale del Civilis Princeps: Nelle Storie di Ammiano Marcellino.* Roma: Cattedra di Filologia bizantina dell'Università di Bologna.

Nesselrath, Heinz-Günther. 1992. "Caesar in den *Caesares:* ein Beitrag zur Text- und Quellenkritik in den Schriften Kaiser Julians." *Rheinisches Museum für Philologie* 135: 352–65.

Nixon, C. E. V. and Barbara Saylor Rodgers, trans. and comm. 1994. *In Praise of Later Roman Emperors: The Panegyrici Latini.* Berkeley: University of California Press.

Nock, Arthur Darby. 1957. "Deification and Julian: I." *The Journal of Roman Studies* 47.1/2: 115–23.

———. 1947. "The Emperor's Divine Comes." *The Journal of Roman Studies* 37.1/2: 102–116.

———. 1930. "Σύνναος Θεός." *Harvard Studies in Classical Philology* 41: 1–62.

———, ed. 1926. *Sallustius: Concerning the Gods and the Universe.* Cambridge: Cambridge University Press.

Nutton, Vivian. 2004. *Ancient Medicine.* London: Routledge.

O'Meara, Dominic J. 2005. *Platonopolis: Platonic Political Philosophy in Late Antiquity.* Oxford: Oxford University Press.

———. 1993. "Aspects of Political Philosophy in Iamblichus." *The Divine Iamblichus: Philosopher and Man of Gods.* H. J. Blumenthal and E. G. Clark, eds. London: Bristol Classical Press. 65–73.

———. 1989. *Pythagoras Revived: Mathematics and Philosophy in Late Antiquity.* Oxford: Clarendon Press.

Onians, John. 1980. "Abstraction and Imagination in Late Antiquity." *Art History* 3: 1–24.

Pack, R. A. 1946. "Notes on the *Caesars* of Julian." *Transactions of the American Philological Association* 72: 151–57.

Pangle, Lorraine. 2003. *Aristotle and the Philosophy of Friendship.* Cambridge: Cambridge University Press.

Parker, Holt N. 1997. "The Teratogenic Grid." *Roman Sexualities.* Judith P. Hallett and Marilyn B. Skinner, eds. Princeton: Princeton University Press. 47–65.

Penella Robert J. 2000. *The Private Orations of Themistius.* Berkeley: University of California Press.

———. 1990. *Greek Philosophers and Sophists in the Fourth Century A.D.: Studies in Eunapius of Sardis.* Leeds: Cairns.

Pépin, J. 1970. "Plotin et le Miroir de Dionysos (ENN. 4.3 [27].12.1–2)." *Revue Internationale de Philosophie* 24: 304–20.

Pergami, F. 1993. *La Legislazione di Valentiniano e Valente (364–375).* Milan: Dott. A. Giuffrè Editore.

Pettersen, Alvyn. 1995. *Athanasius.* London: Geoffrey Chapman.

———. 1990. *Athanasius and the Human Body.* Bedminster, Bristol: Bristol Press.

———. 1987. "Athanasius' Presentation of Antony of the Desert's Admiration for His Own Body." *Studia Patristica* 21: 438–47.

Potter, David. 1994. *Prophets and Emperors: Human and Divine Authority from Augustus to Theodosius.* Cambridge, MA: Harvard University Press.

Price, A. W. 1989. *Love and Friendship in Plato and Aristotle.* New York: Oxford University Press.

Quinn, Kenneth. 1980. *Horace: The Odes.* Walton on Thames, Surrey, United Kingdom: Thomas Nelson and Sons, Ltd.

Rapp, Claudia. 2005. *Holy Bishops in Late Antiquity: The Nature of Christian Leadership in an Age of Transition.* Berkeley: University of California Press.

———. 2000. "The Elite Status of Bishops in Late Antiquity in Ecclesiastical, Spiritual, and Social Contexts."*Arethusa* 33.3: 379–99.

Rappe, Sara. 2000. *Reading Neoplatonism: Non-Discursive Thinking in the Texts of Plotinus, Proclus, and Damascius*. Cambridge: Cambridge University Press.

Rebenich, S. 2002. *Jerome*. New York: Routledge.

———. 1992. *Hieronymus und sein Kreis*. Stuttgart: Franz Steiner Verlag.

Rees, Roger. 2002. *Layers of Loyalty in Latin Panegyric, A.D. 289–307*. Oxford: Oxford University Press.

Reinhold, Meyer. 1970. *History of Purple as a Status Symbol in Antiquity*. Bruxelles: Latomus.

Riccobono, Salvatore and Vincenzo Arangio-Ruiz. 1968. *Fontes Ivris Romani Antejvstiniani*. Florentiae: apud S. A. G. Barbéra.

Richlin, Amy. 1997. "Gender and Rhetoric: Producing Manhood in the Schools." *Roman Eloquence: Rhetoric in Society and Literature*. William J. Dominik, ed. London: Routledge. 90–110.

———. 1993. "Not Before Homosexuality: The Materiality of the Cinaedus and the Roman Law against Love between Men." *Journal of the History of Sexuality* 3.4: 523–73.

———. 1992a (1983). *The Garden of Priapus: Sexuality and Aggression in Roman Humor*. Revised edition. New York: Oxford University Press.

———. 1992b. "Reading Ovid's Rapes." *Pornography and Representation in Greece and Rome*. New York: Oxford University Press. 158–79.

Roberts, Michael. 1989. *The Jeweled Style: Poetry and Poetics in Late Antiquity*. Ithaca: Cornell University Press.

———. 1988. "The Treatment of Narrative in Late Antique Literature: Ammianus Marcellinus (16.10), Rutilius Namatianus, and Paulinus of Pella." *Philologus* 132.2: 181–95.

———. 1985. "Paulinus Poem 11, Virgil's First *Eclogue*, and the Limits of *Amicitia*." *Transactions of the American Philological Association* 115: 271–82.

Robinson, O. F. 1997. *The Sources of Roman Law: Problems and Methods for Ancient Historians*. New York: Routledge.

Rochefort, G. 2003 (1963). *L'Empereur Julien: Œuvres Complètes, Discours de Julien Empereur (VI–IX)*. Paris: l'Association Guillaume Budé.

———. 2003 (1960). *Saloustios: De Deis et Mundo*. Paris: l'Association Guillaume Budé.

Rolfe, John C. 1939. *Ammianus Marcellinus III*. Loeb Classical Library. Cambridge, MA: Harvard University Press.

———. 1937. *Ammianus Marcellinus II*. Loeb Classical Library. Cambridge, MA: Harvard University Press.

———. 1935. *Ammianus Marcellinus I*. Loeb Classical Library. Cambridge, MA: Harvard University Press.

Roper, Michael. 2005. "Slipping out of View: Subjectivity and Emotion in Gender History." *History Workshop Journal* 59: 57–72.

Rosen, K. 2006. *Julian: Kaiser, Gott und Christenhasser*. Stuttgart: Klett-Cotta.

———. 1982. *Ammianus Marcellinus*. Darmstadt: Wissenschaftliche Buchgesellschaft.

Rousseau, Philip. 1985. *Pachomius: The Making of a Community in Fourth-Century Egypt*. Berkeley: University of California Press.

Rousseau, Philip and Jutta Raithel, eds. 2009. *A Companion to Late Antiquity*. Malden, MA: Wiley-Blackwell.

Rousselle, Aline. 1998. *La Contamination Spirituelle: Science, Droit, et Religion dans l'Antiquité*. Paris: Société d'Édition "Les Belles Lettres."

———. 1988 (1983). *Porneia: On Desire and the Body in Antiquity*. Felicia Pheasant, trans. Oxford: Basil Blackwell.

Rubin, Gayle. 1975. "The Traffic in Women: Notes Toward a Political Economy of Sex." *Toward an Anthropology of Women*. R. Reiter, ed. New York: Monthly Review Press. 157–210.

Ruether, Rosemary Radford. 1989. "Sexism and God-Language." *Weaving the Visions: New Patterns in Feminist Spirituality*. Judith Plaskow and Carol P. Christ, eds. San Francisco: Harper & Row. 151–62.

———. 1974. "Misogynism and Virginal Feminism in the Fathers of the Church." *Religion and Sexism: Images of Woman in the Jewish and Christian Traditions*. R. R. Ruether, ed. New York: Simon and Schuster. 150–83.

Russell, D. A. and N. G. Wilson. 1981. *Menander Rhetor*. Oxford: Clarendon Press.

Russell, Kenneth C. 1992. "John Cassian on a Delicate Subject." *Cistercian Studies Quarterly* 27: 1–12.

Rutgers, L. V. 1995. *The Jews in Late Ancient Rome: Evidence of Cultural Interaction in the Roman Diaspora*. Leiden: Brill.

Sabbah, Guy. 1978. *La Méthode d'Ammien Marcellin-Recherches sur la Construction du Discours Historique dans les* Res Gestae. Paris: Société d'Édition "Les Belles Lettres."

Saffrey, H. D. 2000. *Le Néoplatonisme après Plotin*. Paris: J. Vrin.

Saffrey, H. D. and A.-Ph. Segonds. 2013. *Iamblichus: Réponse à Porphyre: (De Mysteriis)*. Paris: Société d'Édition "Les Belles Lettres."

Salzman, Michele R. 2002. *The Making of a Christian Aristocracy: Social and Religious Change in the Western Roman Empire*. Cambridge, MA: Harvard University Press.

———. 2000. "Elite Realities and Mentalités: The Making of a Western Christian Aristocracy." *Arethusa* 33.3: 347–62.

Sardiello, Rosanna. 2000. *Simposio: I Cesari / Giuliano Imperatore*. Galatina (Lecce): M. Congedo.

———. 1997. "Il Marco Aurelio di Giuliano Imperatore." *Rudiae* 9: 257–68.

Savran, David. 1998. *Taking It Like a Man: White Masculinity, Masochism, and Contemporary American Culture*. Princeton: Princeton University Press.

Schehr, Lawrence R. 1997. *Parts of an Andrology: On Representations of Men's Bodies*. Stanford: Stanford University Press.

Schlinkert, Dirk. 1996. Ordo Senatorius *und* Nobilitas: *Der Konstitution des Senatsadels in der Spätantike*. Stuttgart: Franz Steiner Verlag.

Schroeder, Caroline T. 2007. *Monastic Bodies: Discipline and Salvation in Shenoute of Atripe*. Philadelphia: University of Pennsylvania Press.

———. 2006. "Prophecy and Porneia in Shenoute's Letters: The Rhetoric of Sexuality in a Late Antique Egyptian Monastery." *Journal of Near Eastern Studies* 65.2: 81–98.

Schroeder, Frederic M. 1997. "Friendship in Aristotle and Some Peripatetic Philosophers." *Greco-Roman Perspectives on Friendship*. John T. Fitzgerald, ed. Atlanta: Scholars Press. 35–57.

Schweckendiek, Helge. 1992. *Claudians Invektive gegen Eutrop* (In Eutropium)*: Ein Kommentar.* Hildesheim: Olms.

Scott, Joan W. 1986. "Gender: A Useful Category of Historical Analysis." *American Historical Review* 91: 1053–75.

Scott, Stan. 1987. "L'Empereur Julien. Transcendance et Subjectivité." *Revue d'Histoire et de Philosophie Religieuses* 67: 345–62.

Scourfield, J. H. D. and Anna Chahoud. 2007. *Texts and Culture in Late Antiquity: Inheritance, Authority, and Change.* Swansea: Classical Press of Wales.

Scroggs, Robin. 1983. *The New Testament and Homosexuality: Contextual Background for Contemporary Debate.* Philadelphia: Fortress Press.

Seager, Robin. 1986. *Ammianus Marcellinus, Seven Studies in His Language and Thought.* Columbia: University of Missouri Press.

Sedgwick, Eve Kosofsky. 1990. *Epistemology of the Closet.* Berkeley: University of California Press.

———. 1988. "Privilege of Unknowing." *Genders* 1: 102–24.

———. 1985. *Between Men: English Literature and Male Homosocial Desire.* New York: Columbia University Press.

Sells, Michael A. 1994. *Mystical Languages of Unsaying.* Chicago: University of Chicago Press.

Seyfarth, Wolfgang. 1978. *Ammianus: Res Gestae.* 2 vols. Leipzig: Teubner.

Shanzer, Danuta. 2006. "Latin Literature, Christianity and Obscenity in the Later Roman West." *Medieval Obscenities.* Nicola McDonald, ed. York: York Medieval Press. 179–202.

Shaw, Brent D. 1997. "Ritual Brotherhood in Roman and Post-Roman Societies." *Traditio* 52: 327–55.

———. 1996. "Body/Power/Identity: Passions of the Martyrs." *Journal of Early Christian Studies* 4.3: 269–312.

Shaw, Gregory. 1999. "Neoplatonic Theurgy and Dionysius the Areopagite." *Journal of Early Christian Studies* 7.4: 573–99.

———. 1995. *Theurgy and the Soul: The Neoplatonism of Iamblichus.* University Park: The Pennsylvania State University Press.

———. 1993. "The Geometry of Grace: A Pythagorean Approach to Theurgy." *The Divine Iamblichus: Philosopher and Man of Gods.* H. J. Blumenthal and E. G. Clarke, eds. London: Bristol Classical Press. 116–37.

———. 1985. "Theurgy: Rituals of Unification in the Neoplatonism of Iamblichus." *Traditio* 41: 1–28.

Shaw, Teresa M. 1998. *The Burden of the Flesh: Fasting and Sexuality in Early Christianity.* Minneapolis: Fortress Press.

Simpson, Mark and Steven Zeeland. 2001. *The Queen is Dead: A Story of Jarheads, Eggheads, Serial Killers, and Bad Sex.* London: Arcadia Books.

Sivan, Hagith. 1993. *Ausonius of Bordeaux: Genesis of a Gallic Aristocracy.* London: Routledge.

Skinner, Alexander. 2000. "The Birth of a 'Byzantine' Senatorial Perspective." *Arethusa* 33.3: 363–77.

Smith, Andrew. 2012. "Julian's *Hymn to King Helios:* The Economical Use of Complex Neoplatonic Concepts." *Emperor and Author: The Writings of Julian the Apostate.* Nicholas Baker-Brian and Shaun Tougher, eds. Swansea: The Classical Press of Wales. 229–37.

———. 1993. "Iamblichus' Views on the Relationship of Philosophy to Religion in *De Mysteriis*." *The Divine Iamblichus: Philosopher and Man of Gods*. H. J. Blumenthal and E. G. Clark, eds. London: Bristol Classical Press. 74–86.

Smith, J. Z. 2003. "Here, There, and Anywhere." *Prayer, Magic, and the Stars in the Ancient and Late-Antique World*. S. Noegel, J. Walker, and B. Wheeler, eds. University Park: University of Pennsylvania Press. 21–36.

Smith, Rowland. 1995. *Julian's Gods: Religion and Philosophy in the Thought and Action of Julian the Apostate*. New York: Routledge.

Sodano, Angelo Raffaele, trans., introd., comm. 1984. *Giamblico: I Misteri Egiziani: Abammone, Lettera a Porfirio*. Milano: Rusconi.

Sogno, Cristiana. 2010. "Roman Matchmaking." *From the Tetrarchs to the Theodosians: Later Roman History and Culture, 284–450 C.E.* Scott McGill et al., eds. Cambridge: Cambridge University Press. 55–71.

Solomon-Godeau, Abigail. 1997. *Male Trouble: A Crisis in Representation*. New York: Thames and Hudson.

Stahl, William Harris, trans. and comm. 1952. *Macrobius: Commentary on the Dream of Scipio*. New York: Columbia University Press.

Steel, Carlos G. 1978. *The Changing Self. A Study on the Soul in Later Neoplatonism: Iamblichus, Damascius, and Priscianus*. Brussel: Paleis der Academiën.

Straub, Johannes. 1978 (1962). "Die Himmelfahrt des Iulianus Apostata." *Römischer Kaiserkult*. Antonie Wlosok, ed. Darmstadt: Wissenschaffliche Buchgesellschaft. 528–49.

Stroumsa, Gedaliahu G. 1990. "*Caro salutis cardo:* Shaping the Person in Early Christian Thought." *History of Religions* 30: 25–50.

Struck, Peter. 2004. *Birth of the Symbol: Ancient Readers at the Limits of Their Texts*. Princeton: Princeton University Press.

———. 2001. "Pagan and Christian Theurgies: Iamblichus, Pseudo-Dionysus, Religion and Magic in Late Antiquity." *The Ancient World* 32.1: 25–38.

Swain, Simon, ed. 2007. *Seeing the Face, Seeing the Soul: Polemon's Physiognomy from Classical Antiquity to Medieval Islam*. Oxford: Oxford University Press.

Swain, Simon and Mark Edwards. 2004. *Approaching Late Antiquity: The Transformation from Early to Late Empire*. Oxford: Oxford University Press.

Szidat, J. 1995. "Staatlichkeit und Einzelschicksal in der Spätantike." *Historia* 44: 481–95.

Tassi, A. M. 1967. "Costanzo II e la Difesa della Maestà Imperiale nell'Opera di Ammiano Marcellino." *Critica Storica* 6.2: 157–80.

Tate, J. 1934. "On the History of Allegorism." *Classical Quarterly* 28: 105–15.

Teitler, H. C. 1992. "Ammianus and Constantius: Image and Reality." *Cognitio Gestorum: The Historiographic Art of Ammianus Marcellinus*. J. den Boeft et al., eds. Amsterdam: Royal Netherlands Academy of Arts and Sciences. 117–22.

Thom, Johan C. 1997. "Harmonious Equality: The *Topos* of Friendship in Neopythagorean Writings." *Greco-Roman Perspectives on Friendship*. John T. Fitzgerald, ed. Atlanta, GA: Scholars Press. 77–103.

Thomas, Calvin. 1996. *Male Matters: Masculinity, Anxiety, and the Male Body on the Line*. Urbana: University of Illinois Press.

Thomas, Calvin and Catherine A. F. MacGillvray. 2000. "Afterword(s)." *Straight with a Twist:*

Queer Theory and the Subject of Heterosexuality. Calvin Thomas, ed. Urbana: University of Illinois Press. 253–80.

Thompson, E. A. 1952. *A Roman Reformer and Inventor: Being a New Text of the Treatise* De Rebus Bellicis. Oxford: Clarendon Press.

———. 1947. *The Historical Work of Ammianus Marcellinus.* Cambridge: Cambridge University Press.

Thomson, Robert W., ed. and trans. 1971. *Athanasius:* Contra Gentes *and* De Incarnatione. Oxford: Clarendon Press.

Tosh, John. 2011. "The History of Masculinity: An Outdated Concept?" *What is Masculinity?: Historical Dynamics from Antiquity to the Contemporary World.* John H. Arnold and Sean Brady, eds. New York: Palgrave-Macmillan. 17–34.

Tougher, Shaun. 2007. *Julian the Apostate.* Edinburgh: Edinburgh University Press.

Traister, Bryce. 2000. "Academic Viagra: The Rise of American Masculinity Studies." *American Quarterly* 52.2: 274–304.

Trout, Dennis E. 1999. *Paulinus of Nola: Life, Letters, and Poems.* Berkeley: University of California Press.

Turcan, Robert. 1982. *Julius Firmicus Maternus: L'Erreur des Religions Païennes.* Paris: Société d'Édition "Les Belles Lettres."

Valensi, L. 1957. "Quelques Réflexions sur le Pourvoir Impérial d'après Ammien Marcellin." *Bulletin de l'Association Guillaume Budé* 4: 62–107.

Van Dam, Raymond. 2003. *Families and Friends in Late Roman Cappadocia.* Philadelphia: University of Pennsylvania Press.

———. 2002. *Kingdom of Snow: Roman Rule and Greek Culture in Cappadocia.* Philadelphia: University of Pennsylvania Press.

Vanderspoel, John. 1995. *Themistius and the Imperial Court: Oratory, Civic Duty, and Paideia from Constantius to Theodosius.* Ann Arbor: University of Michigan Press.

Van Leer, David. 1989. "The Beast of the Closet: Homosociality and the Pathology of Manhood." *Critical Inquiry* 15: 587–605.

Van Liefferinge, Carine. 1999. *La Théurgie des Oracles Chaldaïques à Proclus.* Liège: Centre International d'Étude de la Religion Grecque Antique.

van Wees, Hans. 1998. "A Brief History of Tears: Gender Differentiation in Archaic Greece" (in Foxhall and Salmon, *When Men Were Men*: 10–53).

Vessey, Mark. 2003. "Sacred Letters of the Law: The Emperor's Hand in Late Roman (Literary) History." *Antiquité Tardive* 11: 345–58.

Vivian, Tim. 1993. "'Everything Made by God is Good.'" *Église et Théologie* 24: 75–108.

Vogel, C. J. de. 1959. *Greek Philosophy: A Collection of Texts.* Vol. 3. Leiden: E. J. Brill.

Waldby, Catherine. 1995. "Destruction: Boundary Erotics and Refigurations of the Heterosexual Male Body." *Sexy Bodies: The Strange Carnalities of Feminism.* Elizabeth Grosz and Elspeth Probyn, eds. New York: Routledge. 266–77.

Wallace-Hadrill, A. 1982. "*Civilis* Princeps: Between Citizen and King." *The Journal of Roman Studies* 72: 32–48.

———. 1981. "The Emperor and His Virtues." *Historia* 30: 298–323.

Wallis, R. T. 1995 (1972). *Neoplatonism.* Indianapolis: Hackett Publishing Company.

Walters, Jonathan. 1997. "Invading the Roman Body: Manliness and Impenetrability in Roman Thought." *Roman Sexualities*. Judith P. Hallett and Marilyn B. Skinner, eds. Princeton: Princeton University Press. 29–43.

Warner, Michael. 1990. "Homo-Narcissism; or, Heterosexuality." *Engendering Men: The Question of Male Feminist Criticism*. Joseph A. Boone and Michael Cadden, eds. New York: Routledge. 190–206.

Watts, Edward. 2010. "Three Generations of Christian Philosophical Biography." *From the Tetrarchs to the Theodosians: Later Roman History and Culture, 284–450 C.E.* Scott McGill et al., eds. Cambridge: Cambridge University Press. 117–33.

———. 2006. *City and School in Late Antique Athens and Alexandria*. Berkeley: University of California Press.

———. 2005a. "Orality and Communal Identity in Eunapius' 'Lives of the Sophists and Philosophers.'" *Byzantion* 75: 334–61.

———. 2005b. "The Student Self in Late Antiquity." *Religion and the Self in Antiquity*. David Brakke et al., eds. Bloomington: University of Indiana Press. 234–52.

Weinstock, Stefan. 1971. *Divus Julius*. Oxford: Clarendon Press.

Whitby, Mary. 1998. *The Propaganda of Power: The Role of Panegyric in Late Antiquity*. Leiden: Brill.

Williams, Craig A. 1999. *Roman Homosexuality: Ideologies of Masculinity in Classical Antiquity*. New York: Oxford University Press.

———. 2010. *Roman Homosexuality*. Oxford: Oxford University Press.

Wimbush, Vincent L. and Richard Valantasis, eds. 1998. *Asceticism*. New York: Oxford University Press.

Winkler, John J. 1990. *The Constraints of Desire: The Anthropology of Sex and Gender in Ancient Greece*. New York: Routledge.

Wormald, P. 1976. "The Decline of the Western Empire and the Survival of its Aristocracy." *Journal of Roman Studies* 66: 217–26.

Wray, David. 2001. *Catullus and the Poetics of Roman Manhood*. Cambridge: Cambridge University Press.

Wright, Wilmer Cave. 2005 (1921). *Philostratus and Eunapius*. Loeb Classical Library. Cambridge, MA: Harvard University Press.

———. 1980a (1913). *The Works of the Emperor Julian (Volume 1)*. Loeb Classical Library. Cambridge, Mass: Harvard University Press.

———. 1980b (1923). *The Works of the Emperor Julian (Volume 3)*. Loeb Classical Library. Cambridge, Mass: Harvard University Press.

———. 1980c (1896). *The Emperor Julian's Relation to the New Sophistic and Neo-Platonism: With a Study of his Style*. London: Spottiswoode & Co.

———. 1969 (1913). *The Works of the Emperor Julian (Volume 2)*. Loeb Classical Library. Cambridge, MA: Harvard University Press.

Zeeland, Steven. 1999. *Military Trade*. New York: Harrington Park Press.

———. 1996. *The Masculine Marine: Homoeroticism in the U.S. Marine Corps*. New York: Harrington Park Press.

———. 1995. *Sailors and Sexual Identity: Crossing the Line between "Straight" and "Gay" in the U.S. Navy*. New York: Harrington Park Press.

———. 1993. *Barrack Buddies and Soldier Lovers: Dialogues with Gay Young Men in the U.S. Military.* New York: Harrington Park Press.

Žižek, Slavoj. 1991. *Looking Awry: An Introduction to Jacques Lacan through Popular Culture.* Cambridge, MA: MIT Press.

INDEX LOCORUM

Aeschylus
  Agamemnon 36, 73n88
Ammianus Marcellinus
  Res Gestae **14.1.4**, 156n57; **14.5.2**, 161; **14.6.1**, 150n35; **14.6.3**, 150–51; **14.6.5**, 151; **14.6.8**, 149–50, 163; **14.6.17**, 162; **4.11.25**, 150; **14.11.28**, 162, 165; **15.1.2**, 148n31; **15.1.3–4**, 148; **15.1.4**, 156; **15.3.3**, 159–60, 164; **15.3.8–9**, 159; **15.5.15–16**, 155, 161; **15.7.1**, 150n35; **15.7.10**, 150n35; **15.8.5–8**, 165–66; **15.8.9**, 166; **15.8.9–10**, 166–67; **15.8.16**, 5, 167; **15.12.6**, 150n39; **16.1.4**, 47n12; **16.10.2**, 143; **16.10.7**, 143; **16.10.8**, 143; **16.10.9–11**, 143–44; **16.10.11**, 147; **16.10.14**, 150n35; **16.10.15**, 143; **16.10.17**, 143; **17.5.2–3**, 157; **17.5.10**, 152n41; **17.7.13**, 150n37; **18.1.2**, 163; **18.1.4**, 154–55; **18.2.7**, 149n33; **18.10.2**, 162; **19.8.2**, 163; **19.10.1**, 150n35; **20.1.2**, 145n25; **20.3.6**, 150n36; **20.5.10**, 154; **21.12.24**, 150n35; **21.14.2**, 154; **21.16.1**, 145; **21.16.9**, 155; **22.7.1**, 146, 147; **22.7.2**, 146–47; **22.7.3–4**, 146, 147; **22.9.3**, 150n35; **22.16.12**, 150n38; **23.1.4**, 150n35; **23.3.3**, 150n35; **23.6.67**, 162; **25.4.2**, 83; **25.4.2–6**, 77n100; **25.4.7**, 149n33, 163; **25.4.18**, 147; **25.8.9**, 86n115; **25.10.3**, 150n36; **25.10.5**, 150n35; **26.3.1**, 150n35; **27.11.2**, 145; **28.1.1**, 150n35; **28.1.4**, 145n26; **28.1.16**, 25n54; **28.1.36**, 150n35; **28.1.56**, 150n35; **28.1.28**, 25n54; **28.4.17**, 149n33; **28.4.27**, 145n26; **28.6.29**, 145n25; **29.1.34**, 163; **29.5.6**, 149n33; **29.6.17**, 150n35; **30.4.3**, 149n33; **31.9.5**, 165

Anthologia Graeca
  12.34, 75n95; **12.222**, 75n95
Apophthegmata Patrum (Alphabetic)
  Achilles 4 (PG 65 125A), 110; Agathon 15 (PG 65 113C), 109; Agathon 23 (PG 65 116B), 114; Ammonas 10 (PG 65 121D–124A), 105n56; Ammoun of Nitria (PG 65 128B), 106; Antony 17 (PG 65 80D), 107; Arsenius 14 (PG 65 92A), 107, 28 (PG 65 97A–B), 105nn52–53; Eudaemon (PG 65 176B), 106; Hyperechius 8 432.3–7 (TLG), 111, 111n47; Isaac of Kellia 5 (PG 65 225A–B), 106n57; Nicon (PG

207

65 309A-C), 105n55; **Sara 4** (PG **65** 420C-D **41–48**), 38n88; **Sisoes 4** (PG **65 392D**), 104

Arnobius
  Adversus Gentes **5.28**, 133n119

Athanasius
  Contra Gentes **2.1–6**, 130; **2.21–27**, 128; **2.24–27**, 134–35; **3.11–12**, 131; **4.1–5**, 131; **4.18**, 92, 128; **8.12–18**, 130; **9**, 131; **9.31–33**, 131n113; **9.31–34**, 131; **9.39–48**, 131; **26.4–7**, 132; **26.7–13**, 93n6, 133; **26.15–19**, 132

  De Incarnatione **4.23**, 92, 128; **5.1–7**, 129; **5.16–34**, 93n7, 134; **5.17–18**, 135

  Vita Antonii **Praef.1**, 94n116; **Praef. 3**, 91, 92; **1.2**, 101n142; **2–3**, 99n37; **2.3**, 98n33; **2.4–5**, 99; **3.1**, 99n34; **5**, 115–16, 127, 153–54; **5.1**, 120; **5.3**, 103, 119, 120; **5.4–5**, 99; **5.4**, 116–17, 118; **5.5**, 118; **5.6**, 120n96; **5.7**, 120; **6.1**, 100, 120; **6.2**, 121; **7.8**, 109; **7.9**, 109; **9.2**, 108; **9.10**, 118n92; **12.5**, 103; **14.6**, 101; **18.2**, 108; **45.1–4**, 102; **45.5–6**, 104, 108; **67.1–2**, 109; **68**, 97; **69–70**, 97; **72.4**, 101n145, 109; **72.5**, 101–102, 109; **78.2**, 101n144; **81.1**, 90, 103; **82**, 97

Augustine
  Confessions **2.2.2**, 27n62; **8.6.15**, 98
  De Mendacio **9.15**, 29n66

Augustus Caesar
  Res Gestae **34.3**, 19n42

Ausonius
  Epistulae **23.51–52**, 14; **24.123–4**, 14

Catullus
  Carmina **116.8**, 16n37

Cicero
  De Fato **22**, 157n60
  Pro Archia Poeta **26**, 146n27
  Pro Quinctio **16.51**, 123
  Tusculan Disputations **1.34**, 146n27

Claudian
  In Eutropium **1.358–70**, 160, 160n68; **1.422–24**, 161

  Panegyricus de Quarto Consulatu Honorii Augusti **214–220**, 158
  Panegyricus de Sexto Consulatu Honorii Augusti **616–17**, 144n21

Clement of Alexandria
  Protrepticus **2.34.3–5**, 133n119

Codex Theodosianus (*CTh.*)
  1.1.5, 22, 25, 139; **1.1.6**, 22; **1.2.12**, 139n8; **1.9.2**, 139n8; **1.12.5**, 152n45; **1.15.4**, 88n117; **1.15.13**, 33n77; **1.16.9**, 33n77; **1.29.1**, 88n118; **1.29.3**, 88n118; **1.29.4**, 88n118

  2.23.1, 139n8; **2.33.4**, 139n8

  3.18.1, 33n77; **3.32.2**, 29n67

  4.22.2, 153n46

  5.7.2.pr., 28n64; **5.12.3**, 139n8; **5.16.31**, 152n45

  6.4.10, 10n21; **6.4.29**, 139n8; **6.4.30**, 152; **6.4.32**, 139n8; **6.14.3**, 139n8; **6.23.3**, 139n8; **6.24.4**, 88n118; **6.24.6**, 153n46; **6.30.23**, 88n118; **6.30.1**, 33n77; **6.30.15**, 139n8; **6.35.6**, 33n77

  7.4.1, 33n77; **7.4.32**, 88n118; **7.4.35**, 88n118; **7.7.4**, 139n8; **7.8.3**, 139n8; **7.22.11**, 33n77

  8.1.13, 139n8; **8.4.18**, 88n118; **8.4.23**, 153n46; **8.5.40**, 139n8; **8.5.57**, 29n67; **8.5.62**, 139n8; **8.7.10**, 88n118; **8.11.5**, 33n77

  9.7.3, 23–24, 24nn52–53, 27n62, 29n68, 39; **9.7.6**, 21, 21n47, 21–22n48, 23, 24n53, 25, 26, 27n62, 28–29, 35, 86; **9.19.3**, 139n7; **9.21.9**, 33n77; **9.27.5**, 33n77; **9.40.11**, 139n8

  10.10.16, 29n67; **10.10.22**, 153n46; **10.20.11**, 153n46; **10.22.3**, 152n43; **10.26.1**, 139n8

  11.1.33, 139n8; **11.16.15**, 10n22; **11.20.5pr.**, 88n118; **11.21.3**, 139n8; **11.28.15**, 139n8; **11.30.49**, 139n8; **11.30.52**, 33n77; **11.36.4**, 25

  12.1.27, 33n77; **12.1.126**, 29n67; **12.1.160**, 152n44; **12.1.175**, 88n118;

INDEX LOCORUM · 209

12.6.17, 33n77; **12.9.2**, 33n77; **12.12.7**, 139n8

13.1.13, 33n77; **13.3.14**, 153n46; **13.5.16**, 152n42; **13.10.8**, 153n46; **13.11.7**, 88n118

14.1.1, 8; **14.4.4**, 153n46; **14.5.1**, 153n46; **14.16.1**, 88n118

15.1.4, 33n77; **15.1.5**, 33n77; **15.1.22**, 33n77; **15.1.33**, 33n77; **15.4.1**, 139n8; **15.5.4**, 88n118; **15.5.5**, 139n8

16.1.4, 153n46; **16.2.37**, 88n118; **16.2.47**, 153n46; **16.4.4**, 139n8; **16.5.5**, 153n46; **16.5.28**, 29n67; **16.5.44**, 33n77; **16.6.4.pr.**, 28n65; **16.8.13**, 139n8; **16.8.22**, 28n65; **16.10.8**, 29n67; **16.10.20**, 153n46

Collatio (*Mosaicarum et Romanarum Legum Collatio*)
5.3.1–2, 19–21, 19–21nn43–46, 22, 23, 25, 26, 27n62, 28, 28–29, 29n68, 30, 30n69, 33, 38, 86, 88, 93, 112, 113, 127, 141, 142, 164

Corpus Inscriptionum Latinarum (*CIL*)
2.4512, 9; **6.1158** (=ILS 731), 151–52, 152n41

Dio Chrysostom
Orations **6.20**, 81n106; **33.53–54**, 26

Diogenes Laertius
Vitae Philosophorum **6.46**, 74n90; **7.173**, 26

Eunapius
The Chronicle after Dexippus **65.1**, 19n42

Lives of the Philosophers **2.2.1.1–2.2.5.1**, 32–33; **5.1.8**, 38n89, 50n21; **6.5.4.6**, 19n42; **6.6.5–10.5**, 38n88; **8.1.5.1**, 19n42

Euripides
Phoenissae **469**, 72n85, 72n86

Evagrius Antiochensis
Vita Antonii **5**, 122

Firmicus Maternus
De Errore Profanarum Religionum **12.4**, 133n119

Gesta Senatus
88n118, 139n6, 152n45

Gregory Nazianzenus/of Nazianzus
Carmina quae spectant ad alios, "To Nemesios" **1572.12–1573.13**, 133n119

Oration **5.32**, 133n119

Oration **21.5.6–7**, 98n32

Poematia Moralia PG **37.3 898–99**, 124–25n102

Heraclitus
Frag. 123, 69n80

Historia Monachorum
Praef.11, 106; **1.4**, 105n54; **15.2–3**, 107; **24.1**, 110; **24.2**, 110; **24.8**, 111; **24.9**, 111; **24.10**, 111

Horace
Odes **3.26**, 31–32n72

Homer
Iliad **2.126**, 42; **2.476**, 42; **3.415**, 83; **6.232–36**, 57; **12.382**, 53; **24.348**, 171n5

Odyssey **10.279**, 171n5

Iamblichus
De Mysteriis **1.12.41 (31.9–15)**, 50n22; **2.3.73 (55.3–17)**, 41–43, 88, 128

Jerome
De Viris Illustribus **106**, 9; **132**, 9

Interpretatio Regulae Sancti Pachomii **7**, 114; **93**, 114; **94**, 114; **95**, 114

Vita Pauli **9.5**, 31

John Chrysostom
Expositiones in Psalmos **160.32–38**, 49n18

Julian, emperor
Epistulae (Note: Wright always first) **17/58**, 19n42; **21/60 380D**, 69–70, 70n81; **77/183** (spurious), 18, 18n40; **1969 (1913), pg. 324/89B 300C–D**, 77n100

Oration 1 (*Encomium to Emperor Constantius*) **1.2.1–7/3C–D**, 52; **1.7.16/9B**, 51n26; **1.12.11/16D**, 49n18; **1.21.13/26C**, 49n18;

1.30.4/37B, 49n18; 1.30.12/37C, 49n18; 1.35.37–38/43D, 51n26; 1.38.16/47B, 51n27

Oration 2 (*Encomium to Empress Eusebia*) 2.5.13/109C, 51n26; 2.5.20/109D, 51n26; 2.12.2–4/117D–118A, 53; 2.12.4/118A, 49n18; 2.17.32/127B, 51n26

Oration 3 (*The Deeds of the Emperor or On Imperiality*) 3.10.4/60D, 49n18; 3.11.10/62B, 49n18, 54n35; 3.11.42/63B, 49n18, 54n35; 3.17/71D, 69; 3.27.9/84B, 49n18

Oration 4 (*Self-Consolation on the Departure of the Most-Excellent Saloustios*) passim, 18n39, 46n5; 4.5.28/247A, 49n18, 54n36

Oration 5 ("Letter to the Athenians") 5.2.5/269D, 49n18, 54n37

Oration 7 (*Against Heracleius*) 7.1/204D–205A, 68; 7.5/210C, 75n96; 7.6/210C–211A, 66; 7.6/210D, 74; 7.7/211B–D, 77–78; 7.7/211D, 84, 87; 7.8/212A, 66; 7.8–9/212C–214A, 65–66; 7.9/214A–B, 72; 7.10/215C–216A, 68n77, 76; 7.10/216A, 75; 7.11/216B, 68, 91; 7.11/216C–D, 69, 72; 7.11/216C, 79n103, 91; 7.11/217A–B, 81; 7.12/217C, 83; 7.12/217C–D, 70; 7.12/217D–218A, 73; 7.14.23/219D, 49n18; 7.16/220D–221A, 72; 7.16/221D–222A, 76; 7.16/221D, 73; 7.17/222C–D, 72; 7.19/225B–C, 74; 7.20/226B–C, 66n72; 7.21/227B, 67, 79; 7.22/227C–234C, 67; 7.22/228B–C, 80; 7.22/228C, 80; 7.22/230C, 80; 7.22/230C–D, 82; 7.22/230D, 81; 7.22/232B, 80; 7.22/232C, 80, 83; 7.23/234C–D, 65; 7.23/235A–B, 74–75; 7.23/235C–D, 66n72

Oration 8 (*To the Mother of the Gods*) 8.10/170A–B, 71n84; 8.19.23–28/179C–D, 53

Oration 9 (*To the Uneducated Cynics*) 9.10.1–4/189B, 54; 9.10.4/189B, 49n18; 9.19/202B–C, 66n74, 74n90

Oration 10 (*Caesares*) 10.1/306A–307A, 46–47; 10.1.10–12/306B, 46n6; 10.1.15–17/306C, 47n7; 10.6/310A–B, 48; 10.6/310C, 48; 10.9/312B–C, 48; 10.10/312D, 48; 10.10/313A, 48; 10.16.2–4/316A, 48n15; 10.17.15–22/317C–D, 47n12, 49–50; 10.17/317D, 88n120; 10.21.15/321B, 49n18; 10.34/333B, 47n12; 10.34.12–15/333B–C, 49n17; 10.34–35/334A–B, 47n12; 10.37.11–12/335D, 47n13; 10.38.16–21/336C, 47

Oration 11 (*To King Helios*) 11.5.12–17/132D–133A, 54–55; 11.5.14/132D, 49n18; 11.13.11–14.5/138D–139A, 55n41; 11.24.7–8/145A, 52n31; 11.24.10/145A, 52n31; 11.24.16/145B, 52n31; 11.30.5/149A, 52n31; 11.37/152B, 52n29; 11.43.5/156D, 52n31; 11.43.9/156D, 52n31; 11.44.4–5/157C, 46n5

Oration 12 (*Misopogon*) passim, 77n100; 12.14.11–12/346A, 51n26; 12.20.38/351A, 51n27; 12.30/359B–D, 76n98

Juvenal
  Satires 9.43, 16n36

Lucan
  Bellum Civile 10.528–29, 16n36

Lucretius
  De Rerum Natura 2.249–60, 157n61

Macrobius
  Commentaria in Somnium Scipionis 1.2.11, 65n70; 1.2.17–18, 65n70

Marinus
  Vita Procli 3, 50n21

Martial
  Epigrammata 1.109.16, 161n70

INDEX LOCORUM · 211

Maximinus
  Elegiae **3.31**, 16n36
New Testament
  Corinthians (1) **15:10**, 116
  Corinthians (2) **12:10**, 109, 110, 111
  Galatians **4:12**, 101
  Matthew **6:34**, 99; **19:21**, 98, 99
  Romans **1:26–27**, 93, 93n8, 133–34
Ovid
  Amores **2.1.33**, 161n70; **3.4.1**, 161n70
Pacatus
  Panegyrici Latini **2[12].33.4**, 161
Paulinus of Nola
  Carmina **19.15**, 50n21
  Epistulae **11.1–5**, 15–16; **11.55–62**, 16–17
De Physiognomonia Liber (Anon. Lat.)
  11, 26; **55**, 162
Plato
  Charmides **153A**, 58n49; **153D**,
    59–60n55; **154C**, 59n51; **154D**,
    58–59n50, 59; **155C**, 59n52; **155D**,
    59n53; **155D–E**, 59; **155E**, 60n56
  Phaedrus **161B**, 172; **227C**, 172; **228D**,
    173n11; **251A**, 118n90; **251C**, 118n90;
    251D, 173n11; **251E**, 118n90, 171n4;
    252C, 118n90, 173n11; **253E**,
    118n90; **255D–E**, 171
  Philebus **47A–B**, 117–18
  Republic **2.377E–3.392A**, 47n8, 62n61;
    6.508D, 60n57; **6.508E–509A**,
    60n57; **10.614B–621D**, 47n9,
    62n61
  Symposium **185D**, 118n90; **188E**, 118n90;
    191C, 18n40; **195A–C**, 173n12;
    196A, 173n12; **206E**, 171n4; **210A–
    211C** ("ladder of love"), 33n75,
    57–58, 135, 165, 175; **215A ff.**, 47n11;
    216D, 47n11; **218D–219A**, 57–58;
    219B, 58; **221E**, 47n11
Plotinus
  Enneads **5.2.1.1–24**, 86n113; **5.5.3.1–15**,
    49n18, 85–86, 144

Plutarch
  Demosthenes **11.1**, 110n70; **23.4–6**, 79
Priapea
  25.6, 16n36
Propertius
  Elegiae **2.25.41**, 161n70
Quintilian
  Institutio Oratoria **11.84–85**, 124n101
Saloustios (Saturninius Secundus Salutius)
  De Deis et Mundo **3.2**, 63–64; **3.3**, 64,
    87; **3.4**, 64, 71n84
Seneca the Younger
  De Beneficiis **2.21.1–2**, 23n51
Septuagint
  Job **40:16**, 115, 119–20, 120n94
  Wisdom **14:12**, 131–32
Sirmondian Constitutions
  1, 34n81; **2**, 34n81; **7**, 34n81; **9**, 34n81;
    12, 34n81; **14**, 34n81; **16**, 34n81
Sophocles
  Oedipus at Colonus **1051**, 73n88
Themistius
  Oration 13 (*Erōtikos ē peri kallous
    basilikou*), **13.161D–163A**, 173n12;
    13.164A, 173n12; **13.164C–165A**,
    171, 173n12; **13.165A–B**, 173n11;
    13.165D, 173, 173n12; **13.166A**,
    173n11, 173n12; **13.166C**, 174n16;
    13.166C–D, 174; **13.168C**, 174n16;
    13.168C–D, 173n12; **13.168D**,
    173n11; **13.175D**, 174n16; **13.176B**,
    172; **13.177B**, 173n13; **13.177B–
    178A**, 173n12; **13.177C**, 174;
    13.177D, 170; **13.178B**, 170, 173n12;
    13.178D, 170; **13.179A**, 174n16;
    13.180A–B, 171n8; **13.180B**, 174n16
Theocritus
  Idylls **12.10–16**, 173; **23.49–53**, 32
Theognis
  1.815, 73n88
Theodosius II
  Novellae **1**, 34n81, 152n45; **3**, 34n81; **4**,
    34n81; **5**, 153n47; **5.1**, 34n80; **5.2**,
    34n81; **5.3**, 34n81; **6**, 153n47; **7**,

153n47; **7.1**, 34n81; **7.2**, 34n81; **7.3**, 34n81; **7.4**, 34n81; **8**, 34n81, 153n47; **9**, 34n81, 153n47; **10**, 153n47; **10.1**, 34n81; **10.2**, 34n81; **11**, 34n81, 153n47; **12**, 34n81; **13**, 34n81, 153n47; **14**, 34n81; **15**, 153n47; **15.2**, 34n81; **16**, 34n81; **17**, 153n47; **17.1**, 34n81; **17.2**, 34n81; **18**, 34n81; **19**, 34n80, 153n47; **20**, 34n81, 153n47; **21**, 34n80, 153n47; **22**, 153n47; **22.1**, 34n81; **22.2**, 34n81; **23**, 34n81; **24**, 34n80; **25**, 34n80; **26**, 34n81, 153n47

Tibullus
  Elegiae **1.4.9**, 161n70; **1.6.33**, 161n70

Valentinian III
  Novellae **1.1**, 34n81, 152n45; **1.2**, 34n81; **1.3**, 139n6; **2**, 153n48; **2.2**, 34n81; **2.3**, 34n81; **2.4**, 34n81; **3**, 34n81; **4**, 34n81; **6.1**, 34n81; **6.2**, 34n81; **6.3**, 34n80; **7**, 153n48; **7.1**, 34n81; **7.2**, 34n81; **7.3**, 34n80; **8.1**, 34n81; **8.2**, 34n81; **9**, 139n6; **10**, 34n81; **11**, 34n81; **12**, 34n81; **13**, 34n81; **14**, 34n81; **16**, 139n6, 153n48; **17**, 34n81, 139n6; **18**, 153n48; **19**, 34n81, 139n6; **20**, 34n81; **21**, 153n48; **21.1**, 34n81; **21.2**, 34n81; **22**, 34n81, 153n48; **23**, 34n81, 153n48; **24**, 34n80; **25**, 34n81; **26**, 34n81; **27**, 34n81; **28**, 34n80; **29**, 34n81; **30**, 34n80; **31**, 34n81; **32**, 34n81, 153n48; **33**, 34n81; **34**, 34n81; **35**, 34n81, 153n48; **36**, 34n81

Victricius
  De Laude Sanctorum **3**, 51n24, 143n18; **5**, 77n101

Virgil
  Eclogues **8.83**, 14n34; **8.89**, 14n34; **8.107–108**, 14
  Georgics **2.32–34**, 126

Vita Antonii (Latin Anon.)
  5, 121–22, 123; **6**, 123n100

Xenophon
  Cyropaedia **8.1.40–42**, 144
  Memorabilia **2.1.29**, 81–82

Zonaras
  Epitome Historiarum **Lib. 13–18 32.16–17**, 24n53

GENERAL INDEX

Adams, J., 16n36

admirability, metaphorized by same-sex sexual attractiveness, 19, 30–34, 39–40, 41, 43, 46, 55, 63, 85, 86, 90, 107, 111, 136, 139–40, 141, 165, 167–68, 170–75

adultery, 24–25, 25n54–55, 64, 110, 132, 133, 133n118, 134

adventus, 51, 51n25, 140, 142–47, 142n15, 142n16, 143n17, 144n21

Against Heracleius (Julian), 4, 45, 62, 65–84, 65n71, 66n75, 74n90, 84

Alcibiades, 43, 47, 55, 56, 57–58, 58n48, 60, 173

Alexander the Great, 47, 48, 79, 148, 156

Alföldi, A., 139n5, 153n49

allegory, 45, 52–53, 52–53n32, 65, 67, 72, 78, 79, 80, 84, 85, 86–87, 119–20, 144

Ambrose, 35, 36, 37

amēchanos, 49n18, 53–55, 55n42, 59n53. See also *kallos amēchanon*

Amerise, M., 48n16

Ammianus Marcellinus, chapter 3 *passim* (but 140–42), 4, 5, 6, 24–25, 25n54, 47n12, 51n25, 77n100, 80, 83, 86n115, 136–37, 176

Amun, Letter to (Athanasius), 97, 97n29

anal penetration, 12n26, 16n36, 19, 23, 29, 44, 56n44, 113, 118, 119, 121, 122–23, 133, 140, 142, 149, 153, 159–61, 160n68, 164. See also *pati muliebria;* same-sex sexual behavior (male); same-sex sexual pleasure (male)

andria (*andreia*), 41–43, 84, 88, 171. See also *vir; virtus*

anēr. See *vir*

anterōs, 171, 172

Antinous, 131–32

Antony of the desert, chapter 2 *passim,* 11n25, 31–32, 37, 38, 70, 139, 153, 168

Aphrodite, 82, 83, 131, 132. *See also* Venus

Apophthegmata Patrum, 38n88, 94, 95, 104, 105, 105n52, 105n53, 105n55, 106, 106n57, 107, 109, 110, 111, 114, 115

Arcadius, emperor, frontispiece, 19, 20, 20n43, 21, 86, 152, 152n43, 152n45, 158

aretē, 52, 66, 74, 75, 115

Aristotle, 18, 18n39, 162

asceticism/ascetics, 13, 37, 50, 50n20, 51, 66, 66n72, 70, 91, 94, 94n11, 94n12, 95, 95n18, 96n22, 97, 98, 98–112, 110n72

213

GENERAL INDEX

aselgeia, 131–32
Athanasius, chapter 2 *passim*, 4, 5, 6, 31n70, 37, 38, 70, 89, 141, 153, 168, 176; body and soul/mind split in, 127–35, 136; his presentation of the *Logos*, 127–35; materiality in, 127–35, 136
Athanassiadi, P., 7n6, 38n90, 47n12, 52n29, 53n32, 54n38, 66n75
Athene (Athena), 67, 80, 83, 171
Attis, 52–53n32, 53, 77n101
Auerbach, E., 169n81
Augustine, 13, 27n62, 29n66, 98
Ausonius, 12, 13–14, 15–17, 18, 19, 20, 26
authority (*auctoritas*/*axiōma*), 1, 3, 4, 5, 6, 12n26, 19n42, 37, 38, 39, 40, 41, 44, 50, 72–78, 79, 84–85, 90, 111, 127, 139, 145, 164, 167, 175; episcopal, 36–37; knowingness of, 3, 4, 5, 19, 29–30, 34–35, 39, 63, 89, 93, 112, 123, 126–27, 136, 141, 142, 164, 168, 175, 176; metaphorized by same-sex sexual attractiveness, 2–3, 18–19, 30–31, 40, 41, 43–44, 55–56, 61, 79, 84–85, 90, 111, 139–40, 165, 167–68, 170–75; projection of, 5, 18–19, 34, 101; transcendent, connection to, 37–38, 50, 86–89, 90, 108, 109, 111, 127, 138–39, 138–39nn5–8, 140, 141, 143, 144, 147, 149, 154, 162–63, 164, 165, 166–67, 168–69. *See also* forbidden knowledge, brandishing of

Bacchus. *See* Dionysus
Baldwin, B., 46n5, 47n12
Barnes, T., 18n40, 77n100, 93n10, 96n20, 96n21, 140n10, 141n11, 155n54
Bartelink, G., 93n10, 94n13, 94n14, 97n30, 119
Barton, C., 123–25, 124n102
Beauty (kallos), 5, 32, 33n74, 41–43, 49, 49n18, 51, 52, 52n30, 53, 54, 55, 57, 58, 59, 60n55, 60n57, 85, 86, 88, 165, 167, 170–75. *See also kallos amēchanon*
Bech, H., 92n2

Behemoth, 119–20
belly's navel (Job 40:16), 119–20
Bertrand, P., 93n10, 94n13
Billerbeck, M., 54n38, 66n73
Blockley, R., 141n11, 142n12, 142n13, 147n30
blush, to/a, 99, 115, 118, 121, 122, 123, 124n102, 125, 126
Børtnes, J., 15n35, 18n41
Boswell, J., 1–2, 2n1, 17, 24n53
Bouffartigue, J., 8n7, 38n90, 47n12, 50, 55n42, 66n75, 71n83, 75n93
Bowersock, G., 47n12, 53n32, 77n100
boy, black (*Vita Antonii*), 100, 100n40, 120–21, 123, 123n100
Brakke, D., 94n12, 94–95n17, 96n22, 96n24, 97, 97n25, 97n27, 97n28, 97n29, 98, 99n36, 100n40, 102n46, 105n54, 111n76, 113, 127n103, 133n118
Branham, R., 81n106
Brennan, B., 97n30
Brisson, L., 62n62, 63n64
Brooten, B., 93n8
Brown, P., 7–8, 8n8, 8n10, 27n61, 27n62, 36, 36–37n86, 37, 50n21, 51n24, 61n59, 94n12, 94n17, 95n18, 99n36, 105n54, 143n18
Burrus, V., 25n57, 31, 35, 36, 37, 37n87, 38n88, 94n12, 96n22, 96n23, 96n24, 97, 97n31, 99n37, 108n64, 127n103, 129

Caesares (Julian), 4, 18, 43, 45, 45–51, 55, 56, 60n57, 62, 63, 66n75, 84–85
Cameron, Alan, 13n30, 142n14
Cameron, Averil, 7n6, 8n8, 8n10, 15n35, 37n86, 93n10, 94n12, 96n22, 97n30, 99n36, 103n48
Campbell, J., 82n109
Camus, P., 140n10, 142n12, 154n50
Caner, D., 94n12
Cantarella, E., 24n53
Castelli, E., 38n88

GENERAL INDEX · 215

charaktēr(es), 69–70, 72, 78–79n103, 91, 92, 94, 96, 98, 107–8, 112. *See* mimesis

Charlesworth, M., 144n20, 153n49

Charmides (Plato), 44, 55, 55n42, 56, 56n43, 58–60, 61, 60n57, 75, 120, 173

Chastagnol, A., 6n3, 8n8, 9n15, 10n20, 13n29

choice of Herakles, 67, 81–83, 84

cinaedus (*kinaidos*), 26–28, 26n59, 162

cingulum (soldier's belt, *zōnē*), 174–75, 174n18

Civiletti, M., 38n88, 38n89, 50n21

civility, 5, 136, 139, 140, 141, 147, 148, 149, 149n33, 150, 153, 154–56, 158, 161, 162, 163, 167, 168, 176

Clark, E., 94n12

Clark, G., 27n62, 38n88, 51n24, 62n59, 143n18

Clarke, E., 63n63, 63n64, 64n68, 65n69, 66n75, 71n83

Claudian, 144n21, 158, 158n64, 160, 160n68, 161

Cleanthes, 26–27, 162

Codex Theodosianus, 22. *See also* Index Locorum

Collatio (*Mosaicarum et Romanarum Legum Collatio*), 19–21, 20–21nn44–47, 23, 25, 26, 27n62, 28, 29, 29n68, 33, 38, 86, 88, 93, 112, 113, 127, 141, 142, 164

Collobert, C., 62n61

competition (*agōn*), 12, 94, 101–3, 106–7, 108, 110, 120, 133, 134

Constans, emperor, 23–24, 24n53, 103

Constantine I, 36n83, 37, 47, 48, 48n16, 53, 67, 72n85, 78–79n103, 80, 96, 103, 138n5, 144, 152

Constantine II, 139n7

Constantius II, 5, 6, 8, 23–24, 51, 51n25, 53, 54, 80, 96, 103, 136–37, 138n4, 140–41, 140n10, 142–49, 142n15, 143n17, 149n33, 150, 151, 152, 152n41, 153–54, 155–63, 155n54, 164–69, 176

Conte, G., 15n35

Contra Gentes (Athanasius), 92–93, 94, 96, 112, 127–35

Conybeare, C., 12n28, 17, 27n62

Cooper, K., 27n62, 176–77, 177n20, 177n21

Copjec, J., 30n69

Corbeill, A., 27n61

Corcoran, S., 8n10, 21n47, 34n80, 88n118, 139n5, 139n7

Cosi, D., 53n32, 71n83, 77n100, 77n101

coturnus, 145–46

Cox, P. *See* P. Miller

Crates, 65, 74

Cremer, F., 38n89

Cribiore, R., 7n6, 8n8

cupid(s), 31–32n72, 44, 86, 87. *See* Missorium (plate)

Cybele. *See* Mother of the Gods

Cynic(s), 45, 54, 54n38, 62, 65–66, 66n73, 68, 74, 74n91, 75, 77, 77n100, 78, 81

Dagron, G., 9n15

Dalla, D., 24n53

Davidson, J., 56n44

Dawson, D., 74n91

de Bonfils, G., 140n10, 168n80

De Incarnatione (Athanasius), 92–93, 94, 96, 112, 127–35

de Jonge, P., 144n21, 157n58

declinare, 148, 156–58, 159, 162

declinatio. *See declinare*

Democritus, philosopher, 148, 156–57

Demosthenes, 79, 80, 109–110

den Boeft, J., 146n27, 154n51

desire, between men and women, 14, 16–17, 27n62, 99–100, 104–5, 110, 112, 113, 118–19, 176–78; female same-sex, 93, 93n8, 133–34; male same-sex, 17, 27n62, 28, 29, 34–35, 38–40, 41, 43, 56–57, 61, 63, 65, 84, 85, 87–89, 90–91, 92, 93, 93n8, 95, 111–12, 114, 119, 125, 126–27,

132–34, 135–37, 139–40, 141, 142, 153–54, 158, 164–65, 167–68, 170–75, 176, 177–78; pederastic, 18, 56–57, 56n44, 92, 100, 100n40, 105–6, 106n58, 112, 113, 119, 133, 165, 172–74. *See also* friendship; metaphor

Devil, the, 90, 92, 99, 100, 105, 108, 112, 113, 115–17, 118–26, 118n92, 123n100, 127, 129

Dexter, Nummius Aemilianus, 3, 7, 8–9, 10–11, 12, 17–18, 177

Dillon, J., 50n20

Diogenes, 62, 65, 66, 66n73, 74, 74n90, 74n91, 77

Dionysus (Bacchus), 66, 72, 73, 76, 82, 133

Dodds, E., 61n58

doubles-entendres, 15–16, 29, 75n95, 160, 160n68, 175

Dover, K., 56n44

duBois, P., 38n88

Dvornik, F., 139n5

Earth, 86–87, 87n116. *See also* Tellus

Ebbeler, J., 13n31

Edmunds, L., 15n35

effeminacy, 5, 6, 20, 76n98, 110, 133, 136, 140, 161

Elm, S., 13n30, 52n29, 53n32, 54n38, 55n41, 66n75, 71n83, 78n103, 81n106, 94n12, 96n22

Elsner, J., 86n114

Epicurus, 157, 157n60

erastēs, 56, 173, 174

erēmos, chapter 2 *passim*, 89

erōmenos, 56, 118n90, 173

Eros, 131. *See also* cupid(s)

erōs, 171, 172, 174

Espejo-Muriel, C., 94n12, 114n78

eternity (aeternitas), 89, 139n7, 140, 148, 148n32, 149–54, 152n43, 152n44, 155, 156, 157, 162, 163

Eunapius, 19n42, 32–33, 33n74, 38, 38n88, 38n89, 50, 50n21, 51

Eutropius, eunuch consul, 160, 160n68, 161

Evans-Grubbs, J., 25n55, 177n21

existent economy, 39–40, 43, 45, 61–62, 61–62nn58–59, 63, 65, 67, 71, 72, 73–74, 77–78, 88–89, 128, 135, 144, 165, 175, 176. *See also* transcendent, the

Feeney, D., 62n62

fellatio, 12n26, 124n101, 160n68

Finn, R., 94n12

Fletcher, G., 142n12

forbidden knowledge, brandishing of, 3, 4, 5, 19, 29–30, 30n69, 34–35, 39–40, 63, 93, 164, 168, 175, 176

Fornara, C., 142n12

fornication, 100, 113, 121, 123n100, 131–32

Foucault, M., 2, 11n24

Fowden, G., 33n74, 38n90, 61n58

Fowler, D., 15n35

Frakes, R., 21n46, 21n47, 24n53, 142n13, 142n14, 142n15

Frank, G., 94n12, 94n17, 108n65

friendship, 13–17, 34, 39–40, 136, 176

Gallus (*caesar*), 53, 140, 147–48, 150, 156, 159, 162, 165, 166; his lanugo, 162

Gallus (priest of the Mother of the Gods), 132, 133n118

Gardner, J., 25n56

Garnsey, P., 22n49

generalitas sacra, 22, 23, 25, 28, 35, 91, 139, 152

genius publicus, 154

Gilliam, J., 46n5

Gizewski, C., 10n20

glamour (frequently masculine), 4, 6, 44, 45, 46, 48, 55, 62, 65, 69, 74, 84, 86,

88, 90, 139–40, 141, 143n17, 151, 165, 167–68, 171, 176
Gleason, M., 7n6, 26n60, 27n61, 35, 37, 37n87
Goehring, J., 94n11, 94n12
Gould, G., 94n12, 106n58, 110n72, 111, 111n74
Goulet, R., 50n21
Gradenwitz, O., 28n63, 28n65, 88n117
Grasso, F., 66n75, 71n83
Gratian, emperor, 8n11, 140, 152, 170–75
Gregory Nazianzenus/of Nazianzus, 18n41, 98, 124–25n102, 133n119
Groß-Albenhausen, K., 10n20
Gunderson, E., 11n25, 30n69

Hadrian, 87n116, 131, 149
Halperin, D., 11n24, 26n59, 27n61, 56n44, 93n9
Halsall, G., 8n10
hand-job, 160n68
Harper, K., 24n53, 27n62
Harpham, G., 94n12, 108n64
Harries, J., 8n10, 21n47, 22n49
Heather, P., 6n3, 8n8, 8n10, 9n12, 9n14, 9n15
hēdonē, 60n57, 117, 131, 131n113
Helen, 67, 79, 83, 84
Helios, 46n5, 49n18, 52, 52n29, 52n30, 55, 54–55n41, 67, 80, 83, 138n5
Henderson, J., 30n69
Herakles, 48, 67, 81, 82, 82n107, 83, 84. See Hercules
Hercules, 49n18, 138n5. See Herakles
Hermes, 46, 48, 49n17, 51, 67, 80, 81, 81n106, 82, 83, 171n5
hero/heroic, 42, 48, 51, 67, 80, 82, 124n102
Hinds, S., 15n35
Hirschfeld, O., 10n20
Historia Monachorum, 51, 94, 95, 105n54, 106, 107, 110, 111, 112n77

Homer, 15, 42, 53, 57, 62n62, 67, 71n84, 83, 84, 170, 171n5
homo, 28, 28n65
homosexuality, 1–2, 11, 11n24, 93n9
homosociality, 1, 2, 3, 5, 6, 11–12, 11n24, 11n25, 13, 17–18, 19, 20, 23, 27n62, 33n74, 34, 39, 41, 58, 84, 85, 86–88, 90, 91, 92, 93, 111, 112, 113, 115, 123, 136, 139, 140, 141, 142, 146, 149, 153, 164, 167, 172, 175, 177–78
Honoré, T., 8n10, 20n44, 21n47, 22n49
Honorius, emperor, 152, 152n44, 152n45, 158
honor-shame dynamic, 12, 12n26, 44, 61, 120, 127
Hoppenbrouwers, H., 121n98
Humfress, C., 22n49
Humphries, M., 7n5
Hunt, D., 47n12
Hunter, D., 51n24, 62n59, 143n18

Iamblichus, 18, 18n40, 30n69, 38, 41–44, 41n1, 49n18, 50, 50n22, 55, 61, 61n58, 66n75, 84–85, 88, 128, 176
idolatry, 130–32, 135
incongruities (*apemphainonta*), 65, 66n75, 67, 70, 71, 71n84, 73, 78, 79, 80, 82, 83, 84, 87
indeclinabilis, 162–63
inserere, 122, 122n99, 125–26
intertextuality, 4, 13, 14–15, 15n35, 18n41, 32, 43, 44, 46, 49n18, 55, 56, 60n57, 61, 67, 72n85, 81, 83, 84, 92, 112, 113, 119, 120, 162, 170–75, 173n11, 173n12, 173n14
itching, obscene, 99, 113, 115, 116–17, 118, 119, 120–22, 127, 130, 153, 168
iustitia, 124n102, 148, 149, 150, 153, 154n52, 155, 156, 157, 162, 163, 174–75

Jacobs, A., 21n47
Jerome, 9, 17, 31–32, 31n70, 36n85, 94, 95, 114, 115, 120n94, 177

Johnston, S., 61n58
Jones, A., 6n3, 7n5, 8n8, 9n12, 9n13, 10n16, 10n19, 10n20, 10n21, 10n22, 12n27, 63n64
Jordan, M., 58n48
Jove, 133n118, 138n5
Joyce, M., 57n45
Julian, emperor, chapter 1 *passim*, 4, 5, 6, 8, 8n11, 13n30, 18, 18n39, 18n40, 18n41, 19n42, 37, 38, 90, 91, 96, 111, 136, 140, 140n10, 141, 143, 146–47, 149, 152, 154, 162–63, 164, 165–68, 173n14, 176; complicated persona of, 72–79, 84; *mythos* of his life, 79–84

Kaldellis, A., 7n6, 8n8, 8n10
kallos amēchanon, 41–44, 48, 49–50, 49n18, 51, 55, 56, 57, 58, 59, 60n57, 84–86, 88, 165, 167. See also *amēchanos*
Kannengiesser, C., 94n12
Kaster, R., 8n8
Kelly, C., 8n10, 86, 86n114, 88n119, 139n5, 139n7, 142n16, 143n17, 143n18
Kelly, G., 15n35, 140n10, 142n12, 142n14, 155n54
kinaidos. See *cinaedus*
King, R., 11n25
kissed, thoroughly, 146, 147
Knight, G., 15n35
know yourself (*gnōthi sauton*), 45, 74, 77–78
Kolb, F., 142n16, 147n30
Krawiec, R., 94n12
Krueger, D., 54n38, 66n73, 94n12
Kuefler, M., 2n1, 24n53, 26n58, 35–36, 36n83–84, 38n88, 158n64

Lacombrade, C., 47n12
ladder of love (*Smp.* 210A–211C), 33n75, 57–58, 135, 165, 175
Lamberton, R., 7n6, 51n23, 62n62, 63n63, 64n68, 66n75, 71n84, 117n88

Late Platonism (Neoplatonism), 4, 35, 48n14, 50, 52n30, 61n58, 62n62, 63, 85, 88, 89, 92, 128, 135, 144, 168, 176. See also Iamblichus; Julian; Plotinus
Layton, B., 94n12, 95, 95n18, 114n78
Leader-Newby, R., 86n114, 87n116
Lendon, J., 10
Lenski, N., 8n8, 9n14, 139n9, 177n21
Lewy, Y., 38n89, 61n58
Leyser, C., 27n62, 94n12
Liebeschuetz, J., 53n32
Liebs, D., 21n47
light, 10, 22, 38, 38n89, 42, 50, 50–51nn21–23, 51, 52, 55, 60n57, 61, 88, 127, 166, 167. See also senate; sun
Lilla, S., 52n30
Lim, R., 97n26
Lloyd, G., 38n88
Löhken, H., 10n20
Long, J., 160n68
Louth, A., 93n10
Luck, G., 61n58
Lysias, 172–73

MacCormack, S., 8n11, 15n35, 138n5, 142n16, 143n17, 152n43
MacMullen, R., 24, 25, 142n16, 143n17
Mamertinus, Claudius, 8n11, 88n117, 146
manhood (elite late-Roman), 1–6, 12, 25–27, 34–38, 44, 65, 83, 84–85, 88–89, 90–91, 93, 95, 97, 98–111, 127, 135–36, 139–40, 164, 176–78. See also competition; homosociality; *paideia;* the transcendent; *vir*
manus divina, 139, 139n6
Marcone, A., 6n3, 8n8, 9–10, 54n38, 177n21
Marcus Aurelius, 4, 43, 44, 46, 47–48, 47n12, 48–50, 49n17, 51, 52, 53, 54, 55–56, 60n57, 61, 62, 84, 88, 90, 141, 149, 165, 166, 167
marriage, 23, 24n53, 177

Marrou, H., 7n6
Martin, D., 94n12
martyr(s), 9, 50n21, 51n24, 108, 109
Mason, H., 10n16
Masterson, M., 11n25, 15n35, 18n39, 18n41, 30n69, 56n43, 92n3, 111n76, 112n77, 173n14
Mastrangelo, M., 15n35
masturbation, 74, 74n90, 79, 81, 81n106, 83, 84, 113
Matthews, J., 6n3, 7n4, 7n5, 8n8, 8n10, 8n11, 13n30, 21n47, 22, 22n49, 85n111, 139n5, 139n6, 139n7, 140n10, 142n16, 144n20, 144n21, 147, 149n33, 152n45, 154n51, 155n54, 177n21
Maximus, philosopher, 146, 147
McCormick, M., 138nn2–3, 142n16, 143n17, 152n41
McDonnell, M., 26n58
McGinn, T., 23n51, 25, 25n57
metaphor, obscene for unknowable, 64–65, 68, 70–71, 78; same-sex sexual desire/pleasure for admirability, 4, 19, 30–34, 33n74, 34–35, 39–40, 55, 63, 84–85, 90, 107, 111, 136, 167–68, 170–75, 176; same-sex sexual desire/pleasure for friendship/non-carnal relations, 4, 17, 18, 34, 39–40, 87, 107, 136, 139, 176. *See also* admirability; authority; friendship
Millar, F., 8n10, 10n16
Miller, P., 33n74, 33n76, 36n85, 38n90, 50n23, 51, 51n24, 61n59, 94n12, 143n18
mimesis, 91, 96, 98, 112, 133, 133n118. See *charaktēr(es)*
Missorium (plate), frontispiece, 44, 86–88, 86n114, 87n116, 103
mollis, 20n46, 159–61, 160n68, 162
Moore, S., 93n8
Mother of the Gods, 52–53, 52n32, 71n84, 77n101, 132, 133, 133n118
Müller, F., 47n10, 47n12, 49n18
myth, 4, 45, 46–47, 46n6, 52n32, 61n59, 62, 62–71, 62nn60–62, 65n70, 66n75, 71n83, 71n84, 72, 72n85, 73, 74, 75, 77n101, 78–79, 78–79n103, 80, 81, 82, 83–84, 91, 168; *mythos* of emperor Julian's life, 79–84

Näf, B., 6n3
negotium, 13
Neoplatonism. *See* Late Platonism
Neri, V., 140n10, 142n15, 142n16, 143n17, 147, 149n33, 154, 155n54
Nicomachus Flavianus, Virius, 20
Nock, A., 63n63, 63n64, 139n5
novellae, 33, 33n79, 34n80, 34n81, 139n6, 152n45, 153
numen, 139, 139n8, 166

obedience (*hypakoē*), 97, 111
obscenity, 4, 30, 30n69, 63, 64, 65, 65n70, 68, 71, 71n83, 78, 113, 141, 160, 164–65, 169, 176
Oenomaus (Cynic), 66, 74, 74n91
Onians, J., 51
Oribasios, 121
Orientius, 20, 21, 23, 29, 33, 88, 90
otium, 12–13, 13n30

Pacatus (Latinus Pacatus Drepanius), 8n11, 158n64, 161
Pachomius, 94, 95, 113–14, 123, 127
Pack, R., 46n5, 48n14
paideia, 3, 4, 7–8, 8n8, 9, 11, 12, 13, 14, 17, 18, 32, 34, 41, 43, 54n38, 55, 63, 66, 66n72, 74–75, 77, 79, 84, 90, 100–101, 110, 115, 117, 126, 139, 142, 167, 170–75
palaestra, 58, 58–59n50, 113, 120
Pan, 65, 68, 81, 81n106, 83
Panegyrici Latini, 8n11, 161
paradox, 3, 4, 6, 35–36, 36n83, 36n84, 43, 44–45, 46, 61, 61n58, 62, 64–65, 66, 66n75, 67, 70–71, 71n84, 72, 73–74, 76,

78–79n103, 79, 84, 86, 87, 88–89, 99, 100–101, 168, 171, 175, 176
paraklausithyra, 31
Parker, H., 12n26, 27n61
pateo, 159–60, 160n67, 160n68, 162, 164, 167
pati muliebria, 29, 122–23, 127
patronus, 2, 12, 23, 36, 47, 90, 99, 99n36
Paul of the desert, 31–32, 31n70
Paul the Simple, 11n25, 110–11, 111n76, 112, 112n77
Paul, saint, 93, 93n8, 133
Paulinus of Nola (Meropius Pontius Paulinus), 3, 12–14, 12n27, 12n28, 13n29, 15–18, 19, 20, 26, 27n62, 28, 39, 50n21
pederasty, 18. See also desire (pederastic)
Penella, R., 38n88
penetrabilis, 159–60, 162, 167
Pettersen, A., 93n10, 94n12, 97n27, 127n103, 128n107, 129, 129n109
Phaedrus (Plato), 33, 118n90, 171, 171n4, 172–73, 173n11
Philebus (Plato), 33, 117–18, 119
Philiscus (Cynic), 66, 74, 74n91
philosophy, 1, 4, 7, 7n6, 32–33, 33n74, 35, 38n88, 38n89, 41n1, 42, 48, 48n14, 52, 54n38, 62n62, 65n70, 66, 68, 68n77, 71n84, 72, 73, 74, 76, 77n101, 85–86, 101–2, 102n46, 109, 128, 146, 156–57, 168, 170, 171, 172, 176. See also Iamblichus; Julian; Late Platonism; Plato; Plotinus
Physiognomy, anonymous Latin, i.e., *De Physiognomonia Liber*, 26–27, 28, 29, 35, 162
Plato, 4, 15, 18, 18n40, 18n41, 33, 33n74, 41, 43, 44, 46, 47, 47n10, 48, 48n14, 49n18, 55, 55n42, 56, 56n44, 57, 59–60n55, 60n57, 62, 75, 86, 90, 92, 100, 112, 113, 117, 118, 120, 129, 135, 165, 170, 171, 171n4, 172–73
Plotinus, 44, 49n18, 51n23, 61n58, 85–86, 88, 144
Porphyry, 41n1, 61n58, 71n84

prostitutes, 19, 20, 23, 25, 25n57, 29
pudor, 20n46, 123–25, 123n100, 124n101

Rapp, C., 8n8, 36–37, 50n20
Rappe, S., 52n30
Rebenich, S., 7n5
Rees, R., 138n1
relics, 45, 50–51, 50–51n23, 61–62, 61–62n59, 63, 143
Republic (Plato), 47, 60n57, 62, 62n61
Rhea. See Mother of the Gods
Richlin, A., 12n26, 23n50, 27n61, 30n69
Roberts, M., 15n35, 140n10, 142n16, 143n17
Robinson, O., 21n47
Rochefort, G., 63n64, 65n71
Romans, Letter to, 93, 93n8, 133–34
Rosen, K., 142n12, 143n17
Rousseau, P., 94n12, 95n18, 114n78
Rousselle, A., 94n12, 114n79
Ruether, R., 38n88
Rutgers, L., 21n47

Sabbah, G., 140n10, 142n12, 142n15, 147, 155n54
Saloustios (Salutius, Sallustius), 45, 46, 46n5, 54, 56n43, 62–65, 63n63, 63n64, 71n84, 87
Salzman, M., 6n2, 6n3, 7n5, 8n7, 8n8, 10n20, 13n30, 86n115
same-sex sexual attractiveness (male), 3, 4, 5, 6, 19, 30–34, 35, 43, 46, 48, 55, 84–85, 86, 90, 136, 140, 141, 165, 167–68, 170–75
same-sex sexual behavior (male), 3, 4, 5, 24, 24n53, 25, 26, 27, 27n62, 29, 35, 39, 46, 61, 63, 89, 92, 92n2, 111, 113–14, 114n78, 149, 159, 176. See also anal penetration; same-sex sexual pleasure (male)
same-sex sexual pleasure (male), 3, 4, 5, 6, 16, 18, 19, 30n69, 34, 35, 36, 38–40, 61,

62, 63, 89, 93, 112, 118, 126, 127, 130, 131, 133, 135–36, 140, 142, 143–44, 164, 176, 177–78. *See also* anal penetration; desire (male same-sex); same-sex sexual behavior (male)

Sapor, king of Parthians/Persians, 152n41, 157–58

Sardiello, R., 46n5, 47n10, 47n12, 49n18

Schroeder, C., 94n12, 95n18, 113

Scroggs, R., 93n8

Seager, R., 154n50

Sedgwick, E., 11, 93n9

Self-Consolation on the Departure of the Most-Excellent Saloustios (Julian), 18n39, 46n5, 49n18, 54, 54n36, 56n43

Sells, M., 52n30

senate, 3, 6–7, 6n3, 9, 9n14, 12, 10, 13, 37, 38, 50, 96, 104–5, 146, 154n51, 170, 171, 172, 175, 177; *clarissimus* (λαμπρότατος), 10, 10n20, 17, 38, 50, 88, 139, 166; *illustris* (ἰλλούστριος), 10, 10n20, 11, 13, 17, 22, 38, 50, 88, 108, 127, 139, 166; *spectabilis* (σπεκταβίλιος/περίβλεπτος), 10, 10n20, 13, 13n29, 17, 22, 38, 50, 88, 139, 166. *See also* light

Septuagint, the, 112, 113, 115, 119

Shanzer, D., 30n69, 120n94

Shaw, G., 33n76, 61n58

Shaw, T., 36n85, 94n12

Shenoute of Atripe, 113

Silenus, 47, 48

Silvanus, 155–56, 161

Sirmondian Constitutions, 33, 33n78, 34n80, 34n81

Sivan, H., 8n11, 177n21

Skinner, A., 9n15

slavery, 23, 27n62, 28, 103–4, 107, 108–9, 146, 162

Smith, A., 52n29

Smith, R., 47n12, 52n29, 53n32, 54n38, 55n41, 61n58, 66n73, 66n75, 71n83, 77n100, 147n30

sneeze of revelation, 26–27, 29, 162

Socrates, 43–44, 47, 55–56, 57–61, 58–59n50, 59–60n55, 60n57, 117, 172–73

Sodano, A., 38n89

Sogno, C., 177n21

soldier(y), 5, 36n84, 66, 72, 75, 76, 76n98, 77, 82n109, 86, 87, 141, 143, 144, 145, 165, 166, 167, 173, 174, 175, 177. *See cingulum*

Solomon-Godeau, A., 11n24

sōphrosynē (temperance), 58, 59, 75

stamp, give a new one to the currency (*paracharaxon to nomisma*), 45, 66, 74, 77–78

Struck, P., 50n21, 61n58

stuprum, 24–25, 25n54, 124n101

submissiveness, 108–111

sun, the, 51n23, 52, 52n29, 52n30, 55, 60n57, 80, 150, 157

swerve. *See declinare; indeclinabilis*

Symposium (Plato), 18n40, 33, 33n75, 43, 43n4, 44, 45, 47, 47n10, 55, 55n42, 56, 57–58, 60, 60n57, 118n90, 165, 171n4, 173, 173n12

symptoms, physical, 6, 92, 115, 116, 127, 153, 156, 157, 168

Taifali, 165

Tassi, A., 140n10, 155n54

Tellus, 86–87, 87n116. *See also* Earth

tener, 161–62

terms of address between *viri/andres*, abstract, 20, 20n46, 29, 29n67, 88, 88n117, 88n118, 90, 103, 108; affectionate, 20, 33–34, 33n77, 34n80, 34n81, 88, 90, 92, 103

theia, ta, 42, 88, 128

Themistius, 170–75

Theocritus, 18n41, 32, 173, 173n14

Theodosius I, frontispiece, 7, 9, 19, 20, 20n43, 21, 44, 86–87, 86n114, 87n116, 142, 142n15, 152, 152n43, 152n45, 158, 161, 164

Theodosius II, 22, 23, 25, 28, 33, 34n80, 34n81, 91, 139, 152, 152n45, 153
theurgy/theurgists, 38n89, 41, 44–45, 50, 50n22, 61–62, 61n58, 63
Thompson, E., 140n10, 141n11, 142n13, 147n30
Thomson, R., 127
transcendent, the, 1, 35, 39–40, 41–43, 46, 52, 55, 63, 65, 67, 69, 70–71, 78, 85–89, 90, 128, 135, 136–37, 141, 144, 154, 164, 168–69, 176; manhood having connection to, 4, 36–38, 41–43, 90, 108, 109; moralized, 5–6, 89, 127–28, 131, 135, 136–37, 141, 153, 154, 162–63, 168–69, 176. See also existent economy
Trout, D., 7n4, 12n28, 27n62

utopia, 92, 95, 112, 112n77, 115

Valantasis, R., 94n12
Valens, emperor, 8n8, 9n14, 96, 139n7, 139n9, 140, 174
Valensi, L., 86n115, 138n4, 139n5, 145n23
Valentinian I, 8n11, 9n14, 98, 139n7, 139n9, 140
Valentinian II, frontispiece, 19, 19–20n43, 20, 21, 86, 152, 152n43
Valentinian III, 33, 34n80, 34n81, 152n45, 153
Van Dam, R., 8n8
van Dijk, G., 79n104
Van Liefferinge, C., 61n58, 66n75, 71n83
Vanderspoel, J., 170n1
Venus, 5, 23, 29n68, 32n72, 141, 167. See also Aphrodite
venustas. See Venus
verecundia, 121–22, 123–25, 124n101
Vessey, M., 8n10, 139n6, 139n7
Victricius, 13, 50–51, 50n23, 51n24, 61n59, 77n101, 143, 143n18

vir (*anēr*), 20, 21, 23–24, 25–29, 28n63, 35–38, 90, 103, 110, 149, 165
Virgil, 14, 16, 18, 126
virtus, 20, 23, 25–26, 127, 148, 149, 150–51, 158
viscera, 15–16, 16n36
Vita Antonii (Anonymous), 94, 94n13, 94n14, 121–27
Vita Antonii (Athanasius), 5, 31n70, 38, 70, 89, 90–93, 93–94, 94n14, 95, 96–98, 98–104, 105, 106, 107, 108–9, 112–13, 115–17, 118–27, 129–30, 135–36, 153–54
Vita Antonii (Evagrius Antiochensis), 94, 94n13, 94n14, 120n95, 121–27, 122n99
Vita Pauli (Jerome), 31–32, 31n70
Vivian, T., 94n12, 97n29, 114n79

wall (around the body), 99, 115, 118, 118n92, 119, 121, 122, 123, 127, 130, 135
Wallis, R., 52n30, 61n58
Walters, J., 12n26
Watts, E., 7n6
Williams, C., 12n26, 24n53, 27n61
Wimbush, V., 94n12
Winkler, J., 27n61, 56n44
women, associated with body, 37–38
Wormald, P., 8n8
wrestling, 92, 113, 115, 119, 120, 127, 153

Xenophon, 81–82, 82n107, 144

Zeeland, S., 92n2
zero-sum game. See honor-shame dynamic
Zeus, 18n40, 47, 48, 65, 67, 68, 72, 80, 81, 83, 132, 133n118, 171
Žižek, S., 29–30, 43
zōnē. See *cingulum*

www.ingramcontent.com/pod-product-compliance
Lightning Source LLC
Chambersburg PA
CBHW020124240426
43673CB00038B/580